# RUSSIA'S WAR ON EVERYBODY

# RUSSIA'S WAR ON EVERYBODY

## And What it Means for You

**Keir Giles**

BLOOMSBURY ACADEMIC
LONDON • NEW YORK • OXFORD • NEW DELHI • SYDNEY

BLOOMSBURY ACADEMIC
Bloomsbury Publishing Plc
50 Bedford Square, London, WC1B 3DP, UK
1385 Broadway, New York, NY 10018, USA
29 Earlsfort Terrace, Dublin 2, Ireland

BLOOMSBURY, BLOOMSBURY ACADEMIC and the Diana logo are trademarks of
Bloomsbury Publishing Plc

First published in Great Britain 2022
Paperback edition published 2024

Cover design by Adriana Brioso
Author photograph by Munira Mustaffa

A catalogue record for this book is available from the British Library.

A catalog record for this book is available from the Library of Congress.

ISBN:   HB:     978-1-3502-5508-1
        PB:     978-1-3504-5260-2
        ePDF:   978-1-3502-5510-4
        eBook:  978-1-3502-5509-8

Typeset by RefineCatch Limited, Bungay, Suffolk
Printed and bound in Great Britain

To find out more about our authors and books visit www.bloomsbury.com
and sign up for our newsletters.

*This book is dedicated to Vladimir Vladimirovich PUTIN with thanks for finally convincing the world of the depths of evil his country is still willing to perpetrate – and of the need to defend itself against them.*

# CONTENTS

# ACKNOWLEDGEMENTS

This book is built around real stories from real people, representing a tiny sample of the vast number of people around the world whose lives have been directly impacted by Moscow's ambition to exert power wherever it can. My thanks go to the friends and colleagues, old and new, from over twenty countries who shared with me their sometimes very personal experiences of finding themselves on the front line of resisting Russia. But in reality, we should thank everybody, worldwide, working to protect themselves, their families, their societies and their countries from the harm Russia wants to do to them and to us.

# PREFACE TO THE PAPERBACK EDITION

Since the first edition of this book was published in late 2022, nearly everything it tries to explain has been proven correct, or got worse, or both.

As I write this, Russia's war on Ukraine continues to drag on with no resolution in sight. And Russia continues to demonstrate on a daily basis in Ukraine some of the most repellent features of how it behaves as a state, and how individual Russians are capable of behaving as people. With the constant indiscriminate missile and drone attacks on Ukrainian cities, causing death and destruction for innocent civilians and children seems just as much one of Moscow's war aims as the grab for territory that prompted the full-scale invasion in February 2022 in the first place. And Russia's treatment of its own soldiers, including convicts who have been sprung from jail and flung into the front lines with no training, shows that the Russian state puts as little value on human life when dealing with its own citizens as with those of the countries it attacks.

And yet, while Russia has not changed its behaviour in Ukraine and around the world, neither it seems has the West learned from the experience of the war. The dominant feature of the choices made by most of the Western coalition backing Ukraine remains timidity and fear of offending Russia. The belief that Russia's nuclear threats are real rather than theatre has constrained major donors like the United States and Germany from providing the full support that Ukraine needs to eject its Russian invaders. That applies not only to withholding specific weapons systems that Ukraine identifies as essential for success, like main battle tanks, or long-range missiles, or at the time of writing combat aircraft. It also dictates the rules that are applied to these weapons systems, when finally, after long delay, the donors are shamed into providing them. The United States in particular still prohibits Ukraine from using the weapons it supplies to strike back into Russia itself, forcing the Ukrainian military to fight with one hand tied behind its back and leaving Russia safe havens from which to strike deep into Ukraine with impunity.

It is not even clear what kind of victory Ukraine's Western supporters are looking for. US and other officials have repeatedly emphasized that they will continue supporting Ukraine for "as long as it takes", without specifying what "it" is - leaving open the possibility of stopping short of the clear and unequivocal setback for Russia that has been identified as the only way to change Moscow's mind about how it should conduct itself in the twenty-first century. Time it again it's been left to the UK to demonstrate leadership, and show that providing the weapons and support Ukraine needs is not going to lead to the catastrophic response from Russia that the US and Germany so fear.

But one realisation that has finally dawned for the western community of nations is that the war in Ukraine is just the front line of a much broader conflict, one that is global in scale. The way in which countries beyond the West failed to condemn Russia's invasion of Ukraine, or even the genocidal atrocities conducted within it, came as a shattering shock to those who assumed that condemnation of aggression would be automatic, and respect for human life would be universal. The way those countries in Africa that were threatened with starvation as a result of Russian blockades of Ukrainian grain failed absolutely to blame Russia for their predicament just underscored how effective Russia had been in some of its campaigns of disinformation and subversion around the world, some of which are described in this book.

Above all it brought home to Western powers the extent to which they had taken their eye off the ball during Russia's long-standing campaign to gain global influence. For years Russia-watchers like me documented the way Moscow had shifted to a broad strategy of seeking friends and dependents wherever it could, far beyond its traditional partners in Africa and Latin America. At the time, we couldn't see where this was leading. But now, the results are very clear - and in mid-2023 the pattern of Russia-friendly coups across central Africa seemed to indicate that globally, Russian power was still advancing rather than retreating.

That global advance of Russian power is the main theme of this book – and in particular, what it means for the individuals who suffer as a result of Russia pushing forward wherever it can, and by whatever means possible. It's the real impact on real people that I wanted to explain in the book, rather than abstract notions of national power that might seem remote from ordinary individuals' everyday life. That's the reason why this book contains interviewees from across the world, demonstrating that nowhere is too remote to be a subject of interest for Russia, and nobody should think that they are protected by distance from the ways in which Moscow can reach out and touch them.

Sadly, it's exactly that focus that leads directly to another key theme of the book that has been proven accurate: the way western countries struggle to deal with the campaigns that Russia mounts against their societies and their people, and the way countermeasures against those campaigns seem faltering and inadequate. There have been successes – not least the exposure of multiple Russian intelligence officers operating under illegal cover across Europe, often with false South American identities. And in the UK, identified in the book as one of the most permissive environments for Russian subversion, new legislation is in place which finally outlaws working as a conscious agent of a hostile state to undermine your own country. Nevertheless, few of the individuals I interviewed for the book would say that they now feel safer from the Russian state.

In cyber warfare, after a brief interlude of transparency, western states seem to have reverted to their previous habits of secrecy, keeping their publics largely in the dark as to the campaigns that are mounted against them. The pattern of suspicious deaths that appeared linked to the Russian practice of murdering inconvenient individuals across Europe and the United States seems to have temporarily abated. But security experts suggest this is because Russia's murder teams are fully occupied behind the lines in Ukraine, conducting targeted assassinations of Ukrainian officials and military officers, meaning that at any point when the war there subsides, the rest of us will be the subject of their attentions once again. Even the UK's long-overdue National Security Act will be of limited use on its own – it may make much of the activity described in this book illegal, at least in one country, but that will achieve little without the political will to resource investigations and prosecutions under the new law.

What is more, few countries seem to have tackled the central problem of the helpers and facilitators for Russian operations that are drawn from among their own populations – which, as you will see from the pages of this book, is an enormous enabling factor for Russia achieving what it wants. It remains hard to distinguish between those working consciously on behalf of Russia, and the "useful idiots" who may think they are doing the right thing out of their own convictions, but end up helping Russia nonetheless. That's why it's vital that national counter-intelligence services take an interest in working out who is who, because the sources of information that make that clear simply aren't available to the public or even to investigative journalists.

It's true that life has got harder for those agents of influence and useful idiots. Some of them have stepped away from supporting Russia, after the nature of the regime they were assisting became clear in the course of the invasion of Ukraine. Others find it hard to keep up with constantly shifting Russian narratives, and how Moscow presents itself to the world. When Putin and Russia abandoned the pretence that its invasions of neighbouring countries were in response to the states of Eastern Europe seeking NATO membership, and instead admitted openly that the assault on Ukraine was a war of colonial reconquest attempting to reverse history and restore the Russian empire, this left some of its backers and propagandists floundering. Some of them have been left behind, and continue making excuses for Russia that Russia has already abandoned. Others resort to increasingly bizarre mental contortions to avoid the truth – or simply disregard the facts altogether. But the net result is that some of the people described in this book have become even more radicalized in their support for Moscow, and in some cases stepped away from any attempt to pretend that they're acting in good faith.

Countries neighbouring Russia also face a new threat, in the form of a revived and invigorated Russian diaspora. This results in particular from two major waves of emigration from Russia, in February and September 2022. In February, several hundred thousand Russians left the country because they were appalled by the full-scale invasion of Ukraine and the growing repression at home. In September, an even greater number departed to avoid conscription into the army after President Putin, in desperate need of more cannon fodder for the war on Ukraine, announced "partial" mobilization. That means the destination countries - especially those with visa-free regimes with Russia - have suddenly acquired hugely increased or substantially new Russian minorities. And the problem with that is that just because somebody has left Russia physically does not mean they have left it mentally, and their new host countries are finding that besides the economic impact, the arrival of a large number of new temporary immigrants with hostile or colonialist attitudes, and no intent to integrate into local society, is fraught with serious social tensions.

What they have left behind in Russia is a country that, as predicted in the book, has continued to regress further back into its dark history of repression and totalitarianism. As time goes on, Russia is showing more and more hallmarks of the feudal society that the rest of Europe left behind centuries ago. In June 2023, the Wagner mercenary group and its leader Yevgeniy Prigozhin left Ukraine, where they had been fighting on the front line for months, and staged an armed mutiny and a march on Moscow, challenging the very core of Russian power. The scenes were extraordinary for today's Europe. And yet, they would have been perfectly normal for the Europe of the middle of the previous millennium - and as such, just another demonstration that in Russia, relations between the state and its subjects have not evolved over the last several hundred years.

This direction of travel for Russia just confirms for the rest of us that the country presents a threat that is both from outside our geographical space and from beyond our time. Returning to its historical default of repression at home and aggression abroad, Russia is now displaying a naked ambition to re-conquer the territory of its neighbours, and has abandoned all pretence otherwise. That means there are still fewer grounds to hope that there may be any such thing as normal, peaceful relations with Moscow in the future. And that applies not only to Russia's immediate neighbours under threat of invasion, but also to those countries further afield that Russia perceives as adversaries – whether they recognise that fact or not.

While Russia's intelligence services and armed forces may have failed in their initial mission in Ukraine, this won't prevent their being central to the coercive activities of the Russian state in the future. That means that for every other country, countering them will remain no less important. Whatever the future trajectory of Russia – whether the long-predicted fall of Putin and fragmentation of the country comes to pass or not – the task for those defending western societies will remain the same: it is to contain the damage from Russia. And that means protecting not only national interests, but also democratic processes, institutions, society, and – as this book tries hard to demonstrate – individual people who may find themselves the target of Moscow's aggression even though they had no previous interest in or involvement with Russia at all.

The final conclusion of the book remains the same: Russia is not going away, and will remain a challenge to us all for the foreseeable future and beyond. But at the end of this new preface for a new edition of the book, there is one important addition I would like to make. The book carries an ironic dedication to Vladimir Putin, since he has made the job of all of us who explain Russia for a living so much easier by removing all doubt as to the hostile, aggressive, backward nature of the regime he leads. But that dedication is incomplete, and by now, it is clear that it needs to be expanded. I would like to dedicate this new edition to Ukraine and to its people, whose courage, steadfastness and solidarity in the face of Russia's onslaught offers the first chance in our lifetimes to check Russia's programme of expanding its power at all our expense. Ukraine is fighting for us all.

*Слава Україні!*

# PREFACE TO THE FIRST EDITION

## *About this book*

The first time I finished writing this book was in October 2021.

As first completed, the book was to have been a warning – that although conflict with Russia had not erupted into open fighting, nevertheless Russia was waging a clandestine war against the West with devastating effects for ordinary people. Then, while the book languished in the publishing doldrums, President Putin enacted one of the worst-case scenarios it described. Russia's assault on Ukraine in late February 2022 confirmed two of the key warnings from the book – not only the Russian state's willingness to use military force in circumstances that are inconceivable for Western countries, but also its willingness once the conflict has begun to embrace the most barbarous and savage means available to win it.

Now, as I finish writing the book a second time in March 2022, far fewer people around the world need to be warned of Russia's intent and nature. The shock of major war in Europe has caused both countries and individuals to reassess their views on Russia, and led to a new willingness to confront the challenges posed by Moscow. The early promise of spectacular reversal of decades of Russia-friendly policy in Germany, for instance, was for some Russia-watchers an even more unexpected development than Russia going to war in the first place.

But while the war on Ukraine grinds on – with its end, at the time of writing, far from clear – so too does Russia's other war. New countermeasures like economic sanctions against Russia and its leadership seek to punish their behaviour in Ukraine, but measures to deal with far longer-running and less obvious campaigns against Russia's adversaries are still patchy – in part, because in contrast to the clear and undeniable nature of Russia's aggression in Ukraine, those other campaigns are far harder to detect and understand.

So as Russia's overt war in eastern Europe continues, this book is telling the story of the other war – the covert war Russia has been waging against the West, and against its people, for years and decades.

The long build-up to Russia's 2022 attack on Ukraine saw confrontation between Moscow and the West steadily growing. Even people who took no interest in the country could not fail to notice how barely a week went by without Russia featuring in the headlines again, doing something outrageous somewhere in the world. Shooting down airliners, poisoning dissidents, interfering in elections, spying and hacking have long seemed to be the Kremlin's daily business. And the question repeatedly put to long-term observers of Russia like me was: what is it all for? Why does Russia consistently behave like this? And what does it achieve?

This book tries to put the pieces of the jigsaw together to explain how and why Russia pushes for more power and influence wherever it can reach, far beyond Ukraine – and what it means not just for governments but for ordinary people. It brings together stories from the military, politics, diplomacy, espionage, cyber power, organized crime and more to describe how Moscow conducts its campaigns across the globe, and how nobody is too unimportant to be caught up in them. I try to lift the lid on the daily struggle going on behind the scenes to protect governments, businesses, societies and people from Russian hostile activity – and in doing so, to show how Russia's aims and objectives are far broader and more ambitious, and the ways it tries to reach them far more pervasive and damaging, than most people can see from media headlines.

In a way, this follows on from a book I wrote in 2019 called *Moscow Rules*. That book dug deep into the underlying factors that have driven Russia to be so permanently hostile to the West throughout the centuries, and explained some of the reasons behind Russian actions today that so many of us find incomprehensible, like the assault on Ukraine and the atrocities committed during it. It's still the case that many of the methods the current Russian government is applying draw from its past experience in manipulating and controlling both its own people and politicians and government officials abroad. Almost everything Russia does that is described in both this book and the previous one is recognizable from previous centuries – just updated as new technology for delivering malign effects becomes available.

But while *Moscow Rules* dealt with *why* Russia attacks the West, this book looks instead at *how* it does so – and in particular, how that affects not just governments and politicians and the armed forces, but a much broader range of people. And importantly, these are often people who might think that because they don't have the slightest interest in Russia, Russia isn't interested in them. Unfortunately, as we see over and over again in the book, this simply isn't true. To show how this works, the book is filled with first-person stories of what it means to face up to Russia.

## About the eyewitnesses

Where possible, I have tried to tell stories that are not well known. There is no shortage of books, articles and studies, explaining individual aspects of how Russia gets its way in great detail – and I wanted to add to them not repeat them. So, you won't find in this book long and detailed descriptions of how Russia used its 'little green men' to seize Crimea, or shot down Malaysia Airlines flight MH17, or is using mercenaries to attempt to rebuild its power and influence in Africa, or attempted to murder Sergei Skripal in Salisbury. All these events and others like it appear in the book, of course, but they are punctuation for a much bigger and longer story. Even the immense and still-unfolding tragedy of the war on Ukraine forms just one case study among many.

So some obvious candidates who could tell us a lot about the impact of Russia's actions only feature in passing in this book. Victims of Russia's assault on Ukraine have suffered the most direct and obvious consequences of Moscow's aggression;

but their harrowing stories are already well established in the public eye. There are many other previous victims too who are not included. The family of Dawn Sturgess, for example, who died as a result of Russian intelligence officers' carefree handling of deadly poison in Salisbury in 2018, have suffered enough and there is no need to ask them to tell their story again. I've also purposely not included interviews with people from organizations like the Bellingcat investigative group, who you might think would be one of the obvious candidates given how effective they have been in exposing Russian activities. But Bellingcat too is already sufficiently well known.

What I wanted to show instead was that behind every high-profile story that reaches the national media in one of the countries targeted by Russia, there are a dozen other stories below the surface that affect real people's lives but never reach public attention. To do that, I spoke to almost forty different people on four continents, ranging from Norway to New Zealand, and most if not all of them you will never have heard of. (Since some interviewees appear in more than one chapter, a reminder list of who they all are can be found at the end of the book.) What all these people have in common is that each in their own way has a story to tell of being on the front line of Russia's campaign against the West. Some placed themselves there deliberately, while others found themselves in Russia's crosshairs entirely unexpectedly. But several of them told me they hoped this book would raise awareness, and perhaps even start a public debate, about what Russia does to Western countries, often unnoticed and without consequences.

So as well as the diplomats, professors and military officers who feature in the early chapters talking about their top-down view of Russia, we'll later also hear from soldiers, police officers, cybersecurity providers and more who talk about the day-to-day experience of the front line. Together, they tell stories ranging from the shocking and dramatic to the mundane and everyday – from the Russian military mounting full-scale operations against its neighbours, to ordinary people at the far end of the continent paying higher car insurance because of the way the Kremlin works with organized crime in their country.

You'll notice that there are no Russian interviewees who actually live in Russia. That's because the majority of people I could have spoken to there would fall into one of two categories. Either they would support the Russian government, in which case they would repeat the weary and familiar propaganda and denials of absolutely everything that we already hear from the Kremlin. Or they would oppose it, in which case – as you will see from Chapter 2 – they would be placing themselves at risk of reprisals in Russia's accelerating and increasingly brutal crackdown on dissent. Some Russia pundits will claim this makes the book worthless, and that none of the people featured in it – despite their combined centuries of working with Russia – understand what they are talking about. But it's better to deal with that claim, as we have done many times before, than to put independent voices within Russia at any more risk than they already are.

A few of the people outside Russia I spoke to needed to be anonymized because they are still in government, military or law-enforcement positions where they are not supposed to be quoted publicly. But disturbingly, just as many of the anonymous or disguised individuals in this book are that way because of what Russia has already done to them or might do in the future. Some have already experienced what it means to be a target of Russian or Russia-backed interference and intimidation and do not want to incur the same consequences again by featuring publicly in a book on the subject. Others were unable to comment because they were involved in legal proceedings launched by Russians linked to the state under defamation laws in two separate countries. Taken together, this group provided a clear indication of how effectively Russia can silence criticism, through intimidation, harassment and exploitation of the courts and in particular the current state of English libel law (see Chapter 6 below).

## About 'Russia' and 'the West'

Writing about what Russia does often means taking pains to explain that you're talking about the country, not ordinary Russians living within it. But you can't add that disclaimer to every sentence without making a book unreadable – it's hard enough trying to make things less tedious by mixing it up and saying 'Moscow', 'the Kremlin' and so on instead of 'Russia'. 'Russia' in this book is a shorthand, standing for the people within the country today who direct its state policy, both for dealing with its own citizens and with foreign countries – and who then put that policy into action.

Some of my interviewees also refer to things done by 'the Russians', and I haven't changed this. Any objective reader will realize that this too is shorthand not crude stereotyping, and even now with apparent widespread support by ordinary Russians for the war on Ukraine, nobody is saying that people living in Russia are pre-programmed robots or clones who slavishly back President Putin in everything. Even after control on public expressions of opinion in Russia tightened dramatically after the launch of the war on Ukraine, there are still dissenting voices there, and critics of the government, and not all Russian citizens share the official view of the West as a mortal enemy.[1] The problem is that as time goes on, the dissenters become more and more irrelevant because they have next to no influence on what Russia's leaders actually decide to do.

Inevitably, talking about 'the West' faces a similar problem. Here we're talking about a hugely diverse group of countries, and it's not always clear who should be included in that group – as evidenced by the fact that this book contains stories from four continents. And each of those countries has their own particular way of dealing with Russia, sometimes subtly different, sometimes in direct opposition to what their immediate neighbours are doing. Again, it's a shorthand, and in this case 'you know it when you see it'. In fact, when considering how Russia deals with 'the West', it's probably easiest to take a Russian view of it, and think of the West not as a precise list of countries but instead as 'a general concept that can refer to

1. 'International Relations: August 2021', Levada-Center, 10 September 2021, https://www.levada.ru/en/2021/09/10/international-relations-august-2021/.

everything that threatens traditional Russian values, questions – implicitly or explicitly – Russia's position as a modern superpower'.[2]

And then there's 'whataboutism', the way defenders of Russia ask 'what about the West', and instead of addressing criticisms of what Russia does, claim that other countries do just the same. Apologists for Russia will immediately scour this book looking for examples where the West, and in particular the United States, can be accused of historically indulging in the kind of behaviour described here. There is no doubt they will find some, and some of them may even be based in fact – although as ever, the conspiracy theorists can be relied on to supply plenty more that are entirely imaginary. But that's not the point. There's no shortage of books detailing mistakes made by the US and other Western countries – it's one of the benefits of their being free and open societies that there is no difficulty in publishing them. This book, on the other hand, is about what Russia does, and what that means for the people it does it to.

## About how we got here

In 2014, Russia sent military intelligence officers under cover into the Czech Republic. They were tasked with attacking an ammunition storage site holding supplies destined for Ukraine. The site duly exploded, killing two Czech citizens. Russia is also the prime suspect for a series of similar explosions in Bulgaria during the same period.[3]

It's worth stopping for a moment and thinking about the nature of those missions. Eight years before the attack on Ukraine woke the world up to the fact that Russia was waging war on Europe, Russian soldiers carried out a destructive sabotage operation in the heart of the continent, attacking a NATO and EU country. As Tom Tugendhat – chair of the UK House of Commons Foreign Affairs Committee and a former British Army officer with operational experience – commented, 'if that is not a war-like act, frankly I don't know what one is'.[4] And four years later, two of those same soldiers, Aleksandr Mishkin and Anatoliy Chepiga, became infamous worldwide as the main perpetrators of the 2018 Salisbury attack using the Novichok nerve agent. Targeted assassinations, sabotage and destruction behind enemy lines are something Westerners normally associate

2. Kati Parppei, 'Enemy Images in the Russian National Narrative', in Katri Pynnöniemi (ed.), *Nexus of Patriotism and Militarism in Russia: A Quest for Internal Cohesion*, Helsinki: Helsinki University Press, https://hup.fi/site/books/e/10.33134/HUP-9/, p. 38.

3. Boris Mitov and Ivan Bedrov, 'Data Shows Alleged Russian Agents in Bulgaria Around Time Of Arms-Depot Blasts', RFE/RL, 22 April 2021, https://www.rferl.org/a/russia-bulgaria-arms-depot-explosions-gru-agents-gebrev/31217945.html.

4. 'Salisbury poisoning suspects wanted over deadly Czech explosion condemned as "war-like act"', Sky News, 18 April 2021, https://news.sky.com/story/czech-police-hunt-two-men-wanted-over-salisbury-novichok-poisonings-12278716.

with wartime, and the activities of organizations like the UK's SOE and the US OSS during the Second World War. And yet, Russia was repeatedly conducting these operations across a peacetime Europe in the twenty-first century.

It's tempting to think that because there are no open military clashes between Russia and NATO countries, this means that there is not a state of hostilities. But while Moscow may not be '*at war*' with the West in conventional terms beyond the conflict in Ukraine, Russia is certainly conducting warfare by different means. And there could be no clearer indicator that Russia is operating as a rogue state than its willingness to use banned chemical weapons of mass destruction against its enemies both within Russia itself and abroad, as in Salisbury.

Throughout this book we will see how conflict and external threat have always featured much more prominently in the minds of Russian leaders and decision-makers than they do for their Western counterparts. In 2007, when most of Europe was blissfully unaware of Russia as a potential threat, and NATO and the EU were speaking the language of 'strategic partnership' with Moscow, Russia's Chief of the General Staff was speaking of 'the immutable axiom that wars and armed conflicts will continue uninterrupted, because they are generated by the unending competition between states'.[5] This mismatch of basic assumptions lies at the root of Russia's drive to attack countries who may not even realize they are viewed as enemies – a problem made worse by the fact that the common ground between Russia and Western countries imagined by Western leaders tends often not to exist. So, Moscow continues to seek means of damaging or outmanoeuvring its adversaries in conflicts that those adversaries may not even recognize are actually under way.[6] In fact, the current leadership in the Kremlin sees itself in a deadly struggle with the West, and with the state of the world that developed under Western leadership – often called the 'rules-based international order'. The Kremlin says it believes that this conflict was actually started by the West, attacking Russia through information and influence operations as well as the spread of 'colour revolutions' bringing about regime change around Russia's periphery.[7] This perception is compounded by two misplaced beliefs: that Russia presents a tempting target for attack, and that Western countries would prefer to see an unstable or even fragmented Russia to a strong coherent state. But whatever the roots of the conflict, the result today is that Russia sees benefit in attacking the West overall. The British Parliament's 'Russia Report', published in July 2020, concluded that 'any actions it can take which damage the West are fundamentally good for Russia'.[8]

5. Andrey Kalikh, 'Nevoyennye ugrozy v Voyennoy doktrine' (Nonmilitary threats in the Military Doctrine), *Nezavisimoye voyennoye obozreniye*, 16 March 2007, http://nvo.ng.ru/concepts/2007-03-16/4_doctrina.html.

6. Oscar Jonsson, *The Russian Understanding of War: Blurring the Lines between War and Peace*, Washington, DC: Georgetown University Press, 2019.

7. http://redstar.ru/vektory-razvitiya-voennoj-strategii/; https://www.rferl.org/a/putin-opens-the-door----wide----to-staying-on-as-president-past-2024/30480215.html.

8. 'Russia', Intelligence and Security Committee of Parliament, 21 July 2020, http://isc.independent.gov.uk/committee-reports.

Russia can only look strong if its enemies are weaker, and President Putin has made this a key plank of his promise to the Russian people. The problem is, when Russia defines its own security through being able to do damage to other countries, that's an immediate problem for the other countries, as Ukraine has found to its immense cost. The fact that this can be hard for the targets of Russia's aggression to realize is in part because many Western countries – especially those physically further away from Russia – have been lulled into a false sense of security by an extended period of peace between themselves. The problem is that 'normal' relations with Russia are not the same as 'normal' relations between European or North American states. Instead, even in notional peacetime, they involve dealing with ongoing hostile, damaging and irresponsible activity by Moscow, with methods as diverse as cyber attacks, economic pressure, dangerous and irresponsible behaviour by warships and combat aircraft, and use of electronic warfare. But still, many Western nations are so accustomed to the notion of being at peace that until 2022, attacks by Russia caused surprise every time they happened. Misguided belief that Russia would recognize and respond to good intentions combined with highly successful campaigns of information warfare and subversion to influence perceptions and the public portrayal of Russian intentions and actions – and the responses to them. For all her experience of dealing with Russia and its leadership, former German Chancellor Angela Merkel was still hurt and outraged when 'on the one hand, I try to improve relations with Russia on a daily basis, and when then, on the other hand, we see that there is hard evidence that Russian forces are operating in such a way'.[9] Serbian President Aleksandar Vučić thought of Russia as 'a friendly and brotherly country'. So, he asked after exposure of a Russian espionage operation against his country in 2019, 'I have one question for our Russian friends. Why?'[10]

In this as in so much else, Russia's behaviour today is returning to what was normal in its Soviet past, and further back into Tsarist times. As we will see in the chapters of this book, descriptions of Moscow's behaviour that date from the Cold War ring instantly true today. At home, Russia is intent on rebuilding a strong state with 'neither moral restraints nor legal embarrassments in the exercise of absolute power'.[11] Abroad, it is using 'every conceivable expedient to break the power, the sense of direction and the unity of the West, at whatever cost in human suffering'.[12] But the part of this that continues to surprise Western countries is the way Russia

9. Hans von der Burchard, 'Merkel blames Russia for "outrageous" cyberattack on German parliament', *Politico*, 13 May 2020, https://www.politico.eu/article/merkel-blames-russia-for-outrageous-cyber-attack-on-german-parliament/.

10. 'Serbia's president Aleksandar Vučić confirms Russian spy operation after bribe video', *Deutsche Welle*, 21 November 2019, https://www.dw.com/en/serbias-president-aleksandar-vucic-confirms-russian-spy-operation-after-bribe-video/a-51359672.

11. Stuart Ramsay Tompkins, *The Russian Mind*, Norman: University of Oklahoma Press, 1953, p. 7.

12. Edward Crankshaw, *Putting up with the Russians*, London: Macmillan, 1984, p. 5.

has decided that it can simply ignore the rules, laws and norms that the West think provide the stable framework for safe and orderly relations between countries.[13] Long-term observer of Russia Paul Goble thinks that 'Russia's national strategy under Vladimir Putin is based on behaving so badly that others don't seem to know how to react.'[14] In fact, Russia's persistent state behaviour is that of an habitual offender, who accepts detection as an occupational hazard and appears to accept the consequences and countermeasures in the same business-like manner. The bottom line is that although the focal point of the conflict is, for now, Ukraine, Russia under President Putin thinks it is already in a stand-up fight with the West, and Putin himself has set out the rules: 'Fifty years ago, I learnt one rule in the streets of Leningrad: if a fight is unavoidable, you have to hit first.'[15]

The rest of this book is about how Russia hits out, and what that means for the people in the path of the blows. In other words, it's about how Russia gets what it wants – but to understand that, first, in Chapter 1, we have to think about what it is that Russia wants from the rest of the world in the first place.

13. Dr James Lewis, Senior Vice President and Director, Strategic Technologies Program, CSIS, at Oral evidence: The Integrated Review – Threats, Capabilities and Concepts, HC 834, House of Commons Defence Committee, 10 November 2020, https://committees.parliament.uk/oralevidence/1174/pdf/.

14. Paul Goble, 'Behaving Badly on Big Things and Small Core of Russia's National Strategy Under Putin', 13 April 2017, http://www.interpretermag.com/april-13-2017/.

15. President Putin in free discussion at Valdai Club meeting in Sochi, 22 October 2015. Available in a different English translation via 'Meeting of the Valdai International Discussion Club', Russian presidential website, http://en.kremlin.ru/events/president/news/50548.

# Chapter 1

## WHAT MAKES RUSSIA DIFFERENT?

*Why does Moscow behave the way it does?*

Paradoxically, in its new dealings with the West and with its own people, Russia is being more open and honest. Not in the sense of giving up its routine denials of everything it is caught doing, but instead no longer trying to even superficially hide the fact that it is a repressive, authoritarian country that is content to behave as a rogue state because it sees the West as its enemy. But throughout the current century, Western leaders' own preconceptions about how countries work together have made it hard for them to recognize and accept the growing evidence that Russia does not share those ideas, and furthermore wants not only to undermine them but to harm the countries that do. The result of this failure or unwillingness to understand the root causes of Russia's strategy against the West has repeatedly been a complete inability to respond appropriately when Russia does something that ought to be unacceptable – as for instance in the wake of the murder of Alexander Litvinenko in the UK in 2006.[1]

The period before the seizure of Crimea was a frustrating one for front-line countries like Poland and the Baltic states, who had watched developments next door in Russia with alarm but felt unable to convince other Western capitals like London of the looming Russia problem – and instead were written off as troublemakers seeking to disrupt positive relations with Moscow. Estonian diplomat Sven Sakkov describes the experience of talking to the EU and NATO about Russia before 2014 as 'horribly difficult, and hugely challenging'. But as so often, it was Russia's own behaviour that proved the point. 'In 2014 we were vindicated,' Sven continues, 'because before, we were pretty much brushed off, very gently and very politely, but it wasn't taken seriously. We were looked at as suffering from historic hallucinations and not being serious. But in 2014 suddenly that changed. We were vindicated, because what we had said about Russia was demonstrated in Crimea and the war against Ukraine. Suddenly we did not any

1. Duncan Allan, 'Managed Confrontation: UK Policy Towards Russia After the Salisbury Attack', Chatham House, 30 October 2018.

more hear as a reply to our concerns that "this is not going to happen because Russia is a partner".

It was not just Russia's international behaviour but also how it was treating its own subjects at home that began finally to remove doubts. According to Robert Pszczel, who was NATO's official representative in Moscow for five years, 'When the embassies are all reporting the same things from Moscow, you can only fight the facts for so long. It became impossible to ignore attacks as they were accumulating, because there were just so many of them. First the Russians doing it to themselves – independent journalists and so on – then any members of the opposition, then progressively more foreigners, and then foreign countries.' Sven's compatriot (and his country's former Defence Minister) Jüri Luik shares this sense of vindication: 'All along this road I have had to explain Russia, and our views about Russia, and also to underline that the Baltic states were not paranoid and not warning about Russian moves because of our own sad history. We simply perhaps had more clarity in seeing what Russia is and what Russia is becoming. And of course now people are often saying to us, my God, you were right.' 'Which doesn't make me happy about it,' he adds.

## Not on the same page

People who work with Russia talk a lot about the difference between there and the West in terms of 'values', by which they often mean very basic ideas about how countries should treat each other, as well as how they should treat both their own people and others. Valeriy Akimenko was born in Ukraine, but after moving to the UK watched Russia for the BBC for over twenty years. He explains that 'there's a real ugly divide between the values ostensibly defended by Russia and the values of the West. You have frequent attacks from the bullhorns of Russian propaganda against all things liberal, with the implication being that it's a facade, hiding the same problems Russia has, corruption, unfair elections, things like that. Meanwhile Russia claims that it stands for, let's call them conservative traditional values, family values, Orthodox Christian values.' An acceptance of a more harsh and authoritarian state goes along with this 'conservative' approach. Westerners who are experienced in dealing with Russia know that like so much else, its attitude to human rights might resemble a European country but only superficially, and on closer inspection has more in common with far more distant societies. Reiner Schwalb is a German Army officer who also spent years posted in Moscow. He recalls how 'In 2003 I was drafting the plans for Germany's Afghanistan mission. Could we establish human rights there from the outside? No, we couldn't. Can we do it in Russia? No.'

But this difference is important not just for individual Russians, but also for how it drives Russia's interactions with the rest of the world. University professor Andrey Makarychev says Russia is rejecting 'all the concepts that have been central for international relations starting from 1991', including globalization, networking, soft power, soft security and more. And Russia is keen to remind people that it is not alone in this, Valeriy says. He points to Russian propaganda channels 'force-feeding the narrative of a friendly China, in a strategic partnership with Russia, and by implication a bloc made up of Russia and China opposed to the world order as we know it'. British MP Tom Tugendhat agrees. 'We are engaged in a challenge over the way the world works,' he says. 'We're seeing autocratic powers like China and Russia challenge the rules and break the agreements we've made to keep us all safe.'[2] According to Russia's latest National Security Strategy, the root cause of the breakdown in relations between Russia and many other countries of the world is 'attempts to isolate Russia and the use of double standards in international politics'.[3] The accusation of 'double standards' is a common one, resurfacing when Russia is caught in behaviour that other countries find unacceptable and renounced long ago. It reflects the Russian belief that the Western commitment to the values it claims to follow are a sham. But it masks a different problem: the genuine Western belief that in many cases there is one standard of what constitutes civilized behaviour, and Russia doesn't come up to it.

The problems start when people in the West, especially political leaders, underestimate these differences with Russia – or fail to understand them altogether. It doesn't help that when they read about Russia, they see words that seem familiar, about a system of government and a notional democracy that seems to resemble their own. But the meaning behind these words – like 'parliament' or 'security' or 'international cooperation' – is vastly different to what they assume. It's impossible to grasp why Russia does what it does without understanding some of these key differences, and the specifically Russian ideas about Russia itself, about the world around it, and how the two interact. A constant plea from Russia-watchers is for the people they are briefing to step away from what 'makes sense', or doesn't, when considering Russia's options. The vital point, they say, is that while it may not make sense *to you*, you are not sitting in Moscow.

Puzzling out Moscow's true motivations and intentions remains a key challenge for Russia-focused analysts and policymakers alike, and the problem of 'mirror imaging' – assuming that the other side thinks and acts the same way you do – has repeatedly caused Western leaders to fundamentally misunderstand Russia. In May 2021, the Chatham House think tank in London published a round-up of some of the most deeply entrenched wrong ideas about Russia that lead to Western politicians making misguided decisions.[4] But this problem also applies in reverse. Russian assessments of the United States and the West are just as prone to being

2. Twitter thread, 12 August 2021, https://twitter.com/TomTugendhat/status/142591 9651469565955.

3. 'A comparison of Russia's National Security Strategies (2009, 2015, 2021)', Aleksanteri Institute, 12 July 2021, https://rusmilsec.files.wordpress.com/2021/07/natsec_comparison_ 2021-1.pdf.

4. 'Myths and Misconceptions in the Debate on Russia: How they Affect Policy: and What Can Be Done', Chatham House, May 2021, https://www.chathamhouse.org/2021/05/myths-and-misconceptions-debate-russia

wildly wrong – and understanding how they are wrong helps us understand still more things Russia says and does that otherwise would be totally inexplicable.

In fact, it is the exact same problem that lies behind a number of Russia's own misconceptions about the West – the idea that really the two are the same and that all the apparent differences are merely superficial. Reiner Schwalb says of Russians, 'In their own view, they are not really different from the West. The Russians believe that their behaviour is the same as Western behaviour. Russia mimics the West, but has never internalized what lies behind what it sees, because Western values and Western principles don't really mean anything to most of them.' This goes along with the assumption that those values and principles don't really mean anything in the West either, and that Western insistence on human rights and freedoms is entirely cynical and simply a ploy to pressure Russia – a 'purely political instrument', as influential Russian foreign policy thinker Fyodor Lukyanov describes it.[5] Alex Grigorievs, a Latvian journalist and former politician, thinks President Putin's willingness to speak the language of liberal democracy and cooperation during his first presidential terms was because he believed this was playing the same game as his Western counterparts. 'He talked the talk,' Alex says. 'Why? Because he believed that Western leaders talked the talk just out of politeness. Then, in reality, they come together in some castle in the mountains and talk for real, and divide the world into spheres of interest like Molotov and Ribbentrop. But then he saw at the end of his first presidency that he was not invited to the castle where the spheres of interests are divided and countries are divided. So he decided that he was simply not taken seriously, that the Western countries, especially America, want to have it all to themselves.'

That refusal to understand that the West is different from Russia lies behind some basic Russian misconceptions about what NATO is and how it works – which Russia in turn uses to persuade itself that NATO is a direct threat to Russia. And this, in turn, formed a central plank of Russia's justification for launching its war on Ukraine.

Vladimir Putin's comment in December 2021 that 'NATO is making dangerous attempts to seize Ukrainian territory' was one of the clearest expressions of his position that rather than countries joining NATO because it serves their own interests, they are forced to do so by the US – much in the same manner that Eastern European countries were brought into the Warsaw Pact by the USSR during the Cold War.[6] Russia consistently refuses to understand that NATO is a mutually agreed alliance of independent states that couldn't accept involuntary members if it wanted to, as it can't coerce nations to join. Reiner Schwalb recalls

5. Fyodor Lukyanov, 'The "Liberal World Order" is dead, but fallout from ill-fated visit of EU's Borrell to Moscow proves much of West still in denial', RT, 9 February 2021, https://www.rt.com/russia/515015-borrell-moscow-visit-fallout/.

6. 'Meeting with US President Joe Biden', Russian presidential website, 7 December 2021, http://kremlin.ru/events/president/news/67315.

how in multiple meetings in Moscow, 'I said, why are talking about NATO expansion? There's no NATO expansion. There are nations who want to become members of NATO. It's their free decision, and their free will, not NATO's initiative. But I don't think the senior Russian military officers I spoke to even understood that.'

Instead, new member states join because they feel threatened – and the greatest threat comes from nowhere else but Moscow. As Sven Sakkov recalls, it was the countries of Eastern Europe that 'forced NATO to start thinking about enlargement', rather than NATO urging them to come aboard. But even the idea that these countries have a will of their own runs counter to some basic assumptions that drive Russian foreign policy. According to Russian Foreign Minister Sergey Lavrov, 'NATO has become a purely geopolitical project aimed at taking over the territories that found themselves ownerless after the disappearance of the Warsaw Pact and after the collapse of the Soviet Union.'[7] The key word here is 'ownerless' – sometimes translated as 'orphaned'. For Russia, these countries do not exist as sovereign, independent, free nations. Instead, they have to have an owner – and that owner should, by rights, be Russia.

These failures to understand also leads to a persistent misreading of Western intentions, and the kind of cooperation that could be on offer if Russia could bring itself to take it. If the assumption that the only way of organizing international relations is 'winner takes all' were correct, Putin would have little reason to think that Western leaders would be any less ruthless or duplicitous than he is in striving to win. Instead, President Putin remains constrained by his Soviet past and his assumption that international relations are, by default, hostile. In his annual state of the nation address in 2021 he promised that 'if somebody interprets our good intentions as weakness, our reaction will be asymmetrical, rapid and harsh' – and provided a classic, and tragic, example of failing to understand the outside world and how different it is from Moscow. It is Russia, not the West, that interprets good intentions as weakness.[8]

The combined effect is to leave Russia consistently misinterpreting both deliberate and accidental messages from the West. Joe Biden's throwaway, and possibly unthinking, confirmation in March 2021 that he considers Vladimir Putin a 'killer' led to wild speculation and spiralling theories of conspiracy in Moscow. The Russian assumption was that the exchange 'must have been pre-planned precisely because that's how they operate'.[9] Moscow-based think-tanker Alexander

7. 'Foreign Minister Sergey Lavrov's interview with Solovyov Live YouTube channel', Russian Foreign Ministry website, 27 December 2021, https://mid.ru/en/foreign_policy/news/1792420/.

8. 'Putin warns of tough Russian action if West crosses "red line"', BBC News, 21 April 2021, https://www.bbc.co.uk/news/world-europe-56828813.

9. Anton Troianovski, 'Russia Erupts in Fury Over Biden's Calling Putin a Killer', *New York Times*, 18 March 2021, https://www.nytimes.com/2021/03/18/world/europe/russia-biden-putin-killer.html.

Gabuyev explains further: 'The Kremlin believes that the question that led to Biden's response [that Putin is a killer] was prearranged and that this was a deliberate provocation to cause an emotional reaction and later blame the deterioration of the US–Russia relationship on Russia.'[10] In this, as in so much else, the Kremlin's view of the outside world is distorted by what British Russia-watcher James Sherr calls its 'conspiratorial view about absolutely everything'.

A project in 2020 comparing Russia and the West's understandings of how the relationship had developed since the end of the Cold War found an almost total mismatch between how the same event was understood and placed in context by each side.[11] Sometimes these different views of the world come into sharp focus at a single event. When Vladimir Putin met Joe Biden one to one in mid-June 2021, both men held press conferences afterwards. But their comments seemed to be describing not just two different meetings, but two different worlds. Whatever mutual understanding they might have reached in private, the picture they painted in the press conferences was as unrecognizable to each other as ever. Many of Putin's comments were in response to questions from the Russian media, and the answers were plainly aimed at a Russian audience. The recurring theme was that the West remains the dangerous, unpredictable, aggressive partner in the relationship. Practised rebuttals of accusations against Russia tapped into a rich seam of 'whataboutism' and accusations against the West. How can you accuse me of being a killer, Putin asked, when so many people are shot on the streets of US cities every day – 'You can't even get a word out before they shoot you, either in the chest or in the back.'

His comments at the press conference showed clearly the gulf in understanding between him and the West, and the mix of half-truth, fiction and delusion that the view of the world that he presents publicly seems to be built on. The political opposition in Russia only exists because it is paid for by Russia's enemies abroad, he suggested. He and Biden didn't discuss coronavirus except in passing, he said – but Putin didn't miss the opportunity to mislead the world by saying Russia had responded to a US plea for critical coronavirus equipment in 2020 by shipping ventilators as 'humanitarian aid' free of charge. Challenged on whether he shared Biden's vision of a 'stable, predictable' relationship between the two countries, Putin lined up another barrage of accusations – and of the Kremlin's own conduct, he said only that 'Russia's response to world events has always been appropriate.' The gulf between the two realities on display starkly illustrated the difficulty in reaching any mutual understanding between Russia and the West. As Finnish President Sauli Niinistö later asked, 'How do you react to behaviour from a different planet?'[12]

10. Tweet by Carnegie Russia, 18 March 2021, https://twitter.com/CarnegieRussia/status/1372594155432644620.

11. 'RUSSIAN–WESTERN BLIND SPOTS: From Dialogue on Contested Narratives to Improved Understanding', *Inmedio*, undated, https://www.contested-narratives-dialogue.org/?p=535.

12. 'Finnish President on Russia: How do you react to behaviour from another planet?', Yle News, 13 February 2022, https://yle.fi/news/3-12326162.

## Same continent, different century

For decades, Western politicians have been persistently confused about what Moscow wants and why it is behaving so destructively in order to get it. They are dealing with a challenge that they cannot understand how to confront, and they cannot understand it because it comes from a previous era beyond their understanding of the world in the current century. In that respect some things haven't changed since the earliest encounters between Russia and the West centuries ago, when, according to Henry Kissinger, western Europeans were taken aback by a country that 'seemed barely able to conceal a primitive force from before and beyond Western civilisation'.[13] Today, Russia continues to behave both at home and abroad as though it was still the twentieth or even the nineteenth century. Reiner Schwalb says part of the explanation lies in significant gaps in Russia's history and social development. 'Russia never experienced the Enlightenment or the Reformation, the two things that lie behind all our modern Western ideas of human rights or even of our democratic system,' he explains. 'The only Russians who really did understand those ideas, the Decembrists in the early nineteenth century and intellectuals later, were all killed or exiled or left the country.' The result is stark differences in attitudes and assumptions from what the West tends to take for granted – like a lengthy national debate in Russia, entering the third decade of the twenty-first century, over whether it was right or wrong to prohibit domestic violence.[14]

In so many respects, today's Russia is returning to patterns of behaviour that are recognizable from Soviet times. For other countries, this might be a cause for concern – Germany, for instance, would be deeply wary of resurrecting practices, rhetoric or attitudes that were associated with the Nazi period. But rather than confront its vicious Soviet past, in dozens of small steps Russia today is celebrating and recreating it. That adds another layer of incomprehension for a generation of Europeans that were quite simply not around to see Soviet times and what they meant both for Russians and for the rest of the world. After all, when the Berlin Wall fell in 1989, French President Emmanuel Macron was only eleven years old.

This process of winding back the clock started slowly, but almost as soon as Vladimir Putin first became president in 2000, one of his first orders was to restore the Soviet national anthem. Since then, both symbolic actions like the anthem and real recreations of Soviet practices have gathered pace. Russia is restoring monuments to mass murderers of Russians, including Feliks Dzerzhinskiy, a Pole who created and led the Cheka and OGPU, Soviet Russia's early secret police forces and the forerunners to the KGB.[15] Stalin consistently tops polls of the 'most notable

---

13. Henry Kissinger, *World Order* (London: Penguin, 2014), p. 50.

14. Bulat Mukhamedzhanov, 'The ongoing fight for protection from domestic violence in Russia', *Riddle Russia*, 15 January 2020, https://www.ridl.io/en/the-ongoing-fight-for-protection-from-domestic-violence-in-russia/.

15. Ivan Rostovtsev, 'В Гусь-Хрустальном восстановили памятник Дзержинскому' (Monument to Dzerzhinskiy restored in Gus-Khrustalny), *Chesnok*, 18 August 2021, https://chesnok.media/2021/08/18/v-gus-hrustalnom-vosstanovili-pamjatnik-dzerzhinskomu/.

figures from history'.[16] In Russian universities, in-residence officers from the FSB security and intelligence service have been installed along the lines of the KGB supervisors from Soviet times.[17] In September 2020, surviving members of the NKVD and other Soviet security forces who had taken part in savage repressions in the Baltic states in the early years of Soviet occupation were awarded 75,000 roubles each in a decree by President Putin.[18] Russia kits out its hockey team pretending to be the USSR – role-playing that should be no more acceptable than if the German national football team took to adorning its kit with Nazi heraldry.[19]

Jüri Luik explains that this is not just a matter of nostalgia; it reflects Putin's 'understanding of how Russia should be organized as a country. He very much harks back to Soviet times, and basically believes that Russia's increasing similarity to the Soviet Union is a source of strength and a sign of vitality of the country, even though anybody else looking would know that's not true. The Soviet heritage sits extremely deeply in his heart and in his mind.'

The Soviet approach extends to ways of persuading Russians that the outside world is hostile – and limiting their knowledge of it. Online, the attempts to gain control over the internet and suppress access to social media are recognizable as old Soviet notions of information security, as exercised by the KGB and its successors.[20] And Russia's latest National Security Strategy has reintroduced the Soviet term 'alien ideals' to describe what the West considers to be universal human values.[21] In some ways these efforts have been effective. Early hopes that Soviet nostalgia would fade with time have been disappointed. Younger generations of Russians who do not have first-hand experience of the Soviet past are less able to discern what is myth and what was reality than those who remember the USSR. This means that far from being repelled by the history of the Soviet era, young

16. 'Putin Plummets, Stalin Stays on Top in Russians' Ranking of "Notable" Historical Figures – Poll', *Moscow Times*, 21 June 2021, https://www.themoscowtimes.com/2021/06/21/putin-plummets-stalin-stays-on-top-in-russians-ranking-of-remarkable-historical-figures-poll-a74280.

17. '"There's A Room Under The Stairs": Russia's FSB Sets Up Resident Agents At Research Institutes', RFE/RL, https://www.rferl.org/a/russia-fsb-sets-up-resident-agents-at-research-institutes/31040751.html.

18. Decree of the President of the Russian Federation No. 544, 2 September 2020, http://www.kremlin.ru/acts/bank/45857.

19. 'Russia Hockey Team Dons Soviet Jerseys in Loss to Finland', *Moscow Times*, 20 December 2021, https://www.themoscowtimes.com/2021/12/20/russia-hockey-team-dons-soviet-jerseys-in-loss-to-finland-a75874.

20. As described at length in Andrey Soldatov and Irina Borogan, *The Red Web: The Struggle Between Russia's Digital Dictators and the New Online Revolutionaries* (New York: PublicAffairs, 2015).

21. Steve Gutterman, 'The Week in Russia: Strategy and Tactics – Putin's "Bleak" New Security Blueprint', 9 July 2021, https://www.rferl.org/a/russia-bleak-new-strategy/31350072.html.

people can at times have an even more positive view of it than their parents or grandparents, especially when Soviet films and propaganda material are presented as historical sources describing how things realistically were during the Soviet Union.[22]

The result is a sharp contrast between Russia and other countries of the former USSR. Andrey Makarychev, living in Tartu, Estonia, points out that 'Russia is the only country out of all fifteen former Soviet Republics that is unhappy about the fall of the Soviet Union. The other countries took the events of 1991 as a kind of new opening – as something that might give a chance to either create a nation state from scratch, or to regain the independence that had been lost decades ago. Russia is different. It's the only country that looks at this as a tragedy.'

## Return to empire

And it is the nature of Russia's relationship with the countries around it that were formerly under Moscow's direct control that lies at the root of many of the tensions between Russia and the West. True to its notions of statehood that also come from previous centuries, Russia considers that as a 'great power' it has the right to dictate to its neighbours how they should behave and in particular how they should conduct their foreign relations. A number of other ideas that seem out of place in the twenty-first century feed into this assumption. Sulev Suvari is a former US Army officer who worked with Russia for much of his career. He suggests that much of Russian behaviour towards its neighbours stems from an inability to adjust to the idea that Moscow no longer has an empire – covering the boundaries of the old Tsarist Russian Empire or those of Soviet control or domination which in many areas were similar. 'They just can't quite give up control. But unlike the French and British empires, the Russian colonies are directly adjacent to Russia. It's even more challenging when they're your neighbour,' Sulev says.

It's true that many of Russia's actions against its neighbours are driven by a failure to adjust to the idea that Moscow no longer rules over lands beyond its borders. But that's a situation Russia wants to correct. Senior Russian officials like the deputy speaker of the State Duma (and at the time, head of the Russian delegation to the Council of Europe) have called for Russia's borders to be revised to their status in 1917, explicitly bringing not only Ukraine but countries like the Baltic states and Finland back under Russian control.[23] Vladislav Surkov, credited

22. 'Vospriyatie molodezhyu novyh nezavisimyh gosudarstv istorii sovetskogo i postsovetskogo periodov', *Yevraziyskiy monitor*, April–May 2009, http://www.eurasiamonitor. org/rus/research/event-162.html.

23. 'Вице-спикер Госдумы призвал расширить Россию до границ 1917 года и объяснился' (Duma deputy speaker calls for Russia to expand to 1917 borders, and explains), Lenta.ru, 13 January 2022, https://lenta.ru/news/2022/01/13/tolstoy/.

with shaping many of the key features of the current Russian regime, has also laid out how the loss of Russia's imperial dominions – the result, as he put it, of the 'shameful' peace treaty that ended Russia's part in the First World War – should be reversed.[24] And President Putin agrees with them. He has not only referred to the end of the USSR as a 'catastrophe',[25] but used the same word to describe the decisions that led to the dissolution of the Russian Empire and the establishment of constituent republics within the USSR – that eventually split off into independent countries.[26] The return to empire is a key part of what Putin calls Russia's 'historical future as a nation' – an apparent oxymoron but one which states clearly his ambition to roll back the clock.[27]

In contrast to other European imperial powers, for Russia the end of empire was postponed. Thanks to Moscow maintaining its control over eastern Europe after defeating Nazi Germany, it finally came not at the end of the First World War, or of the Second, but at the end of the Cold War. Russia is not the only former colonial power to have complex relations with its former dominions in the wake of imperial retreat. However, even given its late start, it has not travelled as far along the path of post-imperial normalization as countries such as the United Kingdom, France or Portugal had a quarter-century after the end of empire. Today, in fact, Russia sees its relations with its former dominions in the way that France or Britain did in the first few years after their power was curtailed – before they suffered the defeats and setbacks that drove home the new limits of their ability to shape the world beyond their own borders.

At the same point in this post-imperial trajectory, Britain had waged a successful campaign against communism in Malaya, but had not yet suffered the humiliating setback of Suez. Russia has achieved success in small wars in Chechnya and Georgia, and projected power more recently in Syria, Kazakhstan and across Africa. Successful military adventurism both close to home and farther afield prolongs Russia's belief in its power and its right to dominate others.

But the first military defeat – which may, just possibly, take place in Ukraine – will have far-reaching consequences. With its control of the information space at home, Russia can spin or explain away political reverses abroad, but not an unarguable military setback that calls into doubt either Russian military power itself or the ability to exercise it unchallenged. It is only this that can constrain

24. Vladislav Surkov, 'Туманное будущее похабного мира' (Murky Future of a Shameful Peace), *Aktualnyye kommentarii*, 15 February 2022, https://actualcomment.ru/tumannoe-budushchee-pokhabnogo-mira-2202150925.html.

25. 'Putin: Soviet collapse a "genuine tragedy"', NBC, 25 April 2005, https://www.nbcnews.com/id/wbna7632057.

26. 'Address by the President of the Russian Federation', Russian presidential website, 21 February 2022, http://en.kremlin.ru/events/president/news/67828.

27. Yasmeen Serhan, 'Vladimir Putin's Self-Serving Revisionist History', *The Atlantic*, February 2022, https://www.theatlantic.com/international/archive/2022/02/putin-russia-ukraine-revisionist-history/622936/.

Russia's future ambition to reassert itself as the dominant power across the countries of eastern Europe, which it sees as its birthright. And it is only significant failure that will encourage Russia's leadership eventually to start to reassess its place in the world. This would be the shock the country needs to start the long, hard process of transitioning from a frustrated former imperial power to a normal country that can coexist with Europe.

Another driver for the urge to exert control over neighbours is the notion of the threat to, and vulnerability of, Russia's borders, which means in order to feel secure, Moscow has to be in command of territory far beyond them. This provides the context for Russia's constant description of NATO enlargement as a threat. Regardless of the fact that countries join NATO for protection from Russia instead of to attack it, NATO 'approaching Russia's borders' is raised again and again in Russia's arguments that it is in danger.[28] According to a guide for history teachers produced by a committee appointed by Putin in 2005, 'The present borders of Russia are unnatural … foremost because they cannot adequately guarantee Russia's security. This inadequacy must be addressed.'[29] Reiner Schwalb recalls how this idea met with incomprehension: 'Russia believes they need a buffer zone between the West and themselves. And we Germans thought it was all nonsense. Why would you need a buffer zone? What for? I mean, we don't want to attack you.'

It's hard to say what depth of buffer zone under its control would be considered satisfactory for Moscow. Discussion of what constitutes 'close to Russia's borders' reveals a very distinctive sense of geography in Russia. Russian Foreign Ministry spokeswoman Maria Zakharova says a Norwegian airport and naval base where the US is considering a greater presence are 'in direct proximity to the Russian border', despite being over 500 kilometres away from Russia even in a straight line.[30] But then, according to Putin, even Israel is also 'in direct proximity to Russia's borders'.[31]

Even at its weakest, Russia never stopped insisting that it has greater rights than other countries around it, or demanding to dictate the foreign policy decisions of countries beyond its borders.[32] The attitude that it is entitled to domination over its

28. As expressed in a wide range of Russian security policy documents, including the December 2014 *Military Doctrine of the Russian Federation* and its predecessors.

29. A.V. Fillipov, *A Latest History of Russia 1945–2006* (Moscow: Prosveshcheniye, 2007).

30. Thomas Nilsen, 'Zakharova erupts in fury over Norway's military deal with the United States', *Barents Observer*, 30 April 2021, https://thebarentsobserver.com/en/security/2021/04/moscow-oslo-destroys-russian-norwegian-relations.

31. 'Путин: палестино-израильский конфликт происходит в непосредственной близости от границ России' (Putin: the Palestinian–Israeli conflict is taking place in direct proximity to Russia's borders), Dozhd TV, 14 May 2021, https://tvrain.ru/news/putin_palestino_izrailskij_konflikt_proishodit_v_neposredstvennoj_blizosti_ot_granits_rossii-529968/.

32. Fiona Hill and Pamela Jewett, *Back in the USSR: Russia's Intervention in the Internal Affairs of the Former Soviet Republics and the Implication for United States Policy toward Russia*, Occasional Paper, Strengthening Democratic Institutions Project (Cambridge, MA: Belfer Center for Science and International Affairs, Harvard Kennedy School, January 1994).

neighbours remains constant regardless of how strong or weak Russia may be at the time. It survived the upheavals of the Bolshevik Revolution of 1917 and the end of the USSR in 1991 intact. A post-mortem published in 1953 of how eastern Europe had been lost to Soviet domination after the Second World War concluded that in the Russian view, 'Stalin was no more than reasserting Russian authority over territories which had long recognized Tsarist rule, and which had been torn away from Russia at the time of her revolutionary weakness after the First World War.'[33] In just the same way after 1991, Moscow continued to act 'as if the Soviet Union had not fallen apart, as if it had only been reformatted, but relations between sovereign and vassal have remained as before'.[34] A key part of the problem is President Putin's belief that in 1991 'Russia voluntarily – I emphasise – voluntarily and consciously made absolutely historic concessions in giving up its own territory'.[35] This notion that other countries may in fact count as Russian territory directly affects how Russia deals with them. In 2005, long before the reality of Russian hostility was recognized beyond the front-line states, a Norwegian researcher trying to understand Russian attitudes to the use of force looked at cases of aggression in Russia's neighbourhood and concluded it was possible that 'Russian decision-makers simply did not consider the former Soviet republics foreign in terms of cases of intervention.'[36]

But Russia's desire to exert control is inherently destructive, because it implies making sure that the countries around it work in the same way as Russia itself. This has real implications for the people living there. An Estonian assessment of the ideal situation in a neighbouring country for Moscow lists 'limited development of the rule of law; absence of free elections; repressed civil society; limited relations with the West; territorial conflict, with Russia as the kingpin; Russian troop presence in the form of a military base or otherwise'.[37] For countries like Estonia, this is a permanent problem, and dealing with problems that in one way or another are created by Russia is a constant drain on their governments and economies. Sven Sakkov explains that throughout his career he has not dealt directly with

33. William Hardy McNeill, *America, Britain and Russia: Their Co-operation and Conflict 1941–1946* (Oxford: Oxford University Press, 1953), p. 406.

34. P. Goble, 'Putin Gives the World His Geography Lesson: "All the Former USSR is Russia"', *The Interpreter*, 28 April 2015, http://www.interpretermag.com/putingivestheworldhisgeographylessonalltheformerussrisrussia/.

35. Ksenia Kirillova, 'Putin practically called Ukraine Russian territory', *Novyy Region 2*, 28 April 2015, http://nr2.com.ua/blogs/Ksenija_Kirillova/Putin-fakticheski-nazval-Ukrainu-territoriey-Rossii-95566.html.

36. Morten Langsholdt, 'Russia and the Use of Force: Theory and Practice', Norwegian Defence Research Establishment, Report 2005/02504, November 2005, www.ffi.no/no/Rapporter/05-02504.pdf.

37. 'International Security and Estonia', Välisluureamet (Estonian Foreign Intelligence Service), February 2021, https://www.valisluureamet.ee/pdf/raport/2021-ENG.pdf.

Russia itself – but everything he has done, especially managing alliances and relationships with allies, has been because of Russia. 'Everything has been influenced by Russia because Russia is the reason why we do all the other things,' he says, and adds, 'The biggest problem for Estonia has been, is and will be our eastern neighbour and its policies. There is no other way to put it.'

Russia doesn't have a history of stable and mutually beneficial relations with many of its western neighbours. And today, if it is incapable of maintaining one even with an ideal neighbour like Belarus under Aleksandr Lukashenka, the hopes for a good relationship with other countries far more inclined to protect their independence and sovereignty are pretty slim – and the risk is even present that they may follow the example of Ukraine and become a victim of direct Russian aggression. President Putin and Foreign Minister Sergey Lavrov have pointed to precedents for constructive Russian involvement in European politics that led to periods of extended peace and stability. The problem is that the precedents they choose – the Congress of Vienna in 1815 and the Yalta Conference agreements in 1945 – are examples of victorious powers in a world war agreeing among themselves how to run the world over the heads of smaller or defeated states. With or without Russia, this template just doesn't fit with European notions of relations between states in the twenty-first century. But still, in pursuing its goal of limiting the options of the countries around it, Russia also seems to assume that major European countries and the United States will still be willing in the twenty-first century to join in old-school agreements to allocate spheres of great power influence that each of them will control.

Russia will only be encouraged in this by Western commentators or academics who propose giving Russia exactly the sphere of influence it wants as a route to a better relationship with Moscow. Michael O'Hanlon is a senior figure at the Brookings Institution, a Washington think tank, and a keen advocate of telling independent countries that they should agree not to seek protection by the West against Russia. 'The core concept should be one of permanent non-alignment for countries of eastern Europe,' he writes. 'Ideally, the zone would include Finland and Sweden.'[38] This is precisely what Russia wants to hear. Former Finnish intelligence chief Pekka Toveri points out that O'Hanlon's notion of Finland being non-aligned is a key element of Russian messaging against the country. 'During political meetings and negotiations Russia always tries to play down Finland's EU membership and point out how NATO is "creeping" to Finland,' he says. 'When Lavrov talks about Finland, he often says that Finland is a "neutral" country, dismissing the whole EU membership and EU's common foreign and security policy.' Under his proposed deal, O'Hanlon explains, 'Russia recognises that Georgia and Ukraine have the right to join any organization other than NATO – e.g. the EU. If Russia agrees to this, then we agree not to expand NATO any further

---

38. Michael E. O'Hanlon, 'To Face Russia and Vladimir Putin, Joe Biden Needs a Smart Strategy', *USA Today*, 28 May 2021.

into the former Soviet space and we lift sanctions.'[39] The whole plan rests on the idea that the United States, and NATO directed by the US, can make deals with Russia about the future of the countries in between without involving those countries at all, still less taking account of what they themselves might desire. This too is entirely in sympathy with Russia's own views on countries like Georgia, Ukraine, Finland, Sweden and a host of others having less right than Russia does to dictate their future.

People actually living in the front-line states, however, would quite like to have a say in that future – especially if they have a clear perception of what the alternative would be if they were once again under Russian rule. Sami Siva is a Canadian photojournalist who has reported on the borderlands in the Baltic states, and recorded what he sees there through the eyes of an outsider with no stake in the argument between Russia and its neighbours. Sami found people had no doubt as to which option they should choose. Narva in Estonia has often been held up as an example of a town and region with a substantial Russian minority that might be expected to side with Russia. 'When Crimea happened in 2014, everyone wondered whether Narva would be next,' Sami says. 'But this won't happen, as the locals clearly don't want to be part of the regime across the river. They see the living and economic conditions of their close family members there.' Linas, from Lithuania, is old enough to remember the Soviet Union, and links the prosperity of his country today directly with joining Western institutions instead of being under Russian control: 'For me as a Lithuanian, I see only the benefits of being part of the European Union and NATO. Baltic countries are a perfect example, that when you join those organizations and union, when we share the values, and when you contribute to those values; you will be prosperous like never before.'

The country where this problem comes most sharply into view is of course Ukraine, which at the time of writing is paying a horrific price for wishing to follow its own ideas about its future, rather than accept Russia's demands. President Putin's view, expressed in multiple interactions with Western leaders and in increasingly bitter essays and speeches, is that Ukraine does not have the right to be a country. Russians, Ukrainians and Belarusians are 'one people', he argues, and Russia needs to protect 'our historical territories' – including Belarus and much of Ukraine. It follows that Ukraine itself is just 'a Russian border province', and Ukrainian statehood from the eighteenth century 'a mutiny' against Moscow.[40] Journalist Sarah Hurst points out that Russia's claim to Russian speakers beyond its borders, including those in Ukraine, is like telling people in Ireland they are British because they speak English.[41]

39. Speaking at 'The Biden Administration and NATO' online event, NATO Defense College, 26 February 2021.

40. Vladimir Putin, 'Об историческом единстве русских и украинцев' (On the historical unity of Russians and Ukrainians), Russian presidency website, 12 July 2021, http://www.kremlin.ru/events/president/news/66181.

41. Tweet by @X Soviet, 8 April 2021, https://twitter.com/xsovietnews/status/138013544889 1260930?s=27.

Historians point out multiple other problems with Putin's view of history, as well as some of the inherent contradictions in Russia's demands on Ukraine – like claiming that Ukrainians are no different from Russians while at the same time objecting strenuously when those Ukrainians that prefer to speak Ukrainian want to communicate in their own language.[42]

But in Ukraine and elsewhere, for as long as the West continues instead to support the independence and sovereignty of Russia's neighbours, and the freedoms of the people living there, there will always be a fundamental disagreement with Moscow. It's simply not possible to humour Russia's demands for what it sees as 'great power' rights to influence the countries around it at the same time as respecting those other countries' rights to independence and to make their own decisions. Russia's drive to dominate Ukraine and dictate its future stems from an implicit assumption of entitlement and exceptionalism. Western optimists may continue to hope for an eventually more benign Russia, one that doesn't terrorize its subjects or threaten its neighbours. But for as long as Russia remains unwilling and unable to accept that its former dominions are now independent countries, and to adapt as other former imperial powers have done, it will continue to fret, posture and lash out to assert its former status. The tragedy is that Russia is still fully willing to send young soldiers to die for the sake of dreams of vanished empire.

## Can't we all just get along?

As well as being repeatedly startled by Russian acts of hostility, Western leaders have been disappointed time and again when attempts to find common ground with Russia and issues on which it's possible to work together with Moscow consistently fail. It is only natural to assume that the Kremlin is interested in cooperation on a shared problem just as a Western country would be; but consistent experience demonstrates that it is not, at least in any accepted Western sense of the word. For Moscow, attempts at cooperation primarily involve trying to make sure Russia's counterparts abroad amend their policies to fit in with Russia's desires or demands (see Chapter 3). Whenever it appears that Russia and the West could work together on a problem, it quickly becomes clear that not only Moscow's understanding of the issue but also its preferred solution and the methods it would favour to deliver it are completely at odds with what the West is hoping for.

Russia's default attitude to cooperative endeavours presents a deep-rooted obstacle to working together on common challenges. Cooperation in itself is a competition for advantage rather than a working together towards shared aims,

---

42. Iryna Matviyishyn, 'How Russia weaponizes the language issue in Ukraine', Atlantic Council, 25 June 2020, https://www.atlanticcouncil.org/blogs/ukrainealert/putin-is-the-only-winner-of-ukraines-language-wars/.

and in the process, any concessions or compromise by the other party is seen as a weakness to be exploited rather than a favour to be repaid in kind. 'The immutable Russian policy is to get whatever they can with the least possible effort, and then ask for more,' Juho Kusti Paasikivi (later President of Finland) wrote in 1891 while he was studying in Russia as a twenty-one-year-old: 'They try to exact a high price for anything that they understand they have to do in any case. They are immune to ethical, humanitarian and abstract juridical arguments, being affected only by practical and realistic points of view.'[43] In the following century, this was repeatedly confirmed when 'the Russians . . . would regard willingness to negotiate as a sign of weakness, and would raise their price for a settlement accordingly.'[44] Still today, Sven Sakkov says, 'when negotiating with Russia you should not assume that your compromise will result in other side compromising'.

The search for ways in which it must be possible to cooperate with Russia has repeatedly come back to counterterrorism. On the face of it, it seems reasonable to assume that since both sides face a threat from terrorism they must have a common interest in countering it. Russia knows this, and recognizes that it can always tempt Western counterparts with offers of collaboration in this area. But this only works for as long as 'the Western hope for partnership [is] based on statements of faith rather than substantive assessment of Russian goals'.[45] The challenge is that the two sides have completely different ideas of what counterterrorism means and who the terrorists are. Russia proved beyond doubt in Chechnya and Syria that its methods for what it calls counterterrorist operations are entirely unpalatable to the West. And by enticing Western states into cooperation, it is this model of savage repression that it wished to export to the world.[46]

Norwegian defence researcher Tor Bukkvoll, like many of the people I spoke to for this book, believes that 'what Russia wants is respect. Respect as a great power.' The key question then, of course, is why Russia persists in doing things that earn it the opposite of respect, instead causing it to be despised or sometimes derided by the rest of the world The answer lies in a very Russian sense of the word 'respect'. 'It's not respect in the Western sense, based on positive attitudes towards you,' Tor goes on. 'For Russia, respect is measured by how you are treated. If they can't convince us to respect them in their way, they can raise the cost of not doing so to a degree that in the end, we will behave in the way they want just because it's too costly for us to do otherwise.'

A surprising amount of Russia's destructive activity is driven, at least in part, by its status anxiety. Russia considers itself to be a great power owed a special status,

43. https://en.wikiquote.org/wiki/Juho_Kusti_Paasikivi.

44. John Gaddis, *Strategies of Containment* (Oxford: Oxford University Press, 1982), p. 86.

45. Andrew Monaghan, *The New Politics of Russia: Interpreting Change* (Manchester: Manchester University Press, 2016), p. 148.

46. Jakob Hedenskog, 'Russia and international cooperation on counter-terrorism – From the Chechen wars to the Syria Campaign', FOI (Swedish Defence Research Agency), March 2020, https://www.foi.se/rest-api/report/FOI-R--4916--SE.

but finds the West fails to grant Russia the respect and superpower status which it feels is its due. Even worse, it objects to Russian behaviour. So, Russia considers the West to be hostile and treats it accordingly. This is because Russia 'never agreed to accept the role the West assigned them in the new framework – the status of a large but second-rank European country'.[47] As Alex Grigorievs points out, a 'second rate country means a country that observes international law' – rather than a great power that can make its own rules.

But if Moscow cannot achieve recognition as a first-rank partner, the next best option appears to be recognition as a first-rank enemy. This obsession with status and the need to sit at the top table drives both high-profile efforts like the continued prioritizing of nuclear capability on a par with the United States, and low-profile angling for direct conversations with the US as equals in many other fields. Cyber expert Raphael Satter thinks one reason the Russian government facilitates Russian cybercrime, instead of trying to crack down on it, is because it provides another means to engage the United States. 'It draws a lot of attention to Russia, and it creates a lot of room for, you know, kind of bilateral summits to discuss how to control hacking and that kind of thing,' Raphael says.[48] Sulev Suvari has also noticed this pattern of looking for any opportunity to engage with the US as an equal. In the Syria ceasefire negotiations, he says, 'they were really pushing for a kind of joint operation centre, a place where the US and Russians could work together to deconflict. They're always looking for [a] way to be treated as equals – equal owners, equal combatants, equal elements of the solution, so to speak. I'm not quite sure if they even cared about Syria itself. It was just an opportunity to be back at the table, equals with the US – the UN in between, and the Russians and the Americans working something out while other nations have to wait to see how it works out.'

Overall, this striving for status makes up a major part of the syndrome described by former Estonian Defence Minister Jüri Luik: 'Russia is never part of the solution but always part of the problem.'[49] In effect, Russia chose to confront the West instead of finding a way of living at peace with it, because peace would mean acceptance of a new place in the world for Russia that its current leaders find utterly unacceptable.

At the same time, a recurring theme in the stories Russia tells itself and the world is of Russia as a victim, not a perpetrator. As Pekka Toveri explains, 'Every time there is a harder Western reaction, Russia can turn on the victim mode, stating that the West is harassing them for no reason. This message is for Russia's

---

47. Fiona Hill, 'Putin: The one-man show the West doesn't understand', *Bulletin of the Atomic Scientists* 72, no. 3 (2016): 140–4.

48. A topic explored at length in Misha Glenny, *DarkMarket: How Hackers Became the New Mafia* (London: Vintage, 2012).

49. 'Russland ist immer Teil des Problems' (Russia is always part of the problem), *Spiegel*, 28 August 2020, https://www.spiegel.de/ausland/estlands-aussenminister-jueri-luik-russland-ist-immer-teil-des-problems-a-459b9f33-e7f3-4189-aaa1-795863fc1c24.

supporters in the West as well as for its own population.' Since the rise of Muscovy, Russia has been a permanent threat to the peoples and territories around it and has pursued a constant policy of expansion when it felt strong enough to do so (a rule proven by the exceptions when it felt too weak and, briefly, stopped or was beaten back). But, Russia says today, relations with the West are only hostile because Western countries are bent on aggression against Moscow – rather than determined to defend themselves against it. According to Putin, the reason for Russia's assaults on Ukraine is that the rest of the world is 'anti-Russian' for supporting Ukraine's aspirations to freedom and independence.[50]

Putin regularly confuses cause and effect in this manner in his public speeches.[51] Jüri Luik explains how this is creates an ongoing cycle of confrontation: 'Permanent tensions around Russia give [Putin] justification for being in power, and of course since other countries try to be friendly he has to initiate those tensions. And when he has initiated them, he makes a sad face and says everybody is against us, everybody is anti-Russian.'

Meanwhile, the attacks on European munitions stores in 2014, Russia's public attempt at the murder of opposition figurehead Alexei Navalny in 2020 and the invasion of Ukraine in 2022 are all part of the same syndrome – instead of being interested in cooperation, Russia feels no constraint in acting as a rogue state. The current state of relations with the West gives no incentive at all for caring what the rest of the world thinks. In fact, Russia's willingness to send its intelligence organizations and agencies out to carry out what are effectively acts of war against the West should have led Europe to the conclusion that Russia is at war with it long before the attack on Ukraine proved the point beyond argument.[52]

Military indoctrination begins early in Russia, in some cases from pre-school age.[53] The tone is uncompromising – after the Victory Day celebrations in May 2021 one Russian school proudly posted videos of small children with dummy rifles marching and chanting 'Oh, Russian land! Those who insult you, your enemies, there is no excuse for them. We are Russians, God is with us! Russians do not betray their country. Give your last breath for the Motherland!'[54] Being taught

50. Vladimir Putin, 'Об историческом единстве русских и украинцев' (On the historical unity of Russians and Ukrainians), Russian presidency website, 12 July 2021, http://www.kremlin. ru/events/president/news/66181.

51. 'As soon as we started to get a bit more stable and to get up off our knees, the politics of containment started.' Vladimir Putin, speaking on Rossiya-24 TV, 10 February 2021.

52. Keir Giles and Toomas Hendrik Ilves, 'Europe must admit Russia is waging war', Chatham House, 23 April 2022, https://www.chathamhouse.org/2021/04/europe-must-admit-russia-waging-war.

53. Kevin Rothrock, 'Russian Military Training. In Kindergarten', *Moscow Times*, 29 March 2017, https://www.themoscowtimes.com/2017/03/29/russian-military-training-in-kindergarten-a57573.

54. Instagram story from 'Vsevolodskaya General Middle School No. 42', @vsevolodskaia_shkola_42, 14 May 2021, reposted on Twitter by Sergej Sumlenny, https://twitter.com/sumlenny/status/1393265801587838983.

to be ready for war goes hand in hand with being taught to fear the evil West. The Night Wolves organization puts on holiday shows for children, funded by the Kremlin (Australian researcher Kira Harris found grant applications promising 'a patriotic atmosphere that combines Russian history, spirituality, and current political events').[55] One of these performances, in 2013, involved a character resembling the Statue of Liberty trying to kidnap Snegurochka, the snow princess who is a companion to Grandfather Frost, the Russian Santa Claus. The Night Wolves save the princess and give the children in the audience an 'alternative to foreign domination' while showing them that 'evil is really scary', Night Wolves leader Aleksandr Zaldostanov explained.[56]

Reiner Schwalb thinks it is instead this programme of indoctrination and preparation that is scary. 'It's frightening, actually, because it is mis-educating a whole generation of young people,' he says. Reiner notes the strong contrast in the entertainment provided for adults too. 'I say to my audiences in Germany that while Germans sit down on a Sunday evening to watch crime series on prime-time TV, Russians watch tank biathlons. That tells you everything about the country,' he adds.[57] The campaigns actively preparing the population, and especially young people, for war reached a new intensity as Russia built up its forces along the Ukrainian border.[58] But their foundations had been laid long before. Besides mass fascist-style rallies in support of the war on Ukraine, Russia's propaganda videos in March 2022 showed educated young people with dead eyes taking turns to publicly back the invasion.[59] None of them would have been old enough to remember a time before relentless and ubiquitous state indoctrination and war propaganda.

Russia's official list of 'unfriendly nations', denounced as enemies on prime-time propaganda shows, continues to grow. Australia was added in April 2021. Far from recognizing that a growing list of enemies might be an indicator of a country's foreign policy being less than ideal, it is a perverse source of pride: television

55. Kira Harris, 'Russia's Fifth Column: The Influence of the Night Wolves Motorcycle Club', *Studies in Conflict & Terrorism* (March 2018), https://doi.org/10.1080/1057610X.2018.1455373

56. Damon Tabor, 'Putin's Angels: The Ride of Russia's Night Wolves', *Rolling Stone*, 26 November 2015, https://au.rollingstone.com/culture/culture-news/putins-angels-the-ride-of-russias-night-wolves-898/.

57. At the same time, Reiner Schwalb presciently told me in mid-2021 that he thought the relentless emphasis on Russian military might tells the opposite story: 'They want to present the picture of how strong they are, again. But if you have to present that picture with that kind of propaganda, I would argue you must be weak otherwise there would be no need. If you were good and capable, you wouldn't have to tell everyone how good you are.'

58. Anton Troianovski et al., 'How the Kremlin Is Militarizing Russian Society', *New York Times*, 21 December 2021, https://www.nytimes.com/2021/12/21/world/europe/russia-military-putin-kremlin.html.

59. Mikhail Khodorkovsky, 10 March 2022, https://twitter.com/mbk_center/status/15018192 69637672960?s=27.

presenter Olga Skabeyeva points out that 'This must be the essence of our greatness ... enemies everywhere.' The danger is not only that the fantasy world created for Russian television viewers reflects the real attitudes of President Putin and his advisers, but that they are turning that fantasy into reality. Russia by its actions continues to pour energy and resources into turning the countries around it into enemies.

Over the period since the end of the USSR, Western analysts have spent vast amounts of time and energy watching, tracking and trying to understand what senior Russian soldiers were saying about war and how to fight it, as well as how what they were saying might translate into what they might do. Oscar Jonsson is a Swedish academic and former soldier whose interest in Russia is long-standing. In his book *The Russian Understanding of War*, Oscar says that 'a distinguishing feature of Russian strategy and warfare is a higher acceptance of risk and a lower threshold for the use of force, be it military or non-military'. In part, this is because 'the traditional Russian understanding of the nature of war as defined by armed violence has broadened to include nonviolent means ... which are now seen to be so effective that they are equivalent to violence, blurring the boundaries of war and peace'.[60] For Ukraine, the question is now academic. But for the rest of Europe and for North America, it is crucial to understanding the means by which Russia seeks to attack without entering an open conflict.

Lars is a serving officer in the counter-intelligence service of a northern European country – and so, naturally, takes a close interest in Russia. He also thinks it is important that 'people should understand Russia does not think about warfare in binary terms like we do in the Western world – that they don't consider there to be some kind of dramatic event when countries are suddenly at war. Rather they have these military tools along with other tools that they use for achieving specific goals.' This means, he says, that Russia does not hesitate to use methods in peacetime that would be off limits for Western countries: 'They are willing to use the kind of tools that we would think are completely off the table unless countries are actually in a crisis going towards war with each other. But Russia is willing to use those tools. Whether it's targeted assassination or sabotage or other means, we have now seen that they hold a lower bar for that. They are more willing to use different parts of that toolkit – so whether it's a dagger or a chainsaw or something in between, applying those military means to the problems without thinking that the country is in an all-out war.'

British Russia expert Mark Galeotti, though, also points to the consequences of Russia thinking the conflict has already begun, and says that because of this wartime mentality, instances where Russia has been fingered as the culprit may not be considered major setbacks. 'We have seen cases or what sometimes look like major blunders. I would suggest that often what we would regard as a blunder, they would not. The Russians are on a wartime footing, and on a wartime footing you

---

60. Oscar Jonsson, *The Russian Understanding of War: Blurring the Lines Between War and Peace* (Washington, DC: Georgetown University Press, 2019), p. 152

care more about not missing opportunities than you do about the potential negative impact of what you're doing. So yes, it leads to a certain amount of international opprobrium, but nonetheless you complete your mission. And they will complete their mission.'[61]

Another perpetual debate among Western Russia-watchers concerns the nature of Russia's overall strategy – or indeed whether it has one at all. Looking at Russia's ability to seize opportunities swiftly in rapidly developing situations, as with the seizure of Crimea or the delivery of military forces to Syria, convinces some people that the approach is completely ad hoc and that there is no overarching master plan. But like many other questions about Russia, the choice presented – being guided by a clear strategy or making it up as you go along – is a false one because the two are not mutually exclusive.

One clear guiding principle is the drive to expand Russian influence or control – and then to fix and consolidate that expansion. When Russia pushes forward and establishes a new principle, or practice, or boundary, the West protests but that then becomes the status quo which Russia seeks to protect, until such time as it pushes forward again. But having an overall guiding plan doesn't prevent Russia from taking opportunities when they present themselves. That mix of long-term principles and short-term opportunism leads to a wide range of metaphors for what kind of game Russia is playing. 'You often hear that the Russians are playing chess and we're playing checkers. I don't know if that's really true,' Sulev Suvari says. 'You can't plan for everything if the world is too complex, so what you do is look for the next right move – what you can do that's in the realm of the possible, and I think the Russians are very good at this. Let's keep on pushing and creating these areas of confusion, seeing how people respond to it, or in the West's case, the lack of response or confusion in response. And then look at those options of, oh well, now we have five different opportunities – this is the best one, let's take that because it could lead to these other things. I see over and over again that they're always doing this sensing and probing.' Lars agrees: 'We shouldn't get too hung up on there being a specific strategy behind that, considering that Russia is pretty nimble in taking advantage of tactical opportunities without necessarily thinking through what the strategic consequences of its actions will be.' Czech journalist and disinformation expert Jakub Kalenský puts it even more pithily: 'We would like to be playing chess, but they are already punching us in the face.'

This pugnacious approach makes a little more sense when you consider that the people within Russia who today decide how it will treat its own citizens and other countries are a small group, almost all of whom are former espionage agents or secret police officers from St Petersburg who grew up in, and benefited from, the Soviet system. It's fair to assume that they share a common understanding of how

61. Mark Galeotti, 'Russian Intelligence & Security Community', *Russia Strategic Initiative*, 12 August 2021, https://community.apan.org/wg/rsi/project-connect/w/events/31576/mark-galeotti-russian-intelligence-security-community/.

the world works based on their very specific professions and experiences, and that that understanding drives how they make decisions for the country. One experienced Western diplomat is convinced that 'Putin and his cabal actually enjoy conflict, relish the undeclared war with the hated "West". They are in their element.'[62]

This raises the question of whether Russia would behave differently if a different leader than Vladimir Putin were in charge. Former US ambassador to Moscow Michael McFaul is an irrepressible optimist, despite decades of experience of Russia. He argues that despite Putin's rhetoric about historic traditions to justify his international behaviour, he has made his own choices in directing Russia's foreign policy. 'Individuals matter. A different Russian leader could have chosen a different path,' McFaul says.[63] The evidence, unfortunately, stands against this. In the 1990s, when nobody had heard of Vladimir Putin, a relatively democratic Russia was already using force against what it called its 'near abroad' (other countries of the former Soviet Union, as opposed to the 'far abroad' rest of the world), interfering in the policies of neighbours and demanding great power status and a geopolitical space where Russian interests reigned. In fact there was no departure from the norm in Russian history, with or without communism, since all of these things were standard practice for Russia's tsars well before the arrival of the Bolsheviks in 1917.[64] The difference is that while in the 1990s former president Boris Yeltsin had the motive to pursue all these aims but was hamstrung by Russia's weakness after the collapse of the Soviet Union, Putin, off the back of the massive influx of oil wealth to Russia in the early part of his presidency, also had the means and the opportunity.

Putin believes not only in the slow demise of the West but also in hastening it where possible, while suppressing dissent at home in pursuit of his vision of restored domestic order, Soviet-style. It's often suggested that the need to keep order at home pushes President Putin to even more aggressive behaviour abroad in order to ensure his popularity and remove any potential challenges to his rule. If that is correct, Ukraine will not be the last victim to suffer Russian aggression, because ensuring stability within Russia means creating even more instability abroad. But the confrontation with the West has become a mission in its own right, and sometimes drives actions to spite it for no evident benefit to Putin or to Russia. In 2011, Putin was present at the signing of a joint venture agreement giving Western oil firm ExxonMobil access to the enormously rich oil and gas fields in Russia's northern Kara Sea.[65]

62. E-mail exchange, April 2021.

63. Michael McFaul, 'Putin, Putinism, and the Domestic Determinants of Russian Foreign Policy', *International Security* 45, no. 2 (Fall 2020): 95–139, https://doi.org/10.1162/isec_a_00390.

64. Henry A. Kissinger, *A World Restored: Metternich, Castlereagh, and the Problems of Peace, 1812–1822* (Boston: Houghton Mifflin, 1957).

65. Tom Parfitt and Dominic Rushe, 'ExxonMobil clinches Arctic oil deal with Rosneft', *Guardian*, 30 August 2011, https://www.theguardian.com/business/2011/aug/30/exxon-rosneft-oil-arctic.

Eyewitnesses said that Putin demanded as a condition 'a rock-solid commitment that not a single cubic metre of that gas would go to Europe'.

Andrey Makarychev says that paradoxically this leads to neglect of Russia's own problems. 'It is very messianic,' he says. 'It is very extrovert, as opposed to being more focused on domestic issues. Russia has so many reasons to be more concerned with what's going on domestically than what's going on in Ukraine, for example.' Tor Bukkvoll suggests this sense of mission may also stem from Putin's own self-esteem. 'You cannot just be a political leader of a country helping yourself to its resources and look yourself in the face in the mirror,' he says. 'You also need to have some bigger goals.' But former diplomat Kyle Wilson points instead to the experience of the end of the USSR for the roots of Putin's apparent obsession. Putin is driven by a burning desire for revenge for the Soviet Union's defeat in the Cold War, Kyle says. 'There is this something seething in there still.'

### To understand Russia, suspend disbelief

One of the most damaging and dangerous misconceptions about Russia is that at some deep level Russian and Western interests must align, and the two sides must fundamentally desire the same end result in their relationship. Putin's 'seething' is one reason why while the idea is seductive, it is wholly wrong. Both at an overall strategic level and in detail on specific issues, Russian objectives and even the underlying assumptions about the nature of relations between states are entirely incompatible with what the West wants, needs and indeed finds acceptable.

Western liberal democracies share a broad consensus about the rules-based international order, based on values which with marginal exceptions are shared across the Euro-Atlantic community and beyond. This consensus is so well established and has become so deeply ingrained over decades, if not centuries, that it takes constant and conscious mental effort to recall that it is one not shared by Moscow. But this effort is essential. Without it, the assumption that there must be common ground between the West and Russia led to a repetitive but doomed cycle of overtures, disappointment and crisis at the level of state-to-state relations, replicated in miniature whenever the West sought to work with Russia on individual apparently shared problems as described above. American historian Stephen Kotkin points to the consistency of this principle over time, something often overlooked by politicians taking a shorter view. 'It is useful to recognize that there has actually never been a period of sustained good relations between Russia and the United States,' he writes. 'This has been due not to misunderstandings, miscommunication, or hurt feelings but rather to divergent fundamental values and state Interests, as each country has defined them.'[66]

66. Stephen Kotkin, 'Russia's Perpetual Geopolitics: Putin Returns to the Historical Pattern', *Foreign Affairs* (May/June 2016): 2–9.

Instead, dealing with Russia requires persistence, patience, a long memory and above all recognition that absolutely none of the normal assumptions of how countries behave hold good. The Kremlin's view of the world is so distinctive from what is taken for granted in Europe and North America that all preconceptions of what is rational or 'makes sense' have to be set aside. This includes the basic assumption that countries by default prefer peaceful and good-neighbourly relations with each other. Russia, instead, assumes the opposite – that the West is engaged in a campaign to destroy it and so it has to wage a struggle in every possible domain to pre-empt that. Russian Defence Minister Sergei Shoygu says that Western policy towards Russia is driven by 'the task that they set themselves – the task of destruction and enslavement of our country'.[67] Paradoxically, if Western leaders had borne in mind that basic assumption of hostility every time they talked to Russia instead of ignoring it and hoping for the best, their relationship with Moscow would have had far fewer unpleasant surprises. Because, for the ruling elite in Moscow, self-preservation means protecting itself and its interests against challenges both from abroad and from within Russia itself – many of which are imaginary.

Perversely, as we will see from repeated examples in later chapters, the methods they choose to do this regularly make the situation worse by turning imagined challenges into real problems. And it's true that Russia has suffered setbacks, long before the initial stages of the assault on Ukraine revealed spectacular errors of intelligence and planning. In each chapter of this book, we will also find examples where, through incompetence or miscalculation, the steps Russia has taken have been counterproductive and achieved the opposite effect to what was intended – or have harmed Russian interests in some other way. But so often, on closer inspection it appears that the downside is something that would matter to other countries but is less significant for Russia – and Russia has come through the experience if not undamaged, then at the very least undeterred. There is no reason for Russia to care about reputational damage in the rest of the world if it considers itself to be already in a state of conflict with those countries that are calling it names. And Western steps after 2014 like sanctions or expelling intelligence officers posing as diplomats may be unfortunate, but were hardly significant compared to major strategic gains like seizing control of Crimea. In fact, Russia seems repeatedly to be following strategies that some Western analysts like to think are self-defeating, but which achieve positive results according to Moscow's own calculations. It's often tempting to call Russian actions irrational. But time and again, the fact that they make sense in Moscow but not in Washington or Brussels comes back to the same root cause: that while Russia is operating to entirely different rules and priorities than Western liberal democracies, it should be no surprise that it has different measures of success.

The fundamental problem is that Russia's aims are inherently destructive. The hope of restoring Russia's power, prestige and influence in the world and in

---

67. Interviewed in *Moskovsky Komsomolets*, 22 September 2019.

particular defending its own self-perceived security needs, including fending off the largely imaginary threat from the West, automatically implies the need to push back Western organizations like the EU as well as individual countries like the US. The ways in which Russia seeks to do this can be hard to understand unless they are seen in this broad overall pattern of needing to weaken the West as a long-term adversary. Repeatedly throughout this book we will see examples of how Russia reaches out to cause damage without any evident additional motive. This includes some of the destructive information campaigns that Russia has launched in attempts to turn Western societies against themselves, like the negative and malicious campaigns over race in the United States, Brexit in the UK, migration throughout Europe, and vaccinations everywhere.

To grasp why this is so, we have to look in more detail at how under President Putin Russia has moved back towards its own historical normality – vicious repression and dictatorship at home, and open confrontation with the West wherever it can reach out and harm it abroad. And that is the subject of the next chapter.

# Chapter 2

## POLITICS: WARFARE BY OTHER MEANS

*Propaganda at home*

It's hard to explain to anybody who hasn't seen it for themselves just how bizarrely different the world looks if you see it through what is shown on Russian television. Just as in Soviet times, a relentless diet of propaganda distorts and conceals what is really happening outside the country. On evening television schedules, even some comedy and chat shows – even though modelled on their Western counterparts – are geared towards portraying the West as a threat to Russia, and attacking its political leadership.[1]

Cynics call the television the *zomboyashchik*, the zombie box or zombifying box. But for obvious reasons, state propaganda continues to be most effective among the generations of Russians who watch television. A video by Alexei Navalny's team showing 'Putin's Palace' in all its gaudy detail, suggestive of corruption on an unimaginable scale, was watched by millions online but made barely any difference to their opinion of Putin. Older people who got their news mainly from state television were inclined to dismiss it, and younger ones that could access a broader range of information online generally believed it – and both groups had already formed their opinions of Putin.[2] The tragic result is that people within Russia are so isolated from reality that even when told by their own children in Ukraine that they were under attack by Russian forces, they refused to believe them.[3]

1. 'Stratcom Laughs: In Search of an Analytical Framework', NATO Strategic Communications Centre of Excellence (NATO StratCom COE), March 2017, https://stratcomcoe.org/pdfjs/?file=/cuploads/pfiles/Full-stratcom-laughs-report_web_15-03-2017.pdf.

2. 'Фильм "Дворец для Путина"' (Putin's Palace film), Levada-Tsentr poll, 8 February 2021, https://www.levada.ru/2021/02/08/film-dvorets-dlya-putina/.

3. Maria Korenyuk and Jack Goodman, 'Ukraine war: "My city's being shelled, but mum won't believe me"', BBC, 4 March 2022, https://www.bbc.co.uk/news/world-europe-60600487.

Robert Pszczel points to the large number of Russians who conform – who echo state propaganda lines, vote for Putin and give him consistently high ratings in opinion polls. 'I very often get this question, do they actually believe, and my answer to that is, at some point, it became immaterial. It doesn't matter.' There can be different motivations for a conscious or unconscious decision to fall into line, Robert says. 'Some people behave out of fear, fear of losing the benefits they have. It's not just government officials, it's anywhere there's lots of money. Other people are just in some kind of collective sense of belonging. You have to speak about this sort of altered state of consciousness, the sort of brainwashing, which is done on an individual level but also on a collective level.' 'In modern Russia it's more difficult not to be aware of the facts, but it's still possible to live within this make-believe world,' Robert goes on. 'Young people are more dangerous in a way, because they have never known anything different and some of them actually believe.'

As ever, it's hard to work out how much of this belief is genuine – especially since shows of belief include students being deceived into taking part in televised demonstrations of loyalty to President Putin, or in some cases being lured there by the promise of higher grades,[4] or tricked into thinking they were going to a concert.[5] But the reaction at home to the assault on Ukraine showed how the relentless bludgeoning of Russians' consciousness through the television held another danger: the normalization of aggression and violence towards the outside world. Long before the invasion, this was an inevitable core component of Russia's propaganda. On the anniversary of 9/11, the chief editor of the Rossiya-24 TV channel was proud to send a friend birthday wishes that 'the World Trade Center should always be burning'.[6] Petr Tolstoy, who represents his country as head of the Russian delegation to the Parliamentary Assembly of the Council of Europe in Vienna, told Russian television in July 2021 that the leaders of Ukraine should be murdered and 'hung from street lights [because] Ukraine is a part of our Great Russia'.[7] Leading propagandist Dmitry Kiselev uses his television show to boast of how Russia could 'reduce the United States to radioactive ash'.[8] (Kiselev also takes

4. 'Студентов обманом заставили участвовать во флешмобе в поддержку Путина', *DOXA*, 6 February 2021, https://news.doxajournal.ru/novosti/studentov-obmanom-zastavili-uchavstvovat-vo-flshemobe-v-podderzhku-putina/.

5. Will Vernon, 18 March 2022, https://twitter.com/bbcwillvernon/status/1504838568514052098?s=27.

6. Fedor Kuzmin, 'Главред "России 24" пожелал башням-близнецам "гореть к ****". Так он поздравил друга' (Chief editor of Rossiya-24 wished for the Twin Towers to 'burn to f***'. That's how he congratulated his friend), *Afisha*, 11 September 2020, https://daily.afisha.ru/news/41408-glavred-rossii-24-pozhelal-bashnyam-bliznecam-goret-k-tak-on-pozdravil-druga/.

7. Video in tweet by Sergej Sumlenny, 8 July 2021, https://twitter.com/sumlenny/status/1413150943923773441?s=27.

8. Stephen Ennis, 'Russian media learn to love the bomb', BBC Monitoring, 23 February 2015, https://www.bbc.co.uk/news/world-europe-31557254.

regular aim at other enemies of Russia, like homosexuals, whose hearts he says should be burned to avoid the risk of them being used for organ donations.)[9]

The cumulative effect is highly toxic. Valeriy Akimenko spent a large part of his career studying and reporting on Russian media, which meant he had no choice but to watch. 'Others could switch it off. I couldn't do that,' he says. 'So it did have a damaging effect on my state of mind and on my attitudes, of course.' Disinformation researcher Jakub Kalenský agrees. 'The most painful part of [the work] was to watch the Russian TV shows,' he says. 'When you watch them for several hours, it affects you physically. You feel the hatred.'

I asked Valeriy to talk me through the propaganda broadcasts, and he painted a picture of an almost constant barrage of hate. 'If we deconstruct it by days of the week, Saturday and Sunday are the days of the heaviest bombardment,' he said. 'It all begins on Saturday with relatively minor propaganda broadcasts like Sergey Brilev's *Vesti v Subbotu* on Rossiya-1, the main state TV channel, and Russian senator Aleksey Pushkov's *Postskriptum* (Postscript) on the second-tier Moscow city government controlled Tsentr-TV. That's Saturday. Then the heaviest salvoes come on Sunday, where we will have a spread of three main propaganda broadcasts of considerable length, every hour on the hour from 7 pm Moscow time. At that time NTV and *Itogi Nedeli* will fire the first broadside. That's a programme more than an hour long. And while that is still on the air, at 8 pm Moscow time, Dimitri Kiselev in his *Vesti nedeli* would unleash his venom on us. That lasts at least two and a half hours, sometimes in excess of three hours. That by far and away was the most poisonous of the broadcasts. And at times all of these are almost exclusively about Ukraine, with a smattering of other news from abroad and very little about Russia. It's just impossible to comprehend. When I describe these kinds of things to my children or to my wife it does not compute.'

'Finally at 9 pm Moscow time would be *Voskresnoye vremya* on Channel One TV, the other main TV channel, also state-controlled. So that will be Saturday and Sunday taken care of. On Sunday, Kiselev's *Vesti Nedeli* would be immediately followed by two other heavyweight propaganda broadcasts: first, *Moscow. Kremlin. Putin* (the name speaks for itself; a quasi-documentary); and then *Voskresny vecher* with Vladimir Solovyev, an aggressively pro-Kremlin and anti-Western talk show of a couple of hours. During the week that will be followed up by other similar formats, such as the now notorious twice-daily 60 Minutes talk show on Rossiya-1, in the mould of *Voskresny vecher* but fronted by a husband-and-wife team, and *Vremya pokazhet* – 'Time Will Tell' – on Channel One TV; as well as various other formats on various other channels. Combined with their regular news bulletin output during the same hours during the day on the three main channels plus second tier channels, the volume of propaganda is colossal,' Valeriy says.

9. Leo Barraclough, 'Russian TV Anchor Rejects Allegations of Homophobia', 12 August 2013, https://variety.com/2013/tv/global/russian-tv-anchor-rejects-allegations-of-homophobia-1200577004/.

The approach will be familiar to anybody who has read George Orwell's *Nineteen Eighty-Four*, except that Orwell's 'Two Minutes Hate' stretches on for hours, and 'Hate Week' is all year round. But Valeriy also noted a peculiarity of the broadcasts: 'There is almost no Russian news content in any of these programs. When Putin speaks, whatever he says is obviously given generous airtime, but that's not exactly Russian news. It's very different from for example BBC or Sky News where there is a lot of local or national news of a meaningful nature. In these programmes nothing of the sort happens,' he says. But the most distinctive feature of this Russian programming is that it is viciously deceitful and negative. 'If you take the picture of the West on Russian TV, it is beset by chaos and degradation and the near collapse of the liberal world order,' Valeriy goes on. 'Of course, that has migrated through various stages – with Trump's election it acquired a very particular slant in defence of Trump, but still drawing attention to lots of negative things about the United States.' Overall, though, he says, 'The whole volume of output is exclusively negative. It's vile and mendacious.'

## *The war on history*

Efforts to isolate the Russian population from a true picture of events both in the outside world and in their own country help the authorities promote the notion of a Russia under threat from an aggressive, expansionist West, by preventing domestic media users from measuring against reality. The result is broad acceptance, at least in public, of the version of reality endorsed by the Russian state. But that alternative reality also involves the rewriting of history, since Russia's past is often just as unacceptable as its present. After a brief period when free discussion of history was possible, Russia has returned both to the Soviet version of its history and to Soviet practices for promoting and enforcing it.[10] This involves enforced amnesia regarding inconvenient events, and promotion of officially-sponsored falsifications. The war on facts goes far beyond just an academic discussion and instead is an integrated part of Russian security policy that has a direct impact both on domestic politics and on Russia's neighbours.[11] Trying to identify the current Russian leadership with moments of Soviet national glory, for instance, offers a reason to support it when there aren't many other reasons available.

Officially promoted fictions cover the whole span of Russia's history from its earliest beginnings to the present day. They begin with one of Russian history's most cherished myths: that the early princes of Muscovy were in some way

10. Jade McGlynn, 'Moscow Is Using Memory Diplomacy to Export Its Narrative to the World', *Foreign Policy*, 25 June 2021, https://foreignpolicy.com/2021/06/25/russia-puting-ww2-soviet-ussr-memory-diplomacy-history-narrative/.

11. Gudrun Persson, 'Controlling the Past', *Frivärld*, 8 May 2020, https://frivarld.se/rapporter/controlling-the-past/.

successors – separated by several hundred miles and a different century – to the entirely different state of Kievan Rus', in what is now Ukraine. Descriptions of Russian history that wish to include Kievan Rus' are forced either to contrive awkward explanations for why that history leaps suddenly hundreds of miles and hundreds of years to Moscow, or simply to ignore the obvious gap altogether.[12] Today, the latest issues of school textbooks bring the revision of history forward to the present day by telling Russian children that Crimea rejoined Russia following a referendum there – but omitting the Russian military operation to seize the peninsula that preceded it, or the fact that the referendum did not offer voters the choice of remaining Ukrainian.[13]

Together with suppressing the history of Soviet repression in the previous century, the enforced ignorance lays dangerous foundations. In early 2022, Russia closed down one of its longest-standing human rights organizations, Memorial, which had been established even before the end of the Soviet Union to preserve the memory of the victims of communist repression.[14] The Russian leadership of today saw this memory as a threat. And they are of course correct: young people knowing nothing about the crimes of Stalin and other Soviet leaders eases the path for a return to authoritarianism. The less people are aware of the extremes to which repression was taken in the past, the less likely they are to oppose it today when President Putin calls for an 'essential self-purification of society', to rid the country of traitors and those whose sympathies lie abroad, in a direct echo of Stalin's purges.[15] And opposing it is already a brave choice – individual Russians are

12. In 2020 I was asked to contribute to a documentary on Russian history produced for the UK's Channel 5 television. We discussed this misguided idea that Kievan Rus somehow turned into Muscovy despite the gap in space and time between them. But that would have meant they no longer had a catchy title about Russia's 1,000-year history – because Russia's history simply isn't that long. So, in the end, the result aired in March 2021 was one we've seen many times before: a discussion of Kievan Rus', then an awkward gap with no explanation as to why you're now moving on to talking about an entirely different remote city-state far to the north-east. The documentary is available to view at https://www.my5.tv/russia-vs-the-world.

13. Halya Coynash, 'Russia did not invade Crimea in new school textbooks edited by Putin adviser', Kharkiv Human Rights Protection Group, 16 August 2021, https://khpg.org/en/1608809430; Keir Giles, 'Crimea's referendum choices are no choice at all', Chatham House expert comment, 10 March 2014, https://www.eureporter.co/world/2014/03/11/opinion-crimeas-referendum-choices-are-no-choice-at-all/.

14. 'Russia's Top Court Upholds Decision To Shut Down Memorial Rights Group', RFE/RL, 28 February 2022, https://www.rferl.org/a/russia-memorial-shutdown-confirmed/31728086.html.

15. 'В Кремле объяснили слова Путина о самоочищении России' (Kremlin explains Putin's words about the self-purification of Russia), RIA Novosti, 17 March 2022, https://ria.ru/20220317/rossiya-1778651331.html.

prosecuted for alluding to historical facts which are inconvenient for current state narratives.[16] The ongoing consignment of inconvenient history to the memory hole has sent Russian bookshops and libraries scrambling to purge their shelves of unapproved books in order to avoid criminal proceedings.[17] In a direct echo of Soviet censorship from the previous century, even before books reach the shops the FSB is confiscating them from printing houses as part of the campaign to suppress historical accounts of Soviet repressions and atrocities.[18]

The most prominent part of the current leadership's borrowing of the Soviet past to legitimize itself is the Great Patriotic War, still ubiquitous in Russian culture and officially promoted memory over seventy years after it ended. But the USSR's conduct before, during and after the war was so horrific that the official myths are at times barely recognizable from real events. Already in the 2010s, the mythologized events of the Second World War played such a central role in Russia's official self-image that genuine historians, including the head of the state archives, who pointed out the gap between fact and fiction found themselves out of a job.[19] In confirmation that Russia does not wish its citizens to know the truth, the military archives covering the war, briefly open, were ordered closed by Defence Minister Sergei Shoygu in 2020.[20] According to Reiner Schwalb, the focus on war history feeds directly into stoking Russia's population for conflict today. 'Stalin is coming back, because Stalin and the military in World War Two were not only strong, but they defeated the Germans,' he says, '– so the new military could do the same, not with the Germans but with NATO. That makes them feel good. And that creates acceptance in the population.'

But Russia's heavy reliance on its censored and idealized history of war heroism also highlights the fact that some of the country's most cherished historical fictions are fragile and highly vulnerable to objective scrutiny. Russia's war story is especially sensitive to the fact that in its campaigns of mass murder and its invasion and subjugation of neighbouring peoples, the Nazi regime it vilifies resembled the USSR itself. As a result of these similarities, pointing this fact out – in fact making any comparison between Nazi Germany and the USSR during the Second World

16. Halya Coynash, 'Russian fined for reposting that the USSR & Nazi Germany invaded Poland', Human Rights in Ukraine, 1 July 2016, http://khpg.org/en/index.php?id=1467327913.

17. Olga Timofeyeva, 'Изыми с глаз моих!' (Get it out of my sight!), *Novaya gazeta*, 15 July 2021, https://novayagazeta.ru/articles/2021/07/15/izymi-s-glaz-moikh.

18. 'The FSB has taken a great interest in reading', *Barents Observer*, 7 September 2021, https://thebarentsobserver.com/en/democracy-and-media/2021/09/fsb-has-taken-great-interest-reading.

19. Tom Balmforth, 'Russian Archive Chief Out after Debunking Soviet WWII Legend', Radio Free Europe/Radio Liberty, 17 March 2016, http://www.rferl.mobi/a/mironenko-state-archive-chief-removed-from-post-panfilov-legend/27619460.html.

20. 'Приказ Министра обороны Российской Федерации от 12.11.2020 № 591' (Order No 591 of the Minister of Defence of the Russian Federation, 12 November 2020), Russian state legal database, http://publication.pravo.gov.ru/Document/View/0001202103220036.

War – is now illegal in Russia.[21] Thus there are now topics that cannot be discussed in public in Russia, in just the same way that it was dangerous to speak freely in the Soviet Union – or in Nazi Germany.

The biggest difference between Hitler's Germany and Stalin's USSR was that one regime was not only destroyed but eradicated, and its ideas completely discredited, while the other survived for another forty-five years until the end of the Soviet Union in 1991.[22] It is hardly surprising that Sergey Lavrov points to 'the Nuremberg trials verdicts as the foundation of today's world order'.[23] Nazi Germany had its Nuremberg reckoning and the Soviet Union had none. An intensive programme of 'de-Nazification' in Germany was briefly, haphazardly and incompletely emulated by Russia in the 1990s, but the results of that process are now steadily being reversed as part of the rehabilitation of the Soviet past described later in this chapter. Nothing could more clearly demonstrate that Russia has no counter-argument to this inconvenient truth than its making the whole conversation illegal. If the two regimes were not so similar, there would be no need to outlaw comparisons between them. After all, nobody is likely to outlaw a comparison between black and white.

And those similarities still echo today. One of the stated aims of Russia's assault on Ukraine was 'de-nazification' of the country, based on Russia's long-standing propaganda campaign claiming that Ukraine and other countries like the Baltic states are run by neo-Nazis.[24] The rest of the world couldn't help but notice that this involved sending the Wagner group, Russian mercenaries with genuine Nazi leanings, to kill Ukraine's Jewish president.[25] And as the war ground on, Russia's embrace of the 'Z' invasion marking symbology came more and more to resemble the ubiquitous swastikas of Nazi Germany, and the fascist-style mass rallies in support of the war became more and more reminiscent of Nazi Party rallies.[26] It

21. 'Путин подписал закон о запрете уравнивания ролей СССР и Германии в войне' (Putin signs law forbidding equating the roles of the USSR and Germany in the war), RIA Novosti, 1 July 2021, https://ria.ru/20210701/voyna-1739359047.html.

22. Robert Conquest, 'Stalin's reputation as a ruthless master of deception remains intact', *Guardian*, 5 March 2003, https://www.theguardian.com/world/2003/mar/05/russia.artsandhumanities.

23. Sergey Lavrov, 'The Law, the Rights and the Rules', Russian MFA website, 28 June 2021, https://www.mid.ru/en/foreign_policy/news/-/asset_publisher/cKNonkJE02Bw/content/id/4801890.

24. Kayleen Devlin and Olga Robinson, 'Ukraine crisis: Is Russia waging an information war?', BBC Monitoring Reality Check, 23 February 2022, https://www.bbc.co.uk/news/60292915.

25. Verity Bowman, 'Russian Wagner mercenaries enter Ukraine to assassinate Volodymyr Zelensky, officials claim', *Daily Telegraph*, 20 March 2022, https://www.telegraph.co.uk/world-news/2022/03/20/russian-wagner-mercenaries-enter-ukraine-assassinate-volodymyr/.

26. Rafi Schwarz, 'Vladimir Putin Holds Giant Nazi-Style "World Without Nazism" Rally', 18 March 2022, https://www.mic.com/impact/putin-rally-crimea-ukraine-nazis.

was as though the Russian authorities had been so diligent about calling everyone around them Nazis that they didn't notice how they had become Nazis themselves.

At the same time, people from the countries of eastern Europe that suffered most from the Second World War were repeatedly shocked at the willingness of German politicians to join in with Russia's erasure of the parts of that history it finds inconvenient. Despite the fact that Ukraine and Belarus bore the brunt of fighting on the eastern Front, and lost a horrifying proportion of their populations in the process, some German policies were driven by the notion that the Second World War was fought between Germany and Russia, not the Soviet Union – and that Germany therefore owed it to Moscow to prioritize Russia's interests over those of Ukraine.[27] The continuing drive to make amends for Germany's conduct in the 1940s has been perversely twisted by collusion in Russia's war on history and now in effect argues that because Germany invaded Poland, Ukraine, Belarus and the Baltic states, it must now support Russia against those same countries. This extends to wilful or deliberate erasure from history of the effects of the joint Nazi–Soviet division of Poland in 1939. In June 2021, German President Frank-Walter Steinmeier built an entire high-profile speech around a supposed first-hand account of the experience of a Russian soldier at the opening of the German offensive in June 1941 that was completely impossible, and could only have been written by somebody who chose to ignore the earlier Soviet invasion of Poland which moved the front line some 300 km west of where Steinmeier's story was supposed to have taken place.[28]

The intensive campaign to enforce a Soviet view of the history of the Second World War on Russians reaches well beyond Russia itself.[29] The restoration of Soviet myths about the 1939–41 period when the USSR collaborated with Nazi Germany to occupy eastern Europe between them has seen the former victim states of Soviet aggression and occupation throughout northern and central Europe subjected to a sustained information barrage, seeking to excuse Moscow's conduct and to shift blame for both the Second World War and its aftermath to those same victims. These campaigns promote the idea of the Soviet Union itself as a victim, not an instigator, of the war, and as a benevolent protector of the nations under its military control.[30] According to Sergey Karaganov, a leading

27. Christian Trippe, 'Opinion: World War II reconciliation gesture still needed in Eastern Europe', *Deutsche Welle*, 19 June 2021, https://www.dw.com/en/opinion-world-war-ii-reconciliation-gesture-still-needed-in-eastern-europe/a-57961269.

28. '80. Jahrestag des deutschen Überfalls auf die Sowjetunion am 22. Juni 1941 und Eröffnung der Ausstellung 'Dimensionen eines Verbrechens. Sowjetische Kriegsgefangene im Zweiten Weltkrieg', German presidential website, 18 June 2021, https://www.bundespraesident.de/SharedDocs/Reden/DE/Frank-Walter-Steinmeier/Reden/2021/06/210618-D-Russ-Museum-Karlshorst.html.

29. Ivo Juurvee et al., 'Falsification of History as a Tool of Influence', NATO Strategic Communications Centre of Excellence, December 2020.

30. Stefan Forss, 'Russia's Victim Narrative', *Frivärld*, 30 November 2020, https://frivarld.se/rapporter/russias-victim-narrative/.

Russian polemicist, Russians are a 'liberating people' who freed the world, and the West only hates Russians because Russia is the only 'viable part' of European civilization.[31]

But this brings the Russian myths head to head not only with abstract discussions of history but with the real and direct lived experience of those nations. Estonia's former president, Kersti Kaljulaid, recalled how her grandmother was imprisoned in Siberia for nine years because her grandfather – not she – had worked for the independent Estonian state before the Soviet annexation. 'All Estonian families have these kind of stories,' she adds.[32] Kersti Kaljulaid's grandparents were, in relative terms, lucky – her grandmother returned to Estonia and lived until 1987, while her grandfather escaped abroad. But former Estonian Defence Minister Jüri Luik's grandfather never returned. He was an officer in the Estonian Army when the Soviet occupation began in 1940, Jüri explains. 'In 1940, he and his fellow officers were arrested and taken to a concentration camp in Norilsk in northern Siberia. And in 1942 he was shot by the Soviet tribunals. I don't know where his grave is.'

For many in the countries formerly occupied by the Soviet Union, Russia's Victory Day is no cause for celebrations; instead, it marks the transition from one oppressor to another. After the liberation of German prison and concentration camps across eastern Europe by the Red Army, Soviet security forces found it convenient to make use of their facilities – including at Auschwitz – to imprison the victims of the new regime.[33] Savage repressions and mass murders of the civilian population in the occupied territories made it plain that the new Soviet overlords could be just as brutal as the old Nazi ones.[34] This is occasionally recognized in accidental outbreaks of honesty by Russian officials – as when Mikhail Ulyanov, Permanent Representative of Russia to International Organizations in Vienna, told Latvian academic Veiko Spolitis, 'There is nothing to celebrate in your case. This is not your Victory. It is ours.'[35] But the savagery also

31. 'The Real Russia. Today. The Nemtsov murder case, political mayhem in Kyrgyzstan, and a neo-isolationist recipe for Russia', *Meduza*, 2 November 2020, https://meduza.io/en/brief/2020/11/03/the-real-russia-today.

32. '"Russia is a threat": Estonia frets about its neighbor', *Washington Post*, 24 March 2017, https://www.washingtonpost.com/opinions/russia-is-a-threat-estonia-frets-about-its-neighbor/2017/03/24/011ad320-0f2b-11e7-9b0d-d27c98455440_story.html.

33. Stuart Dowell, 'After liberation of Auschwitz death camp Stalin's feared NKVD used camp to hold Polish prisoners', *TheFirstNews*, 28 January 2020, https://www.thefirstnews.com/article/after-liberation-of-auschwitz-death-camp-stalins-feared-nkvd-used-camp-to-hold-polish-prisoners-10133; 'The Macikai Complex of a Nazi German prisoner-of-war camp and the Soviet GULAG forced-labour camps (1941–1955)', https://www.silutesmuziejus.lt/maciku-lageriai/the-macikai-complex/.

34. 'World War 2 in Lithuania (1940–1944)', TrueLithuania.com, http://www.truelithuania.com/tag/rainiai-massacre.

35. Tweet by @Amb_Ulyanov, 17 April 2020, https://twitter.com/Amb_Ulyanov/status/1251120241255559168.

extended wherever the Red Army reached – not only Germany as it was conquered, but also countries like Poland that were supposed to have been liberated.[36] The fact that this history, despite being extensively documented at the time,[37] was largely obscured in western Europe for much of the twentieth century stemmed not only from the enforced alliance with the Soviet Union, but also from its roots in a curious oversight by the UK and France in September 1939 – that in going to war ostensibly to protect Poland, they declared war on one of its invaders but not the other.

For Jüri and others, direct family history serves as a constant reminder of what is at stake in resisting Russia. 'Obviously, for me, it had a deep meaning to be the Defence Minister of Estonia and to visit the bases where my grandfather had served,' he says. 'When doing my job, I often thought of him and that what I was doing as Defence Minister had brought me full circle, and showed that in the end the communists lost and we won.' It was not just the countries conquered by the USSR that learned from the experience. At the end of the Second World War, unlike most of eastern Europe the greater part of Finland remained unoccupied by the USSR. But the history of desperate defence against Moscow that bought that freedom still drives a determination to preserve it today. Pekka Toveri says that in Finland, 'support for general conscription is very strong, and willingness to defend one's country against armed attack is the highest in Europe'. This is because 'Finns generally' think that only high readiness to fight for your country gives safety', he says. This attitude stems from the lessons of the twentieth century and its wars fought against the Soviet Union. 'Every Finnish family has lost someone fighting the Russians. Finns have seen what the Soviet occupation meant to smaller nations like our Baltic neighbours, and really don't want to share that fate.'

This knowledge of the stakes and the risks drove diplomats and politicians from the eastern parts of Europe to try to sound the alarm for NATO and the EU over Russia's likely plans. As early as 1994, Estonian president Lennart Meri warned that 'My people and I watch with concern how little the West realizes what is currently brewing in the expanses of Russia.'[38] But as late as 2013, these warnings were not heeded. Jüri recalls how in conversations in Western capitals, 'I had to explain that some of the political moves by Russia are not just benign internal politics, but rather they carried a lot of risks and a lot of echoes from the past. Now, after

---

36. Mindy Weisberger, 'Skeletons of WWII-era nuns murdered by Soviets unearthed in Poland', *LiveScience*, 5 March 2021, https://www.livescience.com/wwii-nuns-murdered-by-russian-army.html.

37. Marcus Papadopoulos, 'British Official Perceptions of the Red Army, 1934–1945', Royal Holloway University of London, 2010, available at https://ethos.bl.uk/OrderDetails.do?uin=uk.bl.ethos.530798.

38. 'Address by H.E. Lennart Meri, President of the Republic of Estonia, at a Matthiae-Supper in Hamburg on February 25, 1994', Estonian presidency website, https://vp1992-2001.president.ee/eng/k6ned/K6ne.asp?ID=9401.

Ukraine, it has become quite easy to explain Russia. But before that, it was quite difficult.' Robert Pszczel too recalls how when he was reporting back to NATO before 2014, he was told 'we respect your judgement and it's interesting what you say but it's a very pessimistic picture' – so, he says, his accurate assessments and predictions of Russia's future steps were dismissed.

The exception that proves the rule is Norway. At the end of the Second World War, instead of remaining as occupiers the Soviet Union withdrew its troops from northern Norway and retreated to territory it had seized from Finland instead. In stark contrast to the rest of Europe, Norwegian journalist Vilde Skorpen Wikan says, 'I think the Second World War made us feel like we could trust Russia … We've not had this experience that other countries have had of being at war with Russia or being part of the Soviet Union. We don't have remnants of Soviet architecture or anything else to remind us about this.'

This leads to a paradox in Norway's attitude to Russia. On the one hand, Vilde says, Norwegians too are highly conscious of the need to protect the country's independence. 'The idea that we have mandatory military service for young women and men is something foreign friends have found a little bit shocking. But to us, it's something that is quite popular. Even though it's mandatory, you have so many volunteers that no one is getting, you know, drafted against their will,' she says. 'A lot of people are eager to contribute to the defence of the country. We also have the Heimevernet, the Home Guard, where people are on standby for military service.' But on the other hand, the far north of the country has a close and friendly cross-border relationship with Russia. 'There is close cooperation, educational exchange programmes, people going out over the border to do their shopping, and so on. So, people in northern areas do find it challenging that maybe the central government emphasizes this hostile aspect of Russia when this maybe differs from their own personal and historic relationship,' Vilde explains.

The unusual success of this cross-border cooperation is only partly due to Norway's equally unusual experience of the Red Army, says Norwegian defence researcher Tor Bukkvoll. 'The Soviet withdrawal has a resonance in the two northernmost counties, those areas that were liberated by the Red Army. That is gradually fading away since it's connected to generations, but today, it's still there to some extent.' It's also connected with deliberate Norwegian policy based on sound pragmatic grounds. 'The cooperation on the civilian side with Russia in the north, starting after the end of the Cold War, was based on an assumption that this would benefit Norway economically, especially in those northern areas of Kirkenes and Finnmark,' Tor explains. 'That cooperation is still there, and it may now be more important than ever. At least to the Russians across the border on the Kola Peninsula, we can show that the West is not out to destroy Russia.'

## Censorship and isolation

But that message doesn't travel far. The Kremlin's default assumption is that dissent or protest in Russia must be inspired from outside. During the election protests in late 2011 and early 2012 President Putin said that he was offended at seeing protesters wearing white ribbons which, in his opinion, had been 'developed abroad'.[39] He also said that protesters had been 'paid to participate', and that these were 'tried and tested schemes for destabilising a society'.[40] This baseless fear of foreign influence provides the context for an ongoing campaign trying to prevent Russians receiving unapproved information from the outside world – and in the process, wiping out the last remnants of a free and independent media in Russia. Russia's crackdown on sources of foreign information following the invasion of Ukraine, including banning Facebook and Twitter and criminalizing reporting on the war, was just another stage in a long process of denying ordinary Russians any access to the reality of the world around them.

Media with any foreign links at all have to carry prominent warnings on their reports that they are created or distributed by 'foreign agents', in the same way packets of cigarettes have to carry graphic warnings of their harmful content and the consequences of consuming them – or the way in Nazi Germany that undesirable elements like Jews, homosexuals or the disabled were badged for ready identification. (Russia claims, falsely, that RT and Sputnik are similarly forced to label their content in the US.)[41] Journalist Sonya Groysman is one of the many Russians who has been labelled in this way. She explains how 'any of our articles in the media, podcasts and even posts on social networks – even stories or comments on Instagram – must be marked with a degrading twenty-four-word disclaimer that you are not merely a journalist and a person, but a foreign agent. The alternative is fines and the prospect of a criminal case.' The designation is effectively a permanent one, since there is no procedure for removing yourself from the list – and meanwhile, Sonya saw her work prospects dwindling, with fewer employers willing to take on the extra burden of hiring 'foreign agents'. A further punishment is to drown them in bureaucracy, including the requirement 'to submit five forty-page reports a year on the source of your income and what you have spent it on'.[42]

Russia genuinely does have plenty to fear from a free, independent media, especially as it continues to commit crimes at home and abroad. One of the ways the British government responded to the chemical weapons attack in Salisbury in 2018 was to release as much detail on the incident as was possible without

39. 'Meeting with participants of the '"seliger-2012" forum', Russian presidential website, 31 July 2012, http://kremlin.ru/transcripts/16106.

40. 'A Conversation with Vladimir Putin. Continued', from live broadcast across all major Russian TV and radio channels on 15 December 2011, Russian presidential website, http://archive.premier.gov.ru/events/news/17409.

41. 'RT America Received More Than $100 Million In Russian Government Funding Since 2017, Filings Show', RFE/RL, 26 August 2021, https://www.rferl.org/a/russia-rt-america-funding/31427870.html.

42. Sonya Groysman, 'I Am a "Foreign Agent"', 17 August 2021, *Moscow Times*, https://www.themoscowtimes.com/2021/08/17/i-am-a-foreign-agent-2-a74815.

compromising the ongoing criminal investigation. Not only was this helpful in mobilizing international support – it also allowed media outlets, including in Russia, to start their own independent investigations into what had happened. The end result was the exposure of hundreds of Russian intelligence officers.[43] There's a clear motivation for the Kremlin to continue its campaign to stamp out this threat – with the added bonus that after independent media are suppressed altogether, there will be nobody to report on repression and persecution of the rest of the population or on Russia's crimes abroad in Ukraine or beyond.

Russia has always been impervious to Western horror and condemnation, which means there is little to constrain it in the atrocities it commits in Ukraine. But there's little likelihood that Russia will be deterred by the prospect of outrage at home either, even if knowledge of what its military is doing abroad filters through to domestic audiences. Moscow has taken steps in advance to ensure the truth does not reach its population. The ban on the Russian media using the words 'war' or 'invasion' to describe the conflict with Ukraine builds on decades of preparation to secure Russia's 'national information space' against inconvenient facts.[44]

But crude and direct censoring or blocking of the media is not the only way Russia controls the information its people receive about the outside world. This isolation of Russian audiences is reinforced by steps as effective and simple as omitting undesirable words from the Russian translations of Western leaders' speeches,[45] or simply refusing altogether to report on controversial issues like the presence of Russian troops abroad where they have no right to be.[46] The danger of Western books can be reduced by producing unauthorized, and subtly altered, versions of these books in Russia.[47] And even in the previous decade, the notion of foreign broadcasters being allowed the kind of access to the Russian media market that RT enjoyed in the West was already impossibly remote.[48]

43. Bellingcat Investigation Team (2018), '305 Car Registrations May Point to Massive GRU Security Breach', Bellingcat, 4 October 2018, https://www.bellingcat.com/news/2018/10/04/305-car-registrations-may-point-massive-gru-security-breach.

44. 'Russia Bans Media Outlets From Using Words "War," "Invasion"', *Moscow Times*, 26 February 2022, https://www.themoscowtimes.com/2022/02/26/russia-bans-media-outlets-from-using-words-war-invasion-a76605.

45. 'Merkel's Remark On "Criminal" Annexation Omitted In Russian Translation', Radio Free Europe/Radio Liberty, 12 May 2015, http://www.rferl.org/content/russiamerkelputintranslationcriminalwordomitted/27011285.html.

46. 'Analysis: "Don't mention the war!" – Russian TV silent on troops near Ukraine', Media analysis by BBC Monitoring, 27 July 2015.

47. Howard Amos, 'Western Experts Cry Foul Over Russian Books Published in Their Names', *Moscow Times*, 9 August 2015, http://www.themoscowtimes.com/news/article/western-experts-cry-foul-over-russian-books-published-in-their-names/527629.html.

48. Keir Giles, 'The information war: how Moscow controls access to Western media', *The World Today*, August–September 2015, p. 19.

Russia has also had some success in censoring the internet, including on occasion with the active help of platforms like YouTube.[49] But the Kremlin's attempts to block access to undesirable information on the internet using purely technical means have a habit of backfiring. Russia's state communications regulator is Roskomnadzor – which translates more literally as Russian communications surveillance, or supervision. In 2018, it tried to shut down the messaging app Telegram, on the grounds that it was being used to spread illegal content. The attempt took thousands of websites offline because they used the same hosting services as Telegram's distributed network. Today, Telegram is still in widespread use in Russia. In early 2021, Roskomnadzor tried again, announcing that Twitter would be 'slowed' because it was failing to follow Russian rules on content. This time the damage was briefer but far more widespread, including making a large number of government websites inaccessible. Researchers later worked out that in trying to restrict traffic to t.co, the domain used to host all content shared via Twitter, Roskomnadzor had accidentally restricted all domains that included that string of four characters – for instance, Microsoft.com.[50] Eventually, Russia moved to block social media platforms altogether in order to suppress information on its war on Ukraine.[51] But to the dismay of counter-disinformation practitioners, removing Twitter from Russia did not have the effect of removing Russia from Twitter, and the country's disinformation outlets continued to shape audiences worldwide unhindered (see Chapter 5).

These attempts at censorship will not be completely successful while Russia still does not have complete control of the internet – or a better developed technical grasp of how to restrict people's access to it, leading to fewer embarrassing mistakes. But despite the growing role of online sources, television is still the main way most sectors of society get their news and information. The propaganda channels Valeriy described form viewers' opinions, which then also spill over into the internet as online providers feel the need to fall into line.[52] Overall, this creates an information environment within Russia that, despite access to a notionally common internet, is steadily retreating still further from the rest of the world and into its own artificial reality.

49. 'Free Speech a "Core Value," YouTube CEO Says After Blocking Russian Opposition Videos', *Moscow Times*, 27 September 2021, https://www.themoscowtimes.com/2021/09/27/free-speech-a-core-value-youtube-ceo-says-after-blocking-russian-opposition-videos-a75153.

50. Dan Goodin, 'Russia's Twitter throttling may give censors never-before-seen capabilities', *Ars Technica*, 6 April 2021, https://arstechnica.com/gadgets/2021/04/russias-twitter-throttling-may-give-censors-never-before-seen-capabilities/.

51. Dan Milmo, 'Russia blocks access to Facebook and Twitter', *Guardian*, 4 March 2022, https://www.theguardian.com/world/2022/mar/04/russia-completely-blocks-access-to-facebook-and-twitter.

52. Christina Cottiero, Katherine Kucharski, Evgenia Olimpieva and Robert W. Orttung, 'War of words: the impact of Russian state television on the Russian Internet', *Nationalities Papers: The Journal of Nationalism and Ethnicity*, March 2015.

Many people's first thought on the reintroduction of censorship and attempts to limit technical means for distributing information is that this is a throwback to Soviet times. It's true that the Russian security services in the 1990s reacted to the arrival of the internet with as much horror as that of the photocopier in the 1970s.[53] But as so often, the roots of this attitude go far deeper in Russian tradition than communist times. Russia has always seen the idea of its subjects enjoying uncontrolled access to news and ideas from abroad as highly dangerous, and throughout its history has tried its hardest to prevent this.[54] The blocks and filters Russia is putting in place today in its attempts to prevent direct access to news from abroad are more of a distorting lens than an information Iron Curtain. But at the same time, Russia has also slowly reinstated soft barriers to direct human contacts between its subjects and the outside world. The foreign agents' law has also been used to cut links between Russian and foreign universities, in ongoing efforts to reduce the ability of foreign organizations to influence Russians.[55] Veteran BBC correspondent Sarah Rainsford says her expulsion from Moscow in 2021 after reporting on Russia for many years was 'a clear sign that things have changed. It's another really bad sign about the state of affairs in Russia and another downward turn in the relationship between Russia and the world – a sign that Russia is increasingly closing in on itself.' She says Russia prefers to host foreign journalists who do not speak the language, and who therefore find it harder to reach real people and hear their stories. 'I really think it is indicative of an increasingly difficult and repressive environment,' she says.[56] Foreigners with friends in Russia now need to tread carefully, since just speaking to an employee working in a sensitive sector of the economy can inadvertently land that friend on a list of foreign agents.[57]

In this as in so much else, the trend is not a new development but a return to old habits. Russia has always felt the need to insulate its population from excessive exposure to foreigners so they are not contaminated with dangerous ideas of political liberty or democracy. A visitor to Russia in the seventeenth century reported that travel abroad by its subjects was punishable by death.[58] Three

53. Soldatov and Borogan, *The Red Web*.

54. This historical approach is explored in more detail in Keir Giles, 'Moscow Rules: What Drives Russia to Confront the West', Chatham House, 2019.

55. Elizabeth Redden, 'Bard College Declared "Undesirable" in Russia', *Inside Higher Ed*, 9 July 2021, https://www.insidehighered.com/news/2021/07/09/bard-grapples-what-it-might-mean-be-declared-%E2%80%98undesirable%E2%80%99-russia.

56. 'Sarah Rainsford on Russia: "I've been told I can't come back – ever"', BBC News, 14 August 2021, https://www.bbc.com/news/world-europe-58213845.

57. Natalia Antonova, 'Scientists Want Out of Russia', *Foreign Policy*, 14 October 2021, https://foreignpolicy.com/2021/10/14/scientists-space-russia-paranoia-elite-corruption/.

58. Adam Olearius, 'The voyages and travells of the ambassadors sent by Frederick, Duke of Holstein, to the Great Duke of Muscovy and the King of Persia begun in the year M.DC.XXXIII. and finish'd in M.DC.XXXIX', https://openlibrary.org/books/OL6951428M/The_voyages_and_travells_of_the_ambassadors_sent_by_Frederick_Duke_of_Holstein_to_the_great_Duke_of_

centuries later, in communist times, the danger of exposure driving these drastic isolation measures was still just as strong, as the Kremlin 'feared direct contact between the Western world and their own, feared what would happen if Russians learned the truth about the world without or foreigners learned the truth about the world within'.[59] The discouragement of foreign contacts steadily grew in many different ways, some of them more subtle than others. In 2021, Russians holding foreign currency bank accounts were in no immediate danger of having their US dollars confiscated – but they were warned that holding them was 'dangerous', as the inevitable decline of the dollar could mean they would lose their savings.[60] (In the event, they lost their savings for the opposite reason – because of the dramatic fall in the rouble exchange rate and currency restrictions introduced after the invasion of Ukraine.)[61] But under Putin, the removal of a BBC correspondent was just one symptom of a persistent pattern of a return to old Russian restrictions not only on what its citizens are allowed to read, but also on who they are allowed to meet.[62]

Despite the challenges of being a country at war, including a drastic curtailment of flights abroad, foreign travel is at the time of writing still technically permitted for most Russians.[63] University professor Andrey Makarychev thinks that while the Kremlin is confident that it can successfully prevent any attempts at organized opposition within the country, it is also perfectly content for the problem to quite literally go away by moving abroad. 'In this sense, Russia is smarter than the Soviet Union,' Andrey says. 'With the exception of Covid, the borders have been open. So, the message is you don't like what is going on here? No problem, go and find your own country and goodbye.' Veteran Australian diplomat Kyle Wilson agrees, and explains that while 'Putin has created an environment in which the fascist current in Russian history is now riding high', there is still a way to go. 'They are edging

59. 'George Kennan's "Long Telegram"', February 22, 1946, http://digitalarchive.wilsoncenter.org/document/116178.

60. 'Россиянам объяснили опасность покупки американских долларов' (Russians are told why it's dangerous to buy American dollars), *Moskovskiy Komsomolets*, 3 May 2021, https://www.mk.ru/economics/2021/05/03/rossiyanam-obyasnili-opasnost-pokupki-amerikanskikh-dollarov.html.

61. Huileng Tan, 'Russians are scrambling to withdraw US dollars at ATMs as the ruble hits a record low on sweeping Western sanctions', *Business Insider*, 28 February 2022, https://www.businessinsider.com/ruble-hits-record-low-russians-rush-withdraw-us-dollars-atms-2022-2.

62. Tatia Lemondzhava, 'In Russia, the Doors Are Closing: How – and Why – Russians Are Losing Their Freedom to Travel Abroad', *Foreign Policy*, 29 April 2016, http://foreignpolicy.com/2016/04/29/in-russia-the-doors-are-closing-tourism-putin-human-rights/.

63. Matthew Mpoke Bigg and Niraj Chokshi, 'Aeroflot says it will suspend international flights', *New York Times*, 5 March 2022, https://www.nytimes.com/2022/03/05/world/europe/aeroflot-russia-international-flights-suspended.html.

steadily towards a more overtly repressive state. But they seem to be still a fair way off totalitarianism because apart from Covid, Russians can still travel.' But with Russia's control over its citizens growing rapidly tighter, there is no telling how soon it might emulate its neighbour Belarus and once again ban most citizens from leaving the country at all.[64]

## *Cracking down*

Restrictions on personal liberties are already well established in Russia, particularly when it comes to the right to express discontent with the way the country is run. Alexei Navalny is by far the most high-profile critic of the current Russian leadership, not least because this has led to at least one attempt by the Russian state to murder him. But close attention to Navalny in the West can overshadow the many other individuals who have suffered severe consequences as a result of showing their support for him or for other opposition figures.[65] Supporters across Russia have been fired from their jobs, or pretexts found to imprison them.[66] One Russian newspaper concluded that the attempt to eradicate Navalny's organization in 2021 indicated a new zero tolerance approach to political opposition: 'the authorities are continuing, or possibly even completing, their operation to remove from politics altogether the opposition that is not willing to compromise'.[67] As so often, the campaign was impervious to irony. By banning an organization fighting corruption and by branding its activities extremist, the Russian leadership effectively confirmed that it considered corruption to be an essential part of the country's system of governance.[68]

---

64. 'Belarus bans most citizens from going abroad', BBC News, 1 June 2021, https://www.bbc.co.uk/news/world-europe-57316838.

65. Nataliya Vasilyeva, 'Navalny activists forced underground as Russia's only opposition crumbles under Kremlin pressure', *Telegraph*, 1 May 2021, https://www.telegraph.co.uk/news/2021/05/01/navalny-activists-forced-underground-political-movement-crumbles/.

66. '"It has to be today": Transcript from secretly recorded meeting shows what it's like to be fired from Moscow's subway for supporting Alexey Navalny', *Meduza*, 14 May 2021, https://meduza.io/en/feature/2021/05/14/it-has-to-be-today.

'Суд назначил бывшему координатору архангельского штаба Навального 2,5 года колонии за репост клипа Rammstein' (Court sentences former coordinator of Navalny staff in Arkhangelsk to 2.5 years in prison for reposting a Rammstein video), *Mediazona*, 29 April 2021, https://zona.media/news/2021/04/29/borovikov.

67. 'Will Russia still have a non-systemic opposition?', *Nezavisimaya gazeta*, 12 August 2021.

68. 'Navalny Groups Vow To Carry On After Moscow Court Suspends "Certain Activities"', RFE/RL, https://www.rferl.org/a/russia-navalny-court-places-restrictions-organizations/31225294.html.

Over the course of 2021, Russia's campaign to suppress political opposition, or in fact most forms of dissent, accelerated rapidly. High-profile arrests of prominent figures like Alexei Navalny were the tip of the iceberg of a much broader campaign of intimidation and repression.[69] Mass detentions at street protests were backed up by hundreds of separate actions against individuals, like a journalist for an opposition outlet charged with 'taking part in unsanctioned rallies' after reporting on a demonstration.[70] In Soviet times, those who considered defying the regime could see newsreels of show trials. Today, the security forces can post to social media video of all stages of brutal arrest and detention in near real-time.[71] The establishment of Rosgvardiya, Russia's 'National Guard', in 2016 confirmed the leadership's deep sense of insecurity, and the threat it perceives from Russia's own population. Although notionally an internal security force, Rosgvardiya is highly militarized and has a wide range of weapons systems for inflicting mass casualties when necessary.[72] In addition, its powers have been steadily expanding, prompting comparisons with the Soviet Union's NKVD.[73] Rosgvardiya's supplementary role of controlling the population in newly-occupied territories meant that its appearance among the Russian troops massing to invade Ukraine in early 2022 was one of the surest indicators that an attempt to occupy the country was about to be launched. But even before suffering severe casualties in Ukraine, the combined effect of paying and arming these organizations represented a colossal drain on the Russian economy, with over 2.5 million people employed by law enforcement and internal security agencies.[74]

69. 'How we got here: Meduza looks back on Russia's most high-profile incidents of repression over the past six months', *Meduza*, 19 July 2021, https://meduza.io/en/feature/2021/07/20/how-we-got-here.

70. 'Корреспондента Дождя забрали в полицию для составления протокола из-за акции 21 апреля' (Dozhd correspondent detained by police for charges over 21 April demonstration), *Dozhd*, 27 April 2021, https://tvrain.ru/news/korrespondenta_dozhdja_zabrali_v_politsiju_dlja_sostavlenija_protokola_iz_za_aktsii_21_aprelja-528956/.

71. Tweet by Kevin Rothrock: 'Highly disturbing video of police in Vladivostok interrogating and humiliating local journalist Gennady Shulga. Cops raided his home and "questioned" him about the opposition's Jan. 23 protests. Especially noteworthy: the police themselves leaked this footage', 6 February 2021, https://twitter.com/kevinrothrock/status/1358122270967922688.

72. Zdzisław Śliwa, 'The Russian National Guard: A Warning or a Message?', National Defence Academy of Latvia, 2018, https://www.baltdefcol.org/files/files/publications/RussianNationalGuard.pdf.

73. Paul Goble, 'Putin Gives National Guard Powers Even NKVD Didn't Have – The Question Now is Why? Gorevoy Says', *Window on Eurasia*, 5 June 2017, http://windowoneurasia2.blogspot.com/2017/06/putin-gives-national-guard-powers-even.html.

74. Vladislav Inozemtsev, 'Не много ли силы? За 15 лет число силовиков выросло более чем вдвое' (Isn't that enough power? In 15 years the number of power ministry employees has more than doubled), *Forbes Russia*, 11 July 2017, https://www.forbes.ru/biznes/346301-ne-mnogo-li-%07sily-za-15-let-chislo-silovikov-vyroslo-bolee-chem-vdvoe.

Censorship doesn't only relate to the war on Ukraine. Soviet-style suppression of basic truths severely affects people's lives if they choose to speak up on other issues too. Kerstin Kronvall has been reporting on Russia's tumultuous changes for a quarter of a century. She has been following the story of Vyacheslav Yegorov, a local civic activist in in Kolomna, south-east of Moscow. Yegorov is no stranger to confrontations with the authorities. His long-standing opposition to uncontrolled official dumping of waste in his home town has seen him arrested and imprisoned multiple times, including on charges of organizing demonstrations that he says he was unaware had even happened. At the beginning of the coronavirus pandemic, he heard of shortages of protective equipment in the city hospital, and decided to help. Provided with a list of essential supplies by the hospital's chief doctor, including gloves and respirators, Yegorov posted the list on a website and tried to start raising funds to buy the hospital what it needed. Shortly afterwards Yegorov – and the chief doctor – were summoned to the FSB for questioning, and accused of causing panic.[75] He was eventually fined 30,000 roubles (about £300, a substantial amount in rural Russia) and placed under house arrest for six months, followed by another six months of 'special conditions' including not being allowed to use the internet.[76]

Long-term Russia-watcher Samantha de Bendern had long advocated a harder line against Russia over its attitude to human rights, in line with past international practice against oppressive regimes. Before the invasion of Ukraine she called for measures against Russia comparable with those faced by South Africa under apartheid – 'the country was basically completely cut off and boycotted and sanctioned by the rest of the world'. At the time of writing, that describes Russia's near-term prospects following ostracism not over domestic concerns but over the attack on Ukraine. But within Russia itself, Reiner Schwalb suggests increasingly firm measures by the authorities are broadly accepted: 'Most Russians seem to believe only a country that is controlled with an iron fist is really stable. Democracy brings chaos. That's their view. Stalin killed millions, but almost nobody cares about that any more.'

Meanwhile Russia's regression to an older style of governance where suppression of any kind of political dissent is the norm is accelerating. As part of the process, Russia is progressively dropping even the pretence to genuine democracy and rule of law. The ways in which Russia's notional 'elections' have now become an entirely cynical routine with little attempt to simulate an actual exercise in democracy were

75. 'I Ryssland straffas initiativ för att hjälpa sjukhus som saknar skyddsutrustning – Vjatjeslav Jegorov blev inkallad till förhör då han försökte få tag på handskar och respiratorer' (In Russia, initiatives to help hospitals that lack protective equipment are punished – Vyacheslav Yegorov was summoned for questioning as he tried to get gloves and respirators), *Yle*, 7 April 2020, https://svenska.yle.fi/artikel/2020/04/07/i-ryssland-straffas-initiativ-for-att-hjalpa-sjukhus-som-saknar-skyddsutrustning.

76. Kerstin Kronvall, 'I Ryssland är det bäst att hålla tyst om missförhållanden om man vill gå ostraffad' (In Russia, it is best to keep quiet about misconduct if you want to go unpunished), *Yle*, 31 July 2021, https://svenska.yle.fi/a/7-10003309.

highlighted in the voting for the State Duma in 2021. Old-school methods of neutralizing the opposition like putting them in jail were joined by new techniques like blocking access to apps and Google Docs tools used for opposition campaigns – and to the dismay of democracy advocates both inside Russia and beyond, Google and Apple assisted the Kremlin in doing so.[77] One candidate standing against Putin's party, Boris Vishnevsky, found that two Photoshopped lookalikes were running in the same election – and just in case that wasn't enough to confuse voters, they had also both been given the name Boris Vishnevsky.[78] Meanwhile the use of criminal law both to punish dissidents and to settle rivalries between individuals close to the heart of power is also becoming more and more transparent and barely even bothering to pretend to legitimacy. When former Economic Development Minister Alexey Ulyukayev was put on trial after being set up to receive a bribe of $2m dollars in cash, he pointed out that if true, the charges meant his government accusers ran a huge off-the-books slush fund of ready cash for facilitating corruption – and that this had been of no interest at all to the prosecutors instructed to take him down.[79]

Throughout all of these rapidly accelerating processes of state control of ordinary citizens, and all the symptoms of a return to the darker, more authoritarian Russia of the past, there is one constant theme: a reminder that now as in past centuries, if Russia is unable to secure the loyalty of its subjects through propaganda, it demands it through force. Strategies for dealing with differences of political opinion have been tried and gradually discarded, leaving only Russia's traditional fallback of oppression.[80]

### Getting poorer

Meanwhile not only the cost of the mechanism of repression at home, but also the obsession with finding foreign enemies – and maintaining Russia's former status in the world – has added direct economic costs to the political ones, and had a

77. Andrew Roth, 'Apple and Google accused of "political censorship" over Alexei Navalny app', *Guardian*, 17 September 2021, https://www.theguardian.com/world/2021/sep/17/apple-and-google-accused-of-political-censorship-over-alexei-navalny-app.

78. Megan Baynes, 'Russia: Opposition politician Boris Vishnevsky says two lookalikes with same name as him running in St Petersburg election in bid to confuse voters', Sky News, 8 September 2021, https://news.sky.com/story/russia-opposition-politician-boris-vishnevsky-says-two-lookalikes-with-same-name-as-him-running-in-st-petersburg-election-in-bid-to-confuse-voters-12402116.

79. 'An elderly gladiator and his cardboard sword', *Meduza*, 7 December 2017, https://meduza.io/en/feature/2017/12/07/an-elderly-gladiator-and-his-cardboard-sword.

80. Anton Troianovski, 'Putin Assails Russians Who Back the West, Signaling More Repression', *New York Times*, 16 March 2022, https://www.nytimes.com/2022/03/16/world/europe/putin-russia-ukraine-protests.html.

catastrophic impact on ordinary Russians' prosperity. Here too, the devastating effect on standards of living of the plummeting rouble exchange rate and restrictions on imports introduced after the attack on Ukraine are just the latest stage of a long trend. Historian Stephen Kotkin pointed out as long ago as 2016 that 'if Russian elites could somehow redefine their sense of exceptionalism and put aside their unwinnable competition with the West, they could set their country on a less costly, more promising course'.[81] Andrey Makarychev agrees: 'Russia is disproportionately much more interested in foreign affairs rather than rebuilding and reconstructing the country. Just imagine how much [military operations] cost, and how much cities and municipalities and townships and other parts of Russia could get from that.'

When President Putin first arrived in power, he pointed at Russia's dependency on energy exports and its failure to innovate and modernize its economy as serious challenges. But high oil prices in the years that followed meant there was little incentive to tackle the problem seriously.[82] Ordinary Russians are now paying the price for that failure to take the opportunity. Still heavily reliant on energy exports, the Russian economy is highly sensitive to changes in the international price of oil. When that price fell sharply in late 2014, the value of the rouble fell with it. The standard of living for ordinary Russians started to fall rapidly and has been doing so ever since. The number of Russians who think they earn more than the bare minimum required to survive has been steadily decreasing, and now stands at only 25% – despite the fact that the official subsistence minimum is just $157 a month.[83]

According to government communications expert Linas, 'the official message to the population is that yes, they will be working hard in order to ensure decent living conditions and so on. But the history shows that they keep saying the same thing year after year after year. And that's why there is huge frustration among the Russian population that basically they are left alone.' Even before 2022, Russia had to resort to introducing price controls and export quotas because essential goods had become unaffordable for such a high proportion of the population.[84] In mid-2021, a poll found almost 40% of Russians saying they have to forgo basic groceries and other essentials.[85]

---

81. Stephen Kotkin, 'Russia's Perpetual Geopolitics: Putin Returns to the Historical Pattern', *Foreign Affairs* (May/June 2016): 2–9.

82. David Clark, 'Russia's biggest enemy? Its own economy', *EU Observer*, 16 September 2021, https://euobserver.com/opinion/152825.

83. 'Evaluation of the Necessary Subsistence Minimum Among Russians', Levada-Center, 31 March 2021, https://www.levada.ru/en/2021/03/31/evaluation-of-the-necessary-subsistence-minimum-among-russians/; 'Russian government sets subsistence level at $157.57 for 2021', TASS, 9 January 2021, https://tass.com/economy/1243017

84. Max Seddon and Henry Foy, 'Kremlin may restrict more food exports to shield it from high prices', *Financial Times*, 6 June 2021, https://www.ft.com/content/07378501-0ab9-4eef-ad13-eb72adff1838.

85. '2 in 5 Russians Can't Afford Necessities – Poll', *Moscow Times*, 26 August 2021, https://www.themoscowtimes.com/2021/08/25/2-in-5-russians-cant-afford-necessities-poll-a74888.

Meanwhile Russia continued to pour funds into not only its military but also its propaganda campaigns abroad.[86] Once again, this is a symptom of how Russia measures its greatness in terms which are unrecognizable in the West. Just as in Soviet times, it prioritizes military might and status symbols to awe the world over basic infrastructure for its own people – including things that most Europeans have taken for granted for most of living memory, like all-weather roads and indoor toilets.[87] Sixty years after the USSR sent Yuri Gagarin into space, reporter Erkka Mikkonen visited the city of Komsomolsk-na-Amure where Gagarin is an honorary citizen. He found people were still living in ninety-year-old 'temporary' barracks with no indoor plumbing or sanitation.[88]

Linas points to the leadership's attitude to Russia's own population as yet another holdover from previous times. 'In Russia the political elites – a really small group of people tightly connected to another really small group of people from the business institutions – are working in order basically to achieve their own personal goals,' he says, 'while the population is left somewhere outside and is being used as a base of resources. That comes from Tsarist Russia, when the domestic population was nothing more than labour for the workforce, or the manpower for going to the wars.'

Where Russians do try to improve their own standard of living, they are faced with a hostile environment for entrepreneurs, where any successful business is a target for corrupt judges, tax officials and police officers. The basic lack of a fair and independent judicial system that can enforce contracts and protect property rights makes it straightforward for businesses to be stolen from their owners. Often, the owner himself is prosecuted as part of the process. And when cases do go to court, it is wise to treat the outcome as a foregone conclusion. US investor Michael Calvey was accused of embezzlement. The distinguishing feature of his trial in 2021 was that no evidence of his crime was presented, and no witnesses testified against him – so state prosecutors argued that all the evidence suggesting his innocence merely proved how well organized the crime had been. To nobody's great surprise, Calvey was still found guilty and given a five-and-a-half-year suspended jail sentence.[89]

According to a survey carried out by the presidential security service the same year, more than three-quarters of Russian businessmen said they felt they were at

86. 'RT America Received More Than $100 Million In Russian Government Funding Since 2017, Filings Show', RFE/RL, 26 August 2021, https://www.rferl.org/a/russia-rt-america-funding/31427870.html.

87. 'Indoor Plumbing Still a Pipe Dream for 20% of Russian Households, Reports Say', *Moscow Times*, 2 April 2019, https://www.themoscowtimes.com/2019/04/02/indoor-plumbing-still-a-pipe-dream-for-20-of-russian-households-reports-say-a65049.

88. Tweet by Erkka Mikkonen, 12 April 2021, https://twitter.com/Erkanomia/status/1381596379022290945.

89. Henry Foy, 'US investor Calvey found guilty of embezzlement by Russian court', *Financial Times*, 5 August 2021, https://www.ft.com/content/b8e222d0-e022-4c1b-bdbb-6fa9af63a182.

risk of unfounded criminal prosecution by the state. Plainly this is a justified fear, since in the same poll 18% of prosecutors agreed with them. The syndrome is so well known that at a high-profile economic conference in St Petersburg, an MP joked that progress was plainly being made towards a healthy investment climate in Russia because they were 'three days into the forum and nobody's been arrested'.[90]

## Paranoia at home and Abroad

But the genuine fear within Russia is matched by a misguided fear of the outside world. So much of Russia's confrontational behaviour is based on a fundamentally wrong assumption: the idea that the West is driven by the desire to 'dismember and destroy Russia'. This keystone belief is regularly stated by figures like former FSB chief and now Secretary of the Security Council Nikolai Patrushev, and is a recurring refrain throughout Russia's propaganda directed at its own people.[91] Robert Pszczel observed a steady progression during his five years in Moscow: 'In a practical sense, yes, they were getting more paranoid. It was beginning to resemble more like the Soviet Union.' In fact the Russian state has never been more secure from external threat than it is today, and yet the new National Security Strategy released in mid-2021 effectively sees 'not just foreign countries as a threat, but the very processes reshaping the modern world'.[92] Once seen through this prism, everything becomes an attempt to bring Russia down. In this view, Western sanctions imposed since 2014 are not only intended to undermine Russia's economy and administer 'punishment' for Crimea, but in fact have the ultimate aim of regime change – even though there is little doubt that uncontrolled regime change in Russia and the ensuing chaos would be the last thing anybody in the West would actually want.[93]

A recurring question in the West is whether Russia's leaders truly believe they are under threat, or whether this is a known fiction maintained in order to keep power through frightening the population with the menace from abroad – and to provide the rationale or excuse for wars of conquest against countries like Ukraine. French academic Bruno Tertrais distinguishes between three different types of Russian paranoia. He points to 'sincere paranoia' (what they really believe),

---

90. Seddon and Foy, 'Kremlin may restrict more food exports to shield it from high prices'.

91. A core element of the 'Vecher [Evening] with Vladimir Solovyev' propaganda broadcast on Rossiya 1 TV, for example. Selection available at https://www.youtube.com/watch?v=bKy4xAC4gKE.

92. 'New National Security Strategy Is a Paranoid's Charter', *Moscow Times*, https://www.themoscowtimes.com/2021/07/05/new-national-security-strategy-is-a-paranoids-charter-a74424.

93. See, for example, interview with Sergey Karaganov in *Rossiyskaya gazeta*, 24 April 2014, http://www.rg.m/2014/04/23/karaganov-site.html.

'internalized paranoia' (what they want their population to believe) and 'instrumentalized paranoia' (what they want the leaders of other countries to think they believe).[94] But from the outside it is hard to discern the lines between them. Andrey Makarychev points out that 'if you keep reiterating certain positions or certain narratives, year after year, even decade after decade, it's just a matter of time when you start seriously believing in that. I don't rule out that some people in the Kremlin do believe in this world that they have produced, because they feel quite comfortable with this fantasy.' And if the Russian leadership has convinced itself that the West is its enemy no matter what, the paranoia becomes self-perpetuating. As Mark Galeotti explains, 'You can't go to Putin and say look, you're wrong about the West. They have no hostile intentions towards you. That will just get you laughed out of the room.' Still worse, Galeotti says, the Russian intelligence services are 'driving this narrative that speaks of an aggressive West actively seeking to constrain Russia abroad, subvert the Kremlin at home, because this works for them. It gives them profile, it gives them budgets, gives them autonomy and gives them a purpose.'[95]

This creates a vicious circle, where the West takes steps in defence of sovereignty or international law, which are interpreted by Russia as further evidence of hostility to Moscow, which then prompts the Kremlin to escalate still further, leading to further Western defensive measures. Whether the Russian leadership truly believes its own propaganda about the West, or whether it is fully conscious that it is based on a myth, the effect is the same: entirely unnecessary confrontation with the West. And the war on Ukraine shows the disastrous consequences of this self-deception.

The acceptance of this delusion also reinforces the belief that Russians who are angry with the regime cannot have been thinking for themselves and must be under the influence of hostile foreign powers that want to destabilize and destroy Russia. Just as in Soviet times, Russia searches for imaginary foreign links lying behind the ever-present threat of radicalization from abroad and attempts at destabilization within the Russian Federation, laying the groundwork for direct attack.[96] In 2019, Chief of the General Staff Valery Gerasimov explained how the US had a 'trojan horse' strategy of using political warfare and information warfare to 'mobilize the protest potential of the population', which would then be combined with precision strikes against critical infrastructure to neutralize Russia.[97] This

94. 'Quelles relations franco-russes?' (What kind of French-Russian relations?), Diploweb. com, 3 February 2021, https://www.diploweb.com/Video-P-Vimont-et-B-Tertrais-Quelles-relations-franco-russes.html.

95. Mark Galeotti, 'Russian Intelligence & Security Community', Russia Strategic Initiative, 12 August 2021, https://community.apan.org/wg/rsi/project-connect/w/events/31576/mark-galeotti-russian-intelligence-security-community/.

96. 'A comparison of Russia's National Security Strategies (2009, 2015, 2021)', Aleksanteri Institute, 12 July 2021, https://rusmilsec.files.wordpress.com/2021/07/natsec_comparison_2021-1.pdf.

97. 'Векторы развития военной стратегии' (Vectors for development of military strategy), *Krasnaya zvezda*, 3 April 2019, http://redstar.ru/vektory-razvitiya-voennoj-strategii/.

attitude even extends to attempts at self-expression for ethnic and national languages within Russia itself that are notionally protected by law.[98] Putin, true to form, sees local self-awareness and the preservation of traditional cultures among the many non-Russian nationalities and ethnicities within Russia as a vulnerability that can be exploited by Russia's enemies.[99]

But it is not only on its own behalf that Russia has consistently pointed to the dangers of regime change sponsored from abroad. Moscow not only prefers to keep its friends in power in autocratic regimes, but also more broadly prefers stability and predictability to sudden changes in geopolitics. In some cases, Russia can justifiably claim it was right. The West was warned before its intervention in the Libyan civil war in 2011 of all the disastrous consequences that would follow, including weapons proliferation, ongoing chaos and mass migration affecting Southern Europe. After Libya, the same concerns prompted Russia's intervention in Syria in 2015, in a successful move to head off another Western attempt to step in. But in all cases, there are two underlying concerns: the fantasy that this is all part of a deliberate and carefully planned Western campaign to overthrow regimes and its eventual target is Moscow; and the reality that when leaders whom the West dislikes are overthrown, as with Saddam Hussein and Muammar Gaddafi, they have a tendency to be lynched.

## Best enemies

Russia portrays itself as being 'surrounded by enemies'. To the extent that that is true in the twenty-first century, it is entirely because Russia has created those enemies. Russia claims it is dismayed by anti-Russian attitudes, but seems unable to grasp that where they exist, they are stoked by Russia's own behaviour.

Where relations with other countries were previously good, Russia has been adept at destroying them. Before 2012, Czechia was an EU state that was relatively friendly to Russian interests. By 2021, the backlash from Russia's covert attack on munitions storage sites in 2014 that killed two Czech civilian employees meant that relations were already in the deep freeze (see Chapter 1). In the same way, even before overt invasion, nothing had done more to push Ukraine toward the West and away from Russia than the Kremlin's actions since 2014. Valeriy Akimenko explained in 2021 how 'I can describe the negative effect of Russian propaganda on me as both a Ukrainian and a resident of the West, but on the plus side no one else

98. Ramazan Alpaut, 'Russky Or Rossiisky: An Activist – And His Native Language – Go On Trial In A Russian Courtroom', RFE/Rl, 17 February 2021, https://www.rferl.org/a/russia-komi-minoroty-language-ivanov-court-russky-rossiisky-navalny-putin/31108182.html.

99. Vladimir Putin, 'Россия: национальный вопрос' (Russia: the nationalities question), *Nezavismaya gazeta*, 23 January 2012, https://www.ng.ru/politics/2012-01-23/1_national.html.

has done more to reawaken my sense of national pride and self-identity than [leading Russian propagandists] Mr Kiselev and Mr Solovyev. I am extremely grateful to them for that.' He went on, 'It's worse than a mistake, it's a crime to allow a wedge to be driven between Russia and Ukraine. It's a manifestation of some kind of tactical genius to regain Crimea, but at the same time a sign of strategic foolishness to lose Ukraine.' Even Russians abroad who observe what Russia does become politically motivated to join the opposition. Kyle Wilson explains how a new group has appeared in Australia calling itself Adekvatnyye Russkiye v Avstralii i Novozelandii (Appropriate Russians in Australia and New Zealand), trying to distance themselves from aggressive Russian nationalists and making clear their preference for a more accountable and representative government back in Russia.

Similarly, Russia's threats against Finland and Sweden over the prospect of joining NATO have also backfired. The proportion of Finns and Swedes in favour of NATO membership had been steadily inching up, as Russia made it more and more plain precisely why a military alliance against it is needed. In addition, even without joining NATO, both countries have focused clearly on the need to boost their own defence spending. According to Pekka Toveri, 'After the occupation of Crimea, the Russians tried to intimidate Finland. There were airspace violations, big exercises nearby, [Russian Chief of the General Staff] General Makarov visiting Finland and basically threatening us for cooperating with NATO, and so on. The result was that the population's attitudes towards Russians got harder, and the government decided to give the Defence Forces money for new fighters for the Air Force and new corvettes for the Navy over and above the defence budget. It was an almost 12 billion euro boost to our defensive capabilities. The Russians learned fast that threatening Finns with military means doesn't work that well.' And now, after Russia's assault on Ukraine starkly highlighted the dangers of not being in a defensive alliance, support for Finland joining NATO has broken all records.[100]

One peculiarity of Russian foreign policy that seems to confirm its confrontational nature is the way the Ministry of Foreign Affairs (MFA), instead of directing it, is routinely sidelined.[101] The intelligence services and the Armed Forces pursue their own policies in countries of interest to Russia without coordination with the MFA.[102] When Russia recklessly destroyed a communications satellite to test one of its anti-satellite weapons in November 2021, endangering its own and others' space operations, Foreign Minister Sergey Lavrov categorically

100. 'Yle poll: Support for Nato membership hits record high', *Yle News*, 14 March 2022, https://yle.fi/news/3-12357832.

101. Mark Galeotti, 'Free Sergei Lavrov!', *Foreign Policy*, 17 February 2016, https://foreignpolicy.com/2016/02/17/free-sergei-lavrov-putin-russia-syria/.

102. Ilgar Musakhanov, 'Внешнюю политику РФ теперь определяют не дипломаты, а силовики?' (Is Russian foreign policy now decided by the power ministers not the diplomats?), *Versiya*, 24 August 2020, https://versia.ru/vneshnyuyu-politiku-rf-teper-opredelyayut-ne-diplomaty-a-siloviki.

denied that this had happened – a few minutes before Russia's own Ministry of Defence confirmed that, yes, it had.[103]

Sergey Lavrov is one of the longest-serving foreign ministers in the world, and foreigners who have watched the effect on him over the years sometimes almost feel sympathy. Mark Galeotti recalls how 'Lavrov was once one of the legends, one of the titans of the diplomatic circuit. But now he's almost become a caricature of himself. He has almost physically shrunk since 2014. He was not involved in the final discussions about taking Crimea, he was required to lie in his teeth, about the little green men.'[104] Robert Pszczel also thinks the need to constantly tell obvious lies after Russia's spies and soldiers commit outrages without consulting or even warning him has had a physical effect. 'It's been years and years and years that he's worked on his face,' he says. 'His nickname is "horse" after spending so long saying ridiculous things with a straight face that, you know, at some point probably you train your muscles so well they stay like that.' The years of practice were put to good use after Russia launched its assault on Ukraine, when two weeks after the invasion began Lavrov was still denying it was happening at all.[105]

Political leaders in western European countries in particular are reluctant to recognize the extent to which their own good intentions are not reciprocated by Moscow; and when this recognition belatedly comes, it is accompanied by profound disappointment and sometimes incomprehension.[106] There are two natural but unfortunate human tendencies at work here. The first is optimism – the assumption that things by default ought to get better, not worse, and that includes Russian behaviour if only Russia is given a chance. The second is a pattern that's repeated by Western leaders and officials at all levels when first coming to the Russia problem: the idea, often born of arrogance as well as a refusal to learn from past experience, that they can succeed where all before them have failed and get the Russia relationship onto a proper, peaceful and stable footing. The trouble is, even a quick survey of past history shows how terribly misguided both of these ideas are.

The unfortunate result is that Western leaders who seek a genuine understanding with Russia come away disappointed, confused and dismayed – but because these leaders are constantly being replaced in Western democracies, the result is their countries coming back to Russia time after time, like a trusting spaniel perpetually confused as to why it is being beaten. The process is fairly predictable, and for all his willingness to reap the benefits of friendships with Russian oligarchs, British

103. 'Russian military admits "destroyed" satellite during test', AFP, 16 November 2021.

104. Mark Galeotti, 'Russian Intelligence & Security Community', Russia Strategic Initiative, 12 August 2021, https://community.apan.org/wg/rsi/project-connect/w/events/31576/mark-galeotti-russian-intelligence-security-community/.

105. 'Russian foreign minister falsely claims that it didn't invade Ukraine', CNN, 10 March 2022, https://edition.cnn.com/europe/live-news/ukraine-russia-putin-news-03-10-22/.

106. Hans von der Burchard, 'Merkel blames Russia for 'outrageous' cyberattack on German parliament', *Politico*, 13 May 2020, https://www.politico.eu/article/merkel-blames-russia-for-outrageous-cyber-attack-on-german-parliament/

Prime Minister Boris Johnson too has experienced it. In December 2017, while serving as Foreign Minister, he went to Moscow looking for a reset, and told Sergey Lavrov that the UK and Russia had 'substantial interests in common'.[107] By mid-September 2018, Johnson described this as the biggest mistake of his career and a 'fool's errand'.[108] In early 2021, the EU's Foreign Affairs chief Josep Borrell followed the same familiar trajectory of heading to Moscow to repair the relationship and returning sadder and wiser. Borrell had pressed ahead with a planned summit meeting with unrealistic expectations against advice not to do so from member states, primarily those from the eastern part of the EU with the longest experience of Russia.[109] Borrell told Sergey Lavrov he had come to Moscow 'to find spaces for understanding and to build mutual trust' including on 'human rights and fundamental freedoms'.[110] But not only did Borrell find his advances spurned and he himself publicly harangued, but on the same day Russia expelled three EU diplomats on the grounds that they had been present at opposition rallies.[111] And so yet another Western politician returned from Moscow bitterly disappointed to discover that hubris and misplaced belief in their own competence did not outweigh the combined experience of centuries of dealing with Russia.[112]

But still, as decades go, by Western leaders continue to succumb to the triumph of hope over experience and believe that a fresh start in relations with Russia will make everything work out this time.[113] They continue to seek 'resets' with Russia,

107. Rob Merrick, 'Boris Johnson clashes with Russian Foreign Minister Sergei Lavrov in Moscow over attacks on Putin regime', *Independent*, 22 December 2017, https://www.independent.co.uk/news/uk/politics/boris-johnson-russia-sergei-lavrov-moscow-visit-putin-foreign-minister-ukraine-uk-a8124021.html.

108. 'A conversation with Boris Johnson', AEI, 13 September 2018, https://www.aei.org/research-products/speech/a-conversation-with-boris-johnson/.

109. James Crisp et al., 'EU chief diplomat accused of kow-towing to Russia for vaccines on embarrassing Moscow visit', *Telegraph*, 5 February 2021, https://www.telegraph.co.uk/news/2021/02/05/eu-chief-diplomat-accused-kow-towing-russia-vaccines-embarrassing/.

110. 'Russia: Remarks by High Representative/Vice-President Josep Borrell at the joint press conference with Foreign Minister Lavrov', EU External Action Service, 5 February 2021, https://eeas.europa.eu/headquarters/headquarters-homepage/92661/russia-remarks-high-representativevice-president-josep-borrell-joint-press-conference-foreign_en.

111. Peter Stubley, 'Russia to expel German, Swedish and Polish diplomats accused of taking part in Navalny protests', 5 February 2021, https://www.independent.co.uk/news/world/europe/russia-diplomats-expel-germany-sweden-poland-navalny-b1798203.html.

112. Mark Galeotti, 'The EU humiliated itself in Moscow', *Spectator*, 5 February 2021, https://www.spectator.co.uk/article/the-eu-humiliated-itself-in-moscow.

113. A report published in late 2011 described in detail the cycle of reset and crisis that had already been repeated several times since the end of the Cold War, and based on that analysis predicted that there would soon be a return to crisis. Sure enough, that crisis turned up in early 2014 in the shape of the confrontation over Ukraine. See *The State of the NATO–Russia Reset*, Conflict Studies Research Centre, September 2011, http://www.conflictstudies.org.uk/files/csrc_nato-russia-reset_preview.pdf.

looking to normalize relations by means of forgiving Moscow its sins. But doing so without addressing the fundamental causes of strife in the relationship is highly damaging, as its sole effect is to confirm to Russia that its policy of hostility toward the West will not only be forgiven but actually rewarded.[114] The US-led Russian 'reset' of 2009 in particular, a few months after Russia occupied the Georgian territories of Abkhazia and South Ossetia, encouraged Russia to think five years later that if there were any international consequences from its seizure of Crimea, they would be only temporary. And in early 2022, the steady procession of Western leaders queuing up to visit Moscow in order to pay court to Putin and try to cajole him out of invading Ukraine were one by one lectured, humiliated and sent home empty-handed, with the net result of the whole exercise being to confirm that there was no conversation to be had.[115] Time and again, Russia has shown that it is not inclined to reciprocate the good faith shown in attempts to improve relations, and that it does not share the West's vision of how the two sides should live with each other.[116] Yet in spite of everything, the idea that you can unilaterally impose a different kind of relationship on Russia when Russia isn't interested seems never to die. If Russia were a woman, these Western leaders would have been called stalkers.

It's hard to see how European politicians hope to restore an amicable relationship with Russia when it's challenging enough even to have a calm, serious conversation. But France and Germany in particular have been consistently intent on trying to drag the rest of Europe back into a closer relationship with Russia, regardless of Russia's behaviour. Where there is a stated reason for this, it's usually a misguided one – like the thoroughly debunked idea that being more friendly to Russia will stop it finding common interest with China. In mid-2021, German Chancellor Angela Merkel and French President Emmanuel Macron startled and dismayed eastern Europe with a surprise proposal for an EU summit with Vladimir Putin. They hadn't thought it necessary to consult other EU leaders on whether this was a good idea. The proposal was eventually shot down in high-level discussion within the EU, but the process revealed still deeper failures by France and Germany to account for, or even realize, the challenges faced by the front-line states. Following a heated debate among EU leaders, Macron said, 'The discussion was complex, it's normal. It's normal because on this issue we don't have the same histories.' But what France and Germany consistently either fail or refuse to grasp is that they and EU countries closer to the Russian border don't share the same

114. Michael McFaul, 'Why deciding to "move forward" with Putin is a big mistake', *Washington Post*, 10 July 2017, https://www.washingtonpost.com/news/global-opinions/wp/2017/07/10/why-deciding-to-move-forward-with-putin-is-a-big-mistake/.

115. Ian Bond, 'Stronger sanctions on Russia: Essential, but not a strategy', Centre for European Reform, 25 February 2022, https://www.cer.eu/insights/stronger-sanctions-russia-essential.

116. Dominik Jankowski, 'With Russia, Transparency No Silver Bullet', *Berlin Policy Journal*, 4 September 2019, https://berlinpolicyjournal.com/with-russia-transparency-no-silver-bullet/.

present either.[117] While this difference of experience of relations with Russia has been forcefully driven home by the assault on Ukraine, past performance suggests that regardless of the outcome of the conflict, France and Germany will once again soon be seeking to restore closer ties with Moscow.

This has been a long-standing challenge for the countries of eastern Europe, who have repeatedly been marginalized by the larger and older members of both NATO and the EU. In 2010, just two years after the short war between Russia and Georgia, NATO held a summit in Lisbon and adopted a 'Strategic Concept' which 'committed NATO to reinforce cooperation with Russia'.[118] The summit included a meeting of the NATO–Russia Council, attended by then Russian president Dmitry Medvedev. Janis, an EU security official present at the meeting, told me how he watched with incredulity the way European heads of state performed for Medvedev. According to Janis, Italian President Silvio Berlusconi's 'whole speech was about him as best friend of Russia – he was basically describing how he had been instrumental in every positive step in developing a good relationship with Russia'. However, the comments by French president Nicolas Sarkozy were not comical, but chilling. 'Sarkozy turned his words toward the allies from the eastern part of NATO, and said you know my friends, I understand that you have had a hard history, and I am very sorry for it, but this is history. Let history be history. We are talking about the future, and the future is Russia at our side as our partner. He didn't say "get over it", but that was the message.'

'And this was in a situation where the heads of state and government had been trying to explain that the problem is not history, and Russia as the Soviet Union, but what Russia is doing *now* – including what it had done just recently to Georgia,' Janis recalled. 'That gave us a good understanding of how a president of France could lecture us, the eastern allies, in front of the Russian president and basically tell us we were stuck in history and should snap out of it. That was quite an experience.'

Russia benefits from a curious mental blind spot routinely displayed by French and German politicians: the idea that the countries in between themselves and Moscow do not matter, or sometimes even do not exist. We'll look more closely in Chapter 6 at the German view that Poland, Ukraine and Belarus count for nothing when Berlin wants to atone for war guilt to Moscow. French Foreign Minister Jean-Yves Le Drian believes too that 'Russia is our neighbour, and we are adamant that we want to find a way to ensure a discussion takes place.'[119] Once again, the combined experience of the millions of people that live in between the two 'neighbours' is entirely disregarded – precisely as the Kremlin would prefer.

117. David Herszenhorn, 'Summit exposes stark clash of EU views on Russia', *Politico*, 25 June 2021, https://www.politico.eu/article/emmanuel-macron-russia-vladimir-putin-european-union/amp/.

118. https://www.nato.int/cps/en/natolive/news_68172.htm.

119. Interview with *France Inter*, 24 January 2021, available at https://twitter.com/franceinter/status/1353304333824229389

Above and beyond 'resets', other Western politicians and policymakers have repeatedly advocated 'dialogue' with Russia regardless of its behaviour; but all too often, without specifying the critically important detail of what is actually to be said during that dialogue in order to discourage, rather than encourage, further Russian hostile activity directed at the West. Here too the repeated offer of a restoration of business as usual with no preconditions served only to confirm for Russia that its actions do not incur long-term consequences, and so could only have helped convince Moscow that despite routine statements of 'concern', in reality Europe would find further aggressive and destabilizing actions by Russia to be acceptable. Once again, it is Ukraine that has felt the tragic consequences.

In April 2000, not long after becoming president, Vladimir Putin visited London. For many in the West at the time the main concern with regard to Russia was renewed fighting in Chechnya, accompanied by fresh and widespread reports of atrocities and human rights abuses. British prime minister Tony Blair felt the best way to deal with these issues was to engage Putin in 'proper dialogue', and later told the public that Putin wanted a strong relationship with the West and 'talks our language of reform'.[120] The subsequent 20 years have seen a pattern of Russia consistently demonstrating that it believes in a form of power from a different place and a different time, that European leaders who believe all conflict can be resolved by dialogue are simply not equipped to deal with.

Both before and after the assault on Ukraine, among European states the UK has been among the most vocally critical of Moscow, and more willing than most to point to Russia as a destructive and destabilizing power. Nevertheless, while direct attacks on British or allied interests or citizens by Russia have occasionally been responded to robustly, the British foreign policy establishment's default state has consistently been to seek cooperation with Moscow despite the very obvious absence of shared values or interests between the two countries. It was not until the attempted murders of Sergei and Yulia Skripal in March 2018 that recognition of Russian hostility became widespread enough to outweigh the notion that relations could be improved through the British side playing nice on its own. But even after 2018, Russian financial and political influence in London remained a serious challenge to dealing with Moscow, as we will see in Chapter 6. Throughout 2021, British policy towards Russia still combined strong words with persistent attempts to offer Russia routes to improving the bilateral relationship, including – still – through talking.

Tellingly, the arguments for dialogue as a means for improving the relationship would fail to stand up when examined with even the slightest knowledge of prior history. German politician Armin Laschet was a repeat offender in this regard during his campaign for the chancellorship, where he was eventually defeated by Olaf Scholz. He claimed that 'Even in the coldest of cold wars there was always . . .

---

120. Nick Hopkins, 'Blair defends "reformer" Putin's visit to No 10', *Guardian*, 17 April 2000, https://www.theguardian.com/world/2000/apr/17/russia.nickhopkins.

a dialogue between civil societies.' Given that the Soviet Union had no civil society in any recognized sense of the term, the comment showed either delusion or a wilful disregard of history.[121] Another of Laschet's key messages was that with Russia 'you have to talk more, not less'.[122] Mistaking more communication for better communication is another fallacy that refuses to die, no matter how often it is disproved.

Advice based on past experience, that approaches to Moscow should be planned with caution and with an end state in mind rather than talking for the sake of it, are repeatedly dismissed by western European politicians on equally spurious grounds. Advocates of renewed wooing of Moscow like French President Emmanuel Macron insist on the notion that '"we" are "pushing Russia away from Europe"', perhaps in the hope that if they repeat it often enough, listeners will overlook the fact that it is completely detached from reality.[123] And politicians who want closer relations with the Russian government – like, again, Armin Laschet – regularly say that those who disagree with them are suggesting Russia should be 'isolated', with all diplomatic relations and channels of communication cut. They know perfectly well that only a tiny fringe of hard-liners hold that view. But this provides a lazy, predictable way of dismissing the conversation instead of actually discussing what should be done.[124]

Even when Russia was interested in talking, it found the habit of countries like France and Germany and organizations like the EU and NATO of presenting dialogue as an end in itself, without necessarily leading to any specific result, deeply frustrating. A decade before Borrell's 2021 visit, NATO and Russia were at a stalemate over plans for missile defence systems in Europe (which Russia opposed, because of the suspicion these were defences against Russian missiles). A meeting of the NATO–Russia Council in Sochi did nothing to resolve the deadlock – but after it, then NATO Secretary-General Anders Fogh Rasmussen 'restated our commitment to pursue [the non-existent] missile defence cooperation ... We are determined to keep up the dialogue and to keep up the work.'[125] The Russian participants who did wish to make progress on specific aspects of cooperation were unimpressed. As British Russia-watcher James Sherr pointed out at the time,

121. Philip Oltermann, 'CDU leader Armin Laschet: "Even in the coldest of cold wars there was dialogue"', *Guardian*, 9 July 2021, https://www.theguardian.com/world/2021/jul/09/cdu-leader-armin-laschet-even-in-the-coldest-of-cold-wars-there-was-dialogue.

122. 'Armin Laschet: With Russia "you have to talk more, not less"', *DW*, 14 June 2021, https://www.dw.com/en/armin-laschet-with-russia-you-have-to-talk-more-not-less/a-57886500.

123. James Nixey and Mathieu Boulègue, 'On Russia, Macron Is Mistaken', Chatham House, 5 September 2019, https://www.chathamhouse.org/2019/09/russia-macron-mistaken.

124. 'Armin Laschet: With Russia "you have to talk more, not less"'.

125. 'NATO–Russia Council makes progress in Sochi', NATO website, 04 July 2011, http://www.nato.int/cps/en/natolive/news_76039.htm

'from Moscow's point of view, negotiations and joint efforts are not exercises in group therapy, but means of advancing national interests'.[126]

The combined result of this dogged drive by the West to restore relations when Moscow has destroyed them is that through the history of the twentieth and twenty-first centuries, Russia has again and again been forgiven for aggression against other countries and its own population. You can hardly blame the Kremlin for concluding that the trend is so consistent it must surely continue, and so Russia is also likely to be swiftly forgiven for any current and future attacks on its neighbours and countries further afield, up to and including full-scale military invasion.

## Read the small print

At the same time, there is a persistent Russian call for 'legally binding' international treaties and agreements that would govern all kinds of different areas of international relations. In December 2021, this was the form in which Russia's demands for 'security guarantees' that formed a precursor to its 2022 attack on Ukraine were presented to the US and NATO. The most striking aspect of the treaties was how entirely unrealistic – and in fact impossible to implement – most of their conditions were.[127]

Reiner Schwalb explains Russia's obsession with signing new treaties at the same time as trying to evade the commitments they have already signed up to through both a belief that a 'global power' stands above international law, and a different understanding of how countries are bound by it. 'When they are looking at international agreements and treaties, they focus on the words of the agreement where we might focus on the ideas or intent behind it,' he explains. Kimberley Marten agrees and has explained in detail how 'Russia has a pattern of not recognizing the "spirit" of an agreement, only its letter. U.S. negotiators . . . have consistently counseled spending the time to make sure that the specifics of what has been agreed are spelled out in great detail, to avoid surprises later.'[128]

Nevertheless, this mismatch of understanding and intent continues to catch Russia's counterparts out. James Sherr observes that 'The Russians are the

126. James Sherr, 'NATO and Russia: doomed to disappointment?', in *NATO Review 2011/5: 'NATO-Russia relations: 20 years after the USSR'*, http://www.nato.int/docu/review/2011/NATO_Russia/EN/index.htm.

127. Alexander Lanoszka, 'How NATO should greet Russia's "draft treaty"', Council on Geostrategy, 20 December 2021, https://www.geostrategy.org.uk/britains-world/how-nato-should-greet-russias-draft-treaty/.

128. Kimberly Marten, 'President Trump, keep in mind that Russia and the West think about negotiations very, very differently', *Washington Post*, 25 July 2017, https://www.washingtonpost.com/news/monkey-cage/wp/2017/07/25/president-trump-keep-in-mind-that-russia-and-the-west-think-about-negotiations-very-very-differently/.

neighbours from hell. If you finally conclude a written agreement that they will stop parking their car on your lawn, don't be surprised if they park their truck there instead.' This leads to a continuing drive by Russia to sign new agreements that constrain its adversaries while leaving Moscow itself a free hand. Reiner Schwalb says Russia 'needs international treaties because of their own weakness. They can only cope with Europe and specifically NATO if NATO countries adhere to those treaties. When the Russians seem to be really interested in treaties, it's because they fear the strength of the West, in every respect. You won't hear that officially from Putin, but the Russian specialists acknowledge it.' The emphasis on written agreements with foreign countries to protect Moscow's interests persists despite past experience of this approach going badly wrong, as during the Second World War, when the Soviet Union's arrangement with Nazi Germany to carve up Europe between them soured when Adolf Hitler turned out to be not as reliable a partner in crime as Joseph Stalin had supposed.

Similar principles apply when Russia takes part in international fora like the UN. Kyle Wilson explains that Russia's aim in being a member of international organizations is not better cooperation. 'For Russia, in the UN, like in any multilateral organisation, *control* is the crucial word,' he says. 'Obviously, the UN Security Council is in a category all by itself. But in other ones, particularly in a region like ours, the Indo-Pacific, where you have organizations like ASEAN, the Asia Pacific security forum, and so on, Russian behaviour is consistent. And that is to infiltrate, to influence, to seek to manipulate, and to use those organisations in any way they can to erode the standing of the enemies, especially the United States.' To do so, Russia exploits its seat at international tables wherever it can. After the seizure of Crimea, Russia found that its new territory was unsustainable because it was not self-sufficient in water. So, Russia tried to engage the UN Human Rights Committee in forcing Ukraine to supply water to the region that it was now claiming was in fact part of Russia.[129] And in February 2022, the world watched the ludicrous spectacle of a UN Security Council resolution condemning Russia's invasion of Ukraine being administered – and vetoed – by Russia.[130]

Moscow's approach to international cooperation is pursued across the board. Russia's abuse of Interpol for pursuing and persecuting its political opponents devalues the system for all its members.[131] The OSCE monitoring mission in eastern Ukraine, which in theory was to receive cooperation from all sides, was

---

129. Halya Coynash, 'Russian occupiers of Crimea want the UN to force Ukraine to give them water', Kharkiv Human Rights Protection Group, 31 August 2020, https://khpg.org/en/1598799338.

130. Michelle Nichols and Humeyra Pamuk, 'Russia vetoes U.N. Security action on Ukraine as China abstains', Reuters, 26 February 2022, https://www.reuters.com/world/russia-vetoes-un-security-action-ukraine-china-abstains-2022-02-25/.

131. Kathy Gilsinan, 'How Russia Tries to Catch Its "Criminals" by Abusing Interpol', *The Atlantic*, 30 May 2018, https://www.theatlantic.com/international/archive/2018/05/russia-interpol-abuse/561539/.

routinely obstructed, with its drones consistently targeted by electronic attacks as well as occasional threats that they would be shot down if launched.[132] Lengthy correspondence by the Russian delegation to the Organization for the Prohibition of Chemical Weapons (OPCW) about the poisoning of Alexei Navalny in October 2020 gave insights into how Russian diplomacy operates, including both trying to rope the OPCW into a scheme to both make it look as though Navalny was poisoned only after he left Russia, and trying to get access to the ongoing investigations. The exchange of letters shows how the OPCW, to its credit, consistently and politely declined as the Russian demands became more strident and irate.[133]

There is one particular circumstance where the different approach to international agreements between Russia and Western countries leads to repeated disaster for the victims of Russian military action. When crises deteriorate to the point of armed conflict, Western powers repeatedly step in to broker ceasefires. But the contrast between Russia's literal approach to interpreting the text of the ceasefire agreements and the West's focus on their spirit and intent has repeatedly led to Russia getting everything it wants from the clash – aided by the Western powers whose main priority is ending the fighting, rather than making sure it comes to a fair or even satisfactory conclusion. In the current century, three separate examples (so far) follow this pattern: Georgia, Ukraine and Syria. On each occasion, ceasefires have been concluded on terms drafted in Moscow, leaving Russia free to interpret them in ways that startle those in the West who hadn't read them properly. It can't be said that there are no precedents to learn from. In precisely the same way, after the Second World War the Western allies protested vigorously at the way Soviet power was extended into Central Europe and the Balkans, saying that this was in violation of the Yalta and Potsdam agreements of 1945 – not to mention the earlier Moscow Declaration which stated that 'After the termination of hostilities [the Allies] will not employ their military forces within the territories of other states except for the purposes envisaged in this declaration and after joint consultation.'[134] But again, although Soviet actions may have been in breach of the Anglo-American interpretation of these ambiguous and imprecise arrangements, their interpretation in Moscow was what counted.

The brief armed conflict between Russia and Georgia in 2008 ended with Russia in control of two regions in the north of the country, Abkhazia and South Osetia, together making up about one-fifth of the territory of Georgia. Then French

---

132. 'Daily Report 99/2021', OSCE Special Monitoring Mission to Ukraine, 30 April 2021, https://www.osce.org/files/2021-04-30%20Daily%20Report.pdf.

133. Correspondence from October 2020 uploaded on Russian Foreign Ministry website, https://www.mid.ru/documents/10180/4510654/%D0%9F%D0%B5%D1%80%D0%B5%D0%BF%D0%B8%D1%81%D0%BA%D0%B0.pdf/.

134. 'The Moscow Declaration by the U.S., U.K., U.S.S.R., China', Moscow, U.S.S.R., 30 October 1943, http://insidethecoldwar.org/sites/default/files/documents/Moscow%20Declaration_1.pdf.

president Nicolas Sarkozy had delivered terms for a ceasefire to Georgia – with the fatal flaw that they had been drawn up in Moscow and not mediated in any way. The effect was that while Sarkozy, and through him the EU, thought that the ceasefire meant Russian troops would return to Russia, there were loopholes in the text of the agreement so big that Russia could drive tanks through them, which it proceeded to do.[135] Russia then declared the occupied territories of Abkhazia and South Osetia to be independent states, and bribed various small and poor countries to recognize this status. The Pacific island state of Nauru maintains this recognition to this day, in return for ongoing Russian support.[136] Over a decade later, states like the UK and Canada were calling on Russia to 'fulfil its obligations' under the August 2008 ceasefire agreement, apparently oblivious to the fact that Russia had done precisely what that agreement – written in Moscow – said it could.[137]

In Ukraine, French President François Hollande and German Chancellor Angela Merkel forced a Russian ceasefire on the victims of Russian aggression in the form of successive 'Minsk peace agreements'. The texts of the agreements conspired in the fiction that the war in Ukraine was an internal matter to which Russia was not a party, demanded that Ukraine surrender key aspects of its national sovereignty and ignored Russia's occupation and annexation of Crimea. And yet, these terms were insisted on by western European leaders as the only possible resolution to the conflict.[138]

Vladislav Surkov was one of the chief designers of Putin's current system of government, and was credited with key roles in the annexation of Crimea and the long war in eastern Ukraine. That's not something he denies: 'I am proud that I was part of the reconquest. This was the first open geopolitical counter-attack by Russia [against the West] and such a decisive one. That was an honour for me.' But he also makes plain how the intent of the Minsk agreements was to break up Ukraine. In June 2021, Surkov echoed the key Russian message to the rest of the world that Ukraine is not actually a real country: 'Ukrainians are very well aware that for the time being, their country does not really exist. I have said that it could exist in the future. The national core exists. I am just asking the question as to what the borders, the frontier should be. And that should be the subject for an international

135. As predicted in 'The Nature of the Georgian Ceasefire', Advanced Research and Assessment Group, Defence Academy of the United Kingdom, 13 August 2008.

136. Bruce Hill, 'What's the deal with Nauru backing the disputed territories of South Ossetia and Abkhazia?' ABC News, 12 May 2018, https://www.abc.net.au/news/2018-05-13/why-is-nauru-backing-south-ossetia-and-abkhazia/9751660.

137. 'Geneva International Discussions on the conflict in Georgia: UK–Canada statement', UK Foreign, Commonwealth & Development Office, 9 July 2021, https://www.gov.uk/government/speeches/geneva-international-discussions-on-the-conflict-in-georgia-uk-canada-statement.

138. Volodymyr Vasylenko, 'The West must not force a Russian "peace" on Ukraine', Atlantic Council, 15 August 2021, https://www.atlanticcouncil.org/blogs/ukrainealert/the-west-must-not-force-a-russian-peace-on-ukraine/.

discussion.'[139] But when talking about revising borders, it seems probable that Moscow would only wish them to be revised in one direction. Russia has no shortage of neighbours whose territory could rightfully be restored after an international discussion of frontiers, following the Soviet annexations of East Prussia from Germany (now the Kaliningrad region), Karelia and Petsamo from Finland, South Sakhalin and the Kuril Islands from Japan, and more. Russia would probably also not wish to encourage discussion of borders too much in order not to encourage China to revive its interest in its former territories now in the Russian Far East. And Russia's founding myth, that the rulers of Muscovy were somehow the inheritors of Kievan Rus', if true would surely imply not that Moscow has claims on Ukraine, but that Russia belongs to Kyiv.

But for years, the existence of a ceasefire (in theory if not in practice) in Ukraine allowed France and Germany to pretend the problem had gone away – and to continue suggesting that if it hadn't, the best way of ending the war in Ukraine would be for Ukraine to give in, rather than for Russia to cease its attacks.[140] In reality the fact that neither of them had the will or the capacity to actually enforce the ceasefire meant that their insistence on Minsk as a resolution to the war meant Russia had no incentive at all to stop waging it.[141]

In both of these cases the driving objective of the Western dignitaries involved has been to stop the fighting. Russia's, by contrast, is to get maximum advantage from it. This means that Russia has ample scope to manipulate the Western fear of escalation, turning up or dialling down the military pressure as the state of negotiations demands – a tactic employed repeatedly during Russia's all-out assault on Ukraine.[142] Throughout this process, Russian information campaigns exploit Western vulnerabilities, assumptions and psychological triggers – especially aversion to conflict, and prioritizing ending the fighting, short attention spans and failure to realize longer patterns, and policy being dictated by media coverage. American Russia-watcher Leon Aron says the Western media idea that not only are there two sides to every story, but that both may be equally valid, leads to a presumption that 'both sides are equally culpable', resulting in not wishing for victory by either side, just 'peace at all costs, including defeat'.[143]

139. Henry Foy, 'Vladislav Surkov: "An overdose of freedom is lethal to a state"', *Financial Times*, 18 June 2021, https://www.ft.com/content/1324acbb-f475-47ab-a914-4a96a9d14bac.

140. Atlantic Council, 'Flawed peace plan for Ukraine doesn't pass muster', 14 February 2020, https://www.atlanticcouncil.org/blogs/ukrainealert/flawed-peace-plan-for-ukraine-doesnt-pass-muster/.

141. Mark Galeotti, 'The Minsk Accords: Should Britain declare them dead?', Council on Geostrategy, 24 May 2021, https://www.geostrategy.org.uk/britains-world/the-minsk-accords-should-britain-declare-them-dead/.

142. Amy J. Nelson and Alexander H. Montgomery, 'Mind the escalation aversion: Managing risk without losing the initiative in the Russia–Ukraine war', Brookings, 11 March 2022, https://www.brookings.edu/blog/order-from-chaos/2022/03/11/mind-the-escalation-aversion-managing-risk-without-losing-the-initiative-in-the-russia-ukraine-war/.

143. Speaking at the Lennart Meri Conference, Tallinn, 24 April 2015.

Former US Army officer Sulev Suvari saw at first hand the effect of these two very different approaches to ending a war. Attached to the US team negotiating a ceasefire for Syria in Geneva in 2016, he observed how even the negotiators sent by each side showed their different priorities. 'On our side was we had some really smart, capable people and individuals from the State Department, with the State Department very much in the lead, as they should be in our system,' he says – by contrast with the Russian side, which was made up primarily of military officers. This was borne out in the content of the negotiations: 'with the military leading all the conversations on the Russian side, you had a sort of breakdown between mindsets and views and goals. The State Department were focused on water and humanitarian rights, and access to medical care. And then the Russian side wanted to talk more about hard security issues and overflights and things of this nature.' It didn't help that because the US team thought the negotiations were about Syria, they sent experts on dealing with Syria not with Russia, Sulev says. 'Our side knew Syria very well. They'd all lived in the area. Almost all of them had also been to Syria at some point, or they'd been to Lebanon or worked in Turkey along the border. So they really understood the space. But nobody had really had any interactions with the Russians and the Russian military, which is a completely different ball of wax. And so that did throw them off sometimes.'

This meant in particular that the US side was under-prepared for Russian negotiating tactics – including the willingness to deny that statements had been made or agreements reached when they were already on the record. 'The Russians would say something, and then two days later say no, that's not what we said. Or, yes, we did say that but it means something different now and we're redefining it. It was Humpty Dumpty in Alice in Wonderland – if you're in charge of the words then you get to make up what the words mean. I saw that threw them off too,' Sulev says of his State Department colleagues. But in addition, Sulev realized that for Russia, the negotiations were not primarily about Syria itself, still less the best interests of its people. 'What I saw them do constantly was confuse and shift on what it really was that they were asking for,' he says. 'Even as I walked away at the end I thought, I don't know what their goal was there. It wasn't clear.'

The final result of the negotiations, though, was clear enough. A ceasefire agreement overseen by former US Secretary of State John Kerry met limited short-term US goals of easing the fighting and allowing delivery of humanitarian aid, and much broader and longer-term Russian aims of cementing its influence in the Middle East and forcing the US to back down on its previous commitment to remove President Bashar al-Assad from power.[144] In effect, because of the very different aims of each side going into the negotiations, both sides got what they wanted – but Russia wanted far more than the US to start with. And once again

---

144. Keir Giles, 'What Russia Learns From the Syria Ceasefire: Military Action Works', Chatham House, 3 March 2016, https://www.chathamhouse.org/2016/03/what-russia-learns-syria-ceasefire-military-action-works.

western European countries – invariably including France – have bought into the fiction that the Russian ceasefire is a positive result for the victim country.[145]

This repeated pattern only confirmed for Russia that armed force is a highly effective means of achieving swift and positive foreign policy results, with limited downside because those results are then broadly accepted by the rest of the world. These ceasefires, rather than punishing the aggressor or even being equitable and ensuring the conflict is resolved, set Moscow's terms and rewarded Russia for military action – and so can only have encouraged Putin in his decision to escalate his war on Ukraine in 2022. Russia repeatedly successfully leveraged the differential between its own and Western attitudes to conflict to cement in place its gains from armed interventions, while the West was just relieved that the active phase of the fighting has stopped. In short, ceasefire agreements of this kind provide Russia with success, and the West with an excuse for looking away. At the time of writing, the fervent hope is that the West will not pressure Ukraine into a similar surrender, to provide an excuse for looking away once again.[146]

But although Russia's military operations are the most dramatic means it can use to intervene beyond its borders, they represent only a small part of the huge range of tools and levers Russia employs to get its way. People living beyond Ukraine are fortunate that they do not – yet – have to face an overt invasion. But for them, it is the hostile actions Moscow can take without overtly going to war that for now are the greater challenge. And those are the subject of the next chapter.

145. Patrick Wintour and Julian Borger, 'Syria Faces Perpetual War unless Russia Extends Ceasefire, France Warns', *Guardian*, 24 September 2018, https://www.theguardian.com/world/2018/sep/24/syria-war-unga-france-warning-russia-extend-ceasefire.

146. James Nixey, 'A negotiated peace with Russia is fraught with danger', Chatham House, 17 March 2022, https://www.chathamhouse.org/2022/03/negotiated-peace-russia-fraught-danger.

# Chapter 3

## NEITHER WAR NOR PEACE

In the previous two chapters I've tried to lay out how Russia behaves as though it is already in a conflict with the West as a whole. But what does 'conflict' look like if Russia isn't actually overtly at war with anybody at present beyond the borders of Ukraine?

The answer lies in Russia adopting every kind of hostility it can that stops short of the West accepting that it is under attack, because then – and only then – its response would be likely to cause Russia serious damage. This approach goes by a number of names, one of which is 'sub-threshold' – in other words, Russia's actions stop short of the point at which its victims can no longer deny that they are at war. Another term is 'grey zone', as in already not at peace, but still not at war. But whatever you call it, that space in between leaves open a huge range of different ways Russia can get what it wants and harm other countries, and their people, in doing so.

And that range also covers different levels of ambition for what Russia wants to achieve. The examples we'll see in this chapter range from low-level attacks and hostile measures for no other reason than to cause damage to Western countries – in effect, petty vandalism – up to the most dangerous Russian goal of all: to change the political direction of a whole country in order to get it to do what Moscow wants without having to fight for it.

### *Direct influence – Trump and Brexit*

The presidency of Donald Trump showed a spectacular example of what Moscow can achieve by having people in positions of influence and power who will make decisions that favour Russia over their own country. Whether or not Russia's attack on the US democratic process in 2016 outweighed domestic factors in leading to Trump's election, the return on investment for Moscow in cultivating Trump over the long term and then assisting his arrival in power was breathtaking.

From before his inauguration to the dying days of his presidency, Trump's actions facilitated many of Russia's long-term goals for the United States, some of which had previously been considered unrealistic. The roll-call of measures implemented or attempted by Trump that assisted Russian objectives ranged from the high-level strategic to the very local and tactical. Strategically, Trump worked hard to reduce the US role in providing security in Europe. Defensive measures against Russia were blocked under various pretexts – linking defensive aid to Ukraine to undermining Joe Biden, or diverting defensive spending earmarked for eastern Europe to Trump's wall project.[1] A strategically and logistically nonsensical order by Trump to reduce the US military presence in Germany was quietly dropped as soon as he was out of office.[2] Local assistance to Russia included ordering the US to abandon allies and territory in north-east Syria to Russian forces.[3] Internally, Trump efforts reduced the effectiveness of the US intelligence community against Moscow by passing classified information to adversaries, leading to the suppression of intelligence reporting on Russia.[4]

In these cases and more, it was primarily the resilience of the US system of government (or, as Trump supporters would describe it, resistance from the 'deep state') that prevented greater damage from being done. The real limitations on what might benefit Moscow were set by those democratic checks and balances that survived Trump's administration, and by officials at all levels of government who continued to work on behalf of US national interests even when this was hard to reconcile with instructions coming from the White House. This process was clearly visible from the outside while it was happening – the dedication for my last book, completed in mid-2018, was 'to all those career US government officials who are working hard to build and deliver a sensible policy on Russia while hoping that President Trump doesn't notice'.

But where Trump achieved undoubted success was in joining Moscow in challenging and undermining Western liberal values, weakening US society and social cohesion, eroding US world leadership and global respect, hurrying on the arrival of a post-truth, post-fact information space and discrediting independent media, and – importantly – treating Russia as a respected partner and equal, satisfying Moscow's perpetual status anxiety. Russia's aspiration to see the US weakened and humbled benefited indirectly from other Trump decisions too, like the February 2020 agreement with the Taliban for US forces to pull out of

1. David Rogers, 'How Trump stiff-armed Congress – and gaslighted the courts – to build his wall', *Politico*, 6 August 2021, https://www.politico.com/news/2021/08/06/trump-congress-wall-pentagon-502652.

2. Isla MacRae, 'Trump and DoD clash over US troop withdrawal from Germany', *ArmyTechnology*, 31 July 2020, https://www.army-technology.com/features/trump-and-dod-clash-over-us-troop-withdrawal-from-germany/.

3. Ben Hubbard, Anton Troianovski, Carlotta Gall and Patrick Kingsley, 'In Syria, Russia Is Pleased to Fill an American Void', *New York Times*, 15 October 2019, https://www.nytimes.com/2019/10/15/world/middleeast/kurds-syria-turkey.html.

4. Natasha Bertrand and Daniel Lippman, 'CIA clamps down on flow of Russia intelligence to White House', *Politico*, 23 September 2020, https://www.politico.com/news/2020/09/23/cia-russia-intelligence-white-house-420351.

Afghanistan with no evident conditions – which laid the groundwork for the chaotic and humiliating scramble to evacuate Kabul eighteen months later, a source of great satisfaction for Moscow.[5] Trump's words and actions would routinely be given a rapturous reception by Russia's propaganda broadcasts – in particular at any of his face-to-face meetings with Putin. Following the G20 summit in July 2019, presenters boasted that 'Putin completely captured Trump. We can now say with complete certainty that Trump is ours. He wants everything in the US to be just like Russia … he says he wants to have everything just like Putin has.'[6]

It's not possible to say – yet – whether Trump was doing this consciously on behalf of the Kremlin, motivated by blackmail or financial dependency, or unconsciously, and it was pure coincidence that his words and actions so consistently promoted Russian policy. People who are not convinced of where Trump's sympathies lie argue that not everything he did was to the benefit of Russia. But the examples they give tend not to stand up to close examination. One classic exception to normal Trump practice that proves the rule is the US joining in with expelling Russian diplomats in solidarity with the UK after the attempted murders of Sergei and Yulia Skripal. Thinking he was agreeing to a limited demonstrative measure, Trump was reportedly enraged when he discovered that the extent of the measures he had approved meant he could be called 'tough on Russia'.[7]

The effect of Russia's back channels of communication to Trump shone through in his repeatedly voicing specific Russian propaganda lines – as in July 2018, when he accused NATO's newest member country Montenegro of being 'very aggressive', despite doubt that he even knew where Montenegro was.[8] But that's not the same as Trump being fully aware that he was being manipulated – a distinction we'll look at in more detail in Chapter 6 when we look at the differences between agents of influence and 'useful idiots'. The investigation into Trump's election campaign by Special Counsel Robert Mueller might have offered an opportunity to find out, but it was fatally hamstrung by being restricted to investigating specific breaches of

---

5. Mary Ilyushina, 'Russia has been engaging with the Taliban for years. The U.S. withdrawal might give it an opportunity to expand its role', CBS News, 21 August 2021, https://www.cbsnews.com/news/russia-taliban-afghanistan-american-withdrawal-opportunity/.

6. '"Все хочу как у Путина!": громкое заявление Трампа из последнего интервью' ('I want everything to be like Putin has' – big Trump statement in his latest interview), *60 minutes*, 2 July 2019, https://www.youtube.com/watch?v=A2HJLJHz36w.

7. Pat Ralph, 'Trump was reportedly furious that his administration was portrayed as tough on Russia after expelling diplomats from the US', *Business Insider*, 16 April 2018, https://www.businessinsider.com/trump-wanted-to-expel-fewer-russian-diplomats-2018-4.

8. Alexander Smith, 'Trump calls out "very aggressive" Montenegro in latest NATO jibe', NBC, 18 July 2018, https://www.nbcnews.com/news/world/trump-calls-out-very-aggressive-montenegro-latest-nato-jibe-n892311.

criminal law rather than including susceptibility to pressure by a foreign intelligence agency.[9] That meant it didn't consider Trump's financial dealings, the means by which his finances were propped up by Russian oligarchs, or other indicators of compromise.[10] And in particular, Mueller's decision not to look at Donald Trump's multiple Russian connections meant that the basis for his complicated relationship with Moscow, laid down long before 2016, was never examined.[11]

Some attempts at malign influence by Moscow succeed, some fail, and in other cases the effect of Russian interference is unknown, sometimes because – as in the case of the 2016 Brexit referendum in the UK – there has been no political will to look too closely at whether it was effective.[12]

It's normally assumed that Russia attempted to influence the Brexit vote towards leaving the EU. In fact, Russia seems to have been agitating both ways, and following its normal procedure of creating conflict in societies by setting both sides against each other. Brexit held both pros and cons for Russia. Although it weakened resistance to Russia overall by removing a prominent critic of Moscow from the EU, it also meant the UK would be in a position to pursue a firmer line in relations with Russia independently because it no longer needed to coordinate policy with Brussels.[13] In particular, the UK's desire for stronger sanctions is no longer frustrated by the need for alignment with Europe – an important enabler when in February 2022, the UK was able to sanction prominent Russian oligarchs previously considered a hard target because they had acquired citizenship in Finland, an EU member.[14]

But either way, Brexit is one of those situations where even if suspicions are completely unfounded, the British government's refusal to address them makes them grow deeper. That in itself is dangerous, because confidence in democracy

9. 'Anne Applebaum Interviews Peter Strzok', *The Atlantic*, 4 September 2020, https://www.theatlantic.com/ideas/archive/2020/09/anne-applebaum-interviews-peter-strzok/616003/.

10. Michael Crowley, 'Trump and the Oligarch: He claims no ties to Russia. Here's how he made millions from one of its wealthiest men', *Politico*, 28 July 2016, https://www.politico.com/magazine/story/2016/07/donald-trump-2016-russian-ties-214116/.

11. Scott Anderson, 'Oldest Living CIA Agent Says Russia Probably Targeted Trump Decades Ago', *Daily Beast*, 5 October 2020, https://www.thedailybeast.com/oldest-living-cia-agent-says-russia-probably-targeted-trump-decades-ago.

12. David Walsh, 'Russia report: UK "actively avoided" probing possible Moscow meddling in Brexit vote', Euronews, 22 July 2020, https://www.euronews.com/2020/07/21/russia-report-findings-of-long-awaited-probe-into-russian-inference-in-uk-politics-release.

13. 'Jeremy Hunt wants "malign" Russia to face tougher sanctions', BBC News, 21 August 2018, https://www.bbc.com/news/uk-politics45250069.

14. Arja Paananen, 23 February 2022, https://twitter.com/KeirGiles/status/1496369100 309897219.

depends on confidence that it has not been compromised. Samantha de Bendern is a former banker and now a specialist in financial crime and corruption. She's angry because of the way Russian money has distorted British politics, a topic we'll come back to in Chapter 6. She is convinced that this includes the Brexit referendum – that the unclear sources of funding for the Leave campaign and relationships with the Russian Embassy indicated a Russian attempt to influence the outcome. But in addition, she says that the British government's outright refusal to investigate whether Russia did in fact intervene in Brexit is symptomatic of a deeper problem, and a broader pattern of malign Russian influence that goes hand in hand with London's reputation as the favoured destination for Russian state and criminal money. 'I'm angry because the British establishment is not reacting in a way that makes any sense to this possible attack against our sovereignty,' she explains. 'In fact, the lack of response from the British government to the allegations of Russian interference is just flabbergasting. And you look at the financial interests of some of the members of the current British government, then that lack of response raises a lot of very worrying questions.'

In the UK in particular, any desire to curb the extent of harmful Russian influence is hamstrung by the lack of any form of legislation to protect British interests against it. Acting as a hostile foreign agent in the UK is, quite simply, perfectly legal, as there is no equivalent to the US Foreign Agent Registration Act, or Australia's nascent Foreign Influence Transparency Scheme.[15] In fact, efforts at malign influence in the UK are effectively presented with an open goal. The report on Russia published by the UK Parliament's Intelligence and Security Committee in July 2020 found to its surprise that there was no designated arm of government, organization or agency actually in charge of countering this kind of activity from Russia.[16] And at the time of writing, despite new efforts to punish Russia and Russians following the attack on Ukraine, a lack of action or interest by the British government has left that goal open at home.

## Subversion and influence

But behind the high-profile, top-level examples like Trump and Brexit lie campaigns of influencing and corrupting politics abroad that run on an ongoing basis rather than being tied to specific events or individuals. Russia uses a wide variety of means to influence political processes and decision-making in adversary countries to its benefit. While well recognized during Soviet times, most of these were relatively neglected in the West while Russia was relatively weak in the two decades

---

15. 'Foreign Influence Transparency Scheme', Australian Government Attorney-General's Department, https://www.ag.gov.au/integrity/foreign-influence-transparency-scheme.

16. 'Russia', Intelligence and Security Committee of Parliament (London: House of Commons, 2020).

after the end of the USSR. Since then, Moscow's methods that use new technology have been closely studied, including in particular interference in democratic processes and attempts to sway mass consciousness through campaigns on social media. But other means of malign influence are not nearly as widely discussed, or their potential for harm understood.[17]

The open, democratic and free nature of Western liberal societies is often claimed to be a strength when facing up the hostile intentions of authoritarian states. But it's also a vulnerability – in fact, a broad and mutually reinforcing range of vulnerabilities and weaknesses that can be exploited by a ruthless adversary. The dedication by Western societies to freedom of expression, freedom of opinion, freedom of assembly and more opens up the playing field for countries like Russia to poison public opinion and political processes. Russia prods public opinion and political processes in one direction or another through genuine or fake media outlets, overt or concealed funding of political parties, purchasing influence through corruption, establishing or exploiting NGOs and think tanks – and in each of these it is aided by local accomplices (see Chapter 6). The process overall is often given the catch-all name of 'malign influence' – and it works best not through high-profile endeavours like the RT and Sputnik propaganda channels, but by targeting individual people. Not all of them will arrive in a position of enormous power like Trump, but Russia has customarily shown itself willing to spread its bets – meaning that far more people will be of interest to Russia than may necessarily realize it.

John Mooney is an Irish author and journalist who focuses on defence, security and organized crime. He says the role of Russia's intelligence services in delivering malign influence is key. 'All countries collect intelligence. What's slightly different about Russia is it seeks to use that intelligence to subvert the countries that it is collecting intelligence on. So here in Ireland at the moment, we have an ongoing situation whereby Russian services are continually targeting people in politics, in business, in the media, in cultural institutions and in scientific research,' John says. But he consistently finds that one of the biggest handicaps in dealing with this challenge is that so few people are aware of it. 'In Europe, I don't think the general public and even politicians fully understand why Russia would have an interest in their respective countries,' he explains. 'I don't think they have much insight into why Russia would seek to undermine the West, that they have that kind of unique political thinking where by destabilizing Europe they think it makes them stronger. I don't think the general public get that at all.'

Russia can reach out to influence individuals of interest directly in the way John describes, or indirectly through what it refers to as 'information warfare' – using any means possible to change what people think in order that they will change what they do. Russia's principles of information warfare offer an enormously long

17. Andrew Radin et al., 'Understanding Russian Subversion: Patterns, Threats and Responses', RAND, 2020, https://www.rand.org/pubs/perspectives/PE331.html.

list of people that should be targeted with this aim, starting with the political leadership, military personnel and their families, the civilian population and certain specific target groups, such as ethnic and religious minorities, opposition groups and businesspeople – in friendly, neutral and hostile foreign countries alike. As the Estonian Foreign Intelligence Service's annual report points out, in effect 'this means that the entire world population outside Russia is a potential target'.[18] The aim, according to Russian information warfare theory, is influence on the mass consciousness of the population – directing people so that the population of the victim country is induced to support the aggressor, acting against its own interests.[19] More precisely targeted campaigns revolve around *informatsionno-psikhologicheskoye vozdeystyviye*, 'information and psychological influence', which the Russian General Staff glossary of information warfare terminology says is the 'complex of measures to influence the intellectual, rational-will and emotional-sentiment domains of the psyche and subconscious of informational-psychological targets, designed for the formation within those targets of predicted opinions and views, specific conditions of world view and psychological state, and behavioural responses' – in short, how Russia fools people into thinking and doing things they otherwise would not.[20]

By comparison with other ways Moscow wages undeclared war, in information warfare it's relatively straightforward to tie campaigns to specific Russian strategies or doctrines. In part, that's because Russia has been very good at writing them down. In 2014, an authoritative Russian military journal listed a set of principles for media campaigns. It's worth quoting the list in full because they are so immediately recognizable from the output both of Russia's domestic propaganda channels and of its propagandists abroad. According to the article:

The primary methods of manipulating information used by the mass media in the interests of information-psychological confrontation objectives are:

- Direct lies for the purpose of disinformation both of the domestic population and foreign societies;
- Concealing critically important information;
- Burying valuable information in a mass of information dross;

18. 'International Security and Estonia', Välisluureamet (Estonian Foreign Intelligence Service), February 2021, https://www.valisluureamet.ee/doc/raport/2021-en.pdf.

19. Yu. Kuleshov et al., 'Информационно-психологическое противоборство в современных условиях: теория и практика' (Information-Psychological Warfare In Modern Conditions: Theory And Practice), *Vestnik Akademii Voyennykh Nauk* 1, no. 46 (2014): 106.

20. 'Словарь терминов и определений в области информационной безопасности' (Dictionary of terms and definitions in the field of information security), *Voyennaya Akademiya General'nogo Shtaba*, 2nd edition (Moscow: Voyeninform, 2008).

- Simplification, confirmation and repetition (inculcation);
- Terminological substitution: use of concepts and terms whose meaning is unclear or has undergone qualitative change, which makes it harder to form a true picture of events;
- Introducing taboos on specific forms of information or categories of news;
- Image recognition: known politicians or celebrities can take part in political actions to order, thus exerting influence on the world view of their followers;
- Providing negative information, which is more readily accepted by the audience than positive.[21]

As well as making full use of the possibilities offered by the internet to reach out to individuals in target countries – something we will also look at in more detail in Chapter 5 – Russia has updated some true old-school techniques for planting what some people now call 'fake news'. 'What's really interesting to me is the historic continuum,' Lars the counter-intelligence officer says. 'Even if you go back decades into what the KGB did with disinformation campaigns, they were seeding articles into, for example, the Far Eastern press. They planted articles and then used those as primary sources for quoting and that would then reach European publications. But now that can be done using these useful idiots or whatever you want to call them. They set up a blog, and they can take these fabricated leaks, and then start disseminating them online. It's the same thing that has taken place since the 1950s or '60s, using today's tools to basically recreate that same process.' These information-planting and laundering tactics are alive and well today, and being used to target real people. Artemiy Panarin is a hockey player for the New York Rangers, who attracted the unwelcome attention of the Russian propaganda machine early in 2021 after he publicly expressed support for Alexei Navalny. A story about Panarin planted by RT contributor Caleb Maupin on a fringe website that describes itself as an 'anti-imperialist tool' included an accusation of sexual misconduct a decade previously.[22] Once planted, the story was picked up and recycled by a range of Russian media – with the accusations in some cases reported as fact.[23] The technique remains precisely the same: what the internet does is make it vastly easier, faster and cheaper – and as a result makes the range of possible targets vastly wider. Former KGB officer Jack Barsky recalls how in the pre-internet

21. Kuleshov et al., 'Информационно-психологическое противоборство в современных условиях: теория и практика' (Information-Psychological Warfare In Modern Conditions: Theory And Practice), p. 107.

22. Caleb Maupin, 'US Media Overlooks NHL Star Artemi Panarin's Ugly History', 16 February 2021, https://www.greanvillepost.com/2021/02/16/us-media-overlooks-nhl-star-artemi-panarins-ugly-history/.

23. Ivan Akimov, 'СМИ указали на избирательность "культуры отмены" и привели в пример Панарина' (Media use Panarin as an example of selective 'cancel culture'), Gazeta.ru, 19 February 2021, https://www.gazeta.ru/social/news/2021/02/19/n_15640850.shtml.

era 'it was pretty hard to disseminate this kind of information. It took a lot of work, and you really had to focus on who you want to do damage to with the resources that you have. Nowadays it's so much easier. Social media makes it possible.'[24]

Another technique of disinformation updated for the online age because it succeeds is 'astroturfing', the term for flooding a conversation with fake supporters to present the impression of widespread popular agreement on a political topic.[25] Sometimes the intended audience can be within Russia itself, as when provocative statements are planted in the online comment sections of genuine British and other Western media outlets, and then repeated by Russian state media as evidence that the public in those countries backs Moscow.[26] But more frequently, it's an attempt to influence any decision-maker in Western countries that is sensitive to public opinion. If done clumsily, this can be counterproductive: when in 2014–15 British parliamentarians started receiving large volumes of duplicated letters arguing against confrontation with Russia, it was sufficiently unsubtle that the only MPs taken in were those who wanted to be.[27] But in other instances it achieves striking success. In late February 2021, Amnesty International announced it no longer considered Alexei Navalny a 'prisoner of conscience' following a Russian campaign to discredit him. Perversely, Amnesty officials knew perfectly well that they were being subjected to an 'orchestrated campaign', but considered even so that 'we had too many requests; we couldn't ignore them'.[28] In doing so, Amnesty confirmed for Russia that mass trolling works, which will inevitably encourage it to do more of the same in the future. Social media are an easy and obvious means of organizing campaigns of this kind too, which makes the habit of some Western governments including the UK of giving in to social media outrage campaigns especially dangerous. Any demonstration that public policy can successfully be influenced by Twitter mobs will only increase Russia's incentives to invest resources in this low-cost, low-risk means of intervening in the internal affairs of other states.

Sometimes the messages Russia transmits to politicians in this way are contradictory, but this only becomes clear if you track the different campaigns and look at them together. Then, we see that Moscow wants us to believe simultaneously both that Russia is a formidable world-class power, and that it is hugely vulnerable

24. Donie O'Sullivan, 'A former KGB spy talks disinformation tactics and the 2020 election', CNN, 31 July 2020, https://edition.cnn.com/2020/07/30/tech/2020-election-russia-disinformation/index.html.

25. Gordon Corera, 'Pro-Kremlin trolls target news website comments, researchers say', BBC News, 6 September 2021, https://www.bbc.co.uk/news/uk-58441662.

26. Tim Shipman, 'Raab: Putin's trolls are targeting national newspapers', *The Times*, 2 May 2021, https://www.thetimes.co.uk/article/raab-putins-trolls-are-targeting-national-newspapers-fzd8hlw65.

27. Private conversations with UK Members of Parliament, September 2015.

28. Sarah Rainsford, 'Amnesty strips Alexei Navalny of "prisoner of conscience" status', BBC News, 24 February 2021, https://www.bbc.co.uk/news/world-europe-56181084.

and has no initiative but only reacts to the hostile challenges of the West. Propagandists argue that it's clear that sanctions on Russia have not had even the slightest effect on Moscow's policy, and that they are in fact utterly meaningless. But they should be removed as soon as possible. And Russia is a rational actor the West can work with. But we also need to remember that excessive criticism of Russia's actions could quickly spiral into a global thermonuclear war, which will certainly be the West's fault. These arguments are then picked up and repeated by a wide range of influential people who are not necessarily working on behalf of Russia. They include well-meaning generalists who completely misunderstand the Russian challenge; accommodationists who argue Russia should be entitled to the 'sphere of influence' over other countries that it demands; and apologists who confuse 'understanding Russia' with giving it a free pass to behave as a rogue state.

Once again, all the methods we see Russia using today echo the Soviet Union's efforts during the Cold War. Unlike in communist times, Russia does not seek to try to spread a precise ideology or set of beliefs, but this hasn't diluted the destructive counterpart to that effort – its determination to undermine the beliefs and values that are broadly common to Western democracies, and set their societies against themselves in the process. Russia works hard to identify fissures or contentious issues in democracies and then play on them to encourage discontent, anger and extremism. This is different from inventing social conflict out of thin air: as disinformation expert Jakub Kalenský points out, 'Russia doesn't create all the problems it exploits, but they are masters in feeding problems and aggravating them.'

To be effective, Russia's approaches have to be tailored to the country they are targeting. Pekka Toveri, the former intelligence chief from Finland, explains that 'Russia also supports a small but noisy group of "useful idiots", who try to create division within Finnish society. These people spread propaganda supporting Russia and attack Finland's Western ties like EU membership and NATO cooperation. They also spread fake news about conspiracies about the "population replacement", rigged elections, deadly vaccinations and so on.' But at the same time, Pekka says, Finland is less susceptible to this kind of approach than many other countries. 'Russia knows that the weakest link in Finland is not the people. The population is well educated and trusts very strongly in the authorities, especially the police and Defence Forces, so fake news doesn't work too well in Finland.' Instead, the preferred tactic is to target individual politicians. 'There is a number of politicians who are willing to "continue the dialogue" in order not to provoke Russia,' Pekka says. 'Therefore, the Russians have returned to the old Soviet habit of using "influencers" to work for them.'

In the US, Russia trying to influence presidential elections, and prodding at divisive issues like race, came as an unpleasant surprise in 2016–17. But the pattern was familiar to those with longer memories. In 1983, Vladimir Kryuchkov, head of the foreign intelligence department of the KGB, 'emphasized the need to analyze contradictions within American society even better in order to find effective opportunities for attack [and] stressed the need for active measures with regard to the presidential elections'.[29] Even further back in history, stirring social conflicts in the West was a preferred tactic for Tsarist Russia too. In 1839, Astolphe de Custine described exactly this process: 'Russia sees in Europe a prey which will sooner or later be delivered to her by our dissensions; it foments anarchy among us in the hope of profiting from a corruption favoured by it because it is favourable to its views'.[30] Edward Lucas is a British journalist and political candidate who has studied Russia's tactics over decades, and finds that some things remain constant. 'The technology has changed – the internet increases the scope, slipperiness and speed of active measures,' he says, 'but the principles behind our adversaries' thinking are the same. Find weaknesses. Exploit them, with money and blackmail where necessary, but mostly using gullibility, impatience and other human frailties. Rinse and repeat'.[31]

## Influence and 'soft power'

The coronavirus pandemic offered plenty of opportunities for Russia's information warfare apparatus. Unlike political issues that are local or regional in nature, Covid-19 affected everybody worldwide. In the early stages of the pandemic, the lack of definitive and reliable information about the virus and how to deal with it provided the most fertile possible ground for information and disinformation campaigns, especially those that fed on fear, uncertainty and doubt. Russia took full advantage.[32] The disinformation system swiftly moved to generating a large number of different stories attempting to undermine confidence in Western institutions and their ability to deal with the crisis.[33] When vaccines were developed, campaigns to discredit Western vaccination programmes – including suggestions that people who took then would turn into monkeys – ran alongside intense

29. Ministry of State Security (Stasi), 'Notes on Statements Made by Comrade Colonel General Kryuchkov', 3 October 1983, Wilson Center Digital Archive, https://digitalarchive. wilsoncenter.org/document/119321.

30. Astolphe-Louis-Léonor, Marquis de Custine, *La Russie en 1839*, vol. 1. In the original: 'La Russie voit dans l'Europe une proie qui lui sera livre tôt ou tard par nos dissensions; elle fomente chez nous l'anarchie dans l'espoir de profiter d'une corruption favorisée par elle parce qu'elle est favorable à ses vues'.

31. Edward Lucas, 'Lenin's doctrines are still dividing the West', *The Times*, 28 September 2020, https://www.thetimes.co.uk/article/lenins-doctrines-are-still-dividing-the-west-cmh2vncqm.

32. Jamie Dettmer, 'Britain Accuses Russia of Vaccine Disinformation Campaign', VOA, 16 October 2020, https://www.voanews.com/europe/britain-accuses-russia-vaccine-disinformation-campaign.

33. https://euvsdisinfo.eu/throwing-coronavirus-disinfo-at-the-wall-to-see-what-sticks/.

campaigns of espionage attempting to steal the research that developed them.[34] Disinformation spread covertly through social media matched that broadcast publicly by Russian state television.[35] But all of these efforts built on resources, and in some cases campaigns, that had been developed long before. Russia's backing of anti-vaccination campaigns pre-dated the coronavirus pandemic, and had already been causing public health challenges in target countries.[36] New, coronavirus-specific vaccine-sceptic propaganda was delivered through well-established routes, including a website targeting US military veterans that had been operating for almost twenty years.[37]

Meanwhile Russia threw its efforts into 'vaccine diplomacy', attempting to win friends and allies through supplies of vaccines. This produced mixed results, as its promises of vaccine help to countries around the world fell flat. Seventy countries initially authorized Russia's Sputnik V vaccine – but a highly suspicious reluctance to publish reliable data on its efficacy, a failure to deliver on time, and reports of corruption, profiteering middlemen and inflated prices caused several of them to pull out of deals to import the vaccine or manufacture it themselves.[38] By May 2021, Russia had produced only 33 million doses of the vaccine, for the 800 million people it had promised to provide vaccines for worldwide.[39] The campaign fell victim to the same problems as Russia's early initiatives delivering PPE to Italy and the US – namely Russia's own ingrained habits of secrecy and fantasy, deceit and corruption. And Russia's promotion of vaccine conspiracies backfired spectacularly, leading to the spectacle of state propaganda outlet RT tying itself in knots when its anti-vaccination campaign collided with Russia's own introduction of the lockdowns and vaccine certificates it had mocked in the West.[40] The propaganda

34. Jamie Grierson and Hannah Devlin, 'Hostile states trying to steal coronavirus research, says UK agency', *Guardian*, 3 May 2020, https://www.theguardian.com/world/2020/may/03/hostile-states-trying-to-steal-coronavirus-research-says-uk-agency.

35. Tom Whipple and Manveen Rana, 'Russian Kirill Dmitriev drops coronavirus "monkey vaccine" jibe', *The Times*, 17 October 2020, https://www.thetimes.co.uk/article/russian-kirill-dmitriev-drops-coronavirus-monkey-vaccine-jibe-g0v2shm38.

36. Laura Halminen, 'OSINT Snapshot: Nordic countries face challenge of anti-vaccination messaging and wider disinformation', *Jane's Intelligence Review*, 29 July 2019.

37. Sasha Ingber, 'Veteran-Focused Website Is Run By Russia And Pushes Vaccine Skepticism', *Newsy*, 18 March 2021, https://www.newsy.com/stories/u-s-veterans-website-secretly-directed-by-russia/.

38. Grace Kier and Paul Stronski, 'Russia's Vaccine Diplomacy Is Mostly Smoke and Mirrors', *Carnegie*, 3 August 2021, https://carnegieendowment.org/2021/08/03/russia-s-vaccine-diplomacy-is-mostly-smoke-and-mirrors-pub-85074.

39. Polina Ivanova and Polina Nikolskaya, 'Big promises, few doses: why Russia's struggling to make Sputnik V doses', Reuters, 14 May 2021, https://www.reuters.com/business/healthcare-pharmaceuticals/big-promises-few-doses-why-russias-struggling-make-sputnik-v-doses-2021-05-14/.

40. Twitter thread by Alexey Kovalyov, 18 June 2021, https://twitter.com/Alexey__Kovalev/status/1405951089434841093.

against vaccines directed at the West too has blown back against Russia's own population, and what is more a profound lack of trust in the government translates into a similar lack of trust in the integrity of Russian science. The combined result was Russians preferring to pay money for fake vaccine certificates rather than receive the Sputnik vaccine for free – because after decades of being lied to by their government, many Russians had little faith that it was safe.[41] In late 2021, doctors in Latvia reported that 80% of Covid patients in hospital were Russian speakers despite their making up only 25% of the population. The problem was that these Russian speakers were relying on misleading Russian state TV reports for their information on vaccination, and suffering severe illness as a direct result.[42]

Russia's failure in promoting a positive self-image of itself on the back of the pandemic is a symptom of its broader inability to use 'soft power'. Coined by American thinker Joseph Nye in the late 1980s, the term soft power broadly means the ability of a country to persuade others to do what it wants without force or coercion. This is often now used to mean gaining support, sympathy and partnership through the power of attraction, for instance through culture and values that others want to emulate, adopt or join. Cultural outreach organizations such as the British Council, Alliance Française, Germany's Goethe-Institut and others provide ways of making that soft power accessible around the world (and a primary reason why the British Council has been banned by Russia).[43] But Russia's persistent practice shows that it does not really understand how to use soft power in this sense, to attract or persuade rather than to coerce. It's hard even to translate the phrase into Russian – it comes out as *myagkaya sila*, but *sila* means force, and is the same word used in the phrase *vooruzhennye sily*, or Armed Forces. So when Russia talks about 'soft power', it often means what in the West would be referred to as 'non-military', and almost invariably is referring to coercion not attraction.

This range of 'non-military' means that Russia has used against its neighbours and other countries further afield include trade embargoes, energy blockades and disruption, cyber and information campaigns, currency and banking manipulation, and social engineering through use of Russian minorities. Sometimes this can be for reasons that seem completely unrelated to what Russia is actually doing. Pekka Toveri explains that causing economic disruption to trade with Finland, including the sanctioning of Finnish food imports to Russia or blocking transit traffic, 'are normal methods. If needed, the Russian authorities arrange problems for the

41. Alexandra Tyan, 'The Infodemic', *Coda*, June 2021, https://mailchi.mp/codastory.com/infodemic-june-8808562.

42. '"Четыре из пяти пациентов с ковидом – русскоговорящие". Врачи в Латвии говорят о провале информационной кампании о вакцинации на русском', *Current Time*, 17 November 2021, https://www.currenttime.tv/a/kazhdye-chetyre-iz-pyati-patsientov-russkogovoryaschie-pochemu-vrachi-latvii-stolknulis-s-russkim-voprosom/31564362.html.

43. 'Statement from the British Council on Russia', British Council, 17 March 2018, https://www.britishcouncil.org/contact/press/statement-british-council-russia.

imports and exports at the borders to force Finns to negotiate with them. During these negotiations they can then raise some other issues to the table. This has happened several times.'[44] Far from being a recent development, this approach by Russia is long-standing. A decade ago, Estonian researcher Kadri Liik explained how Russia creates openings and opportunities for causing disruption at a later date, and then puts them on hold 'like a beer in the fridge just in case'.[45]

But recent efforts like Russia's attempts to exploit the coronavirus pandemic prove the point. In its early stages, Moscow attempted to mount a combined charm offensive and disinformation campaign. Shipments of 'aid' – of questionable utility and quality – went hand in hand with a concerted effort by Russia to have sanctions lifted.[46] These seemed initially to be having some success. Russian state media made clever use of misleading or heavily edited video clips to give the impression that Italy had welcomed shipments of Russian medical supplies (and the accompanying Russian military equipment), while the EU was doing nothing.[47] Russia's claims that it was sending supplies to the United States as 'humanitarian aid' were only belatedly countered by the US State Department pointing out that it had been bought and paid for.[48]

But the effect didn't last and Russia fell victim to its occasional habit of spectacularly misjudging the audiences for its information campaigns. When an Italian investigative journalist found that most of the equipment supplied was inappropriate or unusable, the response by Russian officials was rage and personal threats against the reporter. This laid bare the real nature of the campaign, and immediately alienated many of the people Moscow had sought to win over.[49]

Another feature of Russia's influence campaigns is the way they customarily operate through front organizations in the target country. In some cases, these may be set up by individuals who declare their sympathies with Moscow openly, but just as often, they can at first sight appear genuine and home-grown. That includes not only media outlets established to spread disinformation (see Chapter 5), but also groups or organizations designed to directly influence decisions by Western countries by joining in with policy conversations. In Brussels, 'friendship groups' are subject to limited accountability or public scrutiny, but provide access to the European Parliament for foreign governments.[50] And people attending

44. For a detailed description from 2009 of how this works, see Keir Giles and Susanna Eskola, 'Waking the Neighbour: Finland, NATO and Russia', UK Defence Academy, 2009, https://www.researchgate.net/publication/280611718_Waking_the_Neighbour_Finland_NATO_and_Russia.

45. Speaking at Chatham House, London, 31 March 2011.

46. https://foreignpolicy.com/2020/03/30/russia-china-coronavirus-geopolitics/.

47. https://www.bbc.com/russian/features-52100274.

48. https://www.state.gov/u-s-purchase-of-needed-supplies-from-russia/.

49. https://www.la7.it/tagada/video/maurizio-molinari-sulle-minacce-a-jacopo-jacoboni-la-russia-ha-violato-la-nostra-sovranita-con-un-07-04-2020-318231.

50. Nikolaj Nielsen, 'New oversight rules fail to catch MEP "friendship groups"', *EU Observer*, 3 September 2020, https://euobserver.com./institutional/149312.

international political conferences might not know that they have been organized by a front for the psychological operations division of the GRU.[51]

Johan Bäckman is a Finnish citizen and one of the country's most prominent and hyperactive pro-Kremlin agitators, described by the *New York Times* as 'a tireless supporter of Russian President Vladimir Putin'.[52] He's a serial creator of organizations designed to deceive or confuse, and although sometimes the efforts are comically transparent, they serve a serious purpose. In November 2016, Bäckman registered two NGOs mimicking the names of two genuine organizations, the national journalists' union and the international centre for research on hybrid threats.[53] Both efforts were perfectly legal, since anybody in Finland is entitled to set up NGOs and unions. But the fictitious journalists' union was able not only to set up social media accounts and a website mimicking the official ones, but also to issue fake press cards for supporters who could then pretend to be journalists while harassing opponents of Russia or taking part in anti-vaccine demonstrations. Meanwhile, Bäckman's 'European Center of Excellence for Counteracting Hybrid Threats' not only mimicked the name of the legitimate 'European Centre of Excellence for Countering Hybrid Threats', a multinational outfit set up in Helsinki, but copied its website and social media profiles closely enough to briefly deceive unwary visitors (including me).[54] The copycat organization's main initial activity was organizing speaking opportunities for Russian propagandists in Helsinki, and distributing material like a pamphlet entitled 'EU's Infowar on Russia: Putting in place a totalitarian media regime and speech control'.[55]

Although Bäckman comes from a wealthy family, he has no visible means of financing his various ventures or even of earning a living. The booklets he distributes are printed in Russia, and the accounts of the printing firm are, naturally enough, not transparent, making it impossible to determine who pays for them.

In fact, how propagandists and influencers for Russia support themselves is a common question across multiple countries, and there are grounds to investigate whether the Kremlin keeps its propagandist supporters in the West on its payroll.

51. 'International Security and Estonia', Välisluureamet (Estonian Foreign Intelligence Service), February 2021, https://www.valisluureamet.ee/doc/raport/2021-en.pdf, p. 63.

52. Andrew Higgins, 'Effort to expose Russia's "troll army" draws vicious retaliation', *New York Times*, 31 May 2016. A detailed profile of Bäckman is available at 'The Kremlin's Voice: Johan Bäckman', *UpNorth*, 13 September 2016, https://upnorth.eu/the-kremlins-voice-johan-backman/.

53. Laura Halminen, 'Valemedia MV-lehden puuhamiehet perustivat "Toimittajaliiton", jonka taustalla on Venäjä-yhteyksistään tunnettu Johan Bäckman', *Helsingin Sanomat*, 21 December 2019, https://www.hs.fi/politiikka/art-2000006351322.html.

54. 'Hybrid Threats Target Center To Counter Hybrid Threats', *Medium*, 30 September 2017, https://medium.com/dfrlab/hybrid-threats-target-center-to-counter-hybrid-threats-e7d0160d8b3.

55. Tweet by Johan Bäckman, 10 February 2017, https://mobile.twitter.com/johanbek/status/829958312573681664.

Disinformation and conspiracy theorizing can be a highly profitable business when monetized through social media.[56] But far from every pro-Russian propagandist has done so.

Marcus Papadopoulos is a regular British contributor to RT, who gained access to Members of Parliament, including former Labour Party leader Jeremy Corbyn, through setting up a magazine called *Politics First* and applying for a Parliament press pass.[57] But Papadopoulos still says his main occupation is as editor of the magazine several years after it last appeared, and company records for the publishing house that produced it, owned by Papadopoulos, show it is not generating any noticeable income for him to live off.[58]

Parliamentary accreditation was also the route to influence for a pro-Russia activist in Sweden, often known as Egor Putilov but working and living under a wide range of aliases, and able to show identity documents in several of them.[59] In Putilov's case, at least one source of funding for his activities (although not for his ready supply of passports in different names) became publicly known. In 2014, Putilov contracted to buy a property from 'an influential entrepreneur and now convicted criminal from St. Petersburg' for 6 million Swedish kronor (approximately £520,000) and immediately sold it for its real market value which was double that amount.[60] The obvious implications of foreign compromise were enough for his parliamentary accreditation to be withdrawn and consequently for him to lose his position as an assistant for the Sweden Democrats Party.[61] But it did nothing to hinder Putilov from continuing active and energetic campaigns for Russia and against its critics – as we will see in Chapter 7.[62]

56. Mathew Foresta, 'Meet the Sneakiest Defenders of Vladimir Putin's Ukraine Invasion and China's Xinjiang Repression', Daily Beast, 29 April 2022, https://www.thedailybeast.com/meet-the-sneakiest-defenders-of-vladimir-putins-ukraine-invasion-and-chinas-xinjiang-repression

57. Henry Zeffman, 'Russian propagandist Marcus Papadopoulos should lose his press pass, say MPs', *The Times*, 9 November 2017, https://www.thetimes.co.uk/article/russian-propagandist-marcus-papadopoulos-should-lose-his-press-pass-say-mps-cwqg5ksl0.

58. Hoping to hear from Marcus Papadopoulos in his own words, I asked if he would give an interview for this book, but he declined to respond.

59. Axel Green, 'Egor Putilov lurade sig till svenskt medborgarskap' (Egor Putilov acquired Swedish citizenship by deceit), *Arbetaren*, 18 February 2018, https://www.arbetaren.se/2018/02/18/egor-putilov-lurade-sig-till-svenskt-medborgarskap/.

60. 'SD-tjänstemannen gjorde miljonvinst med rysk affärsman – "potentiell säkerhetsrisk", enligt experter' (SD official made millions in profit with a Russian businessman – 'potential security risk', according to experts), Sveriges Radio, 23 September 2016, https://sverigesradio.se/artikel/6522899.

61. Fredrik Furtenbach and Lova Olsson, 'Putilov nekas ackreditering till riksdagen' (Putilov is denied accreditation to the Riksdag), Sveriges Radio, 25 April 2019, https://sverigesradio.se/artikel/7205950.

62. Chloe Colliver et al., '"Smearing Sweden": International Influence Campaigns in the 2018 Swedish Election', ISD, October 2018, https://www.lse.ac.uk/iga/assets/documents/arena/2018/Sweden-Report-October-2018.pdf.

## *'Active measures'*

But Russia's campaigns against the West extend far beyond information and influence. By the time of Crimea, Russia had been testing out hostile means of targeting its Western neighbours for almost a decade, including gas cut-offs for Ukraine in 2006, the crude cyber offensive against Estonia in May 2007, and ultimately the use of military force against Georgia in 2008.[63] Increased oil revenues from the mid-2000s on gave Moscow not only the funds to rebuild its military and other capabilities, but also increased confidence in its ability to absorb any negative economic impact – like sanctions – from unfriendly actions against the West.[64] And since 2014, Moscow has become more and more willing to reach into Western countries and do direct harm, through sabotage, murders and assassinations, undisguised electronic warfare, false-flag cyber attacks and more. New incidents are uncovered regularly spanning the whole of Europe.[65] Campaigns of this type are often given the name 'active measures', a direct translation of a phrase used by the Russian intelligence services. 'Active measures' cover a wide range of different activities, but their broad theme is any action that can be taken to damage or weaken the target, whether politically, economically, militarily or in some other way.[66]

This approach too has deep roots. According to General Oleg Kalugin, a former senior KGB officer, rather than trying to acquire secret information, 'The heart and soul of the Soviet intelligence was . . . active measures to weaken the West.'[67] Today's Russia is just as unrestrained in attacking the West as the USSR was, if not more so. Mark Galeotti has tracked the attitudes of Russia's intelligence agencies evolving over time, to the point where well before 2022 he was confident they were operating 'under wartime rules'. He says the GRU, the 'Main Intelligence Directorate', as a military entity, has always brought with it a much more risk-tolerant and adventurous approach. 'The GRU is the agency that historically has always been

63. In the middle of the last decade, Chatham House surveyed the unfriendly means Russia adopts to influence its neighbours. See 'Russia's Toolkit' in 'The Russian Challenge', Chatham House, June 2015, http://www.chathamhouse.org/publication/russian-challenge-authoritarian-nationalism.

64. Robert Larsson, 'Russian Leverage on the CIS and the Baltic States', FOI, June 2007, available at www.foi.se/ReportFiles/foir_2280.pdf.

65. Raphael S. Cohen and Andrew Radin, 'Russia's Hostile Measures in Europe: Understanding the Threat', RAND, 2019, https://www.rand.org/content/dam/rand/pubs/research_reports/RR1700/RR1793/RAND_RR1793.pdf.

66. Ivo Juurvee, 'The resurrection of "active measures": Intelligence services as a part of Russia's influencing toolbox', *Hybrid CoE* (April 2018): 3, https://www.hybridcoe.fi/wp-content/uploads/2018/05/Strategic-Analysis-2018-4-Juurvee.pdf.

67. 'Inside the KGB – An interview with retired KGB Maj. Gen. Oleg Kalugin', *Cold War Experience*, CNN, January 1998, http://web.archive.org/web/20070627183623/http://www3.cnn.com/SPECIALS/cold.war/episodes/21/interviews/kalugin/.

sent into the uncontrolled regions, the dangerous locations, whether that's in the middle of a civil war, counter-insurgency, and increasingly that also means cyberspace,' he says. 'There is that sense that they are part of a military institution where the important thing is accomplishing the mission, rather than worrying too much about casualties on the way.'[68]

'Casualties', in today's environment, tends to include meaning detection and exposure. Repeated incidents where the GRU has been relatively carefree about covering its tracks or denying its involvement suggest Mark is right. The US noted already in 2016 that Russia was willing to target critical infrastructure systems and conduct espionage operations 'even when detected and under increased public scrutiny'.[69] But Mark also thinks the GRU's bullish attitude is bringing other, traditionally more cautious, agencies along with it as they have to compete to keep up. 'The SVR tend towards being more subtle, they tend towards more long-term operations. In the past, because they were often embedded in diplomatic missions, they did seem to demonstrate more of an awareness of the need not to be blunt, or to cause diplomatic trouble. But I think we're beginning to see that break down because they have to be able to demonstrate results, and quickly.'[70]

The immediate symptom of this is a willingness by Russia to take any opportunity that presents itself to do harm, based on the belief that 'if there is something that can be learned from the experience of political warfare during the Cold War, it is that what makes Russia stronger weakens the West, and what makes the West stronger, weakens Russia'.[71] That principle may also lie behind suspected, but unconfirmed (at least in public) instigation of public disorder in Western countries like France, whether by backing and encouraging the 'gilets jaunes' protests in 2018 onwards, or targeting British civilians at the Euro 2016 football tournament by means of 'savage and organised' football hooligans delivering violence with 'military organisation'.[72]

68. Mark Galeotti, 'Russian Intelligence & Security Community', Russia Strategic Initiative, 12 August 2021, https://community.apan.org/wg/rsi/project-connect/w/events/31576/mark-galeotti-russian-intelligence-security-community/.

69. James R. Clapper, 'Worldwide Threat Assessment of the US Intelligence Community', Senate Armed Services Committee, 9 February 2016, http://www.armed-services.senate.gov/imo/media/doc/Clapper_02-09-16.pdf (emphasis added).

70. Mark Galeotti, 'Russian Intelligence & Security Community', Russia Strategic Initiative, 12 August 2021, https://community.apan.org/wg/rsi/project-connect/w/events/31576/mark-galeotti-russian-intelligence-security-community/.

71. Ofer Fridman, *Russian Hybrid Warfare: Resurgence and Politicisation* (Oxford: Oxford University Press, 2018), p. 264.

72. Daniel Boffey, 'Russian hooligans were savage and organised, say England fans', *Guardian*, 12 June 2016, https://www.theguardian.com/football/2016/jun/12/russian-hooligans-savage-organised-england-fans-marseille-euro-2016.

Pekka Toveri thinks a key reason why Russia consistently behaves in a hostile and aggressive manner is 'because it works. Putin's regime started to play the game with [the] West in the beginning of the 2010s with a very weak hand. But they noticed soon that by being aggressive and active, they can dance around the West and achieve their goals without any real reactions.' Two case studies from the far North of Europe tell us more about what Russia is willing to do to harm its neighbours and why. Both of Russia's Nordic neighbours, Norway and Finland, have been targeted with two very twenty-first-century forms of unfriendly activity: GPS jamming and migrant dumping.

Russia claims that its Murmansk BN electronic warfare systems deployed next to Finland and Norway on the Kola Peninsula can disrupt communications across Northern Europe, with a range of over 3,000 miles.[73] Although it's called electronic warfare (EW), the targets won't be just military. The task of Russia's EW troops is to 'counter the enemy's advantages in the information and telecommunications space'.[74] This includes activities that we might think a long way from warfighting, such as suppressing broadcast and online media including social media – specifically 'blocking radio and television signals, and message traffic in social networks'.[75]

But the most obvious impact of Russian EW systems is when they are used to jam GPS systems, preventing people in northern Norway and Finland from using their satellite navigation.[76] Disrupting GPS services has a clear military use given the Western military systems that depend on them for navigation or guidance. But a broader attack on GPS would also cause severe disruption for ordinary people, given how broadly the public relies on navigation services.[77] With so much civilian traffic dependent on GPS, roads would be in chaos, and millions of embedded GPS receivers providing faulty information would also wreak havoc in commerce,

73. Jarmo Huhtanen, 'Venäjä julkaisi videon, jossa harjoiteltiin häirintäjärjestelmän käyttöä lähellä Suomen rajaa' (Russia releases video showing training with jamming system near Finnish border), *Helsingin Sanomat*, 13 November 2020, https://www.hs.fi/kotimaa/art-2000007615087.html.

74. Yuriy Lastochkin, 'Солдаты РЭБ на страже эфира' (EW Troops Guarding the Airwaves), *Krasnaya Zvezda*, 15 April 2019, http://redstar.ru/wp-content/uploads/2019/04/041-15-04-2019.pdf.

75. S. G. Chekinov and S. A. Bogdanov, 'Прогнозирование характера и содержания войн будущего: проблемы и суждения' (Forecasting the nature and content of wars of the future: problems and assessments), *Voennaya Mysl'* (Military Thought) 10 (2015): 44–5.

76. Thomas Nilsen, 'Pilots again warned of GPS jamming in Norway's border region to Russia', *Barents Observer*, 10 January 2019, https://thebarentsobserver.com/en/security/2019/01/pilots-again-warned-gps-jamming-norways-border-region-russia.

77. As highlighted by Gen. Sir Patrick Sanders of UK Strategic Command, speaking at 'Defence Space 2020', 17 November 2020, https://www.airpower.org.uk/defence-space-2020/.

logistics and everyday life.[78] Air traffic mostly continues, but is forced to rely on backup systems which in itself causes disruption and delay.[79]

I asked Pekka Toveri from Finland and his fellow military expert Tor Bukkvoll from Norway whether GPS jamming was a deliberate act by Russia, or possibly just an accidental spillover from a test or military exercise. Both of them were in no doubt that these were purposefully disruptive attacks. 'It was deliberate in the sense that they knew this was going to have these effects on the civilian population, on civilian life and on flights and so on, but they did it anyway,' Tor told me.

You might think that an obviously hostile act disrupting civilian life in a foreign country would lead to a firm response. But Tor says in situations like this it's hard for the target country to know best just how to respond. 'It's always a question for every country whether you should object publicly or not when something like this happens,' he says. 'Should you criticize Russia in public? Or should you try to deal with it in other ways? And in this case Norway did both. We did protest publicly, but we also initiated a lot of conversations, not necessarily on the highest level, but trying to find the best level of the Russian bureaucracy to enter discussions.'

But that 'entering discussions' is sometimes exactly what Russia wants as an outcome from its unfriendly behaviour – as we will see again in Chapters 4 and 7. Alex Grigorievs sees a clear pattern of Russian behaviour in causing a crisis in order that people will talk to Moscow. He uses the example of Syria: 'When Putin started making mischief in Syria, Obama started talking to Putin in order to find a solution to the problems that Putin created . . . This is what Putin wants – in order to be taken seriously he has to make these problems.'

Russia followed this pattern in 2015, with a campaign of migrant dumping at the borders with Russia's Nordic neighbours (a tactic replicated in the summer of 2021 by Belarus flying in migrants from Iraq and pushing them across the borders with its European neighbours).[80] The scale of the operation was impressive, especially in the far north. As crossing the border on foot was not permitted by Russian regulations, the migrants arrived in Norway on brand new bicycles – which then piled up in masses on the Norwegian side of the border. In November 2015, 42 tonnes of 'refugee bikes' were sent for recycling as they did not meet

78. Jeff Coffed, 'The Threat of GPS Jamming: The Risk to an Information Utility', *Exelis*, January 2014, p. 1–10, https://www.chronos.co.uk/files/pdfs/cs-an/ThreatOfGPSJamming_V2.0_January2014.pdf; Northrop Grumman, 'Assured Position, Navigation and Timing: The Future Challenge', 2019, p. 1, https://www.northropgrumman.com/Capabilities/AssuredPNT/Documents/NorthropGrumman-APNT.pdf.

79. 'Finland reports GPS disturbances in aircraft flying over Russia's Kaliningrad', *Guardian*, 9 March 2022, https://www.theguardian.com/world/2022/mar/09/finland-gps-disturbances-aircrafts-russia.

80. 'Latvia and Lithuania move to stop migrants arriving via Belarus', Reuters, 11 August 2021, https://www.reuters.com/world/europe/lithuanian-parliament-debate-building-fence-belarus-border-2021-08-10/.

Norwegian safety standards.[81] Tor pointed to a theory that rather than a deliberate act of hybrid warfare, the migrant flows from Russia were the result of a simple administrative change within Russia. 'Russia's laws for how to operate the border changed and this opened a loophole which refugees could use,' he explains. But this theory doesn't explain how as soon as Russia had got the result it wanted, the flow of migrants stopped just as suddenly as it had started.

Instead, later investigation showed that this was an operation 'controlled by the Russian state leadership, in the practical implementation of which the Russian mafia played a significant role from start to finish'. Russia was able to test the responses of the Finnish leadership while adjusting the pressure during various phases of the crisis. In the end it was able to force Finland into a bilateral agreement, which 'served as a principled message that Finland acknowledged its place on the list of countries where Russia could influence political decisions'.[82] In effect, Russia showed that it can deliver migrants to the borders of Europe on demand, depending on whether its wishes in other areas are granted – and then use the migration flows to aggravate social tensions across Europe by amplifying stories, some fact-based, some entirely fictitious, showing how these migrants pose a threat to the societies receiving them.[83]

According to Pekka Toveri, once again what Russia wanted was to flex its muscles just to have other countries ask it to stop. 'The specific outcome was to force the Finnish authorities and political leadership to react and ask help from Putin,' he recalls. 'And that happened. The Finnish president asked for consultations with Putin and after that the issue was solved. It sent a message to the Finnish leadership, that the Russians have a way to hurt us if needed.'

But the episode also clearly illustrated Russia's regularly repeated approach of creating problems and crises in order to extract concessions in exchange for removing them, in a process of blackmail leaving Russia better off than before it started. As a defence official in an English-speaking country who had previously served as ambassador to Moscow wrote in an e-mail, 'Remember the old line? A Russian steals $100 from you. You are outraged. You protest, jump up and down, pound the table, threaten, cajole . . . the Russian looks on, impassive. Then he hands you $20, saying: "There, I've made a concession, now YOU make a concession."'

'We never [expletive deleted] learn,' he added.

81. Sebastian Hagberg, 'Norge skrotar ryska "flyktingcyklar"' (Norway scraps Russian 'refugee bikes'), *Aftonbladet*, 13 November 2015, https://www.aftonbladet.se/nyheter/a/zLVJoO/norge-skrotar-ryska-flyktingcyklar.

82. Kari Alenius, 'Asylum Seekers from Russia to Finland: A Hybrid Operation by Chance?', in Thaddeus Eze (ed.), *ECCWS 2021 20th European Conference on Cyber Warfare and Security*, June 2021.

83. Andrew Rettman, 'Sex and lies: Russia's EU news', *EU Observer*, 18 April 2017, https://euobserver.com/investigations/137595.

## Murder to order

According to former MI6 chief Alex Younger, 'very little is off limits' for the Russian intelligence services.[84] This includes regular acts of murder abroad. Being targeted by Russia's state leadership carries the risk of being put on the list for one of its campaigns of targeted assassination.[85] Once again, in this as in so much else, Russian state behaviour seems to come from a different age. Death can be swift, by gunshot or explosion, or slow and excruciating, by poison, since Russia has updated this medieval method with the benefit of the Soviet Union's extensive research into toxic substances, reportedly including experiments on condemned Gulag prisoners.[86] Russia isn't unique in having been blessed with a ready supply of individuals who will willingly carry out murder to order on behalf of the state. But today it may be unique in the frequency with which it is despatching them around the world and the exoticism of their methods. Investigations in 2019 found that teams of Russian intelligence officers had been roaming Europe to commit murder and sabotage across the continent, periodically regrouping in Haute-Savoie, France.[87]

The UK has seen one of the most consistent patterns of suspicious deaths of individuals connected with Russia – especially those with compromising knowledge of crimes carried out by or for the Russian state. In many cases these deaths have been written off as suicide, although in highly improbable circumstances.[88] Where Russian involvement has been demonstrated beyond doubt, the methods used are staggeringly reckless. Counter-intelligence officer Lars thinks one of the worst aspects of the attacks on Litvinenko and the Skripals was 'the blatant disregard in which the chemical and nuclear agents were used in the UK and allowed to actually spread into the environment. One of the assassins actually poured polonium down the sink in the UK. Consider the effect, the second- and third-order effects, of casually disposing of a chemical or nuclear agent in a foreign country. Were there any consequences to that kind of action? If

84. David Bond, 'UK spy chief says Russia poses "standing threat" to the west', *Financial Times*, 15 February 2019, https://www.ft.com/content/fc0d234e-311d-11e9-8744-e7016697f225.

85. Heidi Blake, 'From Russia With Blood', *Buzzfeed*, 15 June 2017, https://www.buzzfeed.com/heidiblake/from-russia-with-blood-14-suspected-hits-on-british-soil.

86. Andrew Kramer, 'Don't Drink the Tea: Poison Is a Favored Weapon in Russia', *New York Times*, 24 August 2020, https://www.nytimes.com/2020/08/20/world/europe/navalny-poison-russia-kremlin.html.

87. Darko Janjevic, 'Russia posted GRU agents in French Alps for EU ops – report', *Deutsche Welle*, 5 December 2019, https://www.dw.com/en/russia-posted-gru-agents-in-french-alps-for-eu-ops-report/a-51548648.

88. Jane Bradley et al., 'The Man Who Knew Too Much', *Buzzfeed*, 19 June 2017, https://www.buzzfeed.com/janebradley/scientist-who-helped-connect-litvinenkos-murder-to-the.

there were, they seem pretty mild. It is really concerning to me that that is something that we're allowing to happen, that we're giving [Russia] permission to conduct these kind of operations.'

In the case of the Skripals, this effect is known because the reckless handling of lethal substances by the Russian intelligence officers led directly to the death of an entirely innocent victim, Dawn Sturgess, and permanent health damage for others including the first police officer to arrive at Sergei Skripal's house.[89] As journalist Oliver Bullough points out, it is hard to decide which is worse – whether Putin is personally authorizing a campaign of murder across the world, including using highly lethal substances that are then casually discarded regardless of the danger, or whether it is happening without his knowledge and control.[90]

Furthermore, the number of foreign suspicious deaths detected is negligible compared to the number taking place within Russia itself.[91] Opposition activist Vladimir Kara-Murza survived – barely – not just one but two poison attacks.[92] Victims include journalists – not only relatively high-profile individuals like Anna Politkovskaya, murdered in 2006 on Putin's birthday, but dozens of other less well-known names since.[93]

Both and home and abroad, the murder campaigns show how Russia's leaders rule by intimidation, brutality and murder, rather than by law. In December 2020, Alexei Navalny tricked a Russian intelligence officer who had been part of the complex plan to murder him by means of poisoned underpants into revealing details of the planning and execution of the mission. But one of the most chilling moments in the full recording of the surreal conversation is when the officer, Konstantin Kudryavtsev, tries to excuse failure to kill Navalny by repeatedly referring to difficulties that come up 'in our work'. The only possible interpretation for the phrase in Russian is that for this branch of the Russian intelligence services, murder is routine business.[94]

89. 'Salisbury Novichok-poisoned officer Nick Bailey quits', BBC News, https://www.bbc.com/news/uk-england-wiltshire-54582981.

90. Tweet by Oliver Bullough, 2 September 2020, https://twitter.com/oliverbullough/status/1301166211980558339?s=12.

91. 'List of suspicious Russia-related deaths since 2014', *X Soviet*, no date, http://xsovietunion.blogspot.com/2018/03/list-of-suspicious-russia-related.html.

92. Mike Eckel and Carl Schreck, 'RFE/RL Exclusive: Mystery Over Russian's Suspected Poisoning Deepens With New FBI Records', 24 September 2020, https://www.rferl.org/a/rferl-exclusive-mystery-over-russian-suspected-poisoning-deepens-with-new-fbi-records/30856103.html.

93. Karl Dewey, 'Russia's evolving use of poisons in targeted killings', presentation at Kings College London, 23 February 2022.

94. '"If it Hadn't Been for the Prompt Work of the Medics": FSB Officer Inadvertently Confesses Murder Plot to Navalny', Bellingcat, 21 December 2020, https://www.bellingcat.com/news/uk-and-europe/2020/12/21/if-it-hadnt-been-for-the-prompt-work-of-the-medics-fsb-officer-inadvertently-confesses-murder-plot-to-navalny/.

The prominence of apparent failed attacks in public knowledge of Russian activities obscures the number of attacks that are unknown because they were successful. Aleksei Navalny survived his assassination attempt in August 2020 because the pilot of the flight he was on decided to land immediately and the first doctor who saw him, fully aware of the likely cause, administered an antidote without waiting for tests. Sergei and Yulia Skripal survived in March 2018 because they fell ill in a public place instead of in their own home where the deadly agent had been applied to their door handle. Still earlier, in 2015, Bulgarian arms dealer Emilian Gebrev, his son and a director of one of his companies survived an attack using a similar method because of the length of time the poison had been left on the door handles of their cars before they touched them.[95] In all cases, had the victims died as intended, it is far less likely the cause of their death would have been detected – leaving open the question of how many other individuals have been successfully targeted with Novichok or other means without it coming to public notice.

But the ostentatious use of rare chemicals to kill should not distract from Russia's continuing willingness to order murder by far less exotic methods. Less prominent assassinations can be carried out by Russian intelligence officers themselves, or by co-opted Russian or local criminals. Investigation of a campaign of murders of opponents of Russia in Turkey turned up repeated links between the Russian intelligence services and the crime world.[96] State support for the chief suspect in the murder of former Chechen rebel commander Zelimkhan Khangoshvili in Berlin in 2019 included not only training, but removing him from Russian and Interpol wanted lists and issuing him a genuine passport in a false name.[97]

In some cases, even when these attacks are detected they bring no blowback for Russia itself, as with the assassination of another former Chechen leader, Zelimkhan Yandarbiyev, in Qatar in 2004.[98] Two Russian officers were arrested and convicted by the Qatari authorities and returned to Russia to serve their sentences in a

95. 'Three Russian men charged with poisoning Bulgarian arms dealer', *Guardian*, 21 February 2020, https://www.theguardian.com/world/2020/feb/21/three-russian-men-charged-with-poisoning-bulgarian-arms-dealer-emilian-gebrev.

'Post-Mortem of a Triple Poisoning: New Details Emerge in GRU's Failed Murder Attempts in Bulgaria', Bellingcat, 4 September 2020, https://www.bellingcat.com/news/uk-and-europe/2020/09/04/gebrev-survives-poisonings-post-mortem/.

96. 'Have Russian hitmen been killing with impunity in Turkey?', BBC News, 13 December 2016, http://www.bbc.com/news/magazine-38294204.

97. Christo Grozev and Michael Weiss, 'Exclusive: Berlin Murder Suspect's New Ties to Russian Security Services', *New Lines*, 6 August 2021, https://newlinesmag.com/reportage/exclusive-berlin-murder-suspects-new-ties-to-russian-security-services/.

98. 'Ex-Chechen president dies in blast', NBC News, 13 February 2004, https://www.nbcnews.com/id/wbna4261459#.XpbYYsgzbDc.

Russian prison; instead, the murderers were immediately released.[99] More recent Russian operations too have incurred no consequences at all for Moscow, as in the case of the Russian and Russian-backed targeting of British humanitarian James Le Mesurier, resulting in his death in Istanbul.[100]

The fact that some state murders abroad have been detected and exposed has been cited as suggesting the Russian intelligence agencies are lacking in competence and expertise. But this may be measuring success by the wrong criteria. There's a widespread view that Russia does not try too hard to conceal its activities, and may even intend to be detected. According to a report drawn up for the US Congress, 'exposure is not a failure if the attack succeeds in conveying Russia's ability and willingness to carry out targeted attacks'.[101] David Kilcullen, a former Australian Army officer and world-renowned expert on guerrilla and unconventional warfare, explains further: 'The reason they do that is they're sending a message. In the Skripal poisoning case, it's very clever capabilities being displayed. We can reach out into your territory. We can do that with a military unit, insert it into your location with a weapon of mass destruction, and we can kill someone.' Historian Simon Miles agrees: 'There's actually a value to it being known that you can reach out and touch someone, whether that's the Skripals or someone else. There's a value to this imperfect covertness.'[102] Disinformation researcher Gavril thinks that this deliberate posturing extends into online activity. 'Russia has wanted to be caught,' he says of the campaign targeting the US presidential election in 2016. 'They weren't trying to obfuscate very well, the campaigns they were running were not that sophisticated; in the beginning they just used basic marketing campaigns and techniques from the West. And [the troll farms] had been already discovered back in 2013. So if I had to make a guess, I think that they knew full well what the political reaction would be in a country like the US, that they would freak out, that they would overreact and that it would make Russia seem like it's a bigger threat and player than it perhaps really is.'

## What to do about it

As we have seen, while the response to a direct armed assault like the one on Ukraine is obvious, Western countries can struggle to know how to respond when

99. Sarah Rainsford, 'Convicted Russia agents "missing"', BBC News, 17 February 2005, http://news.bbc.co.uk/1/hi/world/europe/4275147.stm.

100. 'The Times view on the death of James Le Mesurier: Assad's Nemesis', *The Times*, 13 November 2019, https://www.thetimes.co.uk/article/2f9b9ba8-0582-11ea-a54d-e177f6bc2c05.

101. Andrew S. Bowen, 'Russian Military Intelligence: Background and Issues for Congress', 24 November 2020, https://crsreports.congress.gov/product/pdf/R/R46616, p. 11.

102. 'Russian Spetsnaz in the Grey Zone', Russia Strategic Initiative, 19 August 2021, https://community.apan.org/wg/rsi/project-connect/w/events/29786/rsi-connect-russian-spetsnaz-in-the-grey-zone/.

under undeclared attack from Moscow. But one approach that has proven successful is closing off as many opportunities as possible for Russia to do damage in the first place. That's because of the way Russia often exploits already existing weaknesses and vulnerabilities in the countries and societies it seeks to harm – and addressing weaknesses and vulnerabilities is basically just a function of good governance. We've already encountered the 'European Centre of Excellence for Countering Hybrid Threats' in Finland.[103] But the name for the centre in Finnish, *hybridiosaamiskeskus*, can be translated as 'hybrid competence centre'.[104] That's a terminology that should be used more widely; because so often it's competence in providing state services and governance that minimizes the openings and vulnerabilities that Russia can exploit through hostile sub-threshold actions. That principle comes through clearly in the range of priorities Sweden has set for bolstering its national resilience in the face of non-military threats. These include focusing on obvious vulnerabilities like security of transport, food and drinking water, and energy, but also on less immediate and tactical issues such as financial resilience, robustness of law enforcement and 'psychological defence' of civilians.[105]

But it's not clear who should be in charge of ensuring resilience like this in the rest of Europe, and western Europe in particular. It isn't a part of NATO's mission, largely because for much of NATO's existence it didn't need to be. During the Cold War, the governments and societies of NATO member states recognized the danger of sabotage, subversion and sub-threshold threats from Moscow, and so took steps to defend themselves. The gap in the West's defences we see today has come about not through a failure of NATO, but because of the two decades when the threat from Russia was less evident, and those same governments and societies just forgot it was there. But where it's NATO's job to bring allies together in countering military threats from Russia and elsewhere, it is the EU that is supposed to be acting as its counterpart and complement for non-military challenges. As we will see in Chapter 6, the EU has completely failed to rise to the task.

Nevertheless, without NATO or the EU, hostile Russian actions, including murders and attempted murders by the state at home and abroad, have sometimes led to international responses. There are plenty of examples that show these responses work best when Western countries show a united front.[106] In the

---

103. https://www.hybridcoe.fi/about-us/.

104. 'Eurooppalaisen hybridiosaamiskeskuksen toiminta käynnistyy Helsingissä', Finnish Ministry of the Interior, 1 September 2017, https://intermin.fi/en/-/eurooppalaisen-hybridiosaamiskeskuksen-toiminta-kaynnistyy-helsingissa.

105. 'Objectives for Swedish total defence 2021–2025', Government Offices of Sweden website, 18 December 2020, https://www.government.se/government-policy/defence/objectives-for-swedish-total-defence-2021-2025---government-bill-totalforsvaret-20212025/.

106. Keir Giles and Kim Hartmann, '"Silent Battle" Goes Loud: Entering a New Era of State-Avowed Cyber Conflict', in T. Minárik et al. (eds), *2019 11th International Conference on Cyber Conflict: Silent Battle* (Tallinn: NATO CCDCOE, 2019).

aftermath of the Salisbury attacks, the UK released partial information about the individuals involved, which allowed media globally and within Russia itself to pull the threads and build up a detailed picture of Russian intelligence operations through their own research – leading eventually to the exposure of entire cohorts of Russian intelligence officers.[107] But in addition, recognizing that there was only so much the UK alone could do to get Russia's attention, the British government organized a highly successful diplomatic effort to persuade allies and partners to join it in expelling Russian intelligence officers and diplomats.

Diplomatic expulsions are a common response by Western countries to hostile or illegal acts by Russia, but it is one that can only be used sparingly.[108] Russia inevitably responds by expelling a similar or greater number of Westerners who are more likely to be genuine diplomats, and given the relative sizes of embassies, this can have a disproportionately greater impact on the Western country's embassy in Moscow than the original expulsion of Russians. (For example, in mid-2021 there were 123 American personnel in Russia, all in the embassy in Moscow. Meanwhile there were over 400 Russian diplomats in the US, spread across an embassy, two consulates and the Mission to the UN).[109] As with so much else, this demands steady nerves and a determination not to back down in the face of Russian threats. In April 2021, Czechia was caught up in an expulsion war after sending home eighteen Russian intelligence officers over the 2014 sabotage attack (see Chapter 1). The eventual result was evisceration of both countries' diplomatic missions to each other, but also a valuable demonstration that neither Czechia nor its close partners would knuckle under to Russian intimidation.[110] In some cases of course this process rebounds against Russian interests – Kyle Wilson points out that expulsions and visa restrictions reducing the size of the Australian Embassy in Moscow indirectly led to Australia doubling the size of its embassy in Kyiv.

Throwing out embassy staff and an accompanying cautious visa policy does help constrain Russia's intelligence reach, although John Mooney is dubious about the value of expulsions in preventing unwelcome intelligence activity, and points out that 'only one set of activities is run via the embassy ... there are others that don't involve it at all'. An alternative approach is exposing, but not expelling, Russian intelligence operatives, making them ineffective while at the same time making their continued presence abroad Russia's problem to deal with rather than the host country's.

107. Thomas Claburn, 'What could be more embarrassing for a Russian spy: Their info splashed online – or that they drive a Lada?', *The Register*, 5 October 2018, https://www.theregister.com/2018/10/05/russian_gru_agents_car_database/.

108. 'Germany expels Russian diplomats after hitman sentenced in Berlin', BBC, 16 December 2021, https://www.bbc.co.uk/news/world-europe-59667937.

109. Tweet from US Embassy Moscow press office, 28 August 2021, https://twitter.com/usembrupress/status/1431272126783295496.

110. 'Prague–Moscow Tensions Escalate as Czechs Slash Russian Embassy Staff and Slovakia Expels Diplomats', RFE/RL, 22 April 2021, https://www.rferl.org/a/czechs-russian-embassy-staff-cut-diplomatic-spat-explosion-vrbetice-kulhanek/31216778.html.

Another common response by Western powers looking to 'do something' is economic sanctions. Until the 2022 invasion of Ukraine, there was an ongoing debate about how and where sanctions were effective in shaping Russian behaviour. In some ways sanctions had been a popular response, primarily as a demonstration of international solidarity. This is in part because there were few other compromises between doing nothing, which would encourage the perpetrator, and doing too much – for instance, a full-scale armed response – which would threaten that international consensus and which in any case public opinion in democracies would find unacceptable.

The tone of that debate changed as dramatically as the sanctions did in the aftermath of the invasion, as the US and other Western powers made good on their threats of a devastating economic impact on Russia if it went ahead.[111] The effect on ordinary Russians of freezing state and personal assets abroad was immediate and dramatic. But at the time of writing it was not yet clear whether sanctions could or would be sustained, or how Russia might succeed in mitigating their impact – in particular by continuing to find willing buyers for its energy exports in Europe and beyond, in order that it could continue to generate hard currency inflows.

Russia, unsurprisingly, had already been waging a long-term and intensive campaign to induce Western nations to lift sanctions (which demonstrates, if nothing else, that they are indeed an effective measure that Russia takes seriously).[112] The coronavirus pandemic saw these efforts stepped up, as official and unofficial lobbying in numerous Western capitals used it as an additional argument to have sanctions eased.[113] In the meantime, as Estonian Prime Minister Kaja Kallas reminded other EU leaders ahead of a summit that would discuss sanctions against Russia, patience is required. 'When we impose sanctions, some ask after six months, "Have they worked?" And if they haven't, "Remove them because they don't work." But actually it is a longer process,' she said.[114] In response, Sergey Lavrov threatened the EU that Russia would 'break off relations' if new sanctions were introduced –

111. Anders Åslund, 'Fortress Russia Crumbles', Project Syndicate, 9 March 2022, https://www.project-syndicate.org/commentary/russia-economic-collapse-shows-that-sanctions-work-by-anders-aslund-2022-03.

112. Nigel Gould-Davies, 'Russia Sanctions: Myths and Lessons', Chatham House, 20 January 2019, https://www.chathamhouse.org/expert/comment/russia-sanctions-myths-and-lessons.

113. Mason Clark et al., 'Russia in Review: Kremlin Attempts to Exploit Covid-19 Crisis to Remove Sanctions on Russia and Its Partners', Institute for the Study of War, 3 April 2020, http://www.understandingwar.org/backgrounder/russia-review-kremlin-attempts-exploit-covid-19-crisis-remove-sanctions-russia-and-its.

114. Charlie Duxbury, 'Estonian PM: EU has to "speed up" with sanctions on Russia', *Politico*, 12 February 2021, https://www.politico.eu/article/estonian-pm-eu-has-to-speed-up-with-sanctions-on-russia-kaja-kallas/.

and in the process acknowledged that sanctions do work, admitting they pose a risk to the Russian economy 'including in its most sensitive areas'.[115]

It's vital also that Western publics should be better informed about the threat they are facing. Increasingly, Russian intelligence officers who carry out attacks have been publicly identified by name, including in formal charges or indictments. The value of doing that has been questioned – after all, they are unlikely ever to appear in a Western court, because they are unlikely ever to reappear in a jurisdiction where they could be arrested and tried. Plus, 'naming and shaming' doesn't have much effect on a country that very obviously feels no shame. But what this practice does do is remind Western publics that the threat is real and present, by sweeping aside the perceived distance or faceless immunity of Russian hostile operations.[116] At the same time, John Mooney says that there are good reasons why much Russian activity is still kept under wraps. 'There's not a lot of disclosure about what's going on right across Europe at the moment,' he says. 'The simple reason is that the various security services that are dealing with this are not going to educate the enemy on what they know about them.' But the problem with that is that publics may then find it hard to understand defensive measures taken by their governments, or countermeasures intended to dissuade or punish Russia. In a democracy, that's a problem, because voters won't support action to deal with threats about which they are mostly unaware. Tor Bukkvoll says the deliberate silence is sometimes for less helpful reasons. 'There is a tendency for those who really don't want conflict with Russia to underplay the dangers of all the actions that Russia is doing towards Western countries,' he says – which sounds a lot like pretending the problem doesn't exist in the hope that it will go away. But Tor also warns against seeing Russia behind everything. 'I meet people who either assume that everything Russia does is geared towards destroying something in other countries, or the opposite – that's it's always our fault, and that Russia is just trying to be a normal state. It's in between the two. We need to be not naive, but also not paranoid,' he says.

Finally, for dealing with the challenge of Russian information warfare, Jakub Kalenský advocates a 'four lines of defence' approach: studying and documenting the threat to understand it better; raising awareness so target audiences are more resistant; reducing systemic weaknesses and vulnerabilities in information ecosystems that can be exploited by attackers; and finally, active deterrence and

---

115. 'Лавров заявил о готовности России разорвать отношения с ЕС' (Lavrov states Russia is ready to break off relations with the EU), *Vedomosti*, 12 February 2021, https://www.vedomosti.ru/politics/news/2021/02/12/857686-lavrov-zayavil-o-gotovnosti-rossii-razorvat-otnosheniya-s-es-v-sluchae-novih-sanktsii.

116. J. Heckman, 'WH cybersecurity coordinator seeks more "naming and shaming" of hackers', Federal News Network, 29 January 2018, https://federalnewsnetwork.com/cybersecurity/2018/01/wh-cybersecurity-coordinator-seeks-more-naming-and-shaming-of-hackers/.

countermeasures against the attackers. 'I believe that we in the West are getting quite close in those first three lines. We are doing a lot of documenting and educating, raising awareness, and working with media literacy programmes. But I think we are still not doing enough in that fourth line – trying to stop the aggressor and trying to make them pay for their aggression,' he says. 'That, of course, is not the story Russia tells itself. In the best traditions of Soviet spy paranoia and whataboutism, Defence Minister Shoygu complains that Russians are recruited by 'centres' in neighbouring countries to create 'information weapons that infiltrate our country and spread through it'.[117] 'I doubt you can name even one centre in our country which prepares specialists for information attacks. We do not train such specialists,' he adds, presumably having forgotten that in 2017 he himself had announced the creation in the Russian Armed Forces of a whole arm of service specifically to carry out information operations.[118] In reality, it appears the closest Europe has come to proper investigation of Russian hostile information campaigns is the British Parliament's 'Russia' enquiry – which proved Jakub's point by finding that the British government had taken no interest at all in whether these campaigns were taking place.

## Preparation for war

But all of these challenges become an entirely different and more immediate threat when Russia takes a confrontation sufficiently seriously that it is prepares for using not only covert active measures, but open military force. Then, all the different levers of power we have seen in this chapter – and more – can be geared towards ensuring in advance that that force is as effective as possible.

If Russia wants to exert military power without actually sending in the army, it has the option of using private military companies (PMCs), the formal term for what most people call mercenaries. Some of these operate in close cooperation with the Russian military – so close that personnel receive military decorations for taking part in operations.[119] But compared to regular Armed Forces, these have the advantage for Moscow of being more deniable (plausibly or implausibly), more

117. 'Генерал армии Сергей Шойгу заявил, что в Риге, Таллине и Варшаве созданы центры пропаганды для подрывной работы в России' (Army General Shoygu says that propaganda centres for sabotaging Russia have been set up in Riga, Tallinn and Warsaw), Russian Ministry of Defence, 6 August 2021, https://function.mil.ru/news_page/country/more.htm?id=12375842@egNews.

118. 'Russia sets up information warfare units – defence minister', Reuters, 22 February 2017, https://www.reuters.com/article/russia-military-propaganda-idUSL8N1G753J.

119. Denis Korotkov, 'Вагнер в Кремле' (Wagner in the Kremlin), 12 December 2016, https://www.fontanka.ru/2016/12/12/064/.

easily deployable, more affordable and especially more expendable.[120] We can tell that Russia is sensitive about war deaths among the military from the lengths it goes to in order to conceal them, both in the war in Ukraine and previously in conflicts in Syria and elsewhere. But deaths among professional mercenaries cause much less political embarrassment. This also has the side effect of these arms-length tools making Russia even more willing to take risks and send in armed groups than if it had to use its 'official' Armed Forces. This has been seen most clearly in Syria, and in Russia's campaign for returning to a position of power in Africa.[121]

Wagner is the best known of all the Russian mercenary companies, and has put significant effort into polishing its brand at home. Attempts to boost the organization's reputation includes shooting films glamourizing its exploits – first *Turist* (The Tourist), set in the Central African Republic, and then *Solntsepek* (Sunbaked), about eastern Ukraine in 2014.[122] But Wagner is only one of a whole constellation of paramilitary groups and other semi-official organizations Russia can use to prepare the ground for overt military action.[123] Another lever Russia is keen to use where possible is the 'compatriots', or Russians already residing abroad. The definition of 'compatriots' is immensely broad, and includes not just recent emigrants but 'descendants [of] peoples historically residing on territories of the Russian Federation'.[124] In the absence of a suitable Russian minority, Russia can create one: issuing Russian passports to individuals in occupied territories and then saying that it will be 'forced to defend' them is a tactic that has been repeated in both Georgia and Ukraine.[125]

120. Valeriy Akimenko and Keir Giles, 'Use and Utility of Russia's Private Military Companies', *Journal of Future Conflict* 1 (Fall 2019), https://www.queensu.ca/psychology/research/journal-future-conflict/journal-future-conflict-issue-01-fall-2019.

121. Sukhankin, Sergey (2020), *The 'Hybrid' Role of Russian Mercenaries, PMCs and Irregulars in Moscow's Scramble for Africa* (Washington, DC: Jamestown Foundation, 2020), https://jamestown.org/program/the-hybrid-role-of-russian-mercenaries-pmcs-and-irregulars-in-moscows-scramble-for-africa/.

122. 'Prigozhin Propaganda? Another Movie Bathes Russian Mercenaries In A Positive Light, This Time In Eastern Ukraine', RFE/RL, 15 August 2021, https://www.rferl.org/a/31411794.html.

123. Christopher Spearin, 'Russian Private Military and Security Companies and Special Operations Forces: Birds of a Feather?', *Special Operations Journal* 7, no. 2 (October 2021): 152–65, https://doi.org/10.1080/23296151.2021.1983944.

124. 'Федеральный закон от 24.05.1999 г. № 99-ФЗ О государственной политике Российской Федерации в отношении соотечественников за рубежом' (Federal Law No. 99-FZ of 24 May 1999 'On the state policy of the Russian Federation towards compatriots abroad'), Russian presidential website, 24 May 1999, http://www.kremlin.ru/acts/bank/13875.

125. Thomas Escritt and Tom Balmforth, 'Merkel tells Putin to pull back troops as Kremlin accuses Ukraine of provocations', Reuters, 8 April 2021, https://www.reuters.com/article/us-ukraine-crisis-kremlin-citizens-idUSKBN2BV1S3.

Russia's move on Crimea and eastern Ukraine in 2014 used methods that startled military planners in NATO, where a focus on operations in theatres like Afghanistan had led to collective amnesia regarding the Russian approach to fighting wars. The result was the emergence of terms like 'Russian hybrid warfare' and the 'Gerasimov doctrine' to describe what NATO was seeing but did not fully understand. These terms briefly dominated the entire discussion of the Russia problem. Sven Sakkov recalls how despite Crimea proving the point he had been making about Russia as a military threat, 'the response now was "well yes, this is all very nice, but the next challenge from Russia will not be in the conventional field, it will be hybrid" – and everything started revolving around hybrid threats'. This had direct consequences in drawing energy and attention away from the immediate conventional military challenges facing eastern Europe.

Experienced Russia analyst Michael Kofman writes that 'the Russian annexation of Crimea in March 2014 led to a scramble for information on the Russian Armed Forces, its military thought, and its doctrine. At first, this yielded faddish terms and malformed interpretations. Over the years the "Gerasimov Doctrine" has become somewhat a professional joke among Russian military analysts, who see it as a litmus test separating those with bona fide expertise from the ever-growing field of self-proclaimed experts on Russian information or political warfare.'[126] Or as a Finnish interviewee told me more succinctly, 'the whole Gerasimov Doctrine terminology should be taken behind the sauna and shot'.

But regardless of what terminology is used for it, in many areas Russia can be seen laying the groundwork for more direct action behind enemy lines in the event of a conflict with the West far beyond Ukraine. Reports from multiple European countries describe Russian 'tourists' straying into restricted military areas while surprisingly well equipped with sophisticated surveillance devices and UAVs. Individuals detected in activities like this are usually made up of 'a mix of Russians disguised as tourists, clandestine operators already resident in the target country, and Russian Embassy staff', a security specialist told me.

In Finland, concern grew over a number of years over a consistent pattern of Russia-linked interests buying land and property next to strategically important facilities and choke points – a process that was entirely legal at the time. The Finnish authorities were eventually able to take action because of the dubious business models of some of the entities involved. In late 2018, tax police backed by military personnel and air surveillance support raided seventeen properties across Finland, in a 'crackdown on money laundering and cheating on tax and pension payments'. The highest-profile raid was on Säkkiluoto, one of the many islands off the western coast of Finland, which had been the site of a wide range of unexplained activity that raised Finnish suspicions. Former military intelligence chief Pekka Toveri explained the danger signs: 'The location was close to important sea lines of

---

126. Michael Kofman, 'Russia's armed forces under Gerasimov, the man without a doctrine', *RIDDLE Russia*, 1 April 2020, https://www.ridl.io/en/russia-s-armed-forces-under-gerasimov-the-man-without-a-doctrine/.

communications and underwater cables. Building a big compound for recreational activities without any visitors didn't seem like a normal business. Since the owners managed to get permission to fly helicopters directly from abroad to the islands, the authorities didn't really have any control on foreigners in the compound. The owner also bought used Finnish Navy boats from auctions, but didn't change the original Navy painting scheme, which is quite unusual. There was also tight security in the island.' The concerns seemed justified: the police raid found an extensive complex with multiple piers, a helipad and 'enough housing to accommodate a small army', plus a stash of cash in multiple currencies including several million euro.[127]

The incident fed enduring concerns that covert networks of Russian enablers have been established in European countries who in time of crisis could be mobilized for direct action in support of a hostile military operation – along the pattern of the Night Wolves in Crimea (see Chapter 5).[128] This includes those established under cover of martial arts clubs, some of them with overt links to Russian special forces or intelligence organizations.[129] Here, too, little has changed since Soviet times, when in addition to KGB and GRU units that were tasked in wartime with sabotage and disruption attacks to destroy important facilities, eliminate key political and military personnel and create panic among the civilian population through terror attacks, the USSR set up agent networks in the target country in advance to support these operations. According to a 1984 US manual, 'The KGB and GRU recruit agents in vital areas of the enemy's social structure – in political circles, in his intelligence services, at all levels of the military, within key industries, in a variety of academic institutions, and in the media – press, radio and television. Some of these agents actively engage in subversion, while others are "sleepers", prepared to act on call.'[130] Pekka Toveri added that the facilities on Säkkiluoto 'reminded me of the Soviet regimental commanders stationed in East Germany who scouted their planned attack routes in West Germany disguised as truck drivers. Islands like that in [the] Finnish archipelago would make it very easy to scout, prepare and exercise wartime sabotage and intelligence activities.'

David Kilcullen also talks about Russia planning for the 'shaping phase' of laying the groundwork for a military option before it begins in a way that should

---

127. Andrew Higgins, 'Finnish soldiers find "secret Russian military bases" after raiding mysterious island', *Independent*, 1 November 2018, https://www.independent.co.uk/news/world/europe/finland-russia-military-bases-sakkiluoto-putin-dmitry-medvedev-police-a8612161.html.

128. 'Putins Geheimtruppe wartet auf ein Signal' (Putin's secret troops are waiting for a signal), *Deutsche Welle*, 18 April 2016, https://www.dw.com/de/putins-geheimtruppe-wartet-auf-ein-signal/a-19195549.

129. Andrew Rettman, 'Fight club: Russian spies seek EU recruits', *EU Observer*, 23 May 2017.

130. 'The Soviet Army: Specialized Warfare and Rear Area Support', FM 100-2-2, US Army, 16 July 1984.

ensure its success. The aim, he says, is that 'by the time an enemy commander realizes they're actually in a conflict, they should have already lost. By the time the first tank rolls, or the first airstrike goes in, the operation should already have got to the point where success is inevitable.' But that also offers the target country an opportunity to prevent it, David goes on, 'The flip side of that is that if they don't believe they've succeeded in that, the tanks may never roll or the airstrike never happen. What that means is the shaping phase is decisive. You're going to win or lose there.'[131]

The apparent absence of this process in Russia's assault on Ukraine, and Moscow's failure to even consider whether it was going to win or lose, is one of the startling ways in which Russia failed to follow its own doctrine – a failure explained in part by the inability of Russia's leaders to grasp that Ukraine is a foreign country (see Chapter 4). Elsewhere, the deliberate creation of uncertainty and ambiguity plays a key role in Russia achieving its aims unchallenged. Sulev Suvari says that keeping their opponents guessing is an equalizer for Moscow: 'They realize that when they are weak, that's the one area that they can make advancement, by creating these areas of puzzlement or confusion and then being able to take advantage of it.' This was shown dramatically in Georgia in 2008 and Ukraine in 2014, where Russia succeeded briefly in preventing Western general publics from seeing what was happening, and for a much longer period succeeded in preventing their governments from delivering a unified, coherent and effective response to the crises. Sulev explains how 'They purposely create confusion because it's an opportunity. NATO is vulnerable because they can't make a decision fast, and Russia uses that to their advantage.'

In operations that aim to stop just short of open warfare, David Kilcullen uses the phrase 'liminal zone' for the time Russia has between its adversary detecting something has happened and the adversary mustering enough understanding and political consensus on what that something is and that Russia was behind it to deliver a response. Russia exploits this delay where possible, David says; 'A Russian style of operations has emerged with a very careful sequencing and integration of different activities to stay in that liminal space, and get done what you need to get done and get back down below the detection threshold before an adversary can respond.' The lack of clear dividing lines between the state, business and crime (see Chapter 7) also aids in this ambiguity because it means no adversary can grasp a clear organizational chart and division of responsibilities within the Russian system. Former FBI agent Peter Strzok explains how this means that 'the Russians have become much more skilled at carrying out operations that can't easily be attributed to them . . . You have people within the formal state apparatus interacting with oligarchs, with various elements in organized crime, plus people within the

131. 'Russian Spetsnaz in the Grey Zone', Russia Strategic Initiative, 19 August 2021, https://community.apan.org/wg/rsi/project-connect/w/events/29786/rsi-connect-russian-spetsnaz-in-the-grey-zone/.

intelligence community floating in and out of all of these different sources of power.[132] The problem is even worse when Western politicians use the uncertainty as an excuse not to take action against Russia at all when it denies involvement in an incident. As Sven Sakkov explains of the Russian troops who seized Crimea in 2014, 'the problem with attribution lay not on the battlefield, but in the heads of people in the West, who did not want to face the facts, but instead to find a way of ignoring them by saying "we do not know who they are"'.

The overall effect is Russia creating confusion among Western decision-makers and then exploiting it to get things done. As well as major campaigns like the seizure of Crimea, this operates on a day-to-day basis in theatres like Syria, where 'Russian forces could overfly U.S. positions – and drop weapons nearby – without eliciting a response from the Air Force because it was near impossible to discern Russian intent'.[133]

Meanwhile, a key aspect of Russia's approach even in notional peacetime is to probe and provoke its NATO adversaries, but not enough to cause military escalation that exceeds the Kremlin's tolerances. This includes the steady drumbeat of Russian activity run against NATO allies and partners – at sea, in the air over the North and Baltic and Black seas, in less visible domains such as space, and cyber and electromagnetic activities – all intended to probe for vulnerabilities, to test reactions, and to prepare for the eventuality of open conflict with the West as a whole. How that conflict may look – and how it might differ from what we have seen in Ukraine – is the subject of the next chapter.

132. 'Anne Applebaum Interviews Peter Strzok', *The Atlantic*, 4 September 2020, https://www.theatlantic.com/ideas/archive/2020/09/anne-applebaum-interviews-peter-strzok/616003/.

133. Aaron Stein and Ryan Fishel, 'Syria, Airpower, and the Future of Great-Power War', *War on the Rocks*, 13 August 2021, https://warontherocks.com/2021/08/syria-airpower-and-the-future-of-great-power-war/.

# Chapter 4

## WHAT THE RUSSIAN ARMY IS FOR

*Russia and its military*

As described in the previous chapter, Russia is developing the means of attacking countries without going to war and exploiting them to the full. But this is as well as, not instead of, having poured vast quantities of money and resources into developing its Armed Forces to be ready for major, full-on war.[1] Some – but far from all – aspects of that development have been in plain view in the early stages of the war on Ukraine.

Military power has always held a unique place in Russia's idea of what it means to be a country, and in particular what it means to be a great power. For Moscow, military power is the absolute foundation of statehood: how much of it you have determines how you can behave as a country. Tsar Alexander III said – regularly, apparently – that Russia had only two allies, its army and its navy. Later, in Soviet times, it was pointed out that the Soviet Union did not *have* a war machine, it *was* a war machine, because every national effort and every sector of the economy was subordinated to sustaining the Armed Forces. From the mid-2000s on, after a brief interlude of national poverty, Russia once again made the rebuilding of its military a core national priority.

Some European nations continue to think that maintaining strong standing armies, and investing in modern capabilities for them, is an old-fashioned way of ensuring your national security. But for as long as Russia clings to a traditional view that possessing brute military force gives you the right to use it, any neglect of military power to match Russia's is a dangerous game. Chief of the General Staff Valery Gerasimov laid out Russia's response to developments in war-fighting, far from turning to focus on sub-threshold efforts, as improving conventional and nuclear readiness for high-end, high-intensity, high-technology war. This included investing in nuclear rearmament, precision guided weapons, electronic warfare,

---

1. A 400-page guide to how the Russian Army is organized to fight, compiled by Lester Grau and Charles Bartles of the US Army's Foreign Military Studies Office, is available at https://www.armyupress.army.mil/Portals/7/Hot%20Spots/Documents/Russia/2017-07-The-Russian-Way-of-War-Grau-Bartles.pdf.

long-range strategic aviation and making sure that the Russian economy was ready to be put on a war footing.[2]

Russia calls the use of non-military tools to attack a country's political stability or economy 'New Type Warfare'. But importantly, it sees these tools as being coordinated with conventional military capabilities that can inflict physical damage, such as missile or air strikes. And under some circumstances, these strikes can be delivered before the actual fighting has begun. According to Michael Kofman, an American researcher who has studied the development of Russia's military tools and thinking extensively, Russia's military is 'geared towards being able to pre-emptively neutralize an emerging threat or deter by showing the ability and willingness to inflict unacceptable consequences on the potential adversary'.[3] While Russia is not necessarily looking for any and all opportunities on a daily basis to strike a military blow against the West, it wants to be fully ready to respond to threats – or opportunities – when they present themselves.[4]

A regularly updated Swedish survey of how Russian military power is developing assessed in 2019 that 'the next ten years will consolidate previous achievements, notably the ability to launch a regional war. Strategic deterrence, primarily with nuclear forces, will remain the foremost priority.'[5] This doesn't just affect Europe. Unsurprisingly, Russia is currently considered the 'primary military threat to the American homeland'. What may be more surprising is that this is not just because of nuclear weapons. After decades of development, 'advanced cruise missiles in Russia's arsenal have the range to strike the United States when launched from inside Russian territory'.[6] (At the same time the US reportedly relies on antiquated analogue systems for transmitting information to command centres, meaning that minutes need to be spent reporting potential incoming strikes by telephone.)[7] And Russia had supposedly taken advantage of combat operations in Syria to learn lessons that are applied all the way up and down the military,

2. Valeriy Gerasimov, 'Мир на гранях войны' (The world on the edge of war), *Военно-промышленный курьер*, 13 March 2017, https://vpk-news.ru/articles/35591.

3. Kofman, 'Russia's armed forces under Gerasimov'.

4. Neal G. Jesse, *Learning From Russia's Recent Wars: Why, Where, and When Russia Might Strike Next* (Amherst, NY: Cambria Press, 2020), pp. 214–15.

5. Susanne Oxenstierna et al., 'Russian Military Capability in a Ten-Year Perspective – 2019', FOI (Swedish Defence Research Agency), December 2019, https://www.foi.se/en/foi/reports/report-summary.html?reportNo=FOI-R--4758--SE.

6. John Grady, 'Russia is Top Military Threat to U.S. Homeland, Air Force General Says', USNI News, 18 August 2021, https://news.usni.org/2021/08/18/russia-is-top-military-threat-to-u-s-homeland-air-force-general-says.

7. Amy McCullough, 'NORTHCOM Presses Case for New Approach to Homeland Defense', *Air Force Magazine*, 18 August 2021, https://www.airforcemag.com/northcom-new-approach-homeland-defense/.

including ongoing efforts within the army to induce junior commanders to 'learn to act unconventionally [and] think outside the box in the fight for superiority'.[8]

But Syria and later Ukraine also illustrated how some traditional features of Russian warfighting remain unchanged. When Russia does go to war, it shows little to no respect for humanitarian concerns or the laws of armed conflict that guide Western armies. In fact, barbarity and atrocities are a consistent feature of Russian campaigning through history, both in total war and in more limited conflicts. In the twenty-first century, this highlights an important difference between abuses carried out by the Russian military and security services, and those carried out by most of their Western counterparts. If US or British forces break the law, or cause civilian casualties, this is a mistake or an aberration, and one that is thoroughly investigated and, if necessary, punished. Russian forces, by contrast, use collateral damage and civilian casualties as a systematic and methodical means of terrorizing the enemy and their civilian support base into submission.[9] The rationale, where one is offered, is that this is the swiftest and most reliable means of winning the conflict and restoring order, and the result of crushing the will to resist is swiftly delivered peace and stability as opposed to enduring chaos and destabilization.

Russia's wars in Chechnya during the 1990s were rife with examples of senseless inhumanity on both sides.[10] But Chechnya's eventual condition once the fighting was over – pulverized and terrorized but stable – was far preferable in Russia's view to before it began, when a degree of autonomy left Chechen bandit groups free to spread terror across southern Russia. Chechnya was eventually reconstructed and is now ruled by a feudal overlord whose loyalty to Moscow is tenuous and expensive, but who keeps order. This model provided a template for Russia's operations and eventual goal in Syria – where Russian and Russian-backed war crimes against civilian targets caused even more widespread horror because they were played out in plain view of the world.[11]

Syria in fact served as the proving ground for an intensive programme for Russia's Armed Forces under operational conditions, including their organization, their logistics, their weapons systems and their people. Innocent civilians suffered

---

8.  A. V. Dvornikov and R. R. Nasybulin, 'Актуальные направления совершенствования боевой подготовки войск с учетом опыта, полученного в Сирии' (Current Ways To Improve Combat Training of Troops Using Experience Obtained in Syria), *Voyennaya mysl'* (July 2021): 100–10, https://vm.ric.mil.ru/upload/site178/pdj6wywh3M.pdf.

9.  Christiaan Triebert et al., 'How Times Reporters Proved Russia Bombed Syrian Hospitals', *New York Times*, 13 October 2019, https://www.nytimes.com/2019/10/13/reader-center/russia-syria-hospitals-investigation.html.

10.  Maura Reynolds, 'War Has No Rules for Russian Forces Fighting in Chechnya', *Los Angeles Times*, 17 September 2000, https://www.latimes.com/archives/la-xpm-2000-sep-17-mn-22524-story.html.

11.  Kavitha Surana, 'Russian Embassy: Grozny is the "solution" for Aleppo', *Foreign Policy*, 17 October 2016, https://foreignpolicy.com/2016/10/17/russian-embassy-grozny-is-the-solution-for-aleppo-syria-war-john-kerry/.

in the process, and especially when Russia used weapons systems that were not obviously suitable for the task at hand in order to assess their performance. After the brief war between Armenia and Azerbaijan in 2020, Armenian Prime Minister Nikol Pashinyan complained publicly that the Russian Iskander missile systems used by the Armenian Army hadn't worked. Russia's Ministry of Defence responded with footage of Iskanders being successfully used in Syria – against a hospital.[12]

But Russia's way of war has remained consistent because it consistently brings success. And that involves targeting populated areas to cause the maximum suffering among civilians and force its victims to submit in order to bring that suffering to an end. Murder, rape, looting and the deliberate engineering of humanitarian disasters to cause the greatest possible human suffering among civilians are the default setting for Russia's Army today just as they have been throughout history. And deportations of Ukrainian citizens to Russia – repeating the programmes of subjugation and exile for the territories Russia occupied during and after the Second World War like Poland and the Baltic states – are another horrifying confirmation that Russia thinks Stalin's methods are the answer to its problems.[13]

The tragedy for Ukraine, and Syria before it, is that these tactics are made all the more devastating by Russia's twenty-first-century weapons of destruction. In Syria, many at first thought that Russian bomb and missile strikes on civilian infrastructure including hospitals, schools and water treatment plants were the result of incompetence or error. They only gradually realized that this was in fact deliberate policy – seeking to bring the conflict to a successful conclusion through ensuring that civilian support for resistance was crushed.[14]

And only five days after the beginning of the war on Ukraine, Russia began to implement what it sees as the war-winning tactic of besieging and bombarding cities and exploiting the destruction of their infrastructure to leave their inhabitants facing intolerable conditions. Russia wants to present its victims with the agonizing calculation of how long civilians who have remained in major cities can survive in underground shelters while Russia does its best to deny them access to food, water and medical supplies. The only restraining factor on Russia's campaign of destruction is likely to be the knowledge that cities that have been reduced to rubble are harder to fight in and capture than ones that can be seized intact.

The systematic adoption of terror and brutality wherever Russia wages war reflects a persistent belief that 'the way you win these things is to be more brutal

12. Tweet by CIT (en), 26 February 2021, https://twitter.com/CITeam_en/status/1365257023521230851

13. 'Mariupol says Russia forcefully deported thousands of people', Reuters, 20 March 2022, https://www.reuters.com/world/europe/ukraines-mariupol-says-russia-forcefully-deported-thousands-its-people-2022-03-20/.

14. 'Syria/Russia: Strategy Targeted Civilian Infrastructure', Human Rights Watch, 15 October 2020, https://www.hrw.org/news/2020/10/15/syria/russia-strategy-targeted-civilian-infrastructure/.

than the Europeans', says Alexander Clarkson, a historian at King's College London.[15] The chilling conclusion was already clear before Ukraine: that in conflict in Europe, there was no reason to think Russian forces would behave there with any less barbarity and savagery against military and civilian opponents alike than they did in the twentieth century.

## Rebuilding the forces

But other things certainly have changed. On 9 May each year Russia holds its Victory Day parade. Alongside the increasing role of historical pageantry in the parade, it's a chance for Russia to flaunt its latest and best military technology – or, at least, what it wants its public and foreign observers to think is the latest and greatest. In May 2013, I was in Moscow late at night standing beside the parade route, watching a rehearsal for the big event. And I was confused. At first I thought that foreign troops had been invited to join in, because the army I was looking at was nothing like the Russian Army that I had by then been studying and writing about for almost a decade. The uniforms, the helmets, the equipment, the vehicles were all new, different and visible improvements on what Russian soldiers had been using up until that time – which had been not much changed since the end of the Soviet Union. And this unrecognizable new Russian military was the one that less than a year later surprised the world by moving on Crimea.

Russia had embarked on a huge, and hugely expensive, programme of rearming, re-equipping and reorganizing its Armed Forces after the conflict with Georgia in 2008 showed serious deficiencies in their performance. Conveniently, this coincided with a huge influx of wealth into Russia, and state budget surpluses, linked to a high and rising oil price. There was a lot of work to be done: Reiner Schwalb recalls how 'the military was in truly a catastrophic state, after not just years, but decades of underfunding and neglect'. But more than a decade later, Reiner too described the Russian Armed Forces as unrecognizable from their previous selves.

Russia was keen to project an image of being more capable than it really is, to bolster its efforts at military intimidation. Before the attack on Ukraine, Reiner Schwalb was one of the few Western observers to note that 'Russia is not as far advanced as they would wish us to believe. The state of the Russian military as we know it is probably halfway between psychological warfare and fact.' Still, the rearmament drive provided the Russian armed forces with hundreds of advanced aircraft and helicopters, thousands of new or modernized armoured vehicles, new submarines, missiles and much more. Service personnel benefited too – there have been huge increases in pay and allowances since 2005 (including tripling

---

15. Jack Losh, 'In Central Africa, Russia Won the War – But It's Losing the Peace', *Foreign Policy*, 21 August 2021, https://foreignpolicy.com/2021/08/21/in-central-africa-russia-won-the-war-but-its-losing-the-peace/.

overnight). But as well as investing in people and capabilities, Russia has rebuilt the way its military is organized, to be more useful in situations other than all-out war. Tor Bukkvoll explains that 'Rearmament was important, but it's still secondary to the reorganisation, from the big mobilization forces to the much smaller but more ready forces that they have today. We have a word in Norwegian, *gripbar*, which means something that you can grab and use immediately.'

That availability for immediate use was honed by repeated exercises practising delivering force to Russia's western borders, as well as by intense training and testing of Russian weapons, organizations and people. US Air Force pilot Nick Caraballo watched this process first-hand in his interactions in the air with Russian fighter pilots. 'In my experience with them over the last five years,' he said in 2021, 'I've seen them improve, and seen them become more professional, more capable; things that they couldn't do previously they can do now.'

The funds poured into redeveloping Moscow's military power have been vast, but affordable. Modernization and renewal throughout the forces has been eased by the fact that by Western standards, in many cases the actual costs are relatively low. Richard Connolly is an economist who has been looking closely at what Russia spends on its military for a number of years. He points out that in almost all cases the way people measure Russia's defence budget against other countries is effectively meaningless, because it uses a market exchange rate into dollars for comparison – but Russia isn't spending dollars. In Russia's relatively self-contained economy, it is what the budget will buy for real that counts rather than translating it into a notional American equivalent. (Some defence analysts say that instead of getting more bang for the buck, Russia gets more rubble for the rouble.) In addition, the direct comparisons overlook the ways in which Western defence budgets are directed sometimes towards very different ends to what Russia actually wants to achieve. Russia's overall spending may not be the highest in the world, but combined with the intent to use it to cause damage it becomes far more potent.

While the process of building and refining the Armed Forces was put to the test in Ukraine – and in many ways found wanting – Russia was still intent on preparing for a much larger conflict. According to an Estonian security report, 'Russia shows no sign of having revised its long-term strategy for the Armed Forces, which is to increase readiness for a full-scale confrontation with NATO.'[16] This is a sharp contrast to what NATO was doing over the same period. Sven Sakkov recalls how 'Basically NATO was fixated on Afghanistan for a long time, and all its military capabilities and thinking needed to deter Russia were atrophying. NATO allies didn't pay attention, and many required military capabilities were left to rot.'

Even before the attack on Ukraine, Russian and NATO forces had begun operating in close proximity to each other in various parts of the world more frequently than they had done since the end of the Cold War. This now happens on

16. 'International Security and Estonia', Välisluureamet (Estonian Foreign Intelligence Service), February 2021, https://www.valisluureamet.ee/pdf/raport/2021-ENG.pdf.

land, at sea, in the air and in the less visible domains of subsea, space, cyber and electronic warfare. But it's in the air that the two sides get the best chance to observe each other closely. Nick Caraballo explains that as well as developing and introducing new and more capable aircraft, Russia has worked hard on improving how it makes use of them. 'They have some formidable capabilities,' he says. 'At least on paper, they are good. Now, what they are working on, I think, is bridging that gap between the technological capabilities and the capabilities in the cockpit. From what I've seen airborne, they're getting better.'

That learning process includes flights that test the responses of likely adversaries. In 2020, there were more Russian air incursions into US air defence identification zones than at any time since the end of the Cold War.[17] The tempo is even more intense in the area around Japan, whose Air Self-Defense Force (JASDF) scrambles on an almost daily basis to intercept and identify Russian aircraft approaching Japan's territorial airspace.[18] When this happens in the UK's area of responsibility, British air power researcher Justin Bronk says, the majority of interactions 'are entirely professional and entirely by the book, they don't violate our airspace. They stick outside in international airspace and with everybody follows the standard procedures and you know, there's some waving and mutual photo taking and that's kind of it.' But at periods of heightened tension, Russia chooses to disrupt civilian air traffic – and does so without consequences.

When Russian military aircraft fly through civilian air corridors around the UK without cooperating with air traffic control (ATC), it puts ordinary airliners at risk and it falls to the RAF to reduce the danger. ATC's 'primary radar' does not give accurate enough position information to ensure aircraft keep at a safe distance from each other in busy airspace, Justin explains. So safety relies on aircraft using transponders that send back information with a radar signal, including accurate height, speed and heading. This means that Russian aircraft that do not switch their transponders on, or file a flight plan, pose a deliberate and distinct danger to other air traffic. 'Flying across civilian airways without transponders on means air traffic control have to reroute things,' Justin goes on, 'especially if the Russians start doing things like changing height bands – because keeping at a safe distance is done as much on height band as it is on horizontal separation.'

Here, as elsewhere, the safety of ordinary people depends on the armed forces of Western countries behaving responsibly while Russia is doing the opposite. 'Without the RAF doing something about it quite actively, that is dangerous. Now, they do it in the knowledge that the RAF will do something about it. That should worry the public,' Justin says. But the UK MOD's reluctance to acknowledge the full nature and extent of Russian hostile activity means that more often than not, the public simply doesn't know.

17.  Grady, 'Russia is Top Military Threat to U.S. Homeland'.

18. 'Warnings and Emergency Takeoffs (Scrambles) in Preparation against Intrusion of Territorial Airspace', in *Defense of Japan 2021* (Tokyo: Japanese Ministry of Defense), p. 28, https://www.mod.go.jp/en/publ/w_paper/wp2021/DOJ2021_Digest_EN.pdf.

Where Russian air activity near the UK is reported in the media, the reports are usually distorted by enduring confusion in media reporting as to what exactly constitutes national airspace – but also as to what exactly the Russian aircraft are doing, and where.[19] The idea persists that in order to pose a threat, a hostile aircraft has to be directly overhead, as in the times of the Blitz and other aerial campaigns during the Second World War. But the picture now is very different. Russian aircraft can launch their cruise missiles from hundreds of kilometres away, well outside the boundaries of national airspace – in exactly the way airstrikes on Ukraine were launched in 2022 from the safety of Russian skies. In Western sources, the Tupolev Tu-160 Blackjack is commonly referred to as a 'bomber', but in Russian, its designation is the far more accurate 'missile carrier'. Tupolev's official website says that it is 'designed to destroy targets in remote geographic areas and deep in the rear of continental theaters of operations'.[20] What this means is that Blackjacks and other similar aircraft do not need to be in close proximity to the UK or any other country to practise their attack runs. This often takes place 'up near the Arctic', Justin Bronk explains. 'They regularly practise sorties out to that part of the world and do launch type drills ... There's quite a wide range of potential targets that could be intended to simulate because [of] the range of the missile. It could be threatening Norway, it could be threatening Sweden, it could be threatening any of Denmark, France, Belgium, UK or the United States. But for the Bears and the Blackjacks, that's their nuclear mission – it's their bread and butter.'

## How the West responds

Western countries seem to work hard to behave responsibly in the face of the growing Russian threat, and look for ways to reduce the likelihood of an actual clash. New arms control agreements have been regularly suggested as a way of calming relations with Russia. But these suggestions are based on the assumption that Russia places the same priority on limiting the number and capabilities of weapons and armaments available to each side. With the trends of military power in Europe firmly in Russia's favour after its epic military overhaul, there was a basic flaw in this idea – there was no reason to think Russia was interested. Until Europe begins to take its weaknesses seriously and starts to show resolve in addressing them, there is still no incentive for the Kremlin to enter into any serious negotiations on any major security issue there.[21]

19. Megan Baynes, 'RAF Typhoons intercept Russian "Cold War era" aircraft flying near UK airspace', Sky News, 6 August 2021, https://news.sky.com/story/raf-typhoons-intercept-russian-cold-war-era-aircraft-flying-near-uk-airspace-12374951.

20. https://www.tupolev.ru/en/planes/tu-160/.

21. Stephen Blank, 'Mission Impossible: pursuing arms control with Putin's Russia', European Leadership Network, 19 January 2018, https://www.europeanleadershipnetwork.org/policy-brief/mission-impossible-pursuing-arms-control-with-putins-russia/.

In addition, proposals for new arms control agreements to replace those that have become void in recent years will go nowhere if they disregard the fact that Russia stepped away from the previous agreements deliberately and for very specific reasons and goals.[22] A prime example is the Intermediate-Range Nuclear Forces (INF) Treaty. Signed in 1987, this was a breakthrough in reducing tensions between the US and the USSR towards the end of the Cold War. It eliminated all US and Soviet nuclear and conventional ground-launched ballistic and cruise missiles with ranges of 500 to 5,500 kilometres. This included the American cruise missiles that during the 1980s had been the subject of extensive protests in Europe, for instance at Greenham Common in the UK – and those missiles' counterparts in the Soviet Union, where any similar protest would have earned swift and vicious reprisals from the KGB.[23]

But after the Cold War ended, Russia found the INF treaty no longer suited its needs. Faced with the deterioration of its conventional military power and the fact that it could no longer comfortably assume victory over NATO – together with the shrinking of its security perimeter back to Russia's own borders, instead of controlling the whole of eastern Europe – Russia felt keenly the lack of the capabilities that missiles of this range would offer. Consequently, Russia spent two decades developing and testing new missiles that were in direct breach of the treaty.[24] Over many years, the US accused Russia of non-compliance with the treaty, but until 2017 was reluctant to present the evidence, possibly because of concerns over revealing their source of information on a missile programme that Russia was still keeping a secret. Finally, Donald Trump announced that the US would be withdrawing from the treaty, and in August 2019 both parties effectively declared the treaty dead.

While Russia had been busy deploying large numbers of its new missiles in Europe, it was also keen to present the US as being at fault for the end of the treaty, and itself as the innocent party.[25] So, shortly afterwards, Russia proposed a new international ban on deploying any more of these same missiles – which it could do quite comfortably, because now it had them, and the US and its allies did not.[26]

22. 'Missile Misdemeanours: Russia and the INF Treaty: Government response to the Committee's Fifteenth Report of Session 2017–19', UK Parliament, 4 June 2019, https://publications.parliament.uk/pa/cm201719/cmselect/cmdfence/2464/246402.htm.

23. 'The Intermediate-Range Nuclear Forces (INF) Treaty at a Glance', Arms Control Association, August 2019, https://www.armscontrol.org/factsheets/INFtreaty.

24. Stefan Forss, 'Russia's New Intermediate Range Missiles – Back to the 1970s', Atlantic Council, 6 April 2017, https://www.atlanticcouncil.org/blogs/natosource/russia-s-new-intermediate-range-missiles-back-to-the-1970s/.

25. 'Russian Compliance with the Intermediate Range Nuclear Forces (INF) Treaty: Background and Issues for Congress', Congressional Research Service, 2 August 2019, https://fas.org/sgp/crs/nuke/R43832.pdf.

26. Joe Gould, 'NATO members set to say they won't deploy land-based nukes in Europe', *Defense News*, 12 June 2021, https://www.defensenews.com/global/europe/2021/06/12/nato-is-preparing-to-ban-land-based-nukes-in-europe/.

This was a pretence at cooperation offered in the classic Russian style: first to change the status quo in its favour, then as a perceived concession to offer to make the change permanent. In other words, a return to treaty arrangements would only 'cement in place Russia's complete missile superiority in Europe, where NATO countries currently have no surface-to-surface short-range missile systems, let alone medium-range ones. Once again, Russia is presenting itself as being open to cooperation by offering concessions that only appear as such.'[27]

Veterans of arms control negotiations say the US and Russia approach the problem from completely different perspectives. The US is altruistic, seeking to improve global security and reduce potential dangers for both sides. Russia, and the USSR before it, saw the process as completely transactional, depending on what the US wants that Moscow can deliver, or vice versa, and what price will have to be paid for it.[28] The second key difference is that Russia's counterparts typically abide by the rules, while Russia routinely violates them. Pekka Toveri describes his experience of arms control verification visits to Russia very simply: 'The Russians lied all the time and didn't show anything.' On the other hand, it's clear when agreements are important for Russia – as shown by the speed with which the Russian parliament ratified a five-year extension to a strategic nuclear weapons treaty (called New START in the US, and START-3 in Russia), agreed with President Joe Biden less than a week after his inauguration. Russia doesn't want to repeat the Soviet experience of bankrupting itself by losing an unlimited arms race with the US. But in addition, the treaty is highly symbolic for Russia. Nuclear weapons are one of the few areas where Russia is on a par with the US as a global power – and one it considers to be a key part of its national status. A direct deal with America ticks all the right boxes.[29]

In other areas, Russia is following an ongoing process of stepping away from treaties that limit not only the numbers of Russian weapons but also what Russia can do with them. Ordinarily, Moscow finds a way to make it look as though the other party to the treaty is at fault for it failing. Another international agreement that follows the same pattern is the Open Skies Treaty, a multinational security arrangement set up immediately after the Cold War. Intended to build contacts and confidence between countries by observing each other's armed forces, the treaty allowed unarmed reconnaissance flights over the territory of each of the countries involved. Just as with INF, the US withdrew from the treaty complaining that Russia was routinely breaching it.[30] A former RAF pilot explained to me how

27. 'International Security and Estonia', Välisluureamet (Estonian Foreign Intelligence Service), February 2021, https://www.valisluureamet.ee/pdf/raport/2021-ENG.pdf.

28. Franklin Miller, speaking at 'Zapad 2021, Biden–Putin Summit, and their implications for U.S. and European security', CSIS, 17 June 2021.

29. Witold Rodkiewicz, 'Russia obtains an extension to the START-3 treaty', OSW, 4 February 2021, https://www.osw.waw.pl/en/publikacje/analyses/2021-02-04/russia-obtains-extension-to-start-3-treaty.

30. 'The Open Skies Treaty at a Glance', Arms Control Association, June 2021, https://www.armscontrol.org/factsheets/openskies.

Russia abused the treaty, using overflights of the UK to examine civilian critical national infrastructure instead of military installations, and then when British missions overflew Russia, having them redirected by air traffic control at the last minute away from the area they wished to photograph and instead to parts of the country completely covered by cloud.

According to Pekka Toveri, that is also the approach taken with arrangements for observers to watch each other's military exercises. 'The Russians got full transparency [from the West], whereas the Russian exercises were either divided into 'different exercises', or just announced as smaller than they actually were. Or the Western inspection teams were taken to exercise fields that were empty,' he says.

Looking at how Western countries deal with non-military threats (see Chapter 3) shows clearly the benefits of being open and honest about what Russia is doing. But NATO militaries and defence ministries are still far from applying this principle when it comes not only to Russian deceptive practices around arms control, but also to ongoing hostile Russian activities against Western armed forces. The extent and volume of Russian hostile activity remains largely outside the public consciousness. And it is not at all clear to people like me, who don't have access to secret information but receive occasional fragmentary and anecdotal glimpses into what is going on, why the UK, NATO and other countries are so reticent and reluctant to let it be known.

As Nick Caraballo puts it, 'In my experience, there is a large gap in public knowledge about what we do in the air force, what the military with the RAF and all the different agencies out there that are NATO are countering, dealing with Russia on a day-to-day basis … Though the public only sees the occasional headline, there's stuff going on all the time in the background.' This has two serious consequences. First, it often allows Russia to set the headlines unchallenged, instead of NATO countries like the UK and US competing for the attention of their publics. Second, those same publics remain critically under-informed about the nature of the threat – and therefore, less likely to support the essential measures (and investment) needed to counter it.

The UK's MOD in particular is habitually highly secretive about what Russia does against the UK and its Armed Forces – at sea, in the air and in cyber and electromagnetic warfare. When I wanted to interview British soldiers deployed to the front-line states about their experiences, it could only be done with the supervision of MOD handlers – who vetoed any questions about direct or indirect ways Russia targets British forces there. Similarly, when reports emerged that the families of Dutch fighter pilots deployed to Estonia were being threatened at home, the Dutch military intelligence service told media that it was 'familiar with this practice, but would not say anything further about it'.[31] Cyber attacks on the British armed forces that cause direct and enormously expensive damage are covered up.

31. '"Russians" threatening Dutch F-16 pilots' family', *NL Times*, 9 August 2017, https://nltimes.nl/2019/08/09/russians-threatening-dutch-f-16-pilots-family.

In early 2021, the Defence Academy of the UK suffered a devastating supply chain hack, which made its email servers unusable and records inaccessible. After several months of limping along, according to both staff and students I spoke to, the decision was taken that the only thing to do with the existing IT system was to 'burn it to the ground and start again'. And yet, there was no public reporting of this major incident until dogged investigation by journalist Deborah Haynes brought the story to light almost a year later.[32]

Instead, the MOD still seems to rely both on obsolete methods and on obsolete measures of success for its information activities – like attaching undue importance to stories appearing in a printed newspaper. This is the only imaginable reason why it repeatedly uses paywalled papers to get out critical messaging, instead of public statements – including to Parliament – that all traditional media outlets, broadcasters and social media can pick up and pass on. At a time when communication is so vitally important, it is hard to fathom why the British government tries to reach people by providing articles to newspapers like *The Telegraph* when in doing so it fails to reach the vast majority of the country that doesn't subscribe to them – or indeed to any hard copy newspaper at all.[33]

As if to prove the rule, when public reporting of military incidents between Russia and Western countries does happen, it repeatedly provides examples of how not to do it. Johnny Stringer was the UK's Air Component Commander in the Middle East in the year to October 2017. After handing over his command, he detailed how overcautious civilian and military leaders had regularly left Russia and others in control of the information space in Syria and Iraq. 'Dignified silences will be filled by other people,' he was quoted as saying. 'If we are not willing to operate in the information space, we cede it to others.'[34] This pattern continues. In June 2021, the Royal Navy warship HMS *Defender* sailed past the coast of Crimea and was challenged by Russia. Russian state media said warning shots had been fired, bombs dropped in *Defender*'s path, and that it had been forced to change course away from Crimea. The UK's response was badly fumbled. Early reporting in major Western media noted 'silence from UK MOD'. This slow reaction allowed Russian storylines to take over and run riot.[35] But worse mistakes followed. In a

32. Deborah Haynes, 'Cyber attack on UK's Defence Academy had "significant" impact, officer in charge at the time reveals', Sky News, 2 January 2022, https://news.sky.com/story/cyber-attack-on-uks-defence-academy-had-significant-impact-officer-in-charge-at-the-time-reveals-12507570.

33. As, for example, Ben Wallace, UK Secretary of State for Defence, 'We have not betrayed Afghanistan', *Telegraph*, 14 August 2021, https://www.telegraph.co.uk/news/2021/08/14/have-not-betrayed-afghanistan/.

34. Tim Ripley, *Operation Aleppo: Russia's War in Syria* (n.p.p.: Telic-Herrick Publications, 2018), p. 192.

35. Dan Sabbagh and Andrew Roth, 'Britain acknowledges surprise at speed of Russian reaction to warship', *Guardian*, 24 June 2021, https://www.theguardian.com/uk-news/2021/jun/24/british-warships-might-enter-crimean-waters-again-says-minister.

departure from its normal habit of secrecy, the UK MOD had given journalists a front-row seat by allowing them to join HMS *Defender* for the most sensitive part of its mission. Breathless first-hand descriptions by BBC correspondent Jonathan Beale on board reported close passes by Russian aircraft, radio warnings that the ship would be fired on, and that HMS *Defender* was harassed by vessels of Russia's coastguard. This seemed to support the Russian story, and was in stark contrast to bland statements downplaying the incident eventually released by the MOD.

After years of deceit and disinformation, the Russian version of any given incident is automatically suspect. But it is also vital for the UK to get its own story straight. The credibility of the UK's Armed Forces relies on honest and truthful reporting of what they are doing. Instead, that essential credibility was challenged by the clear and obvious gap between the MOD version and first-hand accounts from the journalists that it had itself invited on board. In effect, the MOD pretended nothing was happening when it plainly was – precisely what Russia has so often been accused of.

As the security and defence editor for Sky News, Deborah Haynes has to keep in contact with the UK MOD. She says the problem facing the MOD when trying to operate in a modern information environment is an institutional one. 'I feel very protective of MOD press office,' she says. 'I know that the people there are trying their best, but the problem is they're working for a culturally hugely, hugely conservative organization where it's much easier to say no. It's a culture of control – there are situations where the MOD want to be more open but their hands are tied by cautious civil servants and military officers.' In this instance, that culture of control went badly wrong. 'The problem was they went in with a typical mindset where in their minds they control the narrative,' Deborah says. 'It somehow just didn't occur to them that anybody else was involved. My understanding was that everything was supposed to be embargoed [kept under wraps]. HMS *Defender* was supposed to just be tootling along, into those waters off Crimea and out again, and we weren't supposed to find out until a couple of days after it all happened. How ludicrous that when they're doing something they knew would create headlines and have an impact, they didn't consider the possibility that Russia could get in first.'

Perversely, the clearest explanation of what HMS *Defender* was supposed to be doing (and the most reassuring one) came by accident, when a senior civil servant, highly respected by his peers, left secret documents about the planning for the mission at a bus stop. But it is a telling symptom of how inadequate the perception of threat is among the British population that the member of the public who found them thought the appropriate thing to do was to take them not to the police but straight to the media.[36]

---

36. Larisa Brown, 'Civil servant who left files at bus stop was set to be ambassador', *The Times*, 4 August 2021, https://www.thetimes.co.uk/article/civil-servant-in-bus-stop-drop-was-set-to-be-ambassador-3zmc7l9rz.

### Military intimidation

Meanwhile Russia takes opportunities to test the boundaries of what it can get away with using its military forces far beyond Ukraine. This process too is most clearly visible in the air. From the Bering Strait to the Baltic, a consistent pattern of incidents suggests Russian pilots have been instructed to act aggressively – and the only way tragedy is avoided is through the restraint and professionalism of their NATO counterparts.

The occasions when Russia has pushed too far and restraint has not been enough tell us a lot. Pilots explain that these encounters usually progress according to a mutually understood set of rules – a kind of non-verbal language of escalating threat, with a vocabulary including manoeuvring, displays of weapons, different types of radar lock-ons and more. But in November 2015, Turkey shot down a Russian Su-24M bomber after it repeatedly breached Turkish airspace (and after Russia had repeatedly been warned that Turkey would respond). Justin Bronk points out that the lesson from this incident is that when weapons are eventually fired, this can lead to Russia getting the message rather than starting a war. 'The Turks had warned them about it repeatedly,' Justin says. 'And then they clearly just decided, well, fine. You want to test whether this is a proper red line or not? Here we go. And interestingly, the Russian response to what we would see as instinctively very escalatory was oh, okay you mean *that* red line? Fine. And in practice, it's had no effect on Russian–Turkish relations whatsoever besides injecting a bit more respect on the Russian side.' Russia's angry response including taking measures to harm the Turkish economy forced an eventual apology from the Turkish president; but thereafter Russia respected Turkey's military boundaries, and the two countries are now working together more closely than ever before.

Syria reportedly represented the first time that Western and Russian pilots had routinely flown close to one another in combat since the 1973 Arab–Israeli war. 'I was in Iraq and Syria when the Russians first showed up there,' Nick recalls, and explains how the way they did so placed unusual constraints on US pilots in particular, because 'US aircraft were flying in proximity to Russian jets . . . but with rules of engagement that did not classify the Russian Aerospace Forces as a hostile adversary.' These interactions were also taking place within the 'no escape zone' of both Russian air-to-air weapons and Syrian ground air defences.[37] Nick explains how this worked in practice: 'In Syria when it first started, we were directed basically to continue the mission and act as if nothing was there. The policy was, hey, we're going to keep doing this, regardless of what you guys do. Essentially, they were going to have to shoot us down before anything happened.' But this principle made for profoundly uncomfortable missions when Russian aircraft from the Flanker family of fighters used the opportunity to move into position as though

37. Aaron Stein and Ryan Fishel, 'Syria, Airpower, and the Future of Great-Power War', *War on the Rocks*, 13 August 2021, https://warontherocks.com/2021/08/syria-airpower-and-the-future-of-great-power-war/.

they were indeed about to attack. 'As a young dude in a fighter, when you're flying close air support, and literally just flying in a circle around a point on the ground, it's a very vulnerable position,' Nick goes on. 'And so when you're sitting there, and a Flanker rolls up behind you, it's a little bit unnerving. Because there's not a whole lot you can do at that point in time. But we're going to follow the rules and just continue there, with a Flanker in a position that in all of our training, we've been taught to never let them get there.'

Another area where encounters between Russian and NATO aircraft are routine is over the Baltic Sea. Here too the meetings can be tense. 'Particularly around the Baltics, those Russian fighters are usually from Kaliningrad and are armed fairly heavily,' Justin Bronk continues. With today's air-to-air combat technology such as helmet-mounted sights and advanced missiles on both sides, he says, 'both sides are in each other's kill box through the entire encounter. So it's a much more tense kind of encounter.' In addition, the relatively small distances involved mean that speed is important. 'From Kaliningrad it's so quick that you can be inside the airspace of Baltic countries in a couple of minutes from wheels up. If they're not intercepted in time before reaching boundaries, they will do carefully calibrated actual violations of airspace, particularly for Sweden,' Justin says. That's an obvious contrast with the care taken by NATO pilots not to breach Russian airspace. Nick Caraballo explains: 'When we go out to the Baltics, we'll go up to the edge of international waters, which everybody knows is twelve miles out. But we don't cross that, we respect their airspace out there.' Encounters with Russian fighters take place well before anybody reaches Russian airspace. 'They definitely intercept us further out, over those international waters. That being said, our guys would do the same thing. You want to get there early, as opposed to late in this game,' Nick says.

It may be that Russian pilots are selective about their targets for dangerous manoeuvres. A British Typhoon pilot told me after returning from a Baltic Air Policing deployment that Russian fighters liked to 'do stupid stuff up close and see if we will flinch'. And Russian fighters regularly make highly dangerous high-speed passes directly in front of heavier US aircraft, to jolt the target as it passes through the disrupted air.[38] But that's not a behaviour that Nick Caraballo, in a highly capable fighter himself, has seen in the Baltic. 'Personally, I've never had a dangerous encounter with a Russian Flanker or any other type of aircraft,' he says. 'The intercepts I've been a part of have been safe and professional, which probably would surprise most people.' Nick's guess is that Russian pilots feel less at risk targeting larger, less manoeuvrable aircraft instead. 'They're not doing anything super crazy against the fighters, not that I've personally seen anyway. With a fighter, with both of us being highly manoeuvrable, if they put themselves in that position and we manoeuvre in a way that they're not expecting, then there's potential for

38. Barbara Starr, 'Russia intercepts US aircraft flying over the Mediterranean Sea', CNN, 5 June 2019, https://edition.cnn.com/2019/06/04/politics/russia-us-aircraft-mediterranean/index.html.

mid-air collision and all of a sudden you're escalating,' he says. 'A heavy, less manoeuvrable aircraft isn't going to move a whole lot from their current flight path. And so the intercept can potentially be a little bit more aggressive.' Even so, he explains, 'would I go showboating across a B-52 or an AWACS, or anything like that right in front of them, a close pass? No, that definitely then gets into the unprofessional and dangerous realm.'

At sea, too, Russia applies the same pattern of behaviour, in what appears a concerted policy to challenge US and allies' naval operations at any promising opportunity.[39] This too involves brinkmanship that is both dangerous and unnecessary. In a near collision between US and Russian warships in the western Pacific in June 2019, the US cruiser USS *Chancellorsville* and the Russian destroyer *Admiral Vinogradov* came within metres of each other following what US 7th Fleet Commander Clayton Doss called an 'unsafe manoeuvre' by the 'unsafe and unprofessional' Russian vessel.[40] Incidents of this kind continue in various ocean regions, including for example in January 2020 in the North Arabian Sea, when, according to the US Navy, the USS *Farragut* was also put at risk of collision by a Russian Navy warship.[41] The suggestion that Russia only responds with this level of risk to naval movements in waters it claims as its own, as with the incident with HMS *Defender* described above, doesn't hold water. The Netherlands warship HNLMS *Evertsen* was accompanying *Defender* on its Black Sea cruise, but remained further away from Crimea in international waters. Still, it suffered five hours of harassment by Russian aircraft loaded with anti-shipping missiles, flying dangerously low and close, carrying out mock attacks and using electronic warfare equipment against the *Evertsen*'s on-board systems.[42]

Justin Bronk points out that in close encounters with foreign warships, 'Russian pilots are a lot more aggressive than they are with aerial encounters, partly because there's so much less risk of an inadvertent mid-air collision'. They can also rely on NATO warships doing their best to keep things safe. Veteran American arms control negotiator Franklin Miller recalls how 'back in the days of sail when I was

39. Keir Giles, 'Russian High Seas Brinkmanship Echoes Cold War', *Chatham House Expert Comment*, 15 April 2016, https://www.chathamhouse.org/expert/comment/russian-high-seas-brinkmanship-echoes-cold-war.

40. 'Russia and US warships almost collide in East China Sea', BBC, 7 June 2019, https://www.bbc.co.uk/news/world-asia-48553568; Stephen Smith, 'Video shows Russian destroyer nearly colliding with U.S. warship', CBS News, 7 June 2019, https://www.cbsnews.com/news/russian-destroyer-admiral-vinogradov-nearly-collides-uss-chancellorsville-warship-today-2019-06-07/.

41. US 5th Fleet Twitter, 10 January 2020, https://twitter.com/US5thFleet/status/1215658823471501315.

42. 'Russische gevechtsvliegtuigen veroorzaken onveilige situaties bij Zr.Ms. Evertsen' (Russian fighter planes cause unsafe situations at HNLMS Evertsen), Netherlands Ministry of Defence, 29 June 2021, https://www.defensie.nl/actueel/nieuws/2021/06/29/russische-gevechtsvliegen-veroorzaken-onveilige-situaties-bij-zr.ms.-evertsen.

a naval officer, the Soviets would constantly cut in front of US warships knowing that the US skipper would turn away, and thereby showing that we were weak'.[43]

Russia presents this pattern of incidents in the air and at sea as evidence that NATO is being dangerously provocative by operating in international waters and airspace within reach of Russia.[44] The risky behaviour by Russia's pilots and sailors seems to be part of a deliberate policy to influence Western publics and decision-makers towards holding their NATO counterparts back, and in effect allowing Russia de facto air and sea exclusion zones. Squeezing the warships and aircraft of the United States or other major NATO allies out of the Baltic or Black Seas in this way would be a major achievement for Moscow, and a major setback for the front-line states.

But the campaign of intimidation isn't limited to the tactical level of interactions between individual ships and aircraft. More broadly, Russia aims not just to probe and test its adversaries, but to cow them into not responding when it does so.[45] Even before the invasion of Ukraine, there was a barrage of messages both sent officially and distributed through Russia's network of propagandists and influencers that the risk of unintended war was high and rising, and there was a real danger that this could escalate to use of nuclear weapons. Dmitri Trenin, a former Russian military intelligence officer who later worked for a Western think tank in Moscow, explained how the 'world is visibly moving toward military collision between major powers. However, no great power would be willing to accept defeat in conventional conflict at [the] hands of another great power without recourse to nuclear weapons' – the implication being, of course, that nobody should attempt to defeat Russia.[46] The more robustly-minded Russia-watchers in the West refer to this as the 'Don't upset Russia too much or they'll invade a NATO country' trap; 'if we get nuked, it will be our own fault for making Putin feel threatened'. But the messages still find a receptive audience among European audiences instinctively alarmed at the threat of open warfare.[47] At times their fear of escalation can blind

43. Franklin Miller, speaking at 'Zapad 2021, Biden–Putin Summit, and their implications for U.S. and European security', CSIS, 17 June 2021.

44. 'Unsafe, unprofessional intercept of US bomber by Russian aircraft over the Black Sea', DVIDS, https://www.dvidshub.net/news/377080/unsafe-unprofessional-intercept-us-bomber-russian-aircraft-over-black-sea.

45. Konrad Muzyka, 'Russia Goes to War: Exercises, Signaling, War Scares, and Military Confrontations', CSIS, August 2021, https://csis-website-prod.s3.amazonaws.com/s3fs-public/publication/210728_Muzyka_Russia_Goes_to_War.pdf.

46. https://twitter.com/dmitritrenin/status/1404145439616741377.

47. Thomas Frear and Ian Kearns, 'Defusing future crises in the shared neighbourhood: Can a clash between the West and Russia be prevented?', European Leadership Network, 27 March 2017, https://www.europeanleadershipnetwork.org/policy-brief/defusing-future-crises-in-the-shared-neighbourhood-can-a-clash-between-the-west-and-russia-be-prevented/.

them to the underlying motivations for these messages from Russia – and their relationship with reality. When Dmitri Trenin, again, warned that 'Europe is stepping into a new phase of Russian–Western confrontation. Fasten your seatbelts', experienced Swedish politician Carl Bildt reacted immediately and echoed his message: 'I fear Dmitri Trenin has it right. A nervous Russia is reacting aggressively against the European Union mainly due to its domestic vulnerability.'[48]

Carl Bildt is not alone. Even after decades of experience, it is still child's play for Russia to push Western politicians' 'fear of escalation' buttons. Messages are constantly repeated because they work. Moscow has been complaining about NATO creating 'infrastructure' in eastern Europe since the 1990s, but has never actually specified what it means by this – because just talking about it as a threat without saying what it is is enough to alarm Western politicians and provide an excuse or a rationale for opposing defence of the front-line states.[49]

The coordinated campaign of alarmism has other specific goals. It's a highly effective element in the creation of a permissive environment for Moscow, again primarily because of the West's dogged refusal to learn from experience. The West also habitually overlooks the fact that it's just not plausible that Russia genuinely fears military clashes and uncontrolled escalation, since the main cause of confrontations that could turn into serious incidents is Russia's own aggressive behaviour. But the mere suggestion of Russian military power seems sufficient to prevent calm analysis of whether or not it is likely to be used. This too isn't new: in the 1970s a long-term scholar of Russia complained that 'For a century and a half Western statesmen and soldiers, in most matters sane and clear-headed, have allowed themselves to be hypnotised into a state of chronic jitters by the spectacle of Russia's apparently overwhelming armed might.' He then added, in words that apply fully to Russia's performance in Ukraine today, 'armed might, which has invariably, when put to the test, proved inadequate.'[50]

But Russia's attempts to intimidate Western powers into staying out of its war on Ukraine also include an even more powerful trigger for Western jitters. President Putin regularly hints at use of nuclear weapons – and receives the same highly gratifying reaction of near panic from Western media that had forgotten or overlooked the many previous times he had done so.[51]

Often Russia's threats constitute, in the most literal sense, attention-seeking behaviour. In his state of the nation address in March 2018, President Putin listed

48. Tweet by Carl Bildt on 17 February 2021, https://twitter.com/carlbildt/status/1361972565045096455.

49. 'Lavrov points to NATO's infrastructure closing in on Union State's borders', TASS, 15 September 2021, https://tass.com/politics/1338015.

50. Edward Crankshaw, 'The Price Brezhnev should be Asked to Pay', *Observer*, 1977, reprinted in *Putting Up with the Russians* (London: Macmillan, 1984).

51. 'Ukraine war: Could Russia use tactical nuclear weapons?', BBC, 16 March 2022, https://www.bbc.co.uk/news/world-60664169.

a catalogue of new and powerful missiles and weapon systems that he said Russia was introducing. To audience applause and video of missiles raining down on Florida, he added: 'Nobody wanted to listen to us. So listen now.'[52] By constantly driving home warnings of nuclear escalation, Russia seeks to panic the West into giving Russia a free hand, or even rolling back its own security, as a preferable alternative to open warfare.[53] But when this succeeds, it is only because his audience ignores the fact that nuclear threats are a standard part of his repertoire – not a warfighting but a successful diplomatic tactic, deployed whenever he wants Russia to get away with something heinous. When Russia wants operational latitude, mentioning nuclear weapons creates a fear abroad of provoking Putin. But this fear has little basis in an assessment of Russia's real attitudes to nuclear use.[54]

In addition, the logical extension of 'not provoking Putin' is to agree to every Russian demand, for fear any resistance will simply raise the nuclear stakes again. But in that scenario, nowhere is off limits to Russia. In fact, the approach is counterproductive from the start. Precedent shows de-escalation and a willingness to negotiate only convinces Putin he is on the right track, while appeasement spurs him to make further demands.

## Ukraine

And it is in Ukraine that the result of Western powers not wishing to stand up to Putin has been felt most bitterly. The reaction of the US and its closest allies in NATO to Russia's build-up of troops for the invasion was to confirm for President Putin that he had the go-ahead to attack, by almost immediately ruling out direct military support to Kyiv to help it withstand the attack. Moscow will have been delighted, as once again the West helpfully took Russia's greatest fears off the table. It is baffling why Western leaders repeatedly do this – for all it may be unrealistic to expect US or British troops to arrive to defend Ukraine, advertising this fact to Moscow only provides comfort, confidence and encouragement to Russia's planners by instantly removing a wide range of worst-case scenarios from their risk calculus.

One of the many tragedies of this war is that the only thing the West supplied to Ukraine in abundance before it started was missed opportunities. Calls for a

52. 'Russian President Vladimir Putin State of the Nation Address', C-Span, 1 March 2018, https://www.c-span.org/video/?441907-1/russian-president-vladimir-putin-state-nation-address.

53. Jacek Durkalec, 'Nuclear-Backed "Little Green Men": Nuclear Messaging in the Ukraine Crisis', Polski Instytut Spraw Międzynarodowych (PISM), July 2015.

54. Kristin Ven Bruusgaard, 'Understanding Putin's Nuclear Decision-Making', *War on the Rocks*, 22 March 2022, https://warontherocks.com/2022/03/understanding-putins-nuclear-decision-making/.

Western-backed no-fly zone over Ukraine reached a crescendo in the weeks following the invasion. But the only realistic time to have implemented one was before the war started, in response to Russia's demand for 'security guarantees' for itself – which in reality were a demand that the whole of eastern Europe be left at Russia's mercy by having its NATO protections stripped away.[55] Most Western countries displayed a helpless passivity and acquiescence in response to threats based on Putin's carefully constructed fantasy world where the US was preparing to station missiles in Ukraine.[56] And Russia can only have been further encouraged by calls for 'dialogue' and neutrality for Ukraine even after the invasion had begun, and calling diplomacy 'the only option' when Ukraine was already fighting for national survival.[57] As peace talks with Russia continue at the time of writing, in many respects the international community also poses a threat to Ukrainian sovereignty – since as we saw in Chapter 2, the EU in particular has an ugly history of successfully pressuring independent states into making concessions to Russia under duress.

But for all that, Russia still succeeded in grossly miscalculating in its plans to seize Ukraine. The early stages of the campaign reversed all expectations of how Russia's military would perform in real combat. Days before the invasion, experienced analysts predicted a campaign of 'shock and awe'.[58] I myself expected that Ukrainian military resistance would be rapidly crushed by massive air and missile strikes in the opening hours of the conflict, since that was how Russia itself described how it would go about winning a conflict. Instead, the biggest surprise was that Russia simply did not fight the kind of war it had spent a decade and trillions of roubles preparing to fight. Rather than deploying overwhelming force, Russia fed its troops in piecemeal and haphazardly, expecting no serious resistance because their leaders had fallen for their own propaganda.

The Russian assumption that Ukraine would fold like a house of cards showed clearly when Russia's official RIA Novosti news agency accidentally published an article, tagged with a publication date of 8 am two days after the start of the invasion, already celebrating a Russian victory and the collapse of the Ukrainian state. The article triumphantly proclaimed that Vladimir Putin 'took upon himself

55. Keir Giles, 'US must seize the initiative at talks with Russia', Chatham House, 7 January 2022, https://www.chathamhouse.org/2022/01/us-must-seize-initiative-talks-russia.

56. Mark Moore, 'Putin weighing options if security guarantees on NATO expansion in Ukraine not met', *New York Post*, 26 December 2021, https://nypost.com/2021/12/26/putin-looking-at-options-if-security-guarantees-are-not-met/.

57. Jeffrey Sachs, 'Diplomacy Remains the Only Option in Ukraine', Project Syndicate, 9 March 2022, https://www.project-syndicate.org/commentary/diplomatic-compromise-ukrainian-neutrality-for-russia-withdrawal-by-jeffrey-d-sachs-2022-03.

58. Michael Kofman and Jeffrey Edmonds, 'Russia's Shock and Awe: Moscow's Use of Overwhelming Force Against Ukraine', *Foreign Affairs*, 22 February 2022, https://www.foreignaffairs.com/articles/ukraine/2022-02-21/russias-shock-and-awe.

a historic responsibility, by deciding not to leave the resolution of the Ukrainian question to future generations' – and Ukraine would now be 'returned to its natural condition as part of the Russian world'.[59]

Instead, the early stages of the invasion on the approaches to Kyiv displayed not the high-tech, sophisticated military Russia had been showing the world at parades, but a blundering mass of uncoordinated, unprepared and underequipped soldiery and riot police. For long-term observers of the Russian military, the mistakes were shockingly familiar. Isolated units of bewildered and disoriented Russian troops arrived in the centre of Ukrainian populated areas with little idea why they were there, or even that they were not welcome – in exactly the same way they had arrived in the centre of Groznyy in Chechnya twenty-eight years before. And just as in Groznyy, this lack of situational awareness cost them dearly.

As the early days wore on, it became clear that Russia had not made provision to supply its troops with fuel and food, and had widely misled them over where they were going and what they were doing.[60] There were also bewildering failings in important areas of capability like communications and – what had been expected to be a significant Russian strength – electronic warfare. And Russian air power, universally anticipated to win air supremacy in the early hours of the fighting and thereafter be a key enabler for Russian overall victory, simply failed to show up. In fact, the only area of warfighting where Russian forces performed according to expectations was in their embrace of war crimes, atrocities and targeting of civilians.[61]

Russia's overconfidence and under-competence saved Ukraine from swift defeat, even if the long-term outcome of the conflict is far from clear at the time of writing. But they also hold a danger for future victims of Russian aggression. The danger is that Western leaders will look at the abysmal performance of Russia's forces in the opening stages of their campaign in Ukraine and assume that the same would apply if Russia were to attack not a Slavic neighbour, but a NATO or EU state.

This is far from likely to be the case. Russia would not approach a conflict with a NATO country in the same way that it did the war with Ukraine. Its failure to assess that Ukrainian forces and civil society would resist, as opposed to welcoming the invaders with open arms, stemmed not from genuine intelligence failures but from a combination of laziness and arrogance. Russia simply did not assess the

59. Petr Akopov, 'Наступление России и нового мира' (The advent of Russia and a new world), *RIA Novosti*, 26 February 2022, available at https://web.archive.org/web/20220226051154/https://ria.ru/20220226/rossiya-1775162336.html.

60. Carl Schreck, '"Sent As Cannon Fodder": Locals Confront Russian Governor Over "Deceived" Soldiers In Ukraine', RFE/RL, 6 March 2022, https://www.rferl.org/a/russian-soldiers-ukraine-cannon-fodder-governor/31739187.html.

61. William M. Arkin, 'Exclusive: Civilian Casualties in Ukraine 5 Times Higher than U.N. Report', *Newsweek*, 12 March 2022, https://www.newsweek.com/exclusive-civilian-casualties-ukraine-are-5-times-higher-un-report-1685736.

situation on the ground before invading – or if it did, accurate results of this assessment did not reach decision-makers and in particular President Putin. This was in stark contrast to Russia's campaigns in Syria, where detailed and painstaking analysis of human terrain before operations meant that Russia could work with and exploit the populations it was fighting among – making use of clan and faction alliances and rivalries to achieve their aims with the minimum possible armed intervention. And yet, in Ukraine as in previous Russian military interventions in the post-Soviet space, Russia's forces and intelligence officers assumed they knew it all before beginning – falling fully into the trap of Putin's fantasy of Ukraine not being a real country and Ukrainians being no more than frustrated Russians. Russia's planners are highly unlikely to have similar illusions about a country like Finland or Poland.

## Keeping the peace

One reason Russia places so much reliance on military force as a way to get things done is precisely because in all other areas of foreign policy it is such a chronic underachiever. With a limited number of other tools of statecraft, and next to no power of attraction, Russia turns to force as a reliable fallback for getting its way. And it has no hesitation in throwing its military weight around wherever it thinks it can do so without suffering serious consequences. This includes in the fraught atmosphere of campaigns like Syria, where relations between Russian and NATO troops usually stopped just short of open hostility.[62] RAF commander Johnny Stringer recalled disbelief in the coalition air headquarters in Qatar in September 2017 when Russia released satellite imagery of US special forces positions in eastern Syria: 'There was a shaking of heads and people were saying "how could they do this to us". Some of my colleagues were outraged. But you have just got to get over it.'[63] Well into 2020, Russian troops in Syria were still causing American casualties, harassing US patrols and threatening their ground supply lines.[64]

But part of the problem is that whenever Russia achieved success by using its armed forces, that made it more likely that they would be considered as the tool of choice for the next task – as was eventually the case with Ukraine. This trend also enhanced their prestige and their prominence in Russian daily life still further, turning it into an even more militarized society. According to Linas the Lithuanian military officer, Russia rebuilding its military 'also plays a vital role in framing

62. 'Russia's War in Syria: Assessing Russian Military Capabilities and Lessons Learned', Foreign Policy Research Institute, September 2020, https://www.fpri.org/article/2020/09/about-the-book-russia-war-syria/.

63. Ripley, *Operation Aleppo*, p. 192.

64. 'U.S. service members injured in Syria after skirmish with Russian forces', *Politico*, 26 August 2020, https://www.politico.com/news/2020/08/26/us-troops-injured-russian-forces-syria-402347.

social dialogue. Because the patriotism that is built on World War Two narratives is the driving factor pushing the Russian population in one or another direction, and the military plays a significant role in this.' In addition, it's important to see war between Russia and any other country not as a one-off over a single issue, but as a symptom of the enduring problems that set Russia and Europe in inevitable opposition to each other and will continue to do so after the end of any limited conflict. Policy advisers are asked what 'end state' Russia might want from a confrontation. It's a valid question, but it's important also to think where Moscow would like to be at the end of a decade of competition with the West – because only that length of perspective will provide the proper context for where it might wish to be at the end of a short war.

Pekka Toveri from Finland says that to reduce this temptation for Russia to use its military tool, it's critical for other countries too to possess visible and credible military power. 'The first thing is to prevent possible Russian military actions with clear believable deterrence, by building military forces that can stop any aggression in its tracks,' he says. 'As our president says, "a Cossack will take what a Cossack can", so don't give them that possibility.' And there are now practical examples demonstrating the importance of the simple physical presence of military forces for deterring Russia. In Ukraine, training missions by US, British and Canadian troops were withdrawn as the invasion grew closer – with the specific aim of preventing them getting in the line of fire in the event of a Russian attack.[65] This approach is the polar opposite of the way the West protects the Baltic states, where small contingents from multiple NATO member states are embedded in national militaries precisely to ensure that, in the event of Russian aggression, they are directly and immediately involved.

For several years after 2014, the three Baltic states were routinely described as the next likely targets for Russian intervention.[66] There was a dangerous imbalance, between Russia already almost a decade into its intensive programme to rearm and modernize its Armed Forces, and much of the rest of the Baltic Sea region which had taken few defensive preparations at all – and in the case of Sweden, was still reducing its military. That started to change after the Russian move on Crimea. Sven Sakkov recalls how 'exactly ten years after Estonia joined NATO, a company of US sky soldiers arrived in Estonia as [a] symbolic presence of allied forces. And from 1 May 2014 the Danish Air Force started operating from the airbase in Ämari. But it was hard step-by-step work overcoming inertia in NATO.' The result of that hard work was the arrival in the three Baltic states and Poland of NATO's 'Enhanced

65. Murray Brewster, 'Canadian military trainers pulled out of Ukraine before anticipated Russian invasion: sources', CBC, 13 February 2022, https://www.cbc.ca/news/politics/canada-ukraine-military-training-1.6350186.

66. Including in one much-quoted and now-notorious 2016 research paper that promised Russian forces could be on the outskirts of Baltic capitals in sixty hours. David A. Shlapak and Michael Johnson, 'Reinforcing Deterrence on NATO's Eastern Flank', RAND, 2016, https://www.rand.org/pubs/research_reports/RR1253.html.

Forward Presence (eFP)' battalions, a visible reminder to both local populations and to Russia of NATO's commitment to its members' safety. Together with belated moves by Sweden to repair its long-neglected defence capabilities, this means that despite being next door to Russia, Estonia, Latvia and Lithuania are at less risk today than they have been for centuries, and the scenarios for military adventurism by Russia in the region that were so popular in the previous decade are already far less realistic.[67]

But this hasn't led Baltic countries to be complacent. The experience of occupation by Moscow during the twentieth century means that for the front-line states, there are few doubts about the importance of effective resistance. In Latvia, determination to resist is bolstered by the knowledge that in 1939, the only other choice – surrender – brought on exactly the tragedy it was intended to avoid. A grim comparison between the war losses of Latvia and Finland makes the point. In resisting Russian aggression, Finland lost 3.9% of its pre-war population; by not resisting, Latvia eventually lost 12%.[68] As a result, Latvian Minister of Defence Artis Pabriks says, Latvia has decided 'never again'.[69] Today, Latvian seventeen- and eighteen-year-olds in school learn 'crisis response' and 'how to defend the country in dire straits' as part of the national programme of comprehensive defence, and standing instructions to the population are that any message which seems to come from the central authorities with instructions to surrender will be false. The ongoing tragedy is that these are the sort of choices that neighbours of Russia must make at all.

Countries like Norway and Estonia enter a covenant for their security. Demonstrative acts like ensuring that defence spending consistently meets the NATO target of 2% of GDP, or practical ones such as sending men and women to serve alongside allies in Iraq, Afghanistan and Mali, in theory cement the obligation of friends and allies to honour their commitments in return when a crisis threatens closer to home. The UK certainly promises to meet those commitments. Britain offers practical security support to nations directly at risk from Russian hostile action, over and above its NATO commitments. As well as being the main contributor to NATO's rotational deployment in Estonia, and providing small additional forces to the US-led contingent in Poland, it provided direct training and weapons assistance to the Ukrainian armed forces. It is also the lead nation for the Joint Expeditionary Force (JEF), a coalition of ten northern European states intended for crisis response. But the fact the JEF exists at all points to a problem with NATO's capabilities to act swiftly and appropriately in a crisis. It exists at least

67. 'Sweden re-activates conscription', Swedish Ministry of Defence, 2 March 2017, https://www.government.se/articles/2017/03/re-activation-of-enrolment-and-the-conscription/.

68. Presentation by Veiko Spolitis, Latvian National Defence Academy, 7 December 2017.

69. Speaking at Baltic Sea Region Forum 2021, 27 May 2021.

in part to compensate for the possibility that NATO might be unwilling or unable to respond – for instance through having individual member states persuaded not to by Russia. The creation of the JEF as a parallel structure which can respond more swiftly and decisively, and bring in non-NATO partners Finland and Sweden, is an important addition to security for Northern Europe, but it would be better if existing security arrangements meant it was not needed at all. Similarly, the UK faces the enduring self-inflicted challenge of promising security commitments that outstrip its willingness to pay for the military capabilities needed to meet them.[70]

In Estonia, the UK is the 'framework nation' for NATO's eFP deployment. That means it provides the lead and the bulk of the personnel for a multinational battalion attached to the Estonian Armed Forces in order to dissuade Russia from attempting any military attack there.[71] It's not the relatively modest number of troops involved – under 1,000 – that will give Russia pause for thought so much as their simple presence as a demonstration that other NATO allies will support the countries involved – Estonia, Latvia, Lithuania and Poland. Put simply, if other countries' soldiers are already in the fight, there is much less chance that they will shirk their responsibilities to help the front-line states fight Russia off.

The physical presence of British forces in Estonia, and the other NATO contingents across Latvia, Lithuania and Poland, was a major achievement for those countries and their friends in NATO who took the problem of Russia seriously. Sven Sakkov recalls how 'since the Russian war against Georgia, we had very clearly set ourselves the task to see that NATO is present in Estonia with allied forces, with prepositioned equipment and ammunition, and that there are plans for the follow-on forces to come, and that the whole machinery should work. Every single part of that was an uphill battle.' In many ways the UK is a natural fit for Estonia. Support by the Royal Navy played a major role in the country's fight for freedom and independence in 1918–19 – and today the flagship of Estonia's small naval flotilla is not only a former Royal Navy vessel, but is named after a British admiral.[72] The UK was in no position to continue that support in 1940 or at the end of the Second World War when Estonia faced Soviet occupation. But when Estonia once again became free at the end of the Cold War, the UK helped in establishing a functioning state. This included paying out full compensation for

70. Jack Watling, 'By Parity and Presence: Deterring Russia with Conventional Land Forces', RUSI, July 2020, https://rusi.org/sites/default/files/by_parity_and_presence_final_web_version. pdf.

71. UK Ministry of Defence, 'Operation CABRIT explained: Deterring Aggression in Estonia and Poland', *Medium*, 21 December 2020, https://medium.com/voices-of-the-armed-forces/ operation-cabrit-explained-deterring-aggression-in-estonia-and-poland-a4ad5b0e5518.

72. 'Naval Flotilla', Estonian Defence Forces website, https://mil.ee/en/navy/naval-flotilla/.

Estonia's gold reserves deposited with the Bank of England during the previous period of independence – which ensured the country's financial survival and provided vital backing for efforts to set up a new sovereign currency to replace the Soviet rouble.[73]

To try to understand what an ongoing British deployment in Estonia means in practice, I spoke to two people directly involved, but with as different perspectives as you can imagine: Jüri Luik, who had just come to the end of his first term as Estonian Defence Minister, and Peter, a twenty-three-year-old British Army soldier from Worcestershire on his first visit to the country.

Peter is a lance corporal serving in 1st Battalion, The Mercian Regiment. He's an infantryman in the Reconnaissance and Specialist Weapons Support Company, and I spoke to him as he was coming to the end of his battalion's time in Estonia as part of eFP. He says there is a lot more to deployment to Estonia than waiting for anything Russia might throw at the country. 'We're all here to reassure the locals,' he says. 'We're here to work alongside them. And really it's self-development as well. While we're here we're trying to take this opportunity to learn and train to make ourselves better soldiers.' As well as the locals, Peter has had to reassure people at home. 'Initially when I told friends and family that I was going to Estonia, they went, oh, isn't that the border of Russia, won't it be a bit dangerous?' he says. But now, he goes on, 'they're definitely on board' – helped along by Peter emphasizing the training and reassurance part of his job, as opposed to the possibility of having to face the Russian Army.

For British soldiers to be out and about and visible in Estonia is a key part of the reassurance mission. According to Peter, 'The Estonians seem to be happy that we're here. They accept us, especially the soldiers.' Unsurprisingly, Jüri Luik is a lot more emphatic: 'The attitude is overwhelmingly positive. I'm very happy that the Brits as well as the Danes and the French have taken the outreach policy very seriously. Even small public events in small towns and villages, the British military is often there, explaining what they are doing here, waving the Union Jack together with the Estonian flag.' 'On a political or a military level, it's deterrence pure and simple,' Jüri goes on. 'But on a human level it's also reassuring for people to see that our allies are here.'

On a previous deployment, Peter had been involved in a similar task in Ukraine where the British Army was assisting the Ukrainian armed forces with training – a programme that Ukrainian officials credited with significantly bolstering the performance of their armed forces once Russia finally invaded. But unlike in Ukraine, the eFP contingents in Estonia and the other host nations are not just visiting but are attached to the local armed forces. According to Jüri Luik, 'It is also very important that the British battalion has been integrated fully into Estonia's 1st

73. '100 Years of Diplomatic Relations: Estonia and the United Kingdom 1921–2021', Estonian Embassy in London, https://london.mfa.ee/wp-content/uploads/sites/2/2021/01/100_years_of_diplomatic_relations.pdf.

Brigade. It's not only the fact that they are here but the fact that they are integrated to the Estonian defence system. We believe in each other and are ready to go to war together.' As part of this, the British Army contingent trains together with their Estonian hosts. Peter described taking part in Estonia's Exercise Spring Storm, which forms a final test for conscripts finishing their service before they transfer to the reserve.[74] 'For the exercise we were the enemy for them … we were essentially trying to get them. The exercise was really really good because it felt like it was real. Being the reconnaissance group, we were that far forward there was no one with us, there's no help, the enemy could be anywhere, anytime. The challenge was good.' Also, 'it was good to see when we eventually came across the enemy, the enemy being the conscripts, we saw how well they've taken their training and how professional they are. That definitely was the highlight for the tour.'

For Jüri Luik, there's no doubt that rather than being provocative as Russia claims, the presence of allied troops makes Estonia safer. 'There's no doubt that the arrival of eFP has brought an extra layer of stability,' he says. 'That and NATO's Baltic air policing are good examples of a pacifying influence. They are creators of stability and creators of peace. With the exception of Russia, everybody understands that they are a stabilizing factor.'

Above all, initiatives like eFP are a clear answer to the question of what deters Russia. In countless studies analysing Moscow's ambition and how it planned to set about realizing it, I and other Russia-watchers pointed out that real and credible military force – and the demonstrated will to use it – is the Western countermeasure that genuinely causes Russia to think twice and step back from aggression. That countermeasure was not offered to Ukraine, and now Russia has moved in.[75]

74. 'Exercise Spring Storm Unfolds in Estonia', NATO Multinational Corps Northeast, 20 May 2021, https://mncne.nato.int/newsroom/news/2021/exercise-spring-storm-unfolds-in-estonia.

75. Keir Giles, 'What deters Russia: Enduring principles for responding to Moscow', Chatham House, 23 September 2021, https://www.chathamhouse.org/2021/09/what-deters-russia.

# Chapter 5

## NOBODY IS TOO UNIMPORTANT

But while Russia's flexing of military muscle has devastating effects for its victims, its ongoing quieter campaigns continue to affect everybody else. Again and again, we find people unknowingly becoming caught up or affected by Russian hostile operations, even if they had not the slightest interest in Russia beforehand.

There's a huge range of ways this can happen. It can be in ways that seem exotic and improbable, like digital spying, where according to the head of the UK's Security Service (MI5), the targets for 'disguised approaches' online in the form of messages from social media or LinkedIn profiles are 'regular people', not just the senior government or military figures often assumed.[1] Lars the counter-intelligence officer agrees: 'The cyber spying campaigns by Russian intelligence services affect loads of people outside what you might call traditional targets.' Sometimes, Lars explained, somebody suffering unwelcome Russian attention might not even be the actual target themselves. 'They try to get in through so many different vectors that it's hard to even say whether those are the primary targets that they are going after, or are they just trying to find access points into certain circles, that they might exploit later.' In other words, it's easy for innocent people to become targets by proxy, if they are somehow associated with individuals that Russian espionage operations are more interested in. When Bulgaria cracked open a Russian spy ring, the intercepted correspondence showed the Russian handler taking a keen interest, alongside more conventional espionage questions, in the niece of one of his agents.[2]

Ordinary people can also be affected by Russian espionage operations through identity theft. John Mooney explained to me how the Russian Embassy in Dublin had been caught cloning the passports of Irish citizens applying for visas to Russia. An FBI counter-intelligence operation in the US had found the cloned passports being used by Russian intelligence services to 'plant people in America, or work undercover throughout Europe'. 'A certain number of them were caught and

1. Deborah Haynes, 'Head of MI5 Ken McCallum warns "regular people" being targeted by foreign spies', Sky News, Wednesday 14 July 2021, https://news.sky.com/story/head-of-mi5-ken-mccallum-warns-regular-people-being-targeted-by-foreign-spies-12355329.

2. 'Bulgaria uncovers Russian spy network', Eurotopics, 22 March 2021, https://www.eurotopics.net/en/258273/bulgaria-uncovers-russian-spy-network.

detected during that FBI operation,' John says. 'But I think the assessment over here was God only knows how long they have been doing that for, and how many other passports were cloned.' Whether you become a target can even depend on something as simple as where you live. According to researcher Simon Miles, Russian intelligence can target not just NATO military bases but the civilian population around them. 'Russian intelligence services are sophisticated. They know how to penetrate military secrecy and have a global footing. They understand in particular that civilian populations around military installations, and that could be true of facilities in Europe but also in the continental United States, are a really valuable conduit for cultivating a variety of sources that don't require stepping on the turf of the US military.'[3]

Overall, John Mooney explains, it is far easier to be caught up in Russian nefarious activity than people imagine. 'The scale of what's happening is far greater than I think most people will be aware of,' he says. 'It's a lot more pervasive across Europe at the moment than I think anyone realizes, and in the strangest scenarios.'

## Disinformation online

Of all the methods by which Russia reaches out and touches ordinary people in countries it wishes to target, online disinformation is the one that has gathered the most attention. Russian campaigns to influence major political events in Western countries have been either confirmed and documented, as with the US presidential election in 2016 or its French counterpart the following year, or widely suspected and endlessly debated, like the Brexit referendum in the UK. But even though it is the form of Russian influence that most people are most likely to have experienced (whether they are aware of it or not), many people who don't have a direct interest in what Russia does can struggle to understand why it affects them or why they are a target for Russia's efforts.

I asked counter-disinformation activist Jakub Kalenský why Russian disinformation is an issue for ordinary people. 'Because they vote.' he answered. 'And when they vote they elect politicians, so what they think about, say, the conflict in Ukraine or MH17 can influence which politicians they choose and through that the politics of the whole country.' Broadly speaking, that is Moscow's overall objective – to use influence to direct its adversaries' decision-making towards favourable outcomes for Russia; a permissive environment for Russian actions, to either allow notionally unacceptable actions in advance or escape the consequences for them after the fact. But as we saw in Chapter 3, Russia also has the persistent objectives of ongoing subversion and destabilization simply to do damage to the populations and societies it targets. These campaigns are based on

3. 'Russian Spetsnaz in the Grey Zone', Russia Strategic Initiative, 19 August 2021, https://community.apan.org/wg/rsi/project-connect/w/events/29786/rsi-connect-russian-spetsnaz-in-the-grey-zone/

the recognition that, as Russian Chief of the General Staff Valeriy Gerasimov wrote in 2016, 'Information resources have become one of the most effective types of weapon. Their extensive employment enables the situation in a country to be destabilized from within in a matter of days.'[4] The result is that disinformation also affects people on a deeply personal level, Jakub goes on, threatening basic human relationships. 'Two members of my own family are ardent disinformation consumers. We even stopped talking with one of them for six years because of it. Because of the organized spread of this information, this person consumes it day and night. And obviously, even though I'm a family member, I don't have as much time to influence their thinking as the disinformation ecosystem does. So you could see that really influences even basic human relationships, person-to-person relations. And when you have it affecting both personal relations and political decision-making, it's actually seems like quite a big problem that can influence the whole range of human life.' The simple bottom line is that in online disinformation, Russia has found an alternative means of getting its way, at very little risk and cost but with effects that can be just as serious as other forms of attack on Western democracies and their people. Russian propagandist Dmitriy Kiselev puts it plainly: 'If you can persuade a person, you don't need to kill him. Let's think about what's better: to kill or to persuade? Because if you aren't able to persuade, then you will have to kill.'[5]

The efforts to distort, lie and produce fake news pay off, which is why Russia continues to do it. According to a military officer speaking at a discussion of national countermeasures to malign influence, it can be a mistake to refer to a disinformation campaign as an 'information operation' – 'it's not a specific operation, it's just their daily work.'[6] Ariana Gic, a political analyst focused on Ukraine, says that over the long term this is highly effective. 'The Kremlin is wildly successful in putting out disinformation about its victims,' she says. 'What has little place in the world is the truth – it barely has a fighting chance in the heavy fog of lies. For example, in the first eight years of Russia's bloody war of aggression against Ukraine, there was not one single country in the world which formally and officially declared that Russia was the aggressor state waging war on Ukraine. That can only be described as a landmark success for Moscow.'

Russia's types of online disinformation campaign vary widely, as do their objectives. Ghostwriter, a large-scale hack and leak operation targeting Poland, Lithuania and Latvia, combined the aims of discrediting both NATO and individual

4. Valeriy Gerasimov, 'По опыту Сирии' (Based on the experience of Syria), *Voyenno-Promyshlennyy Kur'er*, 9 March 2016, http://vpk-news.ru/sites/default/files/pdf/VPK_09_624.pdf.

5. Speaking on PBS Newshour, 'Inside Russia's propaganda machine', 11 July 2017, http://www.pbs.org/newshour/bb/inside-russias-propaganda-machine/.

6. 'Responding to the Covid-19 "infodemic": Foreign information influence activities in Europe and national countermeasures', Hague Programme for Cyber Norms, 18 June 2021.

politicians who take a firm line on Russia.[7] 'Global Research' belongs to what the US Global Engagement Center (GEC) called a network of proxy sites that, while having no visible ties to Moscow, 'serve no other purpose but to push pro-Kremlin content'.[8] The site is run by Michel Chossudovsky, a discredited former academic who already in 2006 featured in a list of 'Canada's Nuttiest Professors'.[9] But as Canadian disinformation researcher Marcus Kolga points out, the title of professor and apparent links to prestigious universities lend even the most outlandish deceptions an air of plausibility for people who don't look too closely.[10] More recently established Russian influence campaigns have a curious feature in common: they are given clunky and convoluted names like 'Newsroom for American and European Based Citizens'[11] and 'Eliminating Barriers to the Liberation of Africa'.[12] The reason appears to be a puerile sense of humour on the part of their creators. The abbreviations for these two titles, NAEBC and EBLA, as well as the full name of the Peace Data campaign, if read in Russian produce obscenities. Laura Walters is a New Zealand journalist who was drawn into the Peace Data operation. She doesn't know what to make of the real meaning behind the name of the campaign she was unwittingly recruited for. 'I don't know if I love it or hate it,' she told me. 'A little bit of me kind of likes that there's a sense of humour in there, and that they leave these little easter eggs. And then I think no, actually, these are people's lives, you shouldn't be taking the piss and trolling. But you can't help but laugh a little bit. It's ballsy, isn't it?' Either way, it offers a test for journalists considering approaches by new organizations with odd-sounding names: if pronouncing them in a thick Russian accent produces a Russian expletive, chances are they are best left alone.

But in all cases, spreading disinformation online is still made easier by the way social media platforms work and earn money. There are close links between the financial incentives available to advertisers, clicks on sensationalist posts and the

7. Daniel Tilles, 'Hacking of Polish officials linked to Russian security services, says Poland', *Notes from Poland*, 24 June 2021, https://notesfrompoland.com/2021/06/24/hacking-of-polish-officials-linked-to-russian-security-services-says-poland/.

8. 'Pillars of Russia's Disinformation and Propaganda Ecosystem', GEC Special Report, August 2020, https://www.state.gov/wp-content/uploads/2020/08/Pillars-of-Russia%E2%80%99s-Disinformation-and-Propaganda-Ecosystem_08-04-20.pdf.

9. Terry O'Neill, 'Canada's Nuttiest Professors', *Western Standard*, 25 September 2006, https://westernstandard.blogs.com/shotgun/2007/10/here-is-another.html.

10. Thomas Daigle, 'Canadian professor's website helps Russia spread disinformation, says U.S. State Department', CBC News, 21 October 2020, https://www.cbc.ca/news/science/russian-disinformation-global-research-website-1.5767208.

11. Jamie Ross, 'Right-Wing Trumpist News Site Busted as Putin Troll Farm Operation', *Daily Beast*, 1 October 2020.

12. 'IRA in Ghana: Double Deceit', *Graphika*, March 2020, https://graphika.com/reports/ira-in-ghana-double-deceit/.

tendency for users to form 'filter bubbles' where information is pushed to them from accounts that share their own views. The fact that the workings of these platforms is so opaque in particular aids hostile campaigns – a point proven by efforts by Russian state disinformation outlets to challenge transparency measures by Facebook in US courts.[13] And automating disinformation means it can be distributed at enormous scale. Comparitech, a group researching cyber security and privacy, uncovered a Facebook bot farm running multiple fake accounts set up using Russian email addresses. According to researcher Paul Bischoff, bots of this kind can 'scrape users' personal information without consent, fabricate influence campaigns, covertly push agendas, spread disinformation, and make scams more convincing'. The operators used a tool called Selenium to imitate human behaviour, and similarly to other campaigns intended merely to disrupt and divide Western societies, rather than posting overtly pro-Russian messaging, they delivered 'provocative and divisive political content to incite legitimate Facebook users'. But the most striking aspect of the operation was its scale. The bot farm had been used to manage 13,775 unique Facebook accounts, each of them posting on average fifteen times a month, making a total of almost a quarter of a million Facebook posts a year just from this one organization.[14]

I spoke to Anneli Ahonen, a Finnish journalist who until a few months earlier had been in charge of running one of the EU's counter-disinformation efforts. She explained how it was feeling the effects of Russian disinformation campaigns first-hand that motivated her to join in efforts to fight them. 'What led me to thinking about this was all these campaigns targeting Finland, and how Finland is stealing Russian kids from their parents and putting them into concentration camps and discriminating and mistreating them,' she says. 'Where I really felt the real impact from it was that I was in St Petersburg for eight years and then I moved back home to Finland with two kids. And then I realized that even though I knew perfectly well that there is no such thing as the Finnish social services coming to knock on your door and take away your kids, I just caught myself sometimes thinking – but what if it were possible? What if someone did still come and take them away? And that was the moment when I realized that these campaigns do have real impact.'

The most effective disinformation often plays on deeply emotional issues, triggering gut reactions rather than rational thought. Anneli noticed exactly how this worked on her. 'It was the way it captured the emotion inside me – which in a way is the end goal of many of these campaigns. So I realized it's not just some people out there who believe in conspiracy theories, always somebody else but not you yourself. Even for educated and rational people, it does have an effect on you

13. Casey Michel, 'Russian-linked outlet fights Facebook transparency in U.S. courts', *Eurasianet*, 27 August 2020, https://eurasianet.org/russian-linked-outlet-fights-facebook-transparency-in-us-courts.

14. Paul Bischoff, 'Inside a Facebook bot farm that pumps out 200k+ political posts per month', *Comparitech*, 10 May 2021, https://www.comparitech.com/blog/information-security/inside-facebook-bot-farm/.

personally as well.' That's why one of the best recommendations for dealing with information online is taking a pause and a breath to assess it calmly, instead of reacting immediately or spreading it further unthinkingly.[15]

This realization made Anneli determined to do what she could to help. 'It's why I chose to jump from journalism and into an EU job. That choice wasn't easy, because being a journalist is such a huge mission with passion behind it and it's always a question, should you jump to the government side at all. But you can't just pretend that it's not happening, and I had to be able to do something about it. And I felt that I could do more.'

While people like Anneli can understand and feel the effects on themselves, it's been harder to grasp the effects of Russia's ongoing disinformation campaigns against Western countries more broadly. This means there are mixed and sometimes misguided conclusions on whether they are actually achieving any success. Target countries often try to assess their effectiveness by attempting to work out whether they were able to change the minds of significant numbers of people towards a specific political outcome that Russia wanted. Where this could not be shown, it has sometimes been concluded that Russia's efforts were ineffective. But measuring effect by specific short-term goals doesn't take account of long-term Russian campaigns that are not tied to specific events.

Trying to measure specific outcomes from Russian actions also overlooks the campaigns that may not have a specific political objective but are aimed simply at causing harm. Russia watches for any weakness or vulnerability that it can exploit to inflict damage on Western countries and societies, because in its perverse understanding of international relations, anything that weakens them means that in relative terms Russia is stronger. This is what lies behind Russia piling in on trigger issues in other countries – racial tension in the US, migration in Europe, Brexit in the UK and more. The destructive and irresponsible nature of the campaigns is clear from efforts like boosting anti-vaccination propaganda in the middle of a global pandemic.[16]

Anneli says that 'what is important for me would be that people don't underestimate these efforts. It's very easy to say, oh, you're always shouting Russia, Russia, Russia. But people very rarely understand the extent and the impact of what is happening, I think it's very easy to just dismiss it, but it leads into a snowball effect where the influence is growing, and not diminishing.' Understanding this also means recognizing that subversion is a process rather than an event. That requires looking at longer-term trends – for example what is 'normal' in the

15. https://www.newstatesman.com/science-tech/social-media/2020/04/why-we-need-informational-distancing-during-coronavirus-crisis.

16. Lucy Fisher and Chris Smyth, 'GCHQ in cyberwar on anti-vaccine propaganda', *The Times*, 9 November 2020, https://www.thetimes.co.uk/edition/news/gchq-in-cyberwar-on-anti-vaccine-propaganda-mcjgjhmb2; 'Protests in Europe as a consequence of COVID-19 related disinformation', GLOBSEC, 25 November 2020, https://mailchi.mp/globsec/democracyandresilience15-1?e=3d5bba5760.

information space in English-speaking countries in 2022 compared to 2012. Comparisons like this reveal spectacular change over time. Assisted by the policies and algorithms of social media platforms, Russia has ridden and accelerated trends of fragmentation, distrust and the spawning of alternative realities – and is now joined by a wide range of foreign and domestic imitators who choose to emulate Russian tactics for their own political ends, amplifying the damage done. Jakub Kalenský, a former colleague of Anneli's, says of the disinformation challenge that 'We are underestimating the problem. We still make light of it and do not fully appreciate how corrosive it can be.' That corrosion includes the toxic secondary effects of unscrupulous political operators in the West noting the effectiveness of the Russian approach and aping it, and by doing so distorting and corrupting their own country's political processes.[17] The combined result is increased fragmentation in society, with people devolving into alternative realities on a whole range of topics. 'I don't think we really appreciate how deeply they have penetrated our daily debates about problems like the racial question or the migration issue, or, currently, anti-vaccine activism,' Jakub goes on. 'Even on the shooting down of MH17, there are many people who still prefer to believe the Russian disinformation instead of the factual version of events.'

## Suspending disbelief

This belief in the stories Russia tells persists despite the consistency with which they are shown to be complete fiction – and the well-established and predictable routine Russia goes through to tell them. When Moscow is caught in the act of carrying out some outrage, its response has been compared to the widely recognized five stages of grief: denial, anger, bargaining, depression and acceptance.[18] Denial is accompanied by demands for proof. Anger includes a flood of counter-accusations. Bargaining revolves around whataboutism and bringing in unrelated examples to argue that Russia is no worse than any other country. The depression phase portrays Russia as the victim of an external conspiracy intent on weakening or destroying it. And finally, in the acceptance phase, Russia abandons pretence and proudly celebrates its achievement.

---

17. Ashley Parker, 'Trump and allies ratchet up disinformation efforts in late stage of campaign', *Washington Post*, 6 September 2020, https://www.washingtonpost.com/politics/trump-disinformation-campaign/2020/09/06/f34f080a-eeca-11ea-a21a-0fbbe90cfd8c_story.html.

Martin Innes et al., 'The normalisation and domestication of digital disinformation: on the alignment and consequences of far-right and Russian State (dis)information operations and campaigns in Europe', *Journal of Cyber Policy* 6, no. 1 (2021): 31–49, https://doi.org/10.1080/23738871.2021.1937252.

18. 'The Five Stages of Arguing with a Russian Nationalist', *Imgur*, 13 March 2015, https://imgur.com/gallery/0HagQ

At each of these stages, the Kremlin has a credibility problem that isn't a problem. After systematically lying over Crimea, Ukraine, MH17, Syria, the Skripals, the invasion of Ukraine, its own history and many more topics, Russia has devalued its own plausibility to the point where no denial, even if genuine, is likely to be believed. But this is acceptable, because in many cases Kremlin statements and denials are not even intended to be widely believed. Their purpose is to waste the time of Western politicians and serious journalists who engage with them – or indeed any citizen anywhere who takes the time to treat them seriously and attempt to rebut them. This approach was on full display in the aftermath of the attempted murder of Sergey and Yulia Skripal in 2018, when government and independent researchers were hard pressed to keep a tally of all the different implausible explanations for the incident being generated by Russia's propagandists.[19] But the tactic is repeated again and again, as Russian and Russian-backed sources generate implausible denials and contradictory versions of the same event. Some people come to believe each of them. Russia can then sit back and watch as they attack the facts and each other, mainstream media gradually lose interest, and the final conclusion is that the whole thing is very confusing and the truth is probably in the middle somewhere but may never be known.

Even after almost a decade of recognizing the renewed Russian tactic of blanket denials of culpability, Western politicians and media have still not quite figured out how to deal with it. When Vladimir Putin denied in 2014 that Russian troops were in Crimea or in eastern Ukraine, the point was not that what he was saying was plainly untrue – it was that this was a highly effective tactic not only for sowing confusion, as the denials were faithfully repeated by the media, but also for preventing any serious discussion of the problem in face-to-face meetings with his Western counterparts.[20] Today, Russia still sees the usefulness of simply refusing to engage with reality when presented with it. The fact that there is no discomfort at being caught in a lie means Russia also has no difficulty at all in denying facts today that it had previously confirmed during Russia's brief interlude of openness and honesty – as for instance with the story of a lethal anthrax leak from the Soviet Union's huge stockpiles of biological weapons, thoroughly documented in the 1990s but now subject to renewed denial and disinformation.[21]

The denial routine is unconcerned at appearing ridiculous, as with a 2019 letter to the *Irish Times* from Russian Ambassador to Ireland Yuriy Filatov entitled 'Russia stands for a peaceful world order', which wearily ran through the list of

19. 'Russian state media weaponises news to sow confusion and division', King's College London, 1 March 2019, https://www.kcl.ac.uk/news/how-russian-state-media-weaponises-news.

20. Nick Logan, '"Get out of Ukraine": Harper to Putin at G20 Summit in Brisbane', *Global News*, 15 November 2014, http://globalnews.ca/news/1673290/get-out-of-ukraine-harper-to-putin-at-g20-summit-in-brisbane/.

21. Anton Troianovski, 'Soviets Once Denied a Deadly Anthrax Lab Leak. U.S. Scientists Backed the Story', *New York Times*, 20 June 2021.

fictions: 'Russia did not bomb hospitals and other civilian sites in Syria, never used chemical weapons there or elsewhere, it did not invade Georgia, neither it occupied Crimea, nor started the war in the eastern Ukraine. To claim otherwise is just to make false assertion [sic].'[22] Irish journalist John Mooney has seen this routine at first-hand at press conferences: 'They went into this absolute overdrive in terms of denial, deny, deny, deny, deny, it just has all been made up.' The level of denial is absurd – like a toddler denying stealing cookies while their hand is still in the jar – and it would be comical if the stakes were not so high and the consequences so tragic. The pattern is so consistent that experienced Russia-watchers look to the tone and speed of denials to help assess whether Russia is in fact probably culpable in incidents where there is doubt; in fact one of the observations from parodist Darth Putin that is most quoted by professional Russia analysts is 'never believe anything until the Kremlin denies it'.[23]

But this Russian tactic does on occasion work and achieve its effects. Sulev Suvari recalls seeing those effects at first-hand at the Syria ceasefire negotiations in Geneva in 2016. Working alongside US State Department colleagues who had not previously been exposed to Russia, he saw how they were taken aback by the ease with which the Russian negotiators would deny not only facts on the ground in Syria, but even what they had said in the previous meeting. As a seasoned Russia-watcher, he had to explain to them that this was standard practice: 'It was no different than Crimea, like, I don't know who those people are running around in green uniforms, speaking Russian and carrying Russian kit. No idea who they are.'

The effect on his colleagues was heightened because of the knowledge of real human suffering in Syria resulting from ongoing bombing raids and chemical weapons attacks. 'It became very emotional on our side because there was a horrible humanitarian situation. But then the Russians would say something like, we have firm evidence that it's the locals themselves who are actually killing their own people, it was them that poured the chlorine in. Everybody knew it was a lie but there's just nothing you could do about it.'

'For me personally it was just it was just another validation of how they operate,' Sulev says. 'They're just absolute blatant falsehoods that everybody knows is false, but I think they are keenly aware of our vulnerabilities to that because they know how we work.'

Over the years since Russian disinformation became widely recognized as a problem, Western governments and experts have chewed over plenty of possible solutions. These include fact-checking and rebuttals (ineffective), trying to reach Russia's own population with the truth (unworkable) and hitting back at Russia using its own methods (incompatible with Western values). But one set of people

22. 'Russia stands for a peaceful world order', *Irish Times*, 22 October 2019, https://www.irishtimes.com/opinion/letters/russia-stands-for-a-peaceful-world-order-1.4058019.

23. Tweet by @DarthPutinKGB, 22 April 2016, https://twitter.com/darthputinkgb/status/723507863054856192.

that think they have a different answer is the group behind the Darth Putin parody account on Twitter, @DarthPutinKGB. Darth, as I'll call them for short, holds a mirror up to Russian state propaganda. 'We write misworded Kremlinese,' Darth told me. 'We take one of their public statements and change it slightly' – and the effect is to expose its ludicrousness. They think this is a more effective approach to countering Russian state announcements than soberly cataloguing the lies they contain. 'Arguing with it gives it credibility it doesn't deserve. It's not how you respond when somebody is standing there saying that's not a cat lying on the couch. You can get angry about it, which they would really like, because it's helpless ranting and responding to their arguments as though they had merit. We show another way of doing it.'

The lack of self-awareness of many official Russian social media accounts does lend itself to ridicule, like the claim by the Russian Embassy in London that the 'Royal Navy abuses [the] UK's geographic position to intimidate and spy on Russian ships in lawful transit', prompting Twitter users including former Estonian president Toomas Ilves to wonder if they were asking the UK to move.[24] 'As they've retrenched more and more into 'the world is out to get us' paranoia, their statements get more and more ridiculous,' Darth says. 'And we just shine a light on that.' Paradoxically, that can make the job harder. 'It's tricky to mock when it's so blatantly stupid already.'

Still, Darth finds plenty of targets in the increasingly deranged output from the Russian Foreign Ministry, like a press release explaining how the poisoning of Alexei Navalny on a flight over Siberia was a 'pre-planned provocation against Russia'.[25] When the Russian MFA tweeted that 'August 20 marks one year since the emergency hospitalization of Russian blogger Alexey Navalny in Omsk. The actions taken by German authorities over the past 12 months clearly show that a pre-planned provocation was carried out against Russia,' Darth replied: 'August 20 marks one year since a Russian in Russia under close surveillance by Russian intelligence got poisoned by a Russian nerve agent only Russia has while on a plane going from Russia to Russia in "pre-planned provocation by Berlin".'[26]

I mention the proposals from various think tanks calling for serious efforts to counter Russian propaganda online. 'Yes, and bears defecate in the woods. I've seen that. Nearly stood in it once,' says one of the team. 'But we've yet to hear another way of doing this that is as effective as what we do.' This may be true. Darth showed me a number of tweets from Sputnik that had been deleted after their idiocy had been made fun of. Their theory is that this may be due to internal pressure to

24. Tweet by @RussianEmbassy, 6 December 2020, https://twitter.com/RussianEmbassy/status/1335557456307556352.

25. 'Press release on the anniversary of "Alexey Navalny case"', Russian Ministry of Foreign Affairs, 18 August 2021, https://www.mid.ru/en/foreign_policy/news/-/asset_publisher/cKNonkJE02Bw/content/id/4841644.

26. https://twitter.com/darthputinkgb/status/1428586671042347010.

perform. 'We have a feeling that when they have budget meetings, if it looks like all they are doing is getting mocked, that's not great. They have to show progress.' Darth also thinks that a new habit of Russian official accounts putting out 'on this day' anniversary tweets three days early and at odd times of the night is a response to the widespread ridicule.[27] 'They have a flunky tweet at midnight to try to own hashtags.'

In May 2016 the account was banned along with a number of other parody accounts mocking Russian diplomats, following what Darth presumes was pressure from Russia. It was swiftly restored after a mass protest by other Twitter users.[28] Inevitably, the account has also been subjected to multiple hacking attempts, using both crude and highly sophisticated techniques, and efforts to find out who is behind it. I asked the group if they felt personally at risk because of antagonizing the Russian authorities. 'We take a series of precautions,' they said. 'But when you consider what other people in Russia are risking by doing far braver things – jail for the rest of their lives or being killed – I don't think the risk to us should be compared to that.' 'Anyway, both the serious attempts to identify who we are and the wild guesses are all wrong,' Darth added.

Not all of Darth's followers fully support their methods. Ariana Gic, the political analyst focused on Ukraine, thinks it's not right to 'make light of serious matters of life and death, and of freedom and sovereignty. Trivializing a war criminal's actions and the harm which befalls his victims has no critical or cathartic value. It's sophomoric and insensitive at best.' But Darth is fully aware of the serious disinformation problem that lies behind his mockery. 'I worry what would happen if RT actually were a credible news agency, given the successes they have already just by being clowns. Look at all the French and Germans who already think Ukraine is having a civil war.' Darth also thinks part of the problem is Western media repeating Russian statements for the sake of balance, or 'telling both sides of the story'. 'If you don't know anything it can sound plausible, and that's what a lot of journalists do – that's what Russia said and now we cross over to the weather.' This helps Russia's technique of spreading lots of different versions of events they want to deny. 'They don't want you to believe a specific thing,' Darth says. 'They want you to believe nothing, and think that you'll never know. They rely on the fact that most people are too apathetic to care, they have their own problems.'

Despite being intended as parody, Darth has emerged as a highly effective and penetrating short-form commentator on Russian politics and history. Several of their pithy quotes have entered the common language of Russia-watchers abroad because they sum up key aspects of the Russia problem. 'Russia is a peaceful country surrounded by ceasefires,' 'Never believe anything until the Kremlin denies

27. For example, Russian MFA tweet regarding the anniversary of the Molotov–Ribbentrop pact on 23 August, put out on 20 August. See https://twitter.com/mfa_russia/status/1428369500555018243.

28. 'Twitter restores Putin parody account', BBC News, 1 June 2016, https://www.bbc.co.uk/news/blogs-trending-36429074.

it,' and 'The Warsaw Pact is the only mutual defence alliance in history to repeatedly invade itself as members were not permitted to interfere in their own internal affairs' have become recognized shorthand describing some of the basic contradictions driving Russian state behaviour and propaganda. But overall, Darth says, their approach is effective because it does not play the game the Kremlin wants us to. 'The Russian authorities enjoy our helpless rage,' Darth says. 'What they can't stand is being laughed at instead. They take themselves desperately seriously and they want us to as well.'

### Russia and the Western media

Darth Putin is not the only one concerned about how Western media treat stories about Russia. Free and independent media are a vital attribute of Western democracies. But here, too, what is normally described as a strength of Western societies can also be exploited by Russia as a weakness, and a means to extend its reach and influence what ordinary people in the West think and believe.

One of the specific features of respectable Western media that Russia has learned to use to its advantage is the way they apply journalistic ideals of balance and impartiality. Students of journalism tend to say that there are always two sides to every story and the truth usually lies somewhere in the middle. However, this important commitment to objectivity is rendered absurd when one side bases its entire strategy on deceit. Put simply, there can be no meaningful middle ground between deliberate Russian disinformation and reality. Valeriy Akimenko worked for the BBC for more than two decades and is still frustrated by its inability to see the difference between 'balance' and objective reporting of the facts. 'In the UK the BBC would give voices to for example a government source and an opposition spokesman,' he explains. 'By extension the BBC seems to be under the delusion that if it also does that with coverage of Russia, and always includes the voices from the Kremlin, it somehow equates with the notion of balance.' To be fair to the BBC, this approach has evolved under the relentless assault of Russian official fictions. While in 2015 the BBC felt it needed to report seriously Russian allegations that Alexander Litvinenko, poisoned with polonium, might have committed suicide, by 2021 Kremlin denials were routinely being covered by simple addition of the phrase 'a charge which Russia denies'.[29]

But even after eight years of recognizing how Russia uses Western media, it remains necessary to explain repeatedly how 'balance' is one of the Kremlin's best weapons when editors think it means reporting the middle ground between truth and deception, between fact and *maskirovka*. Lars says the problem is that 'in some European countries they still treat Russian media as being normal media, like in other countries, So you might have news outlets actually citing Russian news as

---

29. 'Alexander Litvinenko "may have killed himself", key suspect says', BBC News, 8 April 2015, https://www.bbc.co.uk/news/uk-32221581.

objective truth or something resembling genuine news in terms of trustworthiness. And then those are the kinds of things that seep into public understanding and could shape public opinion. So [the] Western press is used to validate these Russian disinformation narratives.'

While collecting first-hand stories for this book, I approached RT contributors and employees in France, the UK and Russia itself for interviews so they could explain their side of the story. Unfortunately, none agreed (and most did not even respond). They could, if they wished, have told me they were genuine journalists. But in fact it is a widely repeated mistake to call Russian state propaganda outlets like RT, Ruptly and Sputnik 'media', or their employees 'journalists', as this gives them an entirely false aura of legitimacy.

The difference between RT staff and journalists was highlighted in March 2021, when RT employees in Germany were tasked with investigating the Berlin hospital where Alexei Navalny was recovering from being poisoned with Novichok in Russia. The instructions, including operating secretly, covertly photographing the military personnel guarding the hospital, and testing its security, were indistinguishable from reconnaissance for a further attack on Navalny while he lay in his hospital bed. Any suggestion that this was normal journalistic practice was immediately torpedoed by their further instructions not to speak about or publish the story, not to take their equipment with them, and not to say who they worked for.[30]

But an even more challenging problem is for Western media outlets to assess the bona fides and intentions of Russian citizens applying to work for them. Media organizations may not always be best placed to weigh the presumption that applicants are genuine journalists that share their values against wariness over exactly who they are placing in responsible positions. The BBC Monitoring Service is an arm of the BBC whose primary task was originally to collect open-source information for British government customers. There was surprise within the organization when Nikolay Gorshkov, a former Radio Moscow commentator, was appointed head of its outpost in Moscow – a highly responsible position with influence over what information was passed back to UK government customers. There was less surprise when, after Gorshkov left BBC Monitoring under circumstances which one of his contemporaries told me BBC management was 'eager to play down', he went on to lead Sputnik's UK operations.[31]

In some cases the validation process Lars described even appears to take place with the active help of Western news outlets. The Reuters news agency formerly represented an internationally respected gold standard of neutrality and

30. Julian Röpcke, 'Wie Putin "Journalisten" in Deutschland als Spione einsetzt' (How Putin uses 'journalists' as spies in Germany), *Bild*, 9 March 2021, https://www.bild.de/politik/ausland/politik-ausland/geheimbefehl-aus-moskau-wie-putin-journalisten-in-deutschland-als-spione-einsetz-75681168.bild.html.

31. Sarah Hurst, 'Ex-BBC manager at Sputnik sees no evil', Stopfake.org, 15 May 2018, https://www.stopfake.org/en/ex-bbc-manager-at-sputnik-sees-no-evil/.

trustworthy objective reporting. In mid-2020, however, Reuters announced a commercial arrangement with TASS, a Russian (and previously Soviet) state news agency.[32] In theory, this link-up was only about Reuters providing commercial access to a separate feed of TASS material, which would have no impact on core Reuters coverage. In practice, however, alert readers of the agency's material noted Reuters' main feed starting to carry material from Russia that appeared to repeat Russian propaganda points with no comment, caveat or quotation marks.[33]

These stories were labelled as having been produced by Reuters' people in Moscow, but bore no sign of meaningful editorial intervention on their way through the bureau there. In some cases this shone through in the text of the stories, written in not-quite-English. Russians sometimes struggle with when and when not to use 'a' or 'the' in English, as they do not exist in Russian. So when Reuters stories began with phrases like 'Ukraine must show a good will if its wants Russian gas transit to Europe and related fees to remain', it only added to accusations that it was now serving as the Kremlin's tame court reporter as opposed to reporting the news objectively.[34] Fulsome Reuters puff pieces from Russia and Crimea similarly saw it accused of 'broadcasting propaganda from occupied territory'.[35] Worse, some of this reporting played directly into ongoing Russian information campaigns with specific operational aims. In early 2021, as Russia carried out its dry run for the military assault on Ukraine a year later (see Chapter 4), Reuters was content to channel Russian messaging that reflected the Kremlin's fabricated parallel reality, with threats to Ukraine based on Russian resolve to 'defend its citizens' there.[36]

As in so many other instances, cooperation with Russia has been toxic for Reuters' reputation: informed observers of Russia simply no longer consider it a trustworthy source, which is a crushing defeat considering its earlier impeccable reputation. When I asked a Reuters staff member what was going on, they replied 'I'm sorry, I really can't help you with that. Not just because of corporate sensitivities but because I genuinely don't understand it.'

32. 'TASS News Agency joins Reuters Connect', Reuters, 1 June 2020, https://www.reuters.com/article/rpb-tass-connect-idUSKBN2381UQ.

33. Peter Dickinson, 'How Putin made the international media his unwitting accomplices', Atlantic Council, 1 April 2021, https://www.atlanticcouncil.org/blogs/ukrainealert/how-putin-made-the-international-media-his-unwitting-accomplices/.

34. Vladimir Soldatkin and Katya Golubkova, 'Ukraine must show goodwill if it wants Russian gas transit, Putin says', Reuters, 4 June 2021, https://www.reuters.com/business/energy/ukraine-must-show-good-will-if-it-wants-russian-gas-transit-putin-says-2021-06-04.

35. Tweet by Patrik Oksanen, 27 April 2021, https://twitter.com/patrikoksanen/status/1386999917017763841.

36. Thomas Escritt and Tom Balmforth, 'Merkel tells Putin to pull back troops as Kremlin accuses Ukraine of provocations', Reuters, 8 April 2021, https://www.reuters.com/article/us-ukraine-crisis-kremlin-citizens-idUSKBN2BV1S3.

But Moscow also benefits from the largely free and open media marketplace in most Western countries by establishing brand-new propaganda outlets. There are few obstacles to Russia repeatedly setting up fake media organizations apparently based in Western countries – in a way that would be absolutely impossible in Russia itself.

With perfect timing, Laura Walters arrived from New Zealand in London looking for work on 1 March 2020. 'I had lots of friends who were working in media and I just didn't think it was going to be an issue to find a job. But then of course Covid happened. So I sent out hundreds of CVs and got basically nothing back. Then I thought if I update my LinkedIn and Twitter and website and all of that to say I'm a freelance, and I'm looking for work, maybe that will help. And it wasn't long after I did that that I got the message on LinkedIn from Alice Schultz.'

Alice Schultz said she represented a media organization called Peace Data and was interested in having Laura write articles for them on the kind of 'left-leaning' topics she was already interested in. 'And I thought, okay, well, that sounds like a great mission, you know, to write more about human rights and some things that might get left out of everyday reporting,' Laura says. Her work was received enthusiastically, payment was prompt, and there was no reason for her to suspect that Peace Data was in any way connected with Russia. 'You know, I'd studied Russian history in high school, watched all the movies, watched *The Americans* and all of that, but I didn't have any other stronger links. I was no more interested in Russia than anyone, I think.'

But Russia was interested in Laura. The first clue she had that Alice Schultz did not exist and Peace Data was a front for a Russian disinformation operation was a phone call from a fellow journalist following up on Peace Data's removal from Facebook and Twitter after a tip-off from the FBI.[37] I asked Laura how she felt when she realized she had been caught up in a Russian operation. 'It was disbelief to start with,' she says. 'And then surprise. And it sounds weird but I laughed a lot at the start. I was kind of just laughing in disbelief, and I had to keep telling him, I'm not laughing because it's funny. But it kind of is funny, because who does this actually happen to? You see this in the movies, but you never think you're going to be the one who's affected by it.'

'And then in the end, I felt really embarrassed. I don't think I'm particularly gullible. I actually have all the tools and skills at my disposal to check out something like this. I just didn't think to use them, because why would you suspect something like that?'

Laura's more helpful friends and colleagues have reassured her that she did not do anything wrong or foolish by accepting an apparently genuine offer of work. But, she points out, 'If it can happen to me, it can happen to anyone.' Rather than being embarrassed, she is now happy to tell her story because, she says, 'I'd like to

---

37. Jack Stubbs, 'Duped by Russia, freelancers ensnared in disinformation campaign by promise of easy money', Reuters, 2 September 2020, https://www.reuters.com/article/us-usa-election-facebook-russia-idCAKBN25T35E

help stop this kind of thing happening again, by putting a human face on it for people rather than it just being this abstract idea.'[38]

## Targeting individuals

Most people who put their head above the parapet to challenge Russia will be subjected to abuse online. Sometimes this can be relatively mild. Finnish journalist Laura Halminen describes 'fake profiles on Twitter calling me "NATO's whore", mundane stuff. So I was targeted, but not in the worst manner.' Rather than address the points that critics of Russia make, it is common to attack the critics themselves by writing them off as 'Russophobes', who are driven only by a hatred of individual Russians or the country as a whole.[39] This tactic comes and goes in both official Russian statements and online trolling, sometimes with variations in flavour – for instance during 2019 it was briefly the fashion to equate Russophobia with anti-Semitism, by replacing the word 'Russia' in critical comments with 'the Jews'. This didn't persist long, perhaps because some of these replacements showed up the very genuine anti-Semitism of the accusers instead. But the more effort someone devotes to studying and understanding Russia, the greater the likelihood that they will be accused of being either an apologist or a Russophobe. The irony is that so many people who have willingly devoted so much of their working lives to Russia end up being labelled as haters of the country.[40]

Sometimes the effects of online campaigns against individuals can be severe, especially since it is so easy to arrange a mob attack. As disinformation researcher Gavril points out, 'On social media it's really easy for people to whip up a firestorm and attack somebody without thinking about the consequences of what that does to people.' But when abuse and intimidation crosses the line from online to the physical world, the results can range from the merely tedious to the terrifying.

In Moscow itself, Western diplomats from countries that Russia dislikes suffer a level of harassment and aggression that is rarely reported. Robert Pszczel talks of this being a normal part of working in Russia. 'I had some advantages because my family stayed behind at home,' he says. 'But still there's the difficulty of living in

38. See also: Laura Walters, 'I was part of a Russian meddling campaign', *Newsroom*, 4 September 2020, https://www.newsroom.co.nz/i-was-part-of-a-russian-meddling-campaign.

Alicia Wanless and Laura Walters, 'How Journalists Become an Unwitting Cog in the Influence Machine', Carnegie, 13 October 2020, https://carnegieendowment.org/2020/10/13/how-journalists-become-unwitting-cog-in-influence-machine-pub-82923.

39. 'Russophobia in the Kremlin's strategy. A weapon of mass destruction', OSW, 2 November 2015, https://www.osw.waw.pl/en/publikacje/point-view/2015-11-02/russophobia-kremlins-strategy-a-weapon-mass-destruction.

40. Neil Robinson, '"Russophobia" in Official Russian Political Discourse', *De Europa* 2, no. 2 (2019): 61–77, https://ulir.ul.ie/bitstream/handle/10344/8429/Robinson%2c%20Russophobia.pdf.

Mordor. Without going into details, which I can't, there was quite a bit in terms of intimidation of my staff. It's part of the reality you have to accept.' Sulev Suvari was attached to the defence section of the US Embassy in Moscow, and recalled how some new staff members were greeted: 'When it's your first week in Moscow, you're on the metro going in to work and right before the station, two people walk up and just punch you in the stomach, really hard, bending you over, say welcome to Moscow and walk out. It's disconcerting because it says we know exactly who you are, we know what you're doing here and this is our little way of saying welcome.' Sulev himself suffered more mundane harassment, at a level of childish pettiness. This included things as simple as ringing the downstairs doorbell of his ninth-floor apartment 'randomly throughout the late evening and then early morning, so you'll get it at two o'clock in the morning waking you up. And it's one of those doorbells that's more like a fire alarm, so as long as you hold the button, it keeps ringing and ringing and ringing,' he recalled. 'The good thing was over time whoever was assigned to randomly do it started coming around earlier, at about 10.30 every night, so when the bell rang it was more like, all right, time to go to bed.'

Sulev noted that the persecution was systematic but also random. 'I really question if there's any logic to it at all. There's probably just some maniacal person somewhere saying this week let's let the air out of his tyres and see what happens … At the end it's just to throw you off your game, to keep you not focused, and then just looking for those opportunities.' The opportunities are for finding the means of harassment that prove most effective. 'It's a process of seeing how people react, trying to understand the vulnerabilities. And so, if people start to react badly, that goes in your file' as an effective means of pressure to use in the future, Sulev says. Kimberly Marten describes how in negotiations, Russia tries to 'test a partner and look for psychological weaknesses … that could be exploited'.[41] Sulev sees the same process at work in the harassment of American embassy staffers. 'There's always something you learn from those sort of experiments,' he goes on. 'And I think that's really what it is, just probing you to see what works, what doesn't work. You build up a dossier of what frustrates Americans in general, what gets Americans spun up, and then you can use that another time – in a negotiation or in a conversation you say something in a way that will get a reaction. I think that's why they end up looking like they play chess, but it's really because they have taken the time to do their homework.'

When American and European embassy staff's homes are visited while they are out, this is often done not stealthily but in a deliberately obvious way so that the target knows that their home is not a place of safety and privacy. Sulev – and others – say the visitors 'make it very clear that they have been in your apartment. From not flushing the toilet to maybe using some of your items in the kitchen. You

---

41. Kimberly Marten, 'President Trump, Keep in Mind That Russia and the West Think about Negotiations Very, Very Differently', *Washington Post*, 25 July 2017, https://www.washingtonpost.com/news/monkey-cage/wp/2017/07/25/president-trump-keep-in-mind-that-russia-and-the-west-think-about-negotiations-very-very-differently/.

know, so you come back and it just throws you off.' Sulev recalls how when iPads were first released, a close friend bought one but found that each time he bought a charging cable for it, it would be removed from his apartment so the iPad was unusable. 'There was no point in that other than just to be malicious,' Sulev says. Former CIA officer John Sipher tells the story of a US diplomat, a keen runner, who found that every time he bought a new pair of running shoes the clandestine visitors to his apartment would steal one of them from his wardrobe and leave one behind. Faced with a growing collection of useless single shoes, and knowing that he was under constant surveillance, he eventually arrived at a deal by proposing loudly in his apartment for the benefit of the hidden microphones that he would from then on run a predictable route, at a predictable time, to save the Russian intelligence services effort and resources in tracking him. He did so, and his shoes stopped disappearing.[42] But the surveillance itself is a challenge. The knowledge that everything you do or say is being listened to, and may be used against you, is in itself an exhausting drain on daily life. It can lead to married couples waiting months to go abroad before they can have a private conversation.

Diplomats and military personnel posted to Moscow who have children or pets face a particularly difficult moral dilemma because they are placing them in harm's way. The Russian authorities have shown no compunction in targeting children, or using them as instruments of intimidation against their parents. In the period of especially high tensions after the seizure of Crimea, a senior NATO defence attaché's young children went missing for several hours. On leaving school, they had been directed onto 'a different bus', which then drove them around Moscow until late in the evening when they were deposited outside their apartment block. And three separate people attached to the US Embassy in Moscow have told me over a period of years of the pattern of pets being poisoned, including one horrific instance where – just as with the case of the Skripals in Salisbury – the attempt was botched. The two dogs involved had to be put down after days of howling in agony.

Families and children have also been attacked using the technique that has acquired the name 'Havana syndrome' in the West.[43] Primarily affecting US diplomats and other government personnel, the 'syndrome' refers to a pattern of incapacitating long-term brain injuries. How exactly these are inflicted has not yet been clearly described in public – but just as the Novichok used to murder enemies of Russia was a product of the USSR's chemical weapons programme, the methods used to trigger Havana syndrome appear linked to extensive Soviet research on the damaging effects of microwave radiation on the human body.[44]

42. Discussion in Toronto, 2019.

43. Julia Ioffe, 'The Mystery of the Immaculate Concussion', *GQ*, 19 October 2020, https://www.gq.com/story/cia-investigation-and-russian-microwave-attacks.

44. Ana G Johnson Liakouris, 'Radiofrequency (RF) sickness in the Lilienfeld study: An effect of modulated microwaves?', *Archives of Environmental Health* 53, no. 3 (May –June 1998): 236–7.

The syndrome acquired the name Havana after the location where groups of US and Canadian government employees started to suffer from it in numbers large enough to be undeniable. But reports of serious damage to the health of diplomats in the US Embassy in Moscow go back well into the Cold War.[45] They are thought to be linked to the decades-long microwave bombardment of the US Embassy in Moscow – occasionally suspended at times of diplomatic thaws between the two countries – which at the time was suspected to be either efforts to jam American communications or electronic intelligence equipment, or alternatively to trigger or communicate with listening devices planted within the embassy.[46] If so, this follows a pattern of Russia being entirely ruthless in the way it targets foreign diplomats for espionage purposes, regardless of the possible consequences. Another method from the Cold War was the use of carcinogenic 'spy dust' to trace where targeted individuals had been and who they had met.[47] The 'dust' was nitrophenyl pentadien, a barely visible but easily traceable substance known in Russian as *metka*, or 'marker'.[48] Foreigners would pick it up after it was applied to surfaces they were likely to touch, like their car door handles – the same method as used in the Novichok attacks we saw in Chapter 3.

A sign of the growing confidence of Russia's campaigns against the West have been the growing numbers of reported Havana syndrome attacks on foreign soil including the US, Austria and, most recently at the time of writing, Germany.[49] And as public knowledge of the symptoms and effects of the attacks spreads, it seems likely that more countries will disclose that their personnel have been affected. Bill Evanina was a senior US intelligence official when the Havana cases emerged, and stepped down as the head of the National Counterintelligence and Security Center in 2021. 'I would probably put on pause the statement that no one in the UK has experienced any symptoms,' he said in a BBC interview in September of that year – strongly suggesting that 'Havana syndrome' attacks have been carried

45. John R. Goldsmith, 'Epidemiologic Evidence of Radiofrequency Radiation (Microwave) Effects on Health in Military, Broadcasting, and Occupational Studies', *International Journal of Occupational and Environmental Health* 1, NO. 1 (1995): 47–57, https://doi.org/10.1179/oeh.1995.1.1.47.

46. 'Soviet Halts Microwaves Aimed at U.S. Embassy', *New York Times*, 30 May 1979, https://www.nytimes.com/1979/05/30/archives/soviet-halts-microwaves-aimed-at-us-embassy.html.

47. Michael McGuire, '"Spy Dust" Rattles Foreigners in Moscow', *Chicago Tribune*, 25 August 1985, https://www.chicagotribune.com/news/ct-xpm-1985-08-25-8502250501-story.html.

48. Robert W. Pringle, *Historical Dictionary of Russian and Soviet Intelligence* (Lanham, MD: Scarecrow Press, 2006), p. 159.

49. Justin Huggler, 'US diplomats stationed in Germany fall ill with mysterious Havana Syndrome', *Telegraph*, 18 August 2021, https://www.telegraph.co.uk/world-news/2021/08/18/us-diplomats-stationed-germany-fall-mysterious-havana-syndrome/.

out against British citizens or in the UK itself, and this has been discussed with the UK's American allies but not yet disclosed publicly.[50]

## We called, but you were out

The tactic of intimidation by home visits is also not limited to Moscow but shows Russia's ability to reach out and touch its victims abroad. Lawyers for the victim's families in the MH17 case have been 'followed by cars to their homes', homes visited by 'men wearing dark glasses', in incidents that the Dutch national counter-terrorism department assesses were Russian attempts at intimidation.[51] Critics of Russia in different countries of Europe report graffiti on their inside walls, or their laptops smashed while they are out. One activist in Finland recorded multiple home visits, and a series of direct messages like an Orthodox cross painted on his bathroom mirror or a dead bird left on an inside table.[52] One thing that appears consistent between intimidatory home visits in Moscow and abroad is the toilet tactics. Four of my interviewees from four different countries, who do not know each other, told me independently of their uninvited visitors' habit of leaving unmistakeable evidence of their visit in the toilet and not flushing. It's a good example of how many of these tactics are often both confusing and deniable – because anybody hearing the story will question whether, even when somebody is living alone, they might be mistaken as to whether this was the result of an intruder in the house or their own forgotten efforts. Maria, a staff member for the European External Action Service (EEAS) living in Brussels but working directly on the Russia problem, explains how this sows doubts in the victim's own mind. 'No one left a dead rat or bird or a picture of Putin. And there were always things where I couldn't be 100% sure it wasn't me or the family. But there were others where there could be no doubt – as when my computer would have been used while we were away, or once when the window was open when we came home from holiday in the middle of winter. It was a series of things both inside and outside the house.' One of my interviewees found the knowledge that she was not safe in her home country distinctly intimidating – which is, after all, its intent. 'It's not the Russians in Moscow who worry me,' she told me. 'It's their little helpers here. They're the most frightening.'

50. Gordon Corera, '"Havana syndrome" and the mystery of the microwaves', BBC News, 9 September 2021, https://www.bbc.co.uk/news/world-58396698.

51. 'Advocaten MH17-zaak geïntimideerd, hoogstwaarschijnlijk door Rusland', RTL, 28 October 2021, https://www.rtlnieuws.nl/nieuws/nederland/artikel/5262870/advocaten-mh17-zaak-mogelijk-geintimideerd-door-rusland.

52. Laura Halminen, 'Dead birds and multiple crosses: This is what happens when Russian intelligence harasses you in Helsinki, a Finnish activist claims', *Helsingin Sanomat*, 23 August 2015, https://www.hs.fi/sunnuntai/art-2000002847124.html.

Martin Kragh, the Swedish Russia-watcher, became a high-profile target for harassment abroad. In early 2017, he published an academic article about Russian disinformation and malign influence targeting his country.[53] 'From 2014 to 2016, I was able to document an increase in the use of disinformation and forgeries from Russian sources,' he recalls. 'And I inferred from this contextual analysis that there was in fact, a Russian influence campaign, you know, traditional intelligence activity.' The pattern Martin observed was one familiar from previous KGB disinformation practice, updated for the internet. 'All of a sudden, this forgery comes up on an account that is immediately terminated afterwards. It's quoted by nobody, but then it's picked up by some obscure Russian blog, then it's picked up by a Russian news outlet and it's translated for a Russian international English-language outlet, and then all of a sudden it's quoted and circulated everywhere.'

Martin's was one report among many documenting Russian disinformation. But unlike others, his hit the headlines. 'The timing was accidental, but it was when Trump had just been installed as president and there was a huge discussion everywhere in the West regarding Russia and potential influence. So, it became one of the most downloaded academic articles of the year, in the top ten. There was cancer research and research on global warming, and among those articles you find research on Russian influence activities towards Sweden. And so that's basically how I went from a quiet, traditional academic researcher to having requests from CNN.'

The problem was Martin's research touched nerves. A broad combined campaign of threats, media smears and targeted intimidation began, spearheaded by local Russian activists and a Swedish tabloid that Kragh had identified as a regular platform for Russian disinformation. The campaign was effective. 'To be honest, for a few months I was unable to work as normal,' Martin says. 'And I lost weight and I became very careful, and all of that created very negative emotions.' Martin also found that his livelihood was under threat, because the campaign targeted his academic reputation. 'Activists and conspiracy theorists were petitioning my employers and the editors of [the] *Journal of Strategic Studies* to retract my article. There was a huge campaign to have my work retracted, and for a scholar to have an article retracted is basically an academic death sentence.' Another campaign launched an investigation at Uppsala University alleging 'scientific misconduct' by Martin. It eventually cleared him of all accusations, but 'for the whole of 2017 I was in limbo,' Martin says.

Martin experienced online attacks like spearphishing and attempts to register different accounts in his name, as well as simple defamation. 'There were websites created, from addresses in Russia, that were basically just writing all sorts of nonsense about me,' he says. He was struck by the way multiple lines of attack were used at once. 'All of these things were going on at the same time, the various legal

---

53. Martin Kragh and Sebastian Åsberg, 'Russia's strategy for influence through public diplomacy and active measures: the Swedish case', *Journal of Strategic Studies* 40, no. 6 (January 2017): 33, http://dx.doi.org/10.1080/01402390.2016.1273830.

or administrative processes, the media campaigns, the neo-Nazi death threats coming on Messenger and email and through regular mail.'

Martin found that once the campaign against him had begun, there was no shortage of people within Sweden who were happy to join in because they bought into the propaganda against him. 'I think a lot of the things that were going on were sort of spontaneous reactions by people who were not connected to Russia in any formal way, just susceptible to Russian narratives, and able to believe disinformation is true even when it is contradicted by facts.' This included people who call themselves peace activists but 'come from a more sort of anti-imperialist tradition. They support whatever peace Russia is imposing.'

Despite the intensive campaign of intimidation, Martin did not experience any physical attacks. He is very conscious that others have suffered far worse. 'About two years ago I was at a conference in The Hague organized by the Free Russia Foundation,' he says. 'And I was on the same panel as the widow of Alexander Litvinenko, two activists from Donetsk and Vladimir Kara-Murza [see Chapter 3]. And I remember thinking to myself that my experience should be placed in context. Although I lived through some difficult months, where I was constantly attacked and my reputation was undermined, I was reminded of what people from Russia have actually been through.'

But most of all, Martin was struck by the way he suddenly found himself in the line of fire. 'It seems that anyone can be a target. I'm not a decision-maker of any kind. I'm not Bellingcat, not a high-level target. My case is an example of how someone who shouldn't be a target can become one,' he says.

I asked Martin what the response was when he reported death threats to the Swedish police. 'Nothing,' he replied. One alarmingly consistent factor when people experience Russian hostile attention is the lack of official support and protection. Targets of intimidation and harassment often report that they feel they are left with nowhere to turn, as local law-enforcement can be both uncomprehending of the problem and under-resourced to deal with it. Those living alone or in isolated locations feel particularly vulnerable, especially when their personal details are published online. Maria in Brussels was one of the lucky ones: when she started experiencing home intruders and threats, she says, 'I can't accuse my employer of inaction. They did take it quite seriously.' But another of my interviewees who lives alone in a remote area in Southern Europe is reluctant even to mention the problem to the local police, for fear it will not only make her 'look like a paranoid crank' but potentially even make it worse.

After Laura Walters was dragged into her own Russian disinformation scam, she did succeed in making contact with the FBI who had uncovered the operation in the first place. She found the experience surreal. 'It was all like a movie,' she says. 'I met the guy outdoors, and it had to be in a public space. We met in [London's] Borough Market, and then we just walked around and for an hour and a half he asked me a lot of questions but managed to dodge every question I asked about why I was a target, and how they figured out what this was.' Laura is concerned for what people under more direct threat would do. 'I don't know who you would turn to for support and that that does raise an issue, doesn't it?' she wonders. 'For other people who find themselves in more intense circumstances – where would they go?'

But the single biggest deciding factor in how successful Russian intimidation tactics are seems to be the attitude of the victim. According to Martin Kragh, 'You never know beforehand how a person will react. The same treatment can have very different effects on different people.' Sulev, with his experience from Moscow, thinks a positive mental attitude is vital: 'You have to just say it doesn't bother me, it's not that big of a deal.' This seems to be true: the more robust (or the more laid-back) the target, the less effect the harassment has. Maria in Brussels told me 'I took it as part of the job, part of the routine – it's what you can expect if you do this kind of work.' Kyle Wilson in Australia told me about a death threat he received in calm, measured, slightly amused tones. But that approach isn't universal. Gavril was severely impacted and finds that he still needs to keep his head down several years after the harassment campaign peaked: 'It's a hostile environment even though we have tried very much to be objective with them. I generally keep a very low profile and stay out of most fights ... I don't want their attention, and I don't need that in my life because the stress level will be too high,' he says. Laura Halminen in Finland saw the intimidation tactics succeeding. 'Being a journalist dealing with [Russian] issues was a burden after Crimea,' she says. 'During those years I saw fellow journalists react by at best dropping the entire subject, refusing to cover it at all, and at worst losing their mental health due to the amount of hate they faced ... I've seen gaslighting work, and it's really sad.'

It's hard to put a number on the people who have decided to withdraw from the fight, in part because it takes a certain amount of courage to admit that you have done so. Occasionally the effects become clear, as for instance when joint efforts are called for to resist a specific Russian campaign. When Martin Kragh was facing another wave of intimidation, colleagues at Uppsala University wrote a newspaper article in his support. But they concluded, 'Several researchers have expressed their support for this appeal but declined to participate due to fear of becoming targets themselves.'[54] The sad truth is that despite the stoic approach of individuals like Maria and Kyle, harassment campaigns do work, and do achieve their aims.

## *Nobody is too unimportant*

But intimidatory tactics against individuals don't just target people who have particularly annoyed Russia. Service personnel from NATO militaries are targets just because of their jobs – especially if that involves postings to the front-line states. Russia finds it easy to reach out to them at a distance, using military systems for intercepting, jamming or spoofing civilian mobile phone communications,

---

54. 'Vi står bakom Kragh – ta ryska hotet på allvar' (We stand behind Kragh – take the Russian threat seriously), *Svenksa Dagbladet*, 14 February 2019, https://www.svd.se/vi-star-bakom-kragh--ta-ryska-hotet-pa-allvar.

including broadcasting content to smartphones.[55] A Canadian signals NCO serving in Latvia explained to me how Russia tracks the mobile phones of Canadian soldiers – especially those unwise enough to go against instructions and bring over their personal phones with their distinctive North American identification numbers – and mess with them in immediately obvious ways like wiping the content or contacts, or replacing them with junk or Russian information. In the same period, Estonian conscripts taking connected devices near the border with Russia saw their phones attacked, with the data scrambled and starting to play music that one conscript could only describe as 'creepy hiphop'. Russian officers say systems like this have proven to be key tools in carrying out information operations in live conflicts too, as in Syria where they delivered tailored content to opposition fighters intended to demoralize them with suggestions of corruption and embezzlement by their commanders. The tactic has also been used in Ukraine. A collection of messages delivered to Ukrainian soldiers on the front lines in 2015–17 included some aimed at general demoralization, and others with specific and targeted disinformation. The first category came overtly from Russia and included messages like 'UAF [Ukrainian Armed Forces] fighters go home. Nobody will want your children when they're orphans,' or 'UAF soldier! They'll find your body when the snow melts.' But the second pretended to be from Ukrainian soldiers themselves: 'The company commander ran away to Kramatorsk. It smells like trouble. Tonight we are also leaving.'[56]

Russia also makes use of face-to-face encounters, both within Russia itself and abroad. The phrase Laura Halminen uses for an in-person approach for intimidation or confusion is 'live-trolling', and it has a long history. Sulev Suvari recalls how in Moscow, a Russian colonel he had never met before walked up and congratulated him on his daughter's birthday a week previously. 'This was a probe, just saying, we know who you are, we know about your family back home, down to the point where we know your daughter's name and she just had a birthday. It was trying to mess with my mind. I could see where that tactic would create levels of uncertainty and confusion' in the target, Sulev says. For lower-profile targets, Russia does not have to do detailed research when social media are available. A young army captain deployed to eastern Europe with the units sent by America to bolster its defences in 2015 told me of the ways his soldiers were approached by what appeared to be Russian intelligence officers. One had been in line for tickets for a sporting event when the man behind him struck up a conversation about who he was, what he was doing in the country and why – a conversation that

55. Aleksey Ramm and Vladimir Zykov, 'Российская армия получила сотовое оружие' (Russian Army receives mobile phone weapon), *Izvestiya*, 25 January 2017, http://izvestia.ru/news/659503.

56. Collection provided by Raphael Satter. See Raphael Satter and Dmytro Vlasov, 'Ukraine soldiers bombarded by "pinpoint propaganda" texts', AP, 11 May 2017, https://apnews.com/article/technology-europe-ukraine-only-on-ap-9a564a5f64e847d1a50938035ea64b8f.

quickly turned to reeling off the details of the soldier's personal life that could only have been gleaned from detailed study of his Facebook posts. Another had a similar experience on a train through Poland, where another apparent random encounter turned into another demonstration of how careless postings on social media allow soldiers to be identified, tracked and targeted – and how they disclose full details of their families and communities.[57]

Valeriy Gerasimov says a key feature of modern warfare is 'simultaneous effects to the entire depth of enemy territory, in all physical media and in the information domain'.[58] In other words, Russia can use information effects far from what its adversary might think is the front line. This means soldiers don't have to be targeted directly – Russia can just as easily reach their spouses and families with online harassment, intimidation and targeted cyber attacks.[59] The very personal impact of hostile Russian interest has been illustrated by incidents like unsubstantiated allegations of child rape in Russian-backed media against specific named US Army officers visiting Ukraine. The potential effect of interventions like this not only on military units, but also on families and communities at home, is immediate and obvious. In effect, anything that prevents NATO service personnel from doing their job effectively at a critical moment, whether it is interventions against themselves or against their homes or families, would give Russia obvious advantages in a confrontation.[60]

Overall, it is a profound mistake for anybody to assume that they are too unimportant to be a target for Russia, especially online. In 2017, journalist Raphael Satter reported on a rare insight into how Russian intelligence services target individuals for cyber espionage, when the GRU accidentally exposed part of its phishing operation to the internet.[61] Raphael's conclusions from what he observed

57. Jeff Stein, 'How Russia Is Using LinkedIn as a Tool of War Against Its U.S. Enemies', *Newsweek*, 8 March 2017, https://www.newsweek.com/russia-putin-bots-linkedin-facebook-trump-clinton-kremlin-critics-poison-war-645696.

58. V. V. Gerasimov, 'Роль Генерального штаба в организации обороны страны в соответствии с новым Положением о Генеральном штабе, утвержденным Президентом Российской Федерации' (The Role of the General Staff in the Organization of the Country's Defence in Accordance with the New Statue on the General Staff, Approved by the President of the Russian Federation), *Vestnik Akademii Voennykh Nauk* (Bulletin of the Academy of Military Science) 1 (2014): 14–22.

59. Jeff Schogol, 'Report: Russians Posed As ISIS To Threaten Military Spouses, Army Family Readiness Group', *Task and Purpose*, 8 May 2018, https://taskandpurpose.com/bulletpoints/russian-hackers-isis-spouses/.

60. Joseph V. Micallef, 'Russian Harassment of NATO Personnel, Families: The Next Chapter in Information Warfare?' Military.com, 3 September 2019, https://www.military.com/daily-news/2019/09/03/russian-harassment-nato-personnel-families-next-chapter-information-warfare.html.

61. Raphael Satter et al., 'Russia hackers pursued Putin foes, not just US Democrats', AP, 2 November 2017, https://apnews.com/article/technology-entertainment-music-russia-hacking-3bca5267d4544508bb523fa0db462cb2.

were later confirmed by the Mueller Report in the US, which drew on a much wider range of sources – many of them classified – to lead to indictments against specific named GRU officers.[62] But at the time, independent cyber security researchers were able not only to watch hacking attempts in real time, but to study a partial database of the GRU's targets.

Before going public, Raphael showed the database to me and other trusted Russia-watchers. The size of the list, containing roughly 4,700 individuals, gave an indication of the scale of the operation. 'This is a small subset,' Raphael explained. 'We can only see a chunk of the GRU targets who were using Gmail between early 2015 and mid-2016. So we don't see the GRU targets who were using Yahoo or Hotmail. And in fact, we don't see the GRU targets who were hit in different ways. Because phishing is the most basic and the noisiest form of attack. There are many other ways to break into somebody's computer.' But Raphael particularly wanted to hear from Russia specialists about the types of people on the list, because at first sight it made no sense.

'I was very surprised by who was on the list,' Raphael told me at the time, 'in part because it was just so broad and it didn't correspond to what I would have thought of as traditional military intelligence targeting. The meat of the list was composed of military attachés, diplomats, defence contractors, military technology researchers, the kinds of people who would make obvious targets for the GRU and indeed for any military intelligence agency. What didn't make sense to me, or at least not initially, were YouTube influencers like GloZell.'[63]

In light of the social media influence campaigns happening at the same time, Raphael later wondered if the GRU were looking for an insight into what made for a viral YouTube video. But the unexpected targets on the list included even more unlikely people. 'You know, no one was too obscure to be targeted. There was a blogger in Murmansk that I spoke to who blogged about local issues. There was a woman who was running a local charity NGO in Yerevan, Armenia, not at all politically focused. There was another woman who was running a domestic violence NGO in Kyiv. If you were even remotely active in civil society in a country of interest to the Russian government, chances are not bad that the GRU had gone after you. That's kind of sobering. And it was sobering to the people that I talked to, because even though they thought of themselves as politically active, they had no idea that their political activities would bring them to the level of being of interest to the Russian state. That's sobering for anybody who thinks that they're too small a nut to crack.'

Raphael also told me of the large number of religious figures on the list. These included the head of a Ukrainian Jewish association, who at the time was often

62. Andrew Prokop, 'All of Robert Mueller's indictments and plea deals in the Russia investigation', *Vox*, 17 December 2019, https://www.vox.com/policy-and-politics/2018/2/20/17031772/mueller-indictments-grand-jury.

63. 'GloZell's Interview with President Obama', YouTube, 23 January 2015, https://www.youtube.com/watch?v=nQe7o_Gea-4.

quoted by Western media outlets defending Ukraine against Russian charges of anti-Semitism and fascism. But the hackers weren't choosy about denomination: other targets included Protestant missionaries working in the Moscow region, and the Papal Nuncio to Kyiv. But an especially interesting cluster of targets, Raphael said, were the ecumenical Orthodox priests. 'These were very high-ranking members of the Greek Orthodox Church based in Istanbul. Although it's a very small church, relative to, say, the Russian Orthodox Church, they are the first among equals' – and as such, they played a key role in the politically significant decision by the Ukrainian Orthodox Church to split from its Russian counterpart, a source of great concern in Moscow with its preoccupation with being seen as the centre of Orthodoxy and with Ukrainians not being seen as a separate nation.[64]

The use of state intelligence resources to gain an advantage in religious affairs is one symptom of the highly politicized nature of the Russian Orthodox Church, which as well as meeting the needs of worshippers plays a role as a kind of Ministry of Religion. Serving the interests of the state is a normal function for the Church in Russia; the idea that this includes helping Russia in its duty to 'annex lands to Russia, increase the size of the country's territory, incorporate peoples' is not challenged by Church leadership.[65] Statements by the head of the Church, Patriarch Kirill, lend religious weight to Russian state campaigns, as for instance by declaring a visit to Ukraine by the leader of the Eastern Orthodox Church to be a sin.[66] And Russia's invasion of Ukraine saw priests also calling for the reintegration of former Soviet countries like Moldova and Georgia, and threatening dire consequences for the Baltic states, before praying for 'victory over the black hordes'.[67] In this context, it becomes less surprising that priests and missionaries were among the GRU's targets. 'You know, people don't think of religious leaders as targets for spycraft,' Raphael added. 'But they often are, and this was a good illustration of that.' What is more, the use of the Church as a tool to extend Russia's reach is just one aspect of a broad-based campaign to extend Russian influence not just in Europe but around the world.

64. David Masci, 'Split between Ukrainian, Russian churches shows political importance of Orthodox Christianity', Pew Research Center, 14 January 2019, https://www.pewresearch.org/fact-tank/2019/01/14/split-between-ukrainian-russian-churches-shows-political-importance-of-orthodox-christianity/.

65. Paul Goble, 'Russian Orthodox Priest Says State's Task is to Seize Territories and Church's is to Pray over Them', *Window on Eurasia*, 30 August 2021, http://windowoneurasia2.blogspot.com/2021/08/russian-orthodox-priest-says-states.html.

66. 'Патриарх Кирилл назвал греховным визит Варфоломея на Украину' (Patriarch Kirill calls Bartholomew's visit to Ukraine sinful), TASS, 28 August 2021, https://tass.ru/obschestvo/12244505.

67. Kamil Galeev, 12 March 2022, https://twitter.com/kamilkazani/status/1502731079219879944?s=27.

## Going global

Russia claims a right as a 'great power' to a sphere of influence, and to intervene in any decisions by foreign countries which, as the Kremlin sees it, affect Russia. This is enough of a problem in eastern Europe; but since Russia also claims to have global interests, this principle in theory covers the whole planet, giving Russia a right to interfere in anybody's business anywhere. Tor Bukkvoll thinks the logic behind Russia investing in increased presence and influence around the world is simple: 'If we're going to be respected as a great power, we need to act as a great power. And acting as a great power means being involved physically around the world.'

The area where this drive for involvement most commonly reaches the headlines is Africa. Here Russia is using a range of different tools to re-establish itself as an influential power, including most prominently of all the Wagner private military company (PMC), as we saw in Chapter 3. French researcher Julien Nocetti has noted how the new approach to working with Africa is different from what was seen during the Cold War. 'Russian protection does not come free of charge, as it used to in Soviet days,' he says. Instead, it is provided in return for specific things the host country can provide, like energy or arms contracts or – often – a vote for Russia in international organizations like the UN.[68] And in a reflection of the way Russia does business at home, its engagement with Africa is most successful where the target country suffers from weak rule of law and endemic corruption.[69]

Here as elsewhere, Russian officials complain that Western criticism shows 'double standards'. For example, it is nonsense to complain about the activities of organizations like Wagner in Africa when US advisers are there too, they say. But this masks the fact that there are very clearly two different standards of behaviour in play. The methods adopted by Russia's PMCs also reflect the way of doing business at home. In the Central African Republic, Wagner and its affiliates have embedded themselves into the local security structures – and are repeatedly incriminated in random and indiscriminate abductions, torture and murders.[70] The pattern of torture of medieval viciousness and indiscriminate killing repeats

68. Julien Nocetti, Associate Fellow at the Russia/NIS Center, French Institute of International Relations (IFRI), speaking at 'The Bear Returns: Understanding Russia's strategic engagement and policy impact in Africa', South African Institute of International Affairs, 13 May 2021.

69. Dzvinka Kachur, 'Red lights are flashing over Russian dealings with Mozambique and Zimbabwe', South African Institute of International Affairs, 3 December 2020, https://saiia.org.za/research/red-lights-are-flashing-over-russian-dealings-with-mozambique-and-zimbabwe/.

70. 'En Centrafrique, des victimes des exactions russes brisent la loi du silence' (In the Central African Republic, victims of Russian abuses break the law of silence), RFI, 3 May 2021, https://www.rfi.fr/fr/afrique/20210503-en-centrafrique-des-victimes-des-exactions-russes-brisent-la-loi-du-silence.

what had been seen earlier in Syria.[71] In mid-2021, a tablet abandoned by Wagner operators in Libya provided grim details of murders of prisoners and mining and booby-trapping of civilian areas.[72]

Russia also uses African countries as a platform for its online disinformation efforts, whether directed locally or joining in Russia's broader campaign against the West. In October 2019, Facebook shut down a disinformation network spanning eight African countries that had been conducting influence operations in coordination with real-world activities by Wagner.[73] But South African disinformation researcher Jean le Roux says working from Africa provides Russia with another layer of deniability for its campaigns further afield. 'Franchising of disinformation operations – using local actors to propagate disinformation – makes it harder to distinguish what is emanating from Russia. Locals may not even be aware that they are spreading disinformation,' Jean explains. 'Russia uses disinformation in Africa as part of geopolitical competition, to undermine the West, and US and EU interests. By doing this, they are trying to strengthen their own relative position for geopolitical supremacy. This includes using vaccine disinformation targeting their Western competitors.' Just as with malign influence campaigns working against Western countries directly, the activity is not just online but also extends to setting up front organizations. 'Russia is fond of setting up NGOs in Africa because they can operate in the open and pretend to be part of an open and free democracy. They can then use these NGOs to get their narratives across, and at the same time have 'insurance' against being shut down; any actions taken against these NGOs can be reframed as a Western assault on free speech,' Jean says.

But the amount of attention paid to Russia's activities in Africa obscures how far its efforts spread elsewhere, in a truly global programme to reach out and acquire or regain influence.[74] Subversive activities in the United States making use of the Russian diaspora there don't come as much as a surprise.[75] But as if in confirmation

71. Amy Mackinnon, 'New Report Exposes Brutal Methods of Russia's Wagner Group', *Foreign Policy*, 11 June 2020, https://foreignpolicy.com/2020/06/11/russia-wagner-group-methods-bouta-killing-report/.

72. Ilya Barabanov and Nader Ibrahim, 'Wagner: Scale of Russian mercenary mission in Libya exposed', BBC News, 11 August 2021, https://www.bbc.co.uk/news/world-africa-58009514.

73. Nathaniel Gleicher, 'Removing More Coordinated Inauthentic Behavior From Russia', Facebook, 30 October 2019, https://about.fb.com/news/2019/10/removing-more-coordinated-inauthentic-behavior-from-russia/.

74. 'Russia's Global Reach: A Security and Statecraft Assessment', George C. Marshall European Center For Security Studies, http://www.marshallcenter.org/en/publications/marshall-center-books/russias-global-reach-security-and-statecraft-assessment.

75. 'FBI Investigates Russian Diaspora Group for Potential Espionage, Unregistered Political Activity', *Forensic News*, 19 November 2021, https://forensicnews.net/fbi-investigates-russian-diaspora-group-for-potential-espionage-unregistered-political-activity/.

of the Kremlin's global ambition, Ireland and Australia are just two of the far more unlikely targets for Russian interest. Irish journalist and author John Mooney has been tracking the activities of Russian intelligence services in his home country for a number of years. He says a lack of threat perception works in their favour. 'In a place like Ireland, politicians tend to be very open and friendly and courteous to people who seek their help. There's not a big culture of secrecy. It makes us particularly vulnerable, because there's an unawareness of this as a problem, or that the threat is even there.' Nevertheless, John says, the threat to individual people in Ireland is no less than elsewhere. 'Russian services are using lots of different techniques to influence and target people in this country. They're involved in all the type of activities that you would see in other countries. And I have to say, a lot of this is much more acute and serious than people would imagine. They're doing anything and everything to influence thinking and to collect intelligence from people who in many cases might not know that they're vulnerable, or [that] they're being targeted.'

'Because Ireland is a neutral country, the population generally believe that we don't really have enemies, and superpowers like Russia would not have an interest in influencing Irish affairs,' John goes on. But in addition, Ireland itself may not always be the target for Russian intelligence activity carried out on its territory. The scale of operations there came to public attention when the Russian Embassy in Dublin applied for planning permission to extend to more than five times its original size – including a number of suspicious facilities which the planning application claimed would be an (entirely unnecessary) 'underground car park'.[76] At a time when Russian intelligence officers were being expelled from embassies across Europe, the suspicion was that this was to serve as a new operations and signals intelligence hub for multiple countries.

Even John is sometimes surprised by the extent of the Russian activity ongoing in Ireland. 'I've published a number of stories where I've interviewed former officers from the US submarine fleet, who have monitored Russian submarines off the west coast of Ireland, gathering data on the location of the undersea cables that carry internet traffic between North America and Europe,' he says.[77] 'In one interview I was completely astonished when I heard about some of their submarines coming up to periscope depth off the west coast of Ireland, to receive transmissions from people that they have working there.'

For former Australian diplomat Kyle Wilson, 'what's most noteworthy about Russian activities here is that we, though so far away, matter to them enough for them to make such an effort.'

76. John Mooney, 'Intelligence officers search Russian embassy for spy base', *The Times*, 12 February 2021, https://www.thetimes.co.uk/article/intelligence-officers-search-russian-embassy-for-spy-base-5xdj68xd9.

77. John Mooney, 'Russian agents plunge to new ocean depths in Ireland to crack transatlantic cables', *Sunday Times*, 16 February 2020, https://www.thetimes.co.uk/past-six-days/2020-02-16/ireland/russian-agents-plunge-to-new-ocean-depths-in-ireland-to-crack-transatlantic-cables-fnqsmgncz.

Kyle attracted the unwelcome attention of militant members of Australia's Russian diaspora when he wrote an article 'on Australian citizens of Russian origin who have declared themselves to be a "Cossack garrison" in Australia, serving their "Commander-in-Chief", the President of Russia; and to be prosecuting "an information war in a hostile country" on behalf of the Russian state'. The next edition of the group's monthly newsletter devoted six of its forty pages to attacking Kyle, and a front-page sub-headline called him an 'Enemy of Russia'. Inside, a photograph of Kyle was placed next to one of President Putin with the caption 'Funny Guy, I Kill You Last'.[78] While Kyle himself remained relatively relaxed about the implicit threat ('I can't help thinking that this outfit's bark is worse than its bite'), what focused the minds of his university employers was that the group openly identified itself as paramilitary, its website carried pictures of its members receiving weapons training in Russia, and that some members of the group had visited eastern Ukraine and might have fought as Russian proxies there. (There are similar concerns about the Night Wolves organization, with a substantial presence in Australia, which we will look at in more detail in Chapter 7.)

Videos by 'Aussie Cossack', a prominent pro-Russian activist in Australia, refer to Vladimir Putin as 'our president' and assure Russian viewers that 'we are working on it, brothers'.[79] Kyle, meanwhile, is worried about less visible pro-Russian activity. 'What concerns me more than the Cossacks is relatively successful Russian efforts to build a small group of people who are willing to support Russia's policy, to seek to influence the media's presentation of Russia and Australia, and who also presumably seek to influence government policy'. In doing so they face the 'huge obstacle' of Malaysia Airlines flight MH17 predisposing government policy against Russia, as well as Russia's ongoing demonstrations of an aggressive attitude towards Australia, Kyle says, but the pro-Russian campaigns are most effective when they are subtle. 'It's very difficult, but there's been some relative success [for Russia] in influencing the media, and in particular, trying to influence people who might eventually become influential.'

As ever, Western governments are preoccupied with how they can push back against Russia's ongoing campaigns around the world while still not adopting Russia's methods. One possible answer lies in the way that campaigns are sometimes counterproductive and lead to Russia's targets becoming stronger not weaker over the long term.

This applies both to organizations and to people. For two years, Sven Sakkov led NATO's Collective Cyber Defence Centre of Excellence in Tallinn. He recalled how a decade beforehand, the centre's formation had been boosted by the Russian cyber attacks on Estonia in 2007. Estonia had proposed hosting a cyber centre

---

78. 'Putin's Patriots: Russian money and influence in Australia', Four Corners (ABC News), 15 February 2021, https://www.youtube.com/watch?v=u_iLgMy8weA.

79. 'Vladimir Putin praised by Australian politicians: Evidence of "Russian influence" exposed!', YouTube, 31 July 2021, https://www.youtube.com/watch?v=BS2ARn66a6U.

almost as soon as it joined NATO in 2004 – but, Sven says, this was 'met with indifference and the reply that "this is not something NATO does", it's a civilian thing for guys in basements with ponytails and T-shirts. After 2007, the situation changed overnight and the same allies called and said when can you receive our experts?'

More broadly, Russia's actions in Ukraine have succeeded, finally, in focusing the West's attention on its military assertiveness and how to counter it, for instance triggering new deployments and spending on defence within NATO and beyond.[80] Sven goes on, 'We had been making that case to allies for many years, and again we needed Russia to make the case much better than we had been able. And that's been replicated in so many other instances. It takes events on the ground to convince allies what the problem is.'

We saw in Chapter 2 how Russia's campaigns in places like Australia led to a backlash, even among local Russians. Further back in history, Kyle explains how 'When we established diplomatic relations with the Russians in 1942, and they opened an embassy here in 1943, immediately they set up a very effective espionage network. [Their activities] led to the establishment in Australia of our first counter-intelligence organization, the Australian Security Intelligence Organization (ASIO). So you can say that the establishment of our own counter-intelligence organization was a Russian achievement.'

Russia's online efforts too don't always work out. It can misread its audiences in places so apparently familiar as neighbouring Belarus. In the months following the fraudulent re-election of Aleksandr Lukashenko in August 2020, Belarusian journalists resigned en masse. To replace them, propaganda teams were drafted in from Russia. A series of own goals included confusing Belarusian with Ukrainian, and baffling audiences with 'homophobic rhetoric tying EU integration to same-sex marriages', although the protesters had not even been calling for closer ties with the EU.[81] And even at home, Russia can spectacularly misjudge how its messages will be received, especially among a young online audience. Moscow correspondent for the *Independent* newspaper Oliver Carroll described how the 'Russian Foreign Ministry opened [a] TikTok account to try and win back da kids – [but] judging by sarcastic, pro-Navalny comments, they weren't too impressed'.[82] All of these failures offer opportunities for the West to follow the lead of Darth Putin and fight back against Russian online campaigns in the most effective way that has been found to date – by exposing their ludicrousness.

80. Tom Rogan, 'Russia reaps whirlwind with massive Swedish defense spending boost', *Washington Examiner*, 19 October 2020, https://www.washingtonexaminer.com/opinion/russia-reaps-whirlwind-with-massive-swedish-defense-spending-boost.

81. Tatyana Fedosyuk, 'The comic tale of an epic propaganda fail that confirmed Russian intervention in Belarus', *Great Power*, 2 September 2020, https://www.greatpower.us/p/the-comic-tale-of-an-epic-propaganda.

82. Tweet by @olliecarroll, 7 February 2021, https://twitter.com/olliecarroll/status/1358326004352188416.

It's harder to see how the campaigns of direct intimidation of critics of Russia can be countered, except through vastly greater involvement of law enforcement and security agencies in the countries where it is happening. But even for individuals, being the object of malicious Russian attention can end up being a positive experience overall. As we'll see in Chapter 7, Martin Kragh was also among victims of a targeted attack in the UK who found the main result was boosting their own credibility. Laura Walters was concerned that being known for being entrapped by Peace Data would harm her career prospects. 'I was so worried about that,' she says. 'I thought, how do I deal with this? Is this my credibility gone? But it's actually been quite positive. I've had so many people get in touch and be interested in talking to me, and then that's turned into some collaborations and writing about the stuff, and opportunities that I wouldn't have gotten otherwise. I doubt that it was their aim when they started out, but I think they've done me a favour.'

# Chapter 6

## THE WILLING ACCOMPLICES

*MICE and enablers*

There's a common theme to many of the successes Russia has had against democracies and the people who live in them, whether it's harassing individuals into silence or changing the political direction of a whole country. It is that this success would not have been possible without the active help of willing supporters within the target country itself.

One of the areas where this is most visible is in Russia's waging of information warfare. Russia puts out propaganda lines designed to create and foster a permissive environment for Russia to do whatever it pleases domestically as well as abroad – but its storylines are given legitimacy and credibility if they are endorsed by journalists, academics and experts from the countries it targets after they have been being willingly or unwittingly duped into repeating them. A classic example is wordy academic discourse concealing the core message that Russia should be allowed to have its way with independent states along its borders like Ukraine, even suggesting that the status of these countries is 'disputed'.[1] False equivalence and whataboutism – the arguments that Russia behaves precisely the same as Western democracies, because 'the West is just as bad' – is another constantly repeated tactic for deflecting criticism of Moscow. These transmitters of Russian messages must appear as far as possible to be independent, in order to present themselves as authorities in the eyes of the public and policymakers. This is a vital component in ensuring that Russian propaganda lines are not only disseminated through traditional and social media, where they can influence trends and shape what the public thinks about, but are also endorsed for private discussions guiding government policy more directly.

Unlike many other countries (and Russia itself), the UK does not have a 'Foreign Agents Registration Act' to try to prevent this kind of influence. In fact, as

---

1. Richard Sakwa, 'True sovereignty comes not from Europe but from within', Chatham House, 8 December 2016, https://www.chathamhouse.org/2016/12/russia-question-sovereignty-and-legitimacy-post-soviet-eurasia.

Parliament's Intelligence and Security Committee (ISC) discovered to its surprise, 'it is not an offence in any sense to be a covert agent of the Russian Intelligence Services in the UK' – the offence only arises if you acquire damaging secrets and successfully pass them to Russia.[2] But democracies that wish to protect themselves against subversion of this kind need to draft their 'foreign agents' legislation very carefully to avoid trespassing on genuine civil liberties and the democratic process (in distinct contrast with Russia where, as we saw in Chapter 2, the foreign agents law is designed specifically to constrain those liberties).[3] This is because it's important to remember that not everybody who argues in favour of Western government policy that leads to Russia's preferred outcomes is working as a conscious tool of the Kremlin. Before the invasion of Ukraine, academics and think tankers who were arguing that Kyiv should be left to its fate and that there should be no effort to support it against Russia no doubt sincerely believed that they were arguing the pragmatically sensible course of action – whether or not they acknowledged its moral reprehensibility.[4]

At times, people in the West can argue Russia's case to the detriment of their own or others' national security out of a genuine conviction that they are doing the right thing. These unwitting accomplices, often in positions of influence, are referred to among the Russia-watching community as the 'useful idiots'. The phrase is a technical term rather than a deliberate insult, based on what is thought to be a Soviet categorization for influential sympathizers who believe they are acting of their own volition as opposed to 'agents of influence' who are consciously working on behalf of the hostile power. The problem is that while the distinction is important for establishing motivation, it is irrelevant from the point of view of effect, because the two groups of individuals behave outwardly in exactly the same manner with exactly the same results. Mary Dejevsky is a British writer whose newspaper columns closely coincide with the Russian disinformation narratives of the day, whether on Syria and the White Helmets, the attack on Sergey and Yulia Skripal, or most recently preparations for the invasion of Ukraine.[5] Mary has repeatedly assured me over the years that she does this not because she is paid or induced to do so by Russia, but out of her own convictions – just as former British

2. 'Russia', Intelligence and Security Committee of Parliament, 21 July 2020, https://docs.google.com/a/independent.gov.uk/viewer?a=v&pid=sites&srcid=aW5kZXBlbmRlbnQuQuZ292LnVrfGlzY3xneDo1Y2RhMGEyN2Y3NjM0OWFl.

3. Bob Seely, 'Foreign Interference Unchecked: Models for a UK Foreign Lobbying Act', Henry Jackson Society, 10 February 2021, https://henryjacksonsociety.org/publications/uk-foreign-lobbying-act/.

4. Oleksandr Zamkovoi, 'Are We Ready to Die for Kyiv? How Twitter is Helping to Push the West towards Surrendering Ukraine', StopFake.org, 23 November 2021, https://www.stopfake.org/en/are-we-ready-to-die-for-kyiv-how-twitter-is-helping-to-push-to-west-towards-surrendering-ukraine/.

5. 'Mary, Mary, quite contrary', *Private Eye* 1569, 18 March 2022, https://www.private-eye.co.uk/street-of-shame.

MP Matthew Gordon-Banks told me that in his own advocacy of Russian positions 'all I wanted to do was raise the views of Russians and their Leadership. I have never been paid a Ruble [sic] nor had any association with their security services.'[6] Strange as it may seem, I believe Mary – but this lack of malicious intent, unfortunately, does not lessen her usefulness to Russia, a usefulness recognized by a Russian award for 'explaining and promoting understanding'.[7]

The 'idiots' can often be highly intelligent individuals, who for one reason or another simply do not realize the consequences of what they do or say. One example is, once again, academics, when they unintentionally appear to draw false equivalence between Russian malign influence campaigns and those who seek to counter them – accusing the defenders themselves of spreading disinformation. This can in part stem from a lack of understanding of the real-world impact of their academic studies. When a British university project studying RT was caught up in a storm of accusations that the way they presented their research was doing Russia's work for it, one of the startled researchers pointed out that 'our project is for academics. We are not political campaigners, practitioners or activists. If our work is useful for policy analysts and practitioners, it is great, but we do not pro-actively seek this impact.' The problem, of course, was that when their work spilled over into real life, it had a practical effect regardless of whether it was intended or not.[8]

Gavril says the problem of 'lack of exposure to reality' is common among senior academics, including the ones who most enthusiastically promote Russia and its disinformation. 'They've only ever been academics. There's a general belief there that to be truly independent means that you have to be completely untainted by exposure to other places, you can only be an academic so you can't take government money, you can't take industry money, you can't work with government or military or anything that's compromising your credibility and independence.' The result, as with the RT study, can be a failure to fully realize that what they do makes a difference in the real-world conflict going on as well as in their academic debate.

Like me, Gavril prefers to give people who busily promote the Russian point of view the benefit of the doubt for as long as possible. 'I prefer to call them a community of interest, just to try to be respectable,' he says. 'I think they firmly believe in what they're doing.' But it can be hard, or impossible, to discern when working on behalf of Russian interests unknowingly, or by coincidence, becomes a conscious choice and may include direct contact with representatives of the

6. Letter to author, 11 February 2022.

7. Mary Dejevsky, 'Why an award from Russia could complicate my life', *Independent*, 21 October 2021, https://www.independent.co.uk/independentpremium/voices/russia-valdai-prize-journalism-putin-b1942751.html.

8. Keir Giles, 'Defence Against Disinformation is a Team Sport', *Reframing Russia*, 18 May 2020, https://reframingrussia.com/2020/05/18/defence-against-disinformation-is-a-team-sport-guest-blog/.

Russian state. According to a lengthy study based on Russia's own textbooks for recruiting agents of subversion, individuals entrapped into this kind of relationship 'may not even know or allow themself to believe they've been seduced into dancing with the devil'.[9] Other enablers may still be assisting Russian aims without necessarily having any connection to the country at all. Gavril says that often, 'I found no direct evidence to suggest that they're working in concert or on behalf of Russia. That's probably one of the biggest challenges in all of this. Russia doesn't necessarily need to control or even support these voices. All they do is amplify them.' This creates the obvious danger of false accusations, based on leaping to the conclusion that working in parallel with Russian campaigns must necessarily mean collusion. Gavril continues, 'I think it's actually really dangerous that we're quick to label these people, accuse them of being in bed with Russia, because chances are they're not, and we're pushing them into a corner that might make them even less reasonable.' The same principle applies online, where social media accounts that display all the classic symptoms of being fakes, disinformation disseminators and professional Russian trolls can on occasion turn out to be run by real, genuine individuals, who just happen also to be deeply obnoxious.

But whether they are 'in bed with Russia' or not, over and above information operations Moscow gains the most benefit from its 'useful idiots' when they arrive in positions with real and direct political or commercial influence. Politicians from the UK's Labour Party have repeatedly assisted Russia in hack-and-leak attacks intended to discredit its adversaries or influence political processes (see also Chapter 7). In mid-2020, it was then Labour leader Jeremy Corbyn who decided to disseminate classified documents on trade negotiations between the UK and US that had been hacked and posted on the social media platform Reddit by what Reddit called 'a group linked to Russia'.[10] These operations do not succeed without somebody in the target country who is willing to disseminate, promote and act on leaked material; but they seem to have little difficulty in finding individuals naive or unscrupulous enough to do so.

In some cases it is hard to tell from the outside whether campaigns against the West are motivated by naivety or unscrupulousness – for instance when a 'Stop The War' campaign that is ostensibly seeking to stop a war waged by Russia against Ukraine declares that instead its 'focus is on the policies of the British government'.[11] Other cases, however, provide direct evidence of knowing collusion with Moscow.

9. Michael Weiss, 'You Don't Have to Be Recruited to Work for Russian Intelligence', *Newlines*, 4 February 2021, https://newlinesmag.com/reportage/you-dont-have-to-be-recruited-to-work-for-russian-intelligence/.

10. Harry Yorke, 'Russians "played Jeremy Corbyn as a useful idiot" to publicise classified documents', *Telegraph*, 16 July 2020, https://www.telegraph.co.uk/politics/2020/07/16/russians-played-jeremy-corbyn-useful-idiot-publicise-classified/.

11. 'Stop The War Statement On The Crisis Over Ukraine', Stop the War coalition, 18 February 2022, https://www.stopwar.org.uk/article/list-of-signatories-stop-the-war-statement-on-the-crisis-over-ukraine/.

This includes Western organizations posing as media outlets receiving assistance from Russian intelligence services and coordinating with them on how to promote storylines that come from Russia.

Bonanza Media in the Netherlands was founded in early 2019 by former RT employee Yana Yerlashova and Dutch conspiracy theorist Max van der Werff. Reporting by Bonanza initially focused on topics linked to Malaysia Airlines flight MH17, but later pivoted towards Covid-19 disinformation. That the reporting promoted Russian storylines is unsurprising, given that draft articles intended for publication on the Bonanza Media website were sent to Russian intelligence officers for approval.[12] Cooperation with the Russian intelligence services documented by the Bellingcat investigative group included not only close coordination by phone and email, but travel to occupied areas of eastern Ukraine facilitated by Bonanza's handlers, and collaboration on a hack-and-leak attack targeting the MH17 investigation.[13] (Bonanza associates have denied some of the allegations, while accusing Bellingcat itself of spreading disinformation.)[14] Once evidence of the Russian connection was exposed, if the Russian authorities had been inclined to be helpful to van der Werff, they could have denied that he was working on their behalf. Instead, Russian police raided the home of investigative journalist Roman Dobrokhotov (who heads The Insider, a partner organization to Bellingcat, and may well have assisted in collecting evidence showing Bonanza's cooperation with Russian intelligence). Dobrokhotov's passport was confiscated, his parents' home also raided, and charges were drawn up by the aptly named prosecutor Stalina Gurevich that Dobrokhotov had – in a tweet – slandered van der Werff (and the GRU) 'in order to discredit the GRU of the Ministry of Defence of the Russian Federation in the eyes of its Western partners'.[15]

As we'll see later in this book, in some cases when individuals are accused of aiding Russia a lack of shame or self-awareness can lead them to incriminate themselves further, exploiting rather than denying their official Russian connections. But we'll also see that van der Werff's is not the only instance where Russia itself provides the further incrimination, through misguidedly intervening on behalf of its friends. As defence researcher Rob Lee points out in a similar case, 'if someone accuses you of being "paid by the Russians", having a Russian

12. 'Bellingcat: Dutch MH17 journalist is connected to Russian military', DutchNews.nl, 12 November 2020, https://www.dutchnews.nl/news/2020/11/bellingcat-dutch-mh17-journalist-is-connected-to-russian-military/.

13. 'The GRU's MH17 Disinformation Operations Part 1: The Bonanza Media Project', Bellingcat, 12 November 2020, https://www.bellingcat.com/news/uk-and-europe/2020/11/12/the-grus-mh17-disinformation-operations-part-1-the-bonanza-media-project/.

14. Tweet by Eric van de Beek, 12 November 2020, https://twitter.com/beek38/status/1326805727562838017.

15. Application by Stalina Gurevich to open a criminal case against Dobrokhotov, https://twitter.com/bellingcat/status/1420361009995395080/photo/1.

government official leap to your defense on an official Russian government account isn't as useful as you might imagine.'[16]

In effect, you can choose how you prefer to work for Moscow against your own country. You could be a spy for the Russian intelligence services. Or you could take money from RT, which its own director called a weapon of information warfare against the West.[17] The real difference is that the first is a crime and the second is not. But in both cases, there are consistent patterns that explain why most – not all – of the people who decide to work for Russia make that choice. It's a formula that's been laid down as MICE, standing for Money, Ideology, Compromise (or coercion) and Ego – each of them marking a potential motivation, or vulnerability, that Moscow can exploit.[18]

### *Money*

One of the biggest challenges in resisting Russia is the vast quantities of money at Moscow's disposal for corrupting individuals abroad. This applies both to powerful, prominent people and to ordinary individuals. For leading European politicians, being a friend of Russia while in office can lead to highly lucrative appointments with Russian energy companies as soon as you are out. Former Austrian foreign minister Karin Kneissl joined oil giant Rosneft.[19] Former prime minister of France François Fillon went to Zarubezhneft.[20] And the case that stands as a byword for the whole syndrome is that of Gerhard Schröder, who moved seamlessly from one job as chancellor of Germany to the next on the board of the company building the first of the controversial Nord Stream pipelines – under a deal between Russia and Germany which he had hastily agreed shortly before the switch. Since then, Schröder has continued to collect senior positions with Russian energy companies and consistently lobbied for Russian interests.[21]

16. Tweet by @RALee85, 27 May 2021, https://twitter.com/RALee85/status/13979570 26123235341.

17. Benjamin Dubow et al., 'Here's how Russia's RT spread propaganda in the lead-up to the election', *Bulletin of the Atomic Scientists*, 9 November 2020, https://thebulletin.org/2020/11/ heres-how-russias-rt-spread-propaganda-in-the-lead-up-to-the-election/.

18. Chris Smith, 'How ordinary people are convinced to become spies', *The Conversation*, 24 August 2021, https://theconversation.com/how-ordinary-people-are-convinced-to-become-spies-166688.

19. 'Экс-главу МИД Австрии Карин Кнайсль выдвинули в совет директоров "Роснефти"' (Former Austrian foreign minister Karin Kneissl appointed to board of Rosneft), TASS, 3 March 2021, https://tass.ru/ekonomika/10826237.

20. 'Экс-премьера Франции Фийона выдвинули в совет директоров "Зарубежнефти"' (Former prime minister of France François Fillon appointed to board of directors of Zarubezhneft), RBK, 11 June 2021, https://www.rbc.ru/business/11/06/2021/60c3a6c19a79476db6878e7b.

21. 'German ex-chancellor Schröder under fire for Putin link', BBC News, 8 October 2020, https://www.bbc.co.uk/news/world-europe-54462311.

Linas says the warning signs that politicians will eventually be rewarded for a pro-Russia line are often clear in advance. 'They show their friendship with the Russian political establishment, sometimes you hear their official statements or thoughts on Russia, so supportive of Russia's policies, and of course, a number of countries wonder why this is happening. But afterwards these people take their seats on the board. It's obvious that Russia is always looking for those agents of influence, those who have certain leverage on the political processes in their countries.'

Former chess champion turned opposition activist Garry Kasparov makes the point that the process of buying European politicians has become normalized. 'Name me a single European country where no politicians have been corrupted by the Putin regime. It's no big secret, everything is done openly. 20 or 30 years ago, if the press discovered such behavior, these politicians' careers would have been over. Big scandals would have broken out, resignations, court cases. But today, morals have evolved. For Fillon, Russian money is not a problem, neither [is it] for Schröder. For Marine Le Pen, getting Russian funding for her party is no problem. Nobody gets outraged by it. And this is a victory for Putin.'[22] Alexei Navalny agrees. 'Legalised bribery is flourishing, often in the form of board memberships at state-owned companies,' he wrote in a *Guardian* article drafted in prison in August 2021. 'A former German chancellor, or a former Italian prime minister, or a former Austrian foreign minister, can act as background dancers for the Russian dictator, normalising corrupt practices.'[23]

But the ministers and chancellors are only the most high-profile examples of the problem. At a lower level, the corrosive influence of Russian money pervades and perverts the normal processes of politics and justice across a wide range of Western democracies. Former FBI director William Sessions, previously a staunch opponent of organized crime, graduated to acting on behalf of Semyon Mogilevich, one of Russia's most powerful crime lords.[24] Swiss prosecutors closed an investigation into the money-laundering enterprise linked to the 2009 death of Russian lawyer Sergei Magnitsky in prison, just a month after one of the investigators was convicted of taking bribes from Russian prosecutors to do precisely that.[25] A close aide to Italy's deputy prime minister Matteo Salvini held

22. Galia Ackerman, 'Putin's regime represents the West's greatest existential threat', *Desk Russie*, 25 June 2021, https://desk-russie.eu/en/2021/06/25/le-regime-de-poutine-represente. html.

23. Alexei Navalny, 'Only action against corruption can solve the world's biggest problems', *Guardian*, 19 August 2021, https://www.theguardian.com/commentisfree/2021/aug/19/action-against-corruption-russian-sanctions-oligarchs-alexei-navalny.

24. Glenn R. Simpson and Mary Jacoby, 'How Lobbyists Help Ex-Soviets Woo Washington', *Wall Street Journal*, 17 April 2007, https://www.wsj.com/articles/SB117674837248471543.

25. 'Swiss prosecutors drop Russian money-laundering inquiry', Reuters, 27 July 2021, https:// www.reuters.com/world/europe/swiss-prosecutors-drop-russian-money-laundering-inquiry-2021-07-27/.

covert talks with Russian intelligence officers to pump Russian oil money to his far-right party.[26] And these are just examples of the cases that come to light and are publicly reported. As ever, the extent of corrupt activity that remains undetected is likely to be even deeper, broader and worse.

The activity need not necessarily even be illegal. Consultancy and law firms with links to the British establishment can earn impressive sums by lobbying, entirely legally, against EU sanctions on Russia. One of those firms, Debevoise and Plimpton, with offices in Paris and Moscow as well as London, employs Lord Goldsmith, who was the UK Attorney General between 2001 and 2007. Many ordinary people might assume that this would suggest a certain amount of propriety and moral rectitude by Goldsmith. But this was no obstacle to his offering to speak up for Russian customers at risk of being sanctioned, in one case in return for the 'relatively modest fee' of £75,000.[27] And at an even more mundane level, the financial inducement can simply take the form of a better salary than is available elsewhere. New Zealand journalist Laura Walters sees how this sways individuals who do not realize the full implications of signing up with Russian media outlets. 'I think there are a lot of people who haven't had close experience with Russian propaganda, or with influence campaigns or understand how they work, and they just see it as a job,' she says. 'They think this is a chance to work for an outlet that is maybe going to give me the position or promotion that I didn't have in another job. I think they just see it as a good job on paper and don't think more deeply about it. People just go, well, it's a paycheck, isn't it?'

## Ideology

During communist times, misguided idealism also drove sympathizers in the West to support Moscow against their own countries. Perhaps surprisingly, long after the collapse of communism, today's Russia still presents an ideological attraction for their equally misguided descendants.[28] This can be because of their own prejudices, rather than because of an objective assessment of what Russia stands

26. Alberto Nardelli, 'Revealed: The Explosive Secret Recording That Shows How Russia Tried To Funnel Millions To The "European Trump"', *Buzzfeed*, 10 July 2019, https://www.buzzfeednews.com/article/albertonardelli/salvini-russia-oil-deal-secret-recording;     Federico Marconi, 'Soldi russi alla Lega: al tavolo con l'uomo di Salvini anche una spia di Putin' (Russian money to Lega: one of Putin's spies was also at the table with Salvini's man), *Domani*, 25 June 2021,     https://www.editorialedomani.it/politica/italia/soldi-russi-lega-al-tavolo-uomo-salvini-anche-spia-putin-y5mszmfd.

27. Andrew Rettman, 'Illicit Russian billions pose threat to EU democracy', *EU Observer*, 21 April 2017, https://euobserver.com/foreign/137631.

28. Tim Shipman, 'Moscow mules: the left's long romance with Russia', *The Times*, 29 April 2018,     https://www.thetimes.co.uk/article/moscow-mules-the-lefts-long-romance-with-russia-brqp5cw2v.

for. Counter-intelligence officer Lars calls this group 'the traditional anti-imperialist crowd that automatically sees us as evil and everything the US says as dubious, and that is both willing and both susceptible to these Russian narratives about what the West is doing and then going along with it. Some to a certain extent and some to extremes.' In other cases this attraction is to a fictitious version of today's Russia built on a fictitious version of the old Soviet Union. Valeriy Akimenko encounters this delusion regularly. 'There is enduring sympathy with and almost love for the causes that in their view Russia continues to represent,' he says. 'But it's held over from ideas that were formed during the Soviet era when idealists abroad thought Russia represented notions such as social justice, social fairness, equality, even though it was on paper rather than in reality. But by no stretch of the imagination can Russia of the present day be understood to advocate the same values.' Mark Galeotti agrees: 'There are more than a few in the West who see something genuinely admirable in Russia . . . Often, it is less about Russia as it is, and more as Russia as a symbol of not being whatever it is they don't like about the modern West.'[29] Even people who visit Russia, and ought to be able to see for themselves the gap between their ideals and Russian reality, can continue to be seduced by Russia as an idea. Robert Pszczel says he understands how this works. 'Of course, it's exciting and exhilarating. Moscow is very special, it's like a drug. The problem is you can see the Russia of your dreams, you can pick and choose the bits you want, and have Pushkin here and a bit of ballet if you like it and so on. But when you are forced to deal with Russia as it really is, that reality is very, very different.'

## Compromise

The classic mechanism for compromise is blackmail, where Russia gathers *kompromat*, or compromising material on a target in order to induce them to cooperate. One theory is that it is *kompromat* that lay behind Donald Trump's pandering to Moscow at the expense of his own country and its allies. But Samantha de Bendern explains there are more subtle forms of moral compromise that lead people to abandon their principles for Moscow – especially when it comes to service providers in the UK and Europe turning a blind eye to the nature of their Russian customers. 'It's a form of seduction,' she says. 'It's the serpent dangling the apple from the tree. The lawyers, the bankers, the estate agents, get seduced by Russia. It's not just about the money. It's about the Russians turning on the charm, and bringing in the girls – because 95% of all these facilitators are men. So they invite them on business trips to Russia, for beautiful girls and great parties. From getting the 6.56 train to work from God knows what suburb in London, for a week or two every six weeks you fly out to Moscow or St Petersburg and you're made to

29. Mark Galeotti, 'Of MICE and Men in the Berlin Spy Game', *Moscow Times*, 15 August 2021, https://www.themoscowtimes.com/2021/08/15/of-mice-and-men-in-the-berlin-spy-game-a74791'.

feel like a king. A lot of bankers I've worked with got completely sucked in by that glamorous existence.'

The corruption is moral, not financial, she continues. 'Even if there were no envelopes passed under the table, it's a different form of corruption – not one that you can prosecute, because it's not a crime to want to go and have fun when it's offered. But it blinds these bankers and these lawyers to what they're really doing. Because Ivan or Boris or Sergey is so nice and so friendly, I can't possibly believe that he throws people out of aeroplanes when he gets angry with them.'

## *Ego*

Finally, Russia has always been adept at leveraging individual personality defects to induce or seduce people into working against their own countries. Mark Galeotti thinks people persuaded to work, or even spy, for Russia 'might have enjoyed the sense of excitement, the feeling at least someone appreciated his talents. A good case officer, after all, is a skilled field psychologist, who will seek to play on a potential source's discontents, insecurities and frustrations.'[30] One clue to the willingness of Western nationals to promote Russian storylines, appear on RT or wield influence on behalf of Moscow lies in the consistent pattern that before they began working for Russia, many of the most ardent activists and propagandists seem to have led quite sad and lonely lives, filled with failure and repeated reminders of their own personal inadequacies. So when they are embraced by the Russian system, and made to feel not only that they have a role but are valued in it, perhaps it is no wonder that they in return embrace the mission wholeheartedly. Lars agrees that when considering the spectrum of motivations for working for Russia, 'Clearly there's the financial one. But also some people seem to seek validation through this as well. If they're quoted in Russian media, for example, it somehow validates that they're important, as an expert or journalist or whatever.'

The prevalence of personality traits such as 'heightened levels of psychopathic meanness and boldness, dogmatism, disinhibition . . . belief in conspiracy theories' among both far left and far right extremists makes them ideal for recruitment to Russian campaigns, whether through the media or through direct intimidation of Russia's critics in real life (see Chapter 5).[31] And in the same way that social media like Twitter give a global platform to eccentrics who in previous centuries would have reached no bigger audience than shouting at the pigeons in the park, so working as a Russian propagandist gives public visibility to deluded and damaged personalities that previously would have been marginalized. This can accentuate

30. Galeotti, 'Of MICE and Men'.

31. Eric W. Dolan, 'Large study indicates left-wing authoritarianism exists and is a key predictor of psychological and behavioral outcomes', *PsyPost*, 30 June 2021, https://www.psypost. org/2021/06/large-study-indicates-left-wing-authoritarianism-exists-and-is-a-key-predictor-of-psychological-and-behavioral-outcomes-61318.

the problem still further. Gavril has observed at close quarters a process of deluded individuals being pushed even further away from reality. 'I do think they're crazy. I've known some of them enough to have exchanges, and the paranoia levels are really high,' he says. But then it gets worse. 'I think there's a trajectory. They get alienated for questioning things that have become accepted in a mainstream narrative. The more they question established facts, the more they get pushed out, and the more they fall down a conspiracy rabbit hole.'

At times, of course, two or more of these motivating factors overlap in one individual, and when offered the chance to collaborate with the Russian intelligence services, they embrace it.

Professor Paul McKeigue is part of a group of academics in the UK known to the disinformation-watching community as 'the propaganda professors' – not because they study propaganda, but because they relentlessly spread it. Some members of the group are prone to conspiracy theories. One notoriously repellent one promoted by McKeigue holds that a devastating chemical weapons attack in Douma, Syria in 2018 was staged and was in fact a 'managed massacre'[32] – carried out using a method described by a retired pharmacologist who explained in a self-published book how it had come to him in a dream after he had eaten an anchovy pizza.[33]

Bill Wiley works with the Commission for International Justice and Accountability (Cija), a group documenting war crimes in Syria, and consequently a substantial irritant for McKeigue.[34] When Cija became aware that McKeigue was gathering information in an attempt to discredit it, staff members entered a correspondence with him as 'Ivan', who allowed McKeigue to believe he was a Russian intelligence officer.[35] It's reasonable to think that on realizing this, someone with a clear conscience and an appropriate sense of where their loyalties lay would have gone to the police. McKeigue, instead, asked the 'Russian agent' for help discrediting Cija, including personal information on Bill Wiley – 'about a woman he might have slept with, and whether he had a cocaine habit', looking for a means of launching personal attacks regardless of whether his accusations were true or not.[36]

---

32. Paul McKeigue et al., 'Briefing note: the alleged chemical attack in Douma on 7 April 2018, and other alleged chlorine attacks in Syria since 2014', University of Bristol School for Policy Studies, 20 August 2018, https://research-information.bris.ac.uk/en/publications/briefing-note-the-alleged-chemical-attack-in-douma-on-7-april-201.

33. Michael Weiss and Jett Goldsmith, 'How an Email Sting Operation Unearthed a pro-Assad Conspiracy – and Russia's Role In It', *NewLines*, 20 April 2021, https://newlinesmag.com/reportage/how-an-email-sting-operation-unearthed-a-pro-assad-conspiracy-and-russias-role-in-it/.

34. https://cijaonline.org/.

35. Chloe Hadjimatheou, 'The UK professor and the fake Russian agent', BBC News, 26 March 2021, https://www.bbc.co.uk/news/stories-56524550.

36. Hadjimatheou, 'The UK professor and the fake Russian agent'.

McKeigue also passed on information to 'Ivan' on multiple people both in the UK and in Syria who were either critics or opponents of McKeigue's group, or held evidence disproving Russian propaganda. One of these individuals was former British Army officer Hamish de Bretton-Gordon. At the time, de Bretton-Gordon was serving as director of the NGO Doctors Under Fire, which campaigns against attacks on hospitals in war zones – but was fingered by McKeigue as a 'known MI6 agent'. De Bretton-Gordon is fully aware of the dangers involved in crossing the Russian intelligence services, and pointed out angrily to the BBC that 'potentially this guy's putting lots of people's lives [at risk] and potentially one of them is mine'. Nevertheless, the same BBC investigation concluded that McKeigue 'does not seem concerned' about the likely consequences of pointing out targets to what he thought was a Russian intelligence officer.[37] In fact, on at least one occasion when passing on names and addresses, McKeigue asked 'Ivan' to 'attack [them] fast and tough'.[38]

McKeigue's network, the 'Working Group on Syria, Propaganda and Media', brings together academics, conspiracy theorists and hangers-on, few of them with expertise relevant to the topics they publish on. The group routinely accuses people who debunk or ridicule their reporting of working for MI6 or other Western spy agencies. It's unclear whether they sincerely believe this, or whether it is simply a tactic to deflect criticism. But the accusations take on an additional layer of irony in the light of one of their leading members' eagerness to collaborate with, as he believed, Russian intelligence.

And just as with Max van der Werff of Bonanza Media, a lack of either shame or self-awareness led McKeigue to implicate himself still further when invited to explain his conduct. Speaking to the *Observer* newspaper, he said he might have used more 'guarded language' when speaking to 'Ivan' if he had known anybody would find out.[39] And in a personal statement released through the 'Working Group', McKeigue described how he had 'reveal[ed] information provided by others that was not intended to be shared', and that his 'emails were not intended to be made public'.[40]

In other words, according to his own explanation, McKeigue was willing to say things to someone he thought was working for Russian intelligence that he was not willing to be heard saying in public. There could be no more conclusive

37. Hadjimatheou, 'The UK professor and the fake Russian agent'.

38. Weiss and Goldsmith, 'How an Email Sting Operation Unearthed a pro-Assad Conspiracy'.

39. Peter Beaumont and Emma Graham-Harrison, 'The UK professor, a fake Russian spy and the undercover Syria sting', *Observer*, 28 March 2021, https://www.theguardian.com/law/2021/mar/28/the-uk-professor-a-fake-russian-spy-and-the-undercover-syria-sting.

40. 'Personal statement on the CIJA sting: Paul McKeigue', Working Group on Syria, Propaganda and Media, undated, https://syriapropagandamedia.org/personal-statement-on-the-cija-sting-paul-mckeigue.

41. Michael Weiss and Jett Goldsmith, 'Syria Chemical-Attack Deniers Admit Links to WikiLeaks and Russia', *Daily Beast*, 20 April 2021, https://www.thedailybeast.com/syria-chemical-attack-deniers-admit-links-to-wikileaks-and-russia.

demonstration both of malign intent and of conscious betrayal. In addition, it's hard to argue the absence of any Russian connection when according to McKeigue, a reliable means of reaching his British colleagues and co-authors was through a diplomat at the Russian Embassy in Geneva, Sergey Krutskikh. (The co-authors told the BBC that they were not in contact with Krutskikh.)

The discovery that academics in respectable positions at UK universities are willing to work with handlers from Russian intelligence, pointing out individuals in possession of inconvenient evidence for them to 'attack fast and tough' is disturbing enough – especially when they are content to put people in danger because they hold evidence that disproves their theories.[41] Still worse, however, is the fact that they face no visible adverse consequences when this becomes known, and continue in their positions as though their behaviour were entirely acceptable to their employers. McKeigue's colleague at Edinburgh University and another member of his propaganda group, Tim Hayward, along with many other disseminators of Russian disinformation continued to do so even after the Russian invasion of Ukraine, retweeting Russian government claims that the attack on a maternity hospital in Mariupol in early March 2022 was 'fake news' and criticizing the West for not 'considering Russia's legitimate interests'. Edinburgh University still seemed unconcerned, issuing a statement that 'we do not comment on individual members of our staff or their employment' and taking no visible action.[42]

In fact, in a strange and repetitive pattern, when British propagandists for Russia are eventually disgraced, it is nothing to do with their spreading disinformation, but instead for being unable to keep their views on Jewish people to themselves. Another propaganda professor, David Miller, also retained his post at Bristol University despite mounting protests – until finally sacked over comments about Israel and Jewish student groups.[43] Former MPs Matthew Gordon-Banks and Chris Williamson (who we will meet in Chapter 7), both keen promoters of Russian narratives, each found that it was only accusations of anti-Semitism that ended their political careers with expulsion from their respective parties.[44]

42. Theo Usherwood, 11 March 2022, https://twitter.com/theousherwood/status/150223895 1444303872?s=27.

43. 'Bristol University: Professor David Miller sacked over Israel comments', BBC News, 1 October 2021, https://www.bbc.co.uk/news/uk-england-bristol-58765052.

44. John Rentoul, 'How do Labour's disciplinary procedures work, and why has Chris Williamson's case caused uproar?', *Independent*, 7 July 2019, https://www.independent.co.uk/news/uk/politics/williamson-antisemitism-labour-disciplinary-case-a8979611.html.

'Antisemitism in the UK', UK Parliament website, undated, https://publications.parliament.uk/pa/cm201617/cmselect/cmhaff/136/13609.htm.

## London facilitators

The role of London as a favoured destination for the outward flood of Russian money, and the toxic influence on British policy and politics it brings with it, is a perfect illustration of how hazards to personal and national integrity are no less severe for being perfectly legal.[45]

Economist Timothy Ash has studied the outflow of money from Russia over the long term. Based on Russian central bank statistics, he estimates that since 1994, 1.6 trillion – not billion, trillion – US dollars have left the country. Of that, approximately 30%, or $500 billion, is estimated to have gone to the UK. The amount of money flowing out from other countries like Ukraine and Kazakhstan will have boosted this figure still further. The result is billions in fees for UK banks and asset management companies. This is a problem, Timothy says, because of the influence that money brings with it. 'Our systems have been so corrupted by Russian money, it is setting the agenda,' he says. 'We need to understand that Russian capital infiltration is as a big a threat as the latest Putin hypersonic missile. Arguably more dangerous, as it's stealth and goes right to the heart of our governance.'[46]

The problem isn't a new one, of course. Over twenty years ago there were warnings of Russian criminal networks taking 'full advantage of globalisation, ill-equipped law enforcement and lax money-laundering laws – especially in Britain – using the City of London as their onshore gateway to the offshore world'. And it was accurately predicted that this would continue, because 'The City is an absolute cesspool and it will remain a cesspool because the people in charge don't care.'[47] The UK's overseas territories, with laxer rules on financial flows and the added benefit of secrecy in the form of anonymously owned companies, are an even more welcoming environment for Russian money of dubious origins.

Samantha de Bendern worked as a private banker in Switzerland during the first decade of this century. She explains how easy it could be to satisfy rules which were supposed to ensure banks did not handle the proceeds of crime. 'There are a lot of complicated problems with making sure you're not handling dodgy money,' she says. 'So let's take one of the most simple ones. When an individual wants to open an account with a large amount of money, the bank's compliance department is going to want to know where that money comes from. But what does that actually mean, to know where it comes from? They're going to see whether there was a house sold, or an inheritance, or a company sold – some kind of paper

45. 'Ukraine crisis: How much Russian money is there in the UK?', BBC, 11 March 2022, https://www.bbc.co.uk/news/60348046.

46. E-mail exchange in February 2021.

47. Tony Thompson and Paul Farrelly, 'Russian mafia target the City', *Guardian*, 22 August 1999, https://www.theguardian.com/world/1999/aug/22/paulfarrelly.tonythompson.

transaction to show how the money appeared. So if you're a wealthy Russian, and you've sold a company, let's say, or floated your company on the stock exchange, and you've suddenly got 10, 100, 500 million pounds in cash to put into a bank. If you have a transaction that backs up the provenance of that cash there are no further questions . . . asked.'

The point, Samantha goes on, is that there is still little will to dig deeper and find the actual origins of the assets sold. 'I came across clients where basic research showed serious allegations of them belonging to mafia groups, of them having an organized crime past, of links to government structures, but they had just sold a company for 300 million and they wanted to put 300 million in an account in our bank, so well, these 300 million are obviously clean. The billion that came before that might not be clean, but the money that went into our bank is. It was a very narrow-minded view of ticking boxes to show that we had done our due diligence to know where the money comes from, and it missed the whole point of doing it.'[48]

Although the UK criticizes other states for tolerating pervasive corruption, it has paid little attention to its own international accountants, lawyers and external advisors who help construct the complicated illicit schemes to make corruption work and hide the proceeds. 'What happens to a lot of these bankers is a wilful abdication of responsibility,' Samantha says. 'I saw that particularly in Switzerland, where they're so used to hiding money from dodgy people all over the world and they persuade themselves that they're hiding it from the taxman. They don't actually go so far as to think that they are enabling criminal regimes.'

In the UK, one aspect of the problem that may be underestimated is how many people are caught up in dubious Russian schemes without being fully aware what they have got involved in. Not everybody entangled with shady Russian business interests fits the profile of a highly-paid London banker or politician. Ewan Tolladay lives in a modest semi-detached house in a former mining village in the north of England. And the fact that he had set up a series of companies in the UK and Ireland with an interesting range of Russian co-directors would probably never have come to light if one of those companies had not been implicated in an anti-vaccine disinformation campaign run from Russia.

In late May 2021, a number of social media influencers across Europe reported approaches from a marketing company called Fazze, offering lucrative rewards on behalf of their anonymous client if they would join in a campaign highlighting the dangers of Pfizer vaccines, up to and including death.[49] Fazze, it turned out, was a

---

48. Samantha compared this relaxed attitude to accepting enormous sums of money with the onerous requirements for ordinary people wanting to open bank accounts with more modest sums. 'I found myself in the absurd situation of having clients with extremely dodgy backgrounds being able to open accounts in the UK and Switzerland; [but] a year after leaving banking I couldn't get a UK based bank to open an account for my small import business because as a non-resident they claimed they couldn't do due diligence on me,' she recalls.

49. Antoine Daoust, 'La Russie derrière une campagne de lobbying anti Pfizer?' (Russia behind an anti-Pfizer lobbying campaign?), *Factandfurious*, 24 May 2021, https://factandfurious. com/enquetes/moscou-derriere-une-campagne-de-lobbying-anti-pfizer.

subsidiary of a company named Adnow – one of those that had been established in the UK by Ewan, together with one of his Russian co-directors. Fazze was not set up specifically to spread anti-vaccine propaganda. It also markets cryptocurrency and diet pills and, according to one investigation, pushes malware.[50] But it was thrust into the limelight by approaching influencers with a conscience, who chose to blow the whistle instead of taking the money and repeating the anti-vaccine disinformation.

Ewan told BBC journalists the activities of the company he is a director of came as a surprise to him. Fazze, he said, was run by people he didn't know, and neither did he know who the client was that had commissioned the disinformation campaign. In light of what he had learned, Ewan said, 'we are doing the responsible thing and shutting down AdNow here in the UK'.[51] At the time of writing, that hasn't happened. But Adnow did change its registered address in the UK, the day after its Fazze subsidiary was finally banned from Facebook in August 2021.[52] In fact this was the third time it had moved since April the same year.[53]

Samantha also points out the core contradiction between London continuing to welcome Russian money and tough British government rhetoric condemning Moscow's actions. 'Why is that a problem?' she asks. 'Because we're helping support a government that has carried out hostile acts on our territory. Russia has used radiological and chemical weapons against British citizens in the UK, and yet we're helping individuals in that government get richer and richer and stay there. So when we have discussions about how to send a strong message to Russia militarily, like sending a warship to irritate them in Crimea, that absolutely means nothing because with the other hand, we're opening the champagne with them in London and eating their caviar while they send their children to our schools.'

The contradictions are immediately obvious from comparing what the British government says and what the City of London does. In the midst of furious

Facebook, 'July 2021 Coordinated Inauthentic Behavior Report', July 2021, https://about.fb.com/news/2021/08/july-2021-coordinated-inauthentic-behavior-report/.

50. Mark Krutov et al., 'Exclusive: Meet The Murky Russian Network Behind An Anti-Pfizer Disinformation Drive In Europe', RFE/RL, 27 May 2021, https://www.rferl.org/a/russia-pfizer-covid-disinformation-serebryanskaya-murky-vaccine-influencers/31277170.html.

51. Charlie Haynes and Flora Carmichael, 'The YouTubers who blew the whistle on an anti-vax plot', BBC News, 25 July 2021, https://www.bbc.co.uk/news/blogs-trending-57928647.

52. 'COVID-19: Firm that claimed Pfizer vaccine turns people into chimpanzees banned from Facebook', Sky News, 11 August 2021, https://news.sky.com/story/covid-19-network-of-accounts-that-claimed-vaccine-turns-people-into-chimps-taken-down-by-facebook-12378533.

53. I hoped Ewan could explain this pattern of activity to me, and how his part in it was entirely innocent, but multiple messages to his Facebook, LinkedIn and Twitter profiles inviting him to do so went unanswered.

denunciations of Moscow over the Salisbury attack, Gazprom launched a €750 million eurobond issue in London. The next day, Russia floated a $4 billion sovereign eurobond, with British investors making up almost half the buyers. Despite the strong words from the British government, London's business with Russia continued as normal.[54] 'The problem we have in London,' Samantha goes on, 'is that it is the favourite destination for floating national companies. Of the sixty Russian companies that have floated on the London Stock Exchange in the last twenty-five years, I have only found five that have no obvious direct links to the Russian government. And when I say obvious direct links, I mean, not needing any serious investigation but things that you can figure out within fifteen to twenty minutes with Google.'

The British Parliament's ISC has put on the record its concern over 'the extent to which Russian expatriates are using their access to UK businesses and politicians to exert influence in the UK'.[55] The list of members of the House of Lords with direct business links to Russia is long and disturbing – and unlike the House of Commons, there is no requirement to declare those interests.[56] Even when interests are declared, though, this only gives a partial picture. The public can see the extent of donations by individuals at one or two removes from the Russian state to, for example, UK Foreign Secretary Dominic Raab.[57] What it cannot see is what the donors are asking for, or expecting, in return.[58] Neither can it understand the reluctance of the British government to take action to address the inevitable suspicion that it is susceptible to influence through purchase by malign foreign powers.[59]

In the UK at least, this is also not unique to the ruling political party. There has been no direct public allegation that a British politician has taken a course of

54. Duncan Allan, 'Managed Confrontation: UK Policy Towards Russia After the Salisbury Attack', Chatham House, October 2018, https://www.chathamhouse.org/sites/default/files/publications/research/2018-10-30-managed-confrontation-uk-russia-salisbury-allan-final.pdf.

55. 'Russia', Intelligence and Security Committee of Parliament, 21 July 2020, https://docs.google.com/a/independent.gov.uk/viewer?a=v&pid=sites&srcid=aW5kZXBlbmRlbnQuZ292LnVrfGlzY3xneDo1Y2RhMGEyN2Y3NjM0OWFl.

56. A partial list of senior British politicians reported to be in business with Russian oligarchs is available at https://twitter.com/professorshaw/status/1407947733227524098.

57. Mikey Smith, 'Dominic Raab's ex-Russian banker donor runs charity with boss of "Kremlin front group"', *Mirror*, 21 August 2021, https://www.mirror.co.uk/news/politics/dominic-raabs-ex-russian-banker-24810180.

58. Adam Payne, '14 ministers in Boris Johnson's government received funding from donors linked to Russia', *Business Insider*, 23 July 2020, https://www.businessinsider.com/russia-report-donors-boris-johnson-conservative-party-2020-7.

59. Aletha Adu, 'Intelligence Committee's brutal swipe at Boris Johnson for ignoring Russian cash fears', *Mirror*, 15 March 2022, https://www.mirror.co.uk/news/politics/breaking-intelligence-committees-brutal-swipe-26475989.

action because he is under an obligation to Moscow, but as we see in other chapters, there is a pattern of Members of Parliament from the opposition Labour Party, including its former leader Jeremy Corbyn, actively assisting Russian hack-and-leak operations intended to influence elections or discredit opponents of Russia.

But the flood of Russian money distorted markets as well as politics. Service industries including real estate agents, bankers, security services, accountants and public relations and reputation managers thrived on the waves of cash that required managing, investing, and on occasion its origins concealing.[60] In particular, London is still seen as a primary destination for legal tourism. Disputes between Russian oligarchs have repeatedly been settled there, thanks to a distinctive perception of English courts providing both a strong rule of law and the best justice Russian money can buy. In the words of one Russian billionaire, 'All oligarchs have an interest in rule of law and an independent legal system. Because we may have broken the law to make our money, but now we want to keep it.'[61] But while in Russia, the wealthy can bribe a judge, or use political connections to instruct them as to the 'right' verdict, in the UK a comparable end result can be achieved through the ability simply to massively outspend the defendant.[62]

This aspect of the English legal system has had a direct and toxic chilling effect on freedom of speech in the UK and beyond. English libel laws present one of the most powerful tools available for silencing critics of the wealthy and powerful in Russia, with or without direct links to the Kremlin. Books or reporting on how Russia's richest oligarchs and politicians acquired their fortunes are a particular target for legal attempts to suppress their findings, and the oligarchs have waged a seemingly unending defamation lawfare crusade against them.

Catherine Belton was a Moscow correspondent for the *Financial Times* from 2007 until 2013, and wrote a book on how Putin and close associates came to power and wealth.[63] In 2021 it was subjected to a combined legal assault by four oligarchs, which at the time of writing was settled largely in her favour but at enormous cost. *Putin's Kleptocracy: Who Owns Russia?* is a 2014 book by US academic Karen Dawisha on a similar topic, that its original publisher Cambridge University Press declined to publish because of the likelihood of libel suits, regardless of whether they had any basis or not.[64] Earlier, in 2010, oligarch

---

60. 'The UK's kleptocracy problem: How servicing post-Soviet elites weakens the rule of law', Chatham House, 8 December 2021, https://www.chathamhouse.org/2021/12/uks-kleptocracy-problem.

61. Private conversation, June 2021.

62. 'The Power of Money: How Autocrats Use London to Strike Foes Worldwide', *New York Times*, https://www.nytimes.com/2021/06/18/world/europe/uk-courts-russia-kazakhstan.html.

63. Catherine Belton, *Putin's People: How the KGB Took Back Russia and Then Took on the West* (London: HarperCollins Publishers, 2020).

64. 'A book too far', *Economist*, 3 April 2014, https://www.economist.com/eastern-approaches/2014/04/03/a-book-too-far.

Gennadiy Timchenko sued the *Economist* for libel after it put in print widely known details about his financial relationship with Vladimir Putin. The *Economist* won the case – but again, at high risk and extraordinary cost. Overall, Nick Cohen writes, the result of welcoming Russian dirty money 'is we cannot write in our own country about a book on oligarchical wealth without risking legal action in what we naively assumed were our own courts. The UK would have done better to have kept the freedom and lost the estate agent commissions on Mayfair property sales and boosts to partners' profits in London law firms.'[65]

The common factor to all of these lawsuits is the London law firms keen to pursue them. The legal profession too has milked oligarchs for unimaginable sums of money, with little or no thought for distortion of justice that results or the pernicious consequences for their own country.

This is because, according to a professor of Anti-Corruption Practice in the UK, a number of British law firms 'are having navigational problems with their moral compass. They represent clients who are highly lucrative, but should fail any reasonable due diligence test.'[66] It's a professorly way of saying that by providing legal services to oligarchs and silencing their critics through litigation, lawyers and other enablers once again make London a centre of the same corruption that the UK condemns in other countries. London is not the only method or venue. Russia is also attempting, for example, to use French courts to harass French critics of RT.[67] But in all such cases, Russia is showing once again that it can exploit the pillars of a free and democratic society – like its legal system – in ways which run directly counter to the best interests of that society.

As with so many other ways Russia extends its reach into Western democratic societies, it was only the invasion of Ukraine that brought the problem to widespread attention and highlighted the extent of the threat to free speech and democratic processes. In an atmosphere of growing revulsion at dependence on Russian money even within the ruling Conservative Party, statements in the UK's Parliament in March 2022 listed the most prominent lawyers launching 'strategic litigation against public participation', or SLAPPs, aiming to intimidate and silence journalists using English courts.[68] Also in parliamentary hearings, Catherine

65. Nick Cohen, 'The long arm of the Chekists', *The Critic*, July 2021, https://thecritic.co.uk/issues/july-2021/the-long-arm-of-the-chekists/.

66. 'Letter: Britain is damaged by the provision of legal services to dictators', *Financial Times*, 7 September 2021, https://www.ft.com/content/1d984cec-4d34-4ac0-9d32-effac1f84206.

67. Nicolas Tenzer, 'Le régime russe tente d'appliquer dans les démocraties ses pratiques intimidantes' (Russian regime attempts to apply its intimidatory practices in democracies), *Le Monde*, 17 September 2021, https://www.lemonde.fr/idees/article/2021/09/17/le-regime-russe-tente-d-appliquer-dans-les-democraties-ses-pratiques-intimidantes_6094978_3232.html.

68. Harry Cole, 'Lawyers, bankers and city PR firms are "collaborators" of Putin's butchery, top Cabinet minister warns', *Sun*, 2 March 2022, https://www.thesun.co.uk/news/politics/17815063/lawyers-bankers-pr-firms-collaborators-putin-cabinet-minister-warns.

Belton highlighted the role of enablers assisting oligarchs in 'making sure nothing offensive against them is ever printed'.[69] Senior lawyers whose work had previously been largely hidden from the public eye found themselves in the media spotlight, including Nigel Tait of the infamous London law firm Carter-Ruck, best known for his boast of being 'the man who suppresses free speech'.[70] But attempts to remedy the glaringly unjust nature of British defamation law and its scope for exploitation by the wealthy, even if they succeed, come too late to undo decades of chilling effect and self-censorship by journalists and analysts.[71] The fact that the super-wealthy could in effect purchase immunity from criticism or exposure of their wrongdoing will remain an enduring stain on the UK's claims that it is governed by rule of law.

## France, Germany and the EU

But at times the most active facilitator of Russian goals is not an individual but an institution: the EU. We have already seen in Chapter 1 how major European states – primarily France and Germany – rode roughshod over the interests of Russia's neighbours when trying to pursue their own misguided wooing of Moscow. But the same syndrome affects not just member states but the union as a whole.

In the early years of the European External Action Service (EEAS) under then EU foreign policy chief Federica Mogherini, 'internal support was minimal' for work dealing with Russian threats, according to multiple current and former EEAS staff members I interviewed. Former EU official Jakub Kalenský noted the contrast between his work resisting Russia and the attitude of the rest of Brussels. 'I think the best feeling I had was whenever I spoke to Ukrainians; they made us feel that what we were doing in Brussels was important. And they were happy to see that we were on the right side in this conflict. They weren't that used to that from European officials in general.'

Despite the abundance of evidence of Russian intent, major European countries were willing to jeopardize their own security for the sake of selfish and short-term pandering to Moscow – and they brought the EU along with them. It is this approach that led directly to huge spikes in gas prices in late 2021, as Russia restricted supply as part of a game to force through approval of its Nord Stream 2

69. 'Journalist names lawyers who represent Russian oligarchs in Parliament', *PoliticsJOE*, 15 March 2022, https://www.youtube.com/watch?v=2Z90XFW5pu4.

70. Francis Elliott et al., 'Labour gagging orders "are useless"', *The Times*, 9 July 2019, https://www.thetimes.co.uk/article/labour-gagging-orders-are-useless-znd9sf87x.

71. Charlotte Tobit, 'Govt proposes anti-SLAPP clampdown after reporters name UK law firms working with Russian oligarchs to silence journalists', *Press Gazette*, https://pressgazette.co.uk/reporters-name-uk-law-firms-working-with-russian-oligarchs-to-silence-journalists/.

pipeline under the Baltic Sea, designed to deliver Russian gas directly to Germany, bypassing Ukraine and Poland.[72] People living in countries like the UK might think that this has nothing to do with them, because there is no reason for them to consider the link between Russian energy games targeting Ukraine and the huge rises in their own energy bills.[73] But again, Russia's manipulations targeting one country has knock-on effects that impact many others.

Perversely, the use of Nord Stream 2 for blackmail had been predicted from its very inception – but Germany pushed ahead with the project over the protests of European countries closer to Russia that could see clearly it would be disastrous for the energy security of anywhere other than Germany. 'This pipeline must not be used to blackmail Ukraine, or the Baltic States or Poland,' claimed candidate for the German chancellorship Armin Laschet, ignoring the near-unanimous conclusion of Russia-watchers and energy experts that that was precisely the purpose for which it was being built.[74] As the slow-motion but entirely predictable campaign unfolded in August and September 2021, some Western media continued to report that it was 'not obvious why' Russia was restricting supplies to Europe – even though the reason was indeed blindingly obvious and had been described in detail for some time beforehand.[75] By the time the gas price crisis hit hard enough to trigger the collapse of energy companies in the UK, the Russian Embassy there was being entirely overt about the aims of its supply blackmail: 'Early certification of NordStream2 will alleviate the gas crisis in Europe,' it tweeted.[76]

In 2011, Putin called the EU a hamster. The reference was to the EU stuffing its cheeks with new members without being able to swallow them, but it also gives an indication of Putin's assessment of the EU's ineffectual nature.[77] As does occasionally happen, Putin had a point. The EU was founded as an organization of pacifist multilateralism, with no thought for how to exercise hard power and

72. 'Цена газа в Европе превысила $810 за 1 тыс. куб. м' (Gas price in Europe tops $810 for 1,000 cu.m.), *Kommersant*, 15 September 2021, https://www.kommersant.ru/doc/4986113.

73. Lora Jones, 'Ofgem warns soaring gas prices will feed into customer bills', BBC News, 9 September 2021, https://www.bbc.co.uk/news/business-58481330.

74. 'Armin Laschet: With Russia "you have to talk more, not less"', DW, 14 June 2021, https://www.dw.com/en/armin-laschet-with-russia-you-have-to-talk-more-not-less/a-57886500.

75. Sam Meredith, 'Russia is pumping a lot less natural gas to Europe all of a sudden – and it is not clear why', CNBC, 24 August 2021, https://www.cnbc.com/2021/08/24/russia-is-pumping-less-natural-gas-to-europe-as-nord-stream-2-nears-completion.html.

76. Tweet by Russian Embassy in the UK, 28 September 2021, https://twitter.com/RussianEmbassy/status/1442879198956335109.

77. Andrei Kolesnikov, '"Не раздвоится". Владимир Путин поделился с Валдайским клубом своим политическим видением' (It doesn't split in two. Putin shared his political vision with the Valdai Club), *Kommersant*, 14 November 2011, https://www.kommersant.ru/doc/1815727.

designed only to use international rules to get its way. This means it is poorly equipped to deal with a challenger like Russia that both readily resorts to force and consistently shows deep disdain for international rules. As the saying reportedly goes among more hard-headed functionaries in Brussels, like Putin's hamster 'the EU is a vegetarian but we are now in a time of carnivores'. And the EU seems to take every opportunity to demonstrate its sheepishness, even in the face of effective acts of war. The strongest term that European Union (EU) High Representative Josep Borrell could bring himself to use to describe the Russian pattern of behaviour after disclosure of the lethal sabotage attack in Czechia in 2014 was 'disruptive actions'. Even after discussing the attack at a meeting of EU foreign ministers, Borrell mentioned no action beyond a declaration of condemnation and a press conference expressing, as always, 'concern'.[78] The routine expression of 'concern' at each new outrage, widely mocked outside the institution, highlighted the EU's lack of self-awareness as much as its unwillingness to confront reality.[79] As Estonian businessman Kristjan Korsten tweeted in November 2021, '"I'm deeply concerned" is something that's more appropriately told to one's therapist, isn't it? Maybe husband/wife. Why would the general public care about your emotions? We care about your plans of action.'[80]

In terms of actual protection against threats, the benefits of being part of the EU seem more abstract than practical. Sven Sakkov explains that for Estonia, the security aspect of joining the EU meant 'anchoring ourselves in the institutions of the West'. 'We were deprived of our place among our friends and partners and allies for fifty years by the Soviet occupation,' he goes on. 'So it wasn't just NATO and EU – we were trying to join every Western club imaginable, and every organization which wanted us as a member, just in order to anchor ourselves through thousands of different threads into the world, so as not to be ripped away from that again as happened in 1939–40.' When this incentive does not apply, as in the case of Norway, the case for EU membership seems much less clear. 'The EU question is not on the agenda at all,' Tor Bukkvoll says. 'More than 60% of Norwegians are against EU membership. We have the EEC economic agreement, which means that we are economically part of the EU but not politically. That's enough and I think we'll be happy like this for a long time.' The EU just isn't considered a provider of security, he adds. 'I don't think Norwegians are thinking about that really at all. Security for us is our own Armed Forces and it's NATO.' Vilde Skorpen Wikan agrees: 'We don't

78. 'Russia: Declaration by the High Representative on behalf of the European Union in solidarity with the Czech Republic over criminal activities on its territory', Council of the EU, 21 April 2021, https://www.consilium.europa.eu/en/press/press-releases/2021/04/21/russia-declaration-by-the-high-representative-on-behalf-of-the-european-union-in-solidarity-with-the-czech-republic-over-criminal-activities-on-its-territory/.

79. See the busy Twitter account dedicated to EU expressions of 'concern' at https://twitter.com/ISEUConcerned.

80. Kristjan Korsten, 11 November 2021, https://twitter.com/korstenkristjan/status/1458871463226884100?s=27.

really feel that the EU is that relevant, especially when it comes to security cooperation. When it comes to Russia, it's very much the bipolar US versus Russia. And the EU, they're kind of doing their own thing.'

In some circumstances Brussels doing its own thing is preferable to Brussels trying to get involved. In 2019 an otherwise broadly optimistic report from the EU's own security think tank on how the organization is responding to sub-threshold threats included a section entitled 'Lessons: The EU as Its Own Worst Enemy'.[81] Four years earlier, and little more than a year after the covert Russian seizure of Crimea, the Norwegian TV series *Occupied* described a comparable scenario affecting Norway. One key plot element was the EU colluding with Russia and intimidating the Norwegian government into accepting Russian demands. Vilde Skorpen Wikan thinks the show could have been 'upsetting to the EU because they're certainly not used to being painted in the villainous role'. But in Norway itself, this depiction of Brussels caused little surprise – and neither will it surprise anybody who has observed the pattern of European leaders dictating similar terms to the victims of Russian aggression over the last two decades (see Chapter 2). Smaller countries like Lithuania have already found that their interests in withstanding Russia are hostage to Brussels in real life. An assessment of efforts to prevent strategically dangerous Russian efforts to take control of Lithuania's transport sector found that 'so far, Lithuania's actions seem to have helped to prevent some of the companies and individuals associated with Russia from expansion into our country. But when the legal struggle moves to the European Union level, the outcome is hard to predict.'[82]

The EU's inability to effectively withstand Russia, and the unwillingness of its biggest members to admit that Russia needs to be withstood in the first place, came into sharp focus as Russia built up its troops along the Ukrainian border in late 2021. As late as January 2022, Germany was offering Russia cooperation on developing renewable energy supplies in an attempt to cajole it out of the threatened invasion of Ukraine – an offer made doubly ridiculous by the way development of renewable energy supplies is a direct threat to the fossil-fuel-based Russian economy.[83] The EU's foreign affairs chief Josep Borrell meanwhile continued to urge 'dialogue' instead of action. 'The EU believes that dialogue, negotiation, and cooperation are the only means to overcome disputes,' Borrell said, while Russia was already engaged in gas blackmail and massing its troops for invasion.[84]

81. Daniel Fiott and Roderick Parkes, 'Protecting Europe: The EU's response to hybrid threats', European Union Institute for Security Studies Chaillot Paper 151, April 2019, https://www.iss.europa.eu/sites/default/files/EUISSFiles/CP_151.pdf.

82. Marius Laurinavičius, 'Lithuanian Railways: Attack from the East', Vilnius Institute for Policy Analysis, 2019.

83. 'Germany offers cooperation on renewables to defuse tensions with Russia', Reuters, 21 January 2022, https://www.reuters.com/business/energy/germany-offers-cooperation-renewables-defuse-tensions-with-russia-2022-01-21/.

84. 'Putin underlines EU gas needs amid Ukraine threat', *EU Observer*, 24 December 2021, https://euobserver.com./world/153924.

And rather than heeding the warnings from the US and UK about Russia's intentions, Germany and France were alarmed at steps to shore up Ukraine's resilience to the imminent attack.[85] While the UK was urgently shipping anti-armour weapons to Ukraine to bolster its defences against the imminent Russian invasion, Germany was still preventing its NATO allies from sending even second-hand weaponry and munitions to Kyiv.[86] And even after Germany belatedly agreed to support Ukraine, supplies of weaponry fell far short of what had been promised.[87]

After the decades of complacency, Germany's belated awakening to the threat – and the new defence and security policies laid out by Chancellor Olaf Scholz in late February 2022 – constituted a historic change of course that was perhaps even more astonishing than the Russian invasion that triggered it.[88] Proposals for huge increases in defence spending, and a new reality-based approach to Russia, reflected a broader trend across western Europe as the nature of the challenge was finally acknowledged.[89] But the initial flush of enthusiasm for taking steps to register disapproval of Russia ran into inevitable backlash when it became clear what the economic cost would be – and in particular, how difficult it would be to reverse decades of European energy policy which entrenched reliance on Russian fossil fuels more and more deeply.[90] At the time of writing, it remains to be seen just how sustainable Germany's newfound interest in defending itself will turn out to be – and how long the EU would be able to resist the calls for a return, once again, to business as usual. Less than a month after the invasion of Ukraine, amid

85. Anne-Sylvaine Chassany, 'Britain's activism in Ukraine crisis rattles Paris and Berlin', *Financial Times*, 30 January 2022, https://www.ft.com/content/2e003f9c-3ac7-4ae8-ac86-22ccc2799633.

86. 'Germany Blocks NATO Ally From Transferring Weapons to Ukraine', Reuters, 21 January 2022, https://www.wsj.com/articles/germany-blocks-nato-ally-from-transferring-weapons-to-ukraine-11642790772.

87. Klaus Geiger and Hans-Martin Tillack, 'Berlin liefert nur Bruchteil der versprochenen Strela-Raketen', *Welt sm Sonntag*, 18 March 2022, https://www.welt.de/politik/ausland/article237631477/Berlin-liefert-nur-Bruchteil-der-versprochenen-Strela-Raketen-an-Ukraine.html.

88. 'Policy statement by Olaf Scholz, Chancellor of the Federal Republic of Germany and Member of the German Bundestag', German Federal Government website, 27 February 2022, https://www.bundesregierung.de/breg-en/search/policy-statement-by-olaf-scholz-chancellor-of-the-federal-republic-of-germany-and-member-of-the-german-bundestag-27-february-2022-in-berlin-2008378.

89. András Rácz, 'Germany's shifting policy towards Russia: The sudden end of Ostpolitik', FIIA, 17 March 2022, https://www.fiia.fi/en/publication/germanys-shifting-policy-towards-russia.

90. Barbara Moens, Jacopo Barigazzi and Suzanne Lynch, 'Next sanctions round will test EU unity on how hard to hit Russia', *Politico*, 16 March 2022, https://www.politico.eu/article/eu-russia-saction-war-ukraine-trade/.

a flood of businesses quitting Russia, French car-maker Renault was already restarting operations there.[91] The precedent is not good for what may happen a year from now.

The blind spots of London's financial and legal industries, and the failures of the EU to defend itself or its members, would be damaging enough on their own. But both challenges are made worse by an incomplete understanding of Russian state interests and how, and by whom, they are advanced. Western capitals are predisposed to see the threat as coming only from entities that are directly and unquestionably part of the Russian government. But Moscow can get its way not just at a state level, but also through commercial enterprises and even on occasion organized crime. How that works, and the distinctive overlap between the three worlds of business, state and crime in Russia, is the subject of the next chapter.

91. Jasper Jolly and Sarah Butler, 'Renault resumes car production in Moscow as rivals cut ties with Russia', *Guardian*, 21 March 2022, https://www.theguardian.com/business/2022/mar/21/renault-moscow-russia-nestle.

# Chapter 7

## BUSINESS, STATECRAFT AND CRIME

Russia has a bewildering variety of ways it can recruit or persuade foreigners abroad to work against their own country. The target countries often struggle to see this process clearly, because so often the relationship is not with an obvious branch of the Russian government, but instead with a notionally independent commercial organization. But with so many Russian corporations either being directly or indirectly controlled by the state, or finding their roots in organized crime or the intelligence services, any claim that 'it's just business' needs to be carefully evaluated.

The Russian business and crime worlds and the Russian state have overlapping histories and objectives, and far from being directly opposed to each other as in Western countries governed by rule of law, state security officials and criminals routinely operate in close cooperation. As early as 1996, a former director of the CIA had described how difficult this makes it to work out whether you are facing a Russian government official, a criminal or a businessman. 'If an American businessman meets with a nattily dressed and articulate Russian for a business discussion, and the Russian claims that he is with an international trading and banking firm in Moscow and he would very much like to discuss a joint venture that, say, covers the export of Russian oil, such an individual may be what he says he is, or he may be a Russian intelligence officer operating under commercial cover, or he may be an important member of a Russian organised crime group,' James Woolsey explained. 'The really interesting point is that there is a reasonable chance that he is all three and that none of those three institutions sees any problem at all with such an arrangement.'[1] A classic example of this type is Viktor Bout, an arms trader whose life story was the basis for the 2005 Nicolas Cage film *Lord of War*. Bout's career spanned the three worlds of crime, business and intelligence work on behalf of the Russian state – and often all three at the same time.[2]

---

1. R. James Woolsey, former Director of Central Intelligence, speaking to the US House National Security Committee in 1996: 'Challenges Posed by Russia to United States National Security Interests', 13 June 1996, H.N.S.C. No. 104-40, p. 15.

2. Richard Galpin, '"Kremlin links" of alleged arms dealer Viktor Bout', BBC News, 21 January 2011, https://www.bbc.co.uk/news/world-europe-12208961.

Today's Russian state benefits from the legacy of a historically greater willingness to embrace irregular, criminal or subversive methods to achieve political effects during nominal peacetime. As with so much else in Russia, what looks like a new phenomenon has deep roots going back not just to communist times but to Tsarist Russia. The political police have always had an ambiguous relationship with the criminal underworld, fuelled by Russia's permanent state of endemic corruption.[3] And the willingness of the Russian intelligence services to cooperate with organized crime to achieve their objectives goes back to the nineteenth century if not before.[4] But the situation today, where the two worlds have effectively merged, has its roots in the turmoil of the end of the USSR in the early 1990s.

At a time when order was breaking down and there were opportunities to be seized, the two groups that were in the best position to seize them were organized crime and the KGB. They had much in common. The KGB had slush funds to serve as seed capital, including, critically, access to foreign currency overseas. It had networks of power brokers and access to the highest levels of government, and it had experience and initiative. Organized criminal groups similarly had networks, funding, manpower and initiative most of all. The basis of almost all today's economic or political power in Russia – whether its roots lie in the KGB or in crime – was being in the right place at the right time to either sit astride and tap into a financial flow into or out of Russia (for instance foreign aid coming in, or oil exports going out), or seizing and exploiting an asset, like a factory or an oilfield. In effect, the careers of all Russia's major oligarchs were started with an act of crime to climb the vital first rung of the ladder.[5]

During this chaotic time, organized crime filled a vacuum in civil society by providing services that the state could not. Over time, this provision became institutionalized. Protection rackets evolved into a more or less stable and overt market for security services. And in the opposite direction, the hopelessly underfunded and underpaid police and military special forces provided private protection services in competition, or cooperation, with protection rackets. Criminal groups reached understandings with law enforcement agencies that allowed them both to survive – in some cases extending to gangs financially supporting the police for the purpose of 'public relations'.[6] By the mid-1990s,

3. Mark Galeotti, 'Crimintern: How the Kremlin Uses Russia's Criminal Networks in Europe', European Council on Foreign Relations, April 2017, https://ecfr.eu/publication/crimintern_how_the_kremlin_uses_russias_criminal_networks_in_europe/.

4. Victor Madeira, *Britannia and the Bear: The Anglo-Russian Intelligence Wars, 1917–1929* (London: Boydell, 2014).

5. A process detailed in Karen Dawisha, *Putin's Kleptocracy: Who Owns Russia?* (New York: Simon & Schuster, 2014).

6. I. S. Nafikov, *Tenevaia ekonomika i organizovannaia prestupnost' v usloviiakh krupnogo goroda* (Kazan: Poznanie, 2012). Quoted in Kira Harris, 'Russia's Fifth Column: The Influence of the Night Wolves Motorcycle Club', *Studies in Conflict & Terrorism* (2018), DOI: 10.1080/1057610X.2018.1455373.

having already grown wealthy through the protection rackets and other criminal enterprises, gang leaders began to move into the management structures of the companies they protected and to acquire property legally. These attempts to legitimize themselves led to the need to work together with budding politicians following the same goal. At times this process was almost overt. In the early 1990s the advertising slogan of one of Russia's early corporations was *Iz teni v svet*, or 'from the shadows into the light', a reference to its well-known origins in the illegal shadow economy.[7] By the end of the decade, the interwoven nature of crime and statehood was considered irreversible.[8] Each side brought their own special skillset, networks and resources into this symbiotic relationship. Criminal organizations had easy access to private violence and illegal expertise. This could include the use of 'street gangs and thugs to do the sort of dirty work that even spies don't want to touch'.[9] Law enforcement and the intelligence agencies provided favoured groups with official protection in return for their services.[10]

But the end of the 1990s also saw the arrival in power of Vladimir Putin, and a far-reaching campaign of restoring order to Russia. Crucially, though, in many areas this was order as opposed to law and order. Mark Galeotti recalls how 'Many criminals at the time feared that Putin was serious in his tough law-and-order rhetoric, but it soon became clear that he was simply offering (imposing) a new social contract with the underworld. Word went out that gangsters could continue to be gangsters without fearing the kind of systematic crack-down they had feared – but only so long as they understood that the state was the biggest gang in town and they did nothing to directly challenge it.' The eventual result was 'the emergence of a conditional understanding that Russia now had a "nationalised underworld". In short, when the state wanted something from the criminals, they were expected to comply.'[11] The result, over time, has been the assimilation of individuals and organizations with criminal roots into mainstream networks of power and prestige, to the point where they are indistinguishable. In this way Russia has gradually transformed from a country that had a mafia into a mafia that has a country.

7. Photograph available at https://vk.com/wall-72326580_636662.

8. 'Russia's Road to Corruption: How the Clinton Administration Exported Government Instead of Free Enterprise and Failed the Russian People', Speaker's Advisory Group on Russia, United States House of Representatives 106th Congress, September 2000, https://fas.org/irp/congress/2000_rpt/russias-road.pdf.

9. Mark Galeotti, 'The Kremlin's Newest Hybrid Warfare Asset: Gangsters', *Foreign Policy*, 12 June 2017, https://foreignpolicy.com/2017/06/12/how-the-world-of-spies-became-a-gangsters-paradise-russia-cyberattack-hack/.

10. Svetlana Stephenson, 'It Takes Two to Tango: The State and Organized Crime in Russia', *Current Sociology* 65, no. 3 (May 2017): 411–26.

11. Galeotti, 'Crimintern'.

According to Alex Grigorievs, this is facilitated by a criminal mentality on the part of Russia's leaders themselves. 'The group that has seized power in Russia has the psychology and the ethic of a criminal group,' he says. 'And it was clear from the very beginning. Putin was using the criminal jargon, the language of the Russian prison, in his very first speeches. To anybody who is attentive to Russian culture, it was clear.' But Mark Galeotti says this does not mean we should call Russia a 'mafia state'. 'This is not a mafia state in the sense the gangsters control the Kremlin, or the Kremlin completely controls organised crime,' he says. Rather than being fully integrated, the Kremlin calls on the services of organized crime groups. 'We've seen them be used in assassinations in Turkey. We've seen them being used for intelligence gathering in the Baltic states and Scandinavia. We've seen them used to generate *chernaya kassa*, black account monies for political subversion operations.'[12] In effect, the criminal networks operate as state proxies. Russian-based organized crime operating in Europe provides services to the Kremlin like laundering the proceeds of crime and cyber-attacks, trafficking in illicit goods and people, and political assassinations, as well as functions more usually associated with actual governments, like intelligence operations and exerting political influence.

This overlap and blurring of the lines that Western countries think divide these three worlds is routinely used by Russia to get the results it wants. Russia's supposedly covert operations in eastern Ukraine in 2014–16 tapped into a ready pool of current and former GRU and Spetsnaz officers, who might or might not also be convicted criminals who had served time for murder and who would happily engage in slaughtering each other as well as the enemy when Russia felt it needed a change of direction or a new leader.[13] Oligarchs and senior figures in the business world can be called on to lend their personal influence and finances to the war effort.[14] The outsourcing of state functions to private enterprise has the advantages not only of deniability and related confusion for the enemy, but also that if the enterprise goes wrong, it wastes the oligarch's money not the state's. But if it goes right, the return on investment can come in the form of lucrative government contracts, increased access to President Putin and the centre of power, or even directly as spoils of war, as in the case of Russian state-backed mercenaries taking a cut of the profits from the Syrian oil fields they helped recapture.[15]

12. Mark Galeotti, 'Russian Intelligence & Security Community', Russia Strategic Initiative, 12 August 2021, https://community.apan.org/wg/rsi/project-connect/w/events/31576/mark-galeotti-russian-intelligence-security-community/.

13. Jack Losh, 'Is Russia Killing Off Eastern Ukraine's Warlords?', *Foreign Policy*, 25 October 2016, https://foreignpolicy.com/2016/10/25/who-is-killing-eastern-ukraines-warlords-motorola-russia-putin/.

14. Belton, *Putin's People*.

15. Denis Korotkov, 'Вагнер. Первая нефть' (Wagner. First oil.), *Novaya gazeta*, 19 January 2020, https://novayagazeta.ru/articles/2020/01/19/83514-vagner-pervaya-neft.

When considering how private individuals engage in ventures which coincide with the aims of the Russian state, one name constantly crops up. Konstantin Malofeyev is a former banker who became wealthy through telecommunications deals in the mid-2000s. In the period after 2014 he has been providing widespread support to projects that aid the extension of Russian power and influence. These include financial support to the forces fighting in eastern Ukraine,[16] organizing events bringing together representatives of extremist political parties across Europe,[17] setting up the 'International Agency for Sovereign Development'[18] whose 'culturally conservative activists' project Russia's image in Africa as a defender of traditional values,[19] and more. He is president of the 'Katehon' group, made up of 'dedicated supporters of the Imperial Renaissance of Russia' – a fact omitted from the English-language version of its website which provides a platform for a wide variety of international anti-Western activists and conspiracy theorists.[20] Undeterred by the fact that his businesses are reportedly run at a consistent loss, Malofeyev has been reticent in public interviews as to the source of the funding for this impressive range of activity.[21]

But Malofeyev is just one of the most prominent of Russia's oligarchs who provide alternative mechanisms for implementing Russian state policy, including hostile acts against foreign countries. This can mean providing both funding that is off the state books and parallel chains of communication and command.[22] The advantage for Russia is that this is often subject to less scrutiny than direct state action, because of a presumption that the activities of oligarchs are matters of private enterprise. But who is directing Russian commercial enterprises and their activities can often be hidden behind a network of front companies in different

16. Courtney Weaver, 'Malofeev: the Russian billionaire linking Moscow to the rebels', *Financial Times*, 24 July 2014, https://www.ft.com/content/84481538-1103-11e4-94f3-00144feabdc0.

17. Andrew Rettman, 'Illicit Russian billions pose threat to EU democracy', *EU Observer*, 21 April 2017, https://euobserver.com/foreign/137631.

18. 'Konstantin Malofeev:"Russia is a partner of strategic importance to Africa"', Roscongress, 15 October 2019, https://roscongress.org/en/materials/konstantin-malofeev-rossiya-dlya-afrikanskikh-stran-yavlyaetsya-prioritetnym-partnerom/.

19. Presenter at 'The Bear Returns: Understanding Russia's strategic engagement and policy impact in Africa', South African Institute of International Affairs, 14 June 2021.

20. 'О нас' (About Us), Katehon, https://katehon.com/ru/o-nas.

21. Irina Pankratova, 'Russia's "Orthodox tycoon" is bankrolling a monarchist movement – but where does he get his money?', *The Bell*, 22 November 2019, https://thebell.io/en/russia-s-orthodox-tycoon-is-bankrolling-a-monarchist-movement-but-where-does-he-get-his-money/.

22. Linnea Hylén, '"Dark, Dirty and Secret": A Qualitative Study on Russia's Financial Active Measures', Uppsala University Institute for Russian and Eurasian Studies (IRES), 4 June 2021, http://www.diva-portal.org/smash/get/diva2:1569656/ATTACHMENT01.pdf.

countries around the world. This not only conceals the way these enterprises can exert political and financial influence, but can also facilitate espionage operations by providing cover for Russian intelligence officers in businesses apparently unconnected to Russia. In addition, according to Alexei Navalny, failure to recognize that notionally private enterprise is perfectly capable of working on behalf of the Russian state constitutes a major blind spot in challenging Russian hostile actions: 'The west needs to free itself of a semantic mindset where the label "businessman" acts as an indulgence,' he writes.[23] Pekka Toveri agrees, and says that in Finland, 'It is still difficult for some authorities and politicians to understand how intermingled these activities are for Russians, and that a oligarch can do things that are stupid and unprofitable from a business point of view in order to support other aims.'

These stupid and unprofitable things sometimes coalesce into a clear pattern that has obvious security risks for the target country. Governments along Russia's western borders have noted an ongoing interest by Russian corporations linked both to the state and to organized crime in gaining control of transport infrastructure. Lars says that 'the pawprints of the bear are here and there. It's clear that the Russian criminal money is involved across Europe, and it seems like it's often related to infrastructure, things like ports.' The threat is threefold. First, direct or indirect criminal control of freight forwarding and shipping companies facilitates the illegal movement of goods or people across borders. Second, Russian control of or influence on national transport systems such as rail links poses a national security threat in the event of a worsening confrontation with Russia.[24] Third, these interests inevitably bring with them an increased level of corruption and malign influence in the target country.[25] This affects not just Russia's immediate neighbours with land borders. Mark Galeotti noted in 2017 that 'Stockholm port is a notorious maritime smuggling link with St. Petersburg, and the city's primary organised crime group – Tambovskaya – has a long-standing presence there.'[26]

But efforts to restrict the activities of front companies for Russian interests, whether state or criminal, are hampered if there is no direct evidence of ongoing illegality. According to Laura Halminen, 'there are multiple companies operating in Finland with apparent connections to Russian intelligence as well as oligarchs

23. Alexei Navalny, 'Only action against corruption can solve the world's biggest problems', *Guardian*, 19 August 2021, https://www.theguardian.com/commentisfree/2021/aug/19/action-against-corruption-russian-sanctions-oligarchs-alexei-navalny.

24. Marius Laurinavičius, 'Lithuanian Railways: Attack from the East', Vilnius Institute for Policy Analysis, 2019.

25. Emmet Tuohy, 'Cinema Vérité: Corruption Scandals and Russian Influence in the Baltic', International Centre for Defence and Security, undated, https://icds.ee/wp-content/uploads/2014/Emmet_Tuohy_-_Corruption_Scandals_and_Russian_Influence_in_the_Baltic.pdf.

26. Galeotti, 'Crimintern'.

close to Kremlin. By just scratching the surface of these companies the straw men appear easily, but there isn't much we can do as long as they don't break the law.' And if they are interdicted, she adds, a change of name or front company can ensure operations are not disrupted for long. 'There's a case where the US sanctioned a Russian deep-water tech company supplying to the FSB and Russia's MOD and applied sanctions to the company's Finnish freight forwarding partner, but new fronts keep on going and delivering the same goods with no US reaction.'

At other times the link between Russian state employees and criminal activity is not too difficult to deduce, because the crimes are being carried out by staff posted to Russian embassies abroad. The range of ambition appears to stretch from high-profile international crime worth tens of millions of dollars, like the cocaine smuggling ring operating out of the Russian Embassy in Buenos Aires,[27] to far more mundane criminal enterprises like a member of the consulate in Strasbourg boosting his salary by selling stolen bicycles on the French small ads site Leboncoin.[28] On occasion the conduct of Russian diplomats is not only criminal but also deeply unpatriotic, as with the Russian Consul-General in Narva, Estonia, who arranged to jump the coronavirus vaccination queue in suspicious circumstances in order to receive the Pfizer vaccine, condemned by Russia as dangerous, before returning to Russia – apparently because he had little faith in Russia's own Sputnik vaccine.[29] And in some cases, the interaction between business, government and crime is so blatant that it confirms Russia's leadership is barely even bothering to pretend to legitimacy. Private military companies are illegal in Russia – but one of Russia's best-known exports is the Wagner private military company. This contradiction was touched on by President Putin in his 2018 annual press conference, where he said that 'if Wagner violates something, the Prosecutor General should draw up a legal opinion on it. But if they don't break Russian laws, they can push on with their business interests anywhere in the world.' But Putin is perfectly well aware that Wagner is breaking Russian laws simply by existing.[30]

27. 'Russian Lawmakers Ensnared in Argentine Cocaine Scandal – Report', *Moscow Times*, 21 September 2020, https://www.themoscowtimes.com/2020/09/21/russian-lawmakers-ensnared-in-argentine-cocaine-scandal-report-a71496.

28. 'Le chauffeur d'un diplomate russe de Strasbourg soupçonné de recel de vélos volés', *France Bleu*, 22 March 2021, https://www.francebleu.fr/infos/faits-divers-justice/le-chauffeur-d-un-diplomate-russe-de-strasbourg-soupconne-de-recel-de-velos-voles-1616438763.

29. 'Doctor who vaccinated Russian diplomat ahead of schedule loses job', ERR, 4 February 2021, https://news.err.ee/1608096889/doctor-who-vaccinated-russian-diplomat-ahead-of-schedule-loses-job.

30. 'Кудрин, повар, ЧВК Вагнера, женитьба: что важного и странного сказал Путин на пресс-конференции' (Kudrin, the chef, the Wagner PMC, marriage: all the important and strange things Putin said at his press conference), *The Bell*, 20 December 2018, https://thebell.io/kudrin-povar-chvk-vagnera-zhenitba-chto-vazhnogo-i-strannogo-skazal-putin-na-press-konferentsii.

*'The insurance will cover it'*

But it's not just state-on-state attacks, sending in mercenaries or high-level corruption that make use of Russia's willingness to provide a hospitable home base for crime directed abroad. Ordinary people in other countries also suffer as a result of far more mundane and old-school criminal activity that benefits from Russia turning a blind eye, or actively helping.

Nicola (not her real name) is an experienced officer in a British law enforcement agency. She explained to me how organized crime groups (OCGs) with Russian state cover run a network of 'chop shops' in the east of England, where stolen vehicles are disguised for selling on or, more frequently, broken down for parts. The vehicles and parts are then exported to Lithuania and sold, she explained, with the money earned going to accounts in Russia. The chop shops are manned by Lithuanian passport holders recruited from the east of the country (where the country's Russian minority is concentrated), whose cooperation is ensured by threats against their families at home. If arrested, they are briefed to say that they have been trafficked, which triggers a different handling process as they are then considered a victim of modern slavery practices rather than the perpetrator of a crime. Repatriated to Lithuania, they can soon return to start again.

The net effect is millions of pounds of value being extracted from the UK, monetized and delivered to Russian-controlled bank accounts in the full view of the authorities. Insurers have to cover the cost, but – just as with the example of gas bills in Chapter 6 – few British drivers probably stop to consider that when their vehicle insurance premiums go up, part of the increase is indirectly going to Russia.

According to Nicola, this process is well known to law enforcement but there are no resources to mount arrests and prosecutions. It is not a high-priority crime for under-resourced local forces as it receives little publicity, but at the same time it is not a big enough problem for the National Crime Agency, even when factoring in the illegal migration and trafficking aspects. Part of the problem is that because the impact is indirect, the process is classed as 'victimless crime'. 'They call it victimless,' Nicola says. 'But tell that to the small trader who's lost his van.'

One area where the common interests between Russian criminal enterprises and the Russian state are clearest is cyber crime. In part this is because the methods and tools used by cyber criminals to steal money are broadly the same as the ones used by cyber spies to steal national secrets, and by cyber activists to steal embarrassing or compromising information that can be made public – in all cases, the key is extracting private information from the target computer. It makes sense for Russia's intelligence agencies to tap into the readily available cyber skills of organized criminals, because of the ease with which they can be turned to state needs.[31] And

---

31. 'Dark Covenant: Connections Between the Russian State and Criminal Actors', Insikt Group, 9 September 2021, https://go.recordedfuture.com/hubfs/reports/cta-2021-0909.pdf.

in return, Russia has traditionally turned a blind eye to cyber crime operations – as long as they are directed outside and not within Russia itself.[32]

Even without counting the damage caused by successful espionage operations, just the financial costs imposed on the victims of successful cyber attacks are staggering. Just as with the attack on the UK Defence Academy described in Chapter 4, the UK Foreign Office was hit by a 'serious cyber security incident' in 2021. This cost the department £467,000 just for analysis by one outside contractor, even before counting the cost of mitigating damage and restoring secure systems.[33]

But even when cyber criminals attack Western targets on their own initiative and for their own profit, it helps the Russian state in its overall campaign to harm the West. Lars, the counter-intelligence officer, points to the harm done to Europe and North America by ransomware gangs operating out of Russia. Even when they are not tools of the state, he says, 'they certainly are something that the state could clamp down on if it chose to do so. [But] it's in Russia's interest to let these gangs inflict billions of dollars of damages across Europe and the US.' In 2021, three-quarters of all the funds extorted through ransomware attacks worldwide went to Russian hacking groups.[34] And tracing that money repeatedly led cyber-security experts to front companies in a prestigious office high-rise in central Moscow, that by pure coincidence also housed Russia's Ministry of Digital Development, Signals and Mass Communications.[35]

Adam Blake is a British cyber-security expert. His company, Threatspike, helps businesses in the UK protect themselves against cyber attack. This means he sees just how broad the range of targets is – and how devastating the effect can be. 'We deal with many different types of companies,' Adam says. 'There are private aviation companies, factories, retailers, people like this. But when they get hit, they are all businesses who aren't able to do business. For as long as it takes, they're simply unable to function.' In addition, Adam says, 'It takes an incredibly long time to recover. We see people who are still recovering six months later from these types of issues. And so it can be incredibly costly.'

After years when national security experts had been sounding the alarm about how vulnerable essential services are to hacking, it was a Russian ransomware

32. Maggie Miller, 'Top FBI official says there is "no indication" Russia has taken action against hackers', *The Hill*, 14 September 2021, https://thehill.com/policy/cybersecurity/572184-top-fbi-official-says-there-is-no-indication-russia-has-taken-action.

33. Alexander Martin, 'Foreign Office was targeted by "Serious cyber security incident"', Sky News, 8 February 2022, https://news.sky.com/story/foreign-office-was-targeted-by-serious-cyber-security-incident-12536181.

34. '74% of ransomware revenue goes to Russia-linked hackers', BBC, 14 February 2022, https://www.bbc.co.uk/news/technology-60378009.

35. Kartikay Mehrotra and Olga Kharif, 'Ransomware HQ: Moscow's Tallest Tower Is a Cybercriminal Cash Machine', Bloomberg, 3 November 2021, https://www.bloomberg.com/news/articles/2021-11-03/bitcoin-money-laundering-happening-in-moscow-s-vostok-tower-experts-say.

attack in early 2021 that shut down Colonial Pipeline, the company delivering much of the petrol, diesel and jet fuel used on the US East Coast, that finally focused public attention on the chaos that could be caused by cyber disruption to critical national infrastructure. Russia took the opportunity to press for a summit meeting between presidents Putin and Biden – something that Russia-watchers consistently warn should not be provided to Russia as a reward for bad behaviour.[36] Lars had seen the pattern before, where Russia uses cyber crime committed from its territory as 'a kind of leverage they can use when negotiating with the West, to extract concessions in return for their help with shutting down these ransomware gangs that are inflicting considerable damage there'.

Meeting Putin in June 2021, Joe Biden presented a list of sixteen areas of essential infrastructure that he said were off-limits – as well as asking Putin to rein in the amount of cyber crime being launched from Russia.[37] But once talks on cyber crime began with the United States, not only did they have no visible effect on the number of attacks, but Russia also tried hard to broaden them out to other issues beyond the specific problem of ransomware. As ever, Russia excelled at creating a problem and then presenting itself as the solution – but a solution that brings with it other, unrelated gains for Moscow. For several decades Russia has been arguing for treaties governing cyberspace, with terms that Western powers have long found unacceptable. Russia's latest proposal for an international agreement on cyber crime would mean Western countries signing up to Russia's ideas on domestic control of the internet.[38] Belgian cyber law researcher Nathalie Van Raemdonck explains why this is a problem: 'Russia wants sovereignty over its internet and wants to be able to censor dissidents, so in a nutshell, it's exactly what we don't want: to break up the "free and open" internet.' Moscow tries to persuade other countries that this is a good idea by telling them two contradictory stories, Nathalie says. 'Russia pushes the idea that Western countries are weak for not being able to control the problem of online extremists. But then they also push the idea that the Western world is hypocritical for restricting freedom of speech while condemning other countries, like Russia, for doing just the same.'

Andrew Kramer, 'Companies Linked to Russian Ransomware Hide in Plain Sight', *New York Times*, 6 December 2021, https://www.nytimes.com/2021/12/06/world/europe/ransomware-russia-bitcoin.html.

36. Joseph Menn, 'Analysis: Murkiness of Russia's ransomware role complicates Biden summit mission', Reuters, 14 June 2021, https://www.reuters.com/technology/murkiness-russias-ransomware-role-complicates-biden-summit-mission-2021-06-14/.

37. Julian E. Barnes and David E. Sanger, 'After Biden Meets Putin, U.S. Exposes Details of Russian Hacking Campaign', *New York Times*, 1 July 2021, https://www.nytimes.com/2021/07/01/us/politics/biden-putin-russia-hacking.html.

38. Elena Chernenko, 'Синдром киберответственности: Как Россия предлагает миру бороться с преступностью в интернете' (Cyber irresponsibility syndrome: how Russia suggests the world fights crime on the internet), *Kommersant*, 20 July 2021, https://www.kommersant.ru/doc/4920377.

Along with online disinformation, cyber crime is perhaps the clearest example of how anyone, no matter how remote from Russia, can be a target for Russian hostile action. According to former British cyber-security chief Ciaran Martin, 'organised Russian crime is bombarding the west with national security levels of harm, in healthcare, energy and food supplies, education and more'.[39] But behind the headline stories of attacks lies the impact on real people. In the aftermath of a spate of attacks in the United States in mid-2021, it was declared that the 'national impact was small as critical infrastructure was not hit' – but life was paralysed for ordinary people in many different locations around the world.[40] This included attacks on hospitals and threatening care for critically ill patients. 'It's like asking what's the point of putting a bomb in an elementary school,' one nurse told American reporter Ellen Barry. 'There is a lot of evil in the world.'[41] Often, as with ransomware incidents, there is a clear financial incentive. But in other cases, including failed or successful attacks on the Olympic Games, it can be hard to discern any motivation for attacks beyond pure spite and malice from Moscow.[42]

Any online presence presents a method by which people can be targeted. LinkedIn remains a favourite means both of identifying targets and attacking them. As well as rudimentary attack methods that exploit a user's poor security, sophisticated advanced techniques have been used to deliver cyber attacks via LinkedIn messages.[43] And Russia has developed the means of completely denying access to the internet for ordinary users, including through exploits like the VPNFilter and Cyclops Blink malwares, capable of permanently disabling home and small office internet connections on demand.[44] Adam Blake says that even

39. https://twitter.com/ciaranmartinoxf/status/1423240637000859655?s=27.

40. 'Russian hackers are targeting small towns in the US. See what happened in Maryland', CNN, 16 July 2021, https://www.cnn.com/videos/tech/2021/07/16/leonardtown-maryland-cyberattack-kaseya-marquardt-dnt-ebof-vpx.cnn.

41. Ellen Barry and Nicole Perlroth, 'Patients of a Vermont Hospital Are Left "in the Dark" After a Cyberattack', *New York Times*, 26 November 2020, https://www.nytimes.com/2020/11/26/us/hospital-cyber-attack.html.

42. 'Six Russian GRU Officers Charged in Connection with Worldwide Deployment of Destructive Malware and Other Disruptive Actions in Cyberspace', US Department of Justice, 19 October 2020, https://www.justice.gov/opa/pr/six-russian-gru-officers-charged-connection-worldwide-deployment-destructive-malware-and.

43. Dan Goodin, 'iOS zero-day let SolarWinds hackers compromise fully updated iPhones', *Ars Technica*, 14 July 2021, https://arstechnica.com/gadgets/2021/07/solarwinds-hackers-used-an-ios-0-day-to-steal-google-and-microsoft-credentials/.

44. Liam Tung, 'FBI to all router users: Reboot now to neuter Russia's VPN Filter malware', ZDNet, 29 May 2018, https://www.zdnet.com/article/fbi-to-all-router-users-reboot-now-to-neuter-russias-vpnfilter-malware/.

'New Sandworm malware Cyclops Blink replaces VPNFilter', UK National Cyber Security Centre, 23 February 2022, https://www.ncsc.gov.uk/news/joint-advisory-shows-new-sandworm-malware-cyclops-blink-replaces-vpnfilter.

people and companies that take their cyber security seriously cannot be fully protected. 'All the common Microsoft, Apple, Google software has "zero day" vulnerabilities that are being exploited and nobody even knows about it,' he says. 'And once vulnerabilities become known, they'll be used in a matter of minutes.'

Adam explains how once an individual has been tricked into clicking a link or downloading an infected attachment, the malware ransacks their computer for passwords. This means that people can be targeted not because of who they are themselves, but where they might have access to – which rewards the hackers for casting the net as widely as possible. 'It's a case of spray and pray and find out what you've got later on. And the thing is, this has turned into such a marketplace that if you get access to something, you just sell it to somebody else,' Adam adds. 'Somebody happens to work for Gatwick Airport, for example. They click a link, and the attacker has access to their work passwords. Potentially that person won't have any interest in that at all, but they just sell that access to somebody else who can actually then go and do something with it.'

### *Choose your target*

In the vast majority of cases, these attacks are simply opportunistic and will take any target that presents itself online, including using simple techniques like computerized password guessing.[45] But when they have a specific objective, other methods come into play, including human intervention to try to ensure the attack succeeds. The Organization for the Prohibition of Chemical Weapons (OPCW) is a high-value target for Russia: it plays a key role in investigations that Russia would prefer not to happen, such as into chemical warfare in Syria or Russia's use of banned chemical weapons to attempt to murder Sergei Skripal or Aleksey Navalny. So Russia sent a GRU cyber team to the OPCW's headquarters in the Netherlands to hack into its internal systems by tapping into the wi-fi network from just outside the building.[46] Attempted attacks on far less significant targets can also be pressed home by people acting in person as well as online. Shortly before publication of my last book, *Moscow Rules*, several of my colleagues at Chatham House were invited to read and review a set of sample chapters, sent to them by email. But the document was a fake, with a poisoned payload. Most people were alerted when shortly after the e-mail, they received a phone call on their private numbers from someone claiming to be my personal assistant, wanting to make sure they had downloaded

45. 'Russian GRU Conducting Global Brute Force Campaign to Compromise Enterprise and Cloud Environments', National Security Agency Cybersecurity Advisory, July 2021, https://media.defense.gov/2021/Jul/01/2002753896/-1/-1/0/CSA_GRU_GLOBAL_BRUTE_FORCE_CAMPAIGN_UOO158036-21.PDF.

46. 'How the Dutch foiled Russian "cyber-attack" on OPCW', BBC News, 4 October 2018, https://www.bbc.co.uk/news/world-europe-45747472.

the attachment. For friends and colleagues, the exotic notion that I might have a personal assistant was as much of a giveaway as the caller's thick Russian accent.

With all three of Russia's main intelligence agencies – the SVR, the GRU and the FSB – now engaged in cyber attacks, the head of Google's Threat Analysis Group, Shane Huntley, says 'It is important to note that everyone draws actor boundaries differently' – cyber-security speak indicating that not everybody agrees which attack has been carried out by which Russian intelligence agency.[47] The SolarWinds attack, found in December 2020 to have affected 18,000 companies and government agencies by hacking widely distributed network management software, was attributed to the SVR. But of the different agencies, the GRU appears to be the most prolific and destructive. A single group within the organization was identified as being behind a campaign of mayhem across multiple countries, including causing power outages in Ukraine, huge financial losses to US healthcare and pharmaceutical companies and an attack on the 2018 Winter Olympics in China.[48] For Adam Blake, though, the difference is academic. Adam follows the investigations and attributions of Russian attacks carried out by bigger cyber-security firms and governments, but his own company doesn't trace back who is attacking its customers. This is largely because the customers simply don't care. 'At the end of the day, to the customer it doesn't make any difference who it is,' Adam says. 'They're not even treating it as a crime – they're almost just taking it as this is a cost of doing business on the internet. In the past, people would say can we contact the local authorities in that country and engage them, and maybe we should contact the Metropolitan Police and their cyber division, and they'll help. But people have lost a lot of interest in doing that. Because it's so prevalent, people are way more focused on getting their business up and running than they are on who did it.'

The impact of this normalization of crime is not just on the small businesses that are taken out of business, but on everybody that pays for insurance against cyber attacks. Premiums are rising constantly, along with the number of payouts insurers are making. According to Adam, 'It's like having your car stolen. The availability of the insurance means that people are less impacted financially. But it also causes the whole thing to speed up because if people can recover, and get over it and get back to business, and the people who are doing the attacks get the money, then everybody's happy and it just starts all over again.' But just as in the example of car crime described by Nicola, the net effect is ordinary people in the UK paying for the huge amounts being stolen or extorted and ending up in Russia.

According to Raphael Satter, there are technical means by which Russian cyber criminals try to limit the impact within Russia itself. 'Some ransomware groups write it into their code that they do not deploy against machines that run Russian

---

47. Goodin, 'iOS zero-day let SolarWinds hackers compromise fully updated iPhones'.

48. Pete Williams and Kevin Collier, 'Russian hackers charged with targeting foreign elections', NBC, 19 October 2020, https://www.aol.com/2020-10-19-russian-hackers-charged-with-targeting-foreign-elections-24656402.html.

on their keyboards,' he says. 'And so that gives you some idea of what may be some informal deals being struck between the state or elements of the state and cyber criminal groups.' As cyber-security expert Brian Krebs points out, given how much malware is designed not to affect computers using Russian keyboards, a quick extra level of protection for ordinary users is to activate the Russian keyboard on their operating system even if they do not speak Russian and will never use it.

But for as long as Russia permits its intelligence services and its cyber criminals to sow mayhem across the rest of the world, ordinary people will continue to bear the cost. There have often been questions about the extent to which the Kremlin directs the operations of Russian hackers who may not be directly employed by the government. But these questions miss the point that Russia is culpable in what they do simply by allowing them to do it. Whether it is all centrally commanded or not, if President Putin wanted to stop it, it would stop.

The result of this interplay between levers of influence that Western countries tend to believe should be entirely separate means that Russia is ready to take hostile action in ways that the West appears still not to fully understand. In Chapter 6 we saw the corrosive power of Russian money being accepted in financial centres like London that are willing to turn a blind eye to whether or not it came from legitimate sources – and how the Russian state and its corporations continue to raise funding there. But even crime that has no pretension to legality can harm Western societies with few effective countermeasures. Mark Galeotti explains how harmful Russian criminal enterprise slips through the gaps in law enforcement systems, both in the UK and elsewhere. 'Police services are primarily tasked with keeping the streets safe,' he says. 'Ironically, Russia-backed organised crime is rarely a high priority, given that such groups are less likely to be operating directly at street level. Rather, they are simply facilitating the gangs whose activities most directly impact society. The temptation is for over-worked and under-resourced police officers to leave them for another day.'[49]

Effective defences against this kind of multifaceted threat requires close interaction and common understanding between different security and law enforcement agencies, such as police, state counter-intelligence services and, in particular, financial watchdogs – and all of this has to be integrated as a key element of a country's total defence (see Chapter 3). But as in so many other areas, the essential first step is a change of mindset. To properly protect countries, societies and people against the way Russia integrates business, statecraft and crime to harm them, Western governments need to step away from the idea that cyber attacks from Russia are 'just crime' or that incentivizing European officials with high-earning positions in Russian companies is 'just business'. A proper, overall, strategic understanding of the challenge means recognizing that often, when it comes to Russia, there is no such thing.

---

49. Galeotti, 'Crimintern'.

## Putting it all together

What is more, none of these threats can be dealt with in isolation. Russia mixes and matches its methods flexibly, choosing from a buffet of belligerence and deploying them in different combinations to suit specific situations. The seizure of Crimea was a demonstration of how Russia used levers of power that appeared to be non-governmental and which were only reinforced by state capabilities like the Armed Forces, to initiate civil unrest and secure physical territory. The operation combined five elements of national power: economic pressure; information operations; conventional military presence and posturing; unconventional destabilization; and political activities.[50] Crimea also exemplified how to use a fifth column made up of groups embedded in a population with the intent of helping the outside aggressor. This can be through political subversion and agitation, or in the event of open hostilities, providing the manpower already in place to hamper defensive preparations by setting up roadblocks, seizing government buildings, or destroying communications networks and other unprotected facilities. Later, the study of Russian malign influence in Sweden that caused Martin Kragh so much unwelcome attention highlighted 'the blurring of boundaries between public diplomacy and active measures; document phenomena such as forgeries, disinformation, military threats and agents of influence'.[51]

Two years after the events we looked at in Chapter 5, Martin was caught up in another multi-pronged Russian campaign, but this time targeting the UK. The Integrity Initiative was a group set up with a headquarters in London to try to bring together international expertise in countering disinformation. This, naturally enough, was unwelcome news for Russia; so, when after operating on a shoestring for a period the group was allocated a substantial grant from the UK Foreign Office to develop its activities, Russia mounted a highly successful combined operation to discredit it. Hackers targeted the organization using a method which reportedly closely resembled the one used by the GRU to target the World Anti-Doping Agency the previous year.[52] Then, posing as members of the Anonymous hacking group, they uploaded stolen documents onto a public website, which was the cue for Russia's propaganda outlets, RT and Sputnik, to go to work publicizing them.[53] Genuine Integrity Initiative paperwork was mixed in with subtly altered material and outright forgeries in order to back up the Russian allegations that the group had been set up by the British intelligence services to wage information

---

50. Nicholas Barber, 'A Warning from the Crimea: Hybrid Warfare and the Challenge for the ADF', *Australian Defence Force Journal* 198 (April 2015): 11–22.

51. Kragh and Åsberg, 'Russia's strategy for influence through public diplomacy and active measures', 773–816.

52. Lucy Fisher, 'Russia linked to hacking of anti-propaganda initiative', *The Times*, 11 December 2018, https://www.thetimes.co.uk/article/russia-linked-to-hacking-of-anti-propaganda-initiative-cd3w2ng7c.

53. Sarah Hurst, 'From the editor: Who is the real Anonymous?', *The Russia Report*, 12 March 2021, https://therussiareport.substack.com/p/the-russia-report-6a0.

warfare against Russia. The organization had grouped contacts by country into so-called 'clusters', and these lists were presented as evidence that everybody on them had been part of a British conspiracy – much to the surprise of the supposed cluster members, some of whom had never even heard of Integrity Initiative.

One of these was British journalist Deborah Haynes, now Defence Editor for Sky News. 'I had never heard of it,' she told me. 'I didn't know anything about Integrity Initiative until I suddenly found myself being accused of being part of it.' At first, Deborah was dismayed – 'I felt really sick, because it was so untrue. And I remember just thinking this is the ultimate nightmare for a journalist. For an impartial journalist to be accused of being a kind of stooge would be really damaging for your reputation,' she says. But then she realized that instead of credible allegations, the torrents of abuse she was receiving online were 'complete nonsense'. Deborah continued, 'When I realized the actual kind of people that were piling in, I was much, much more relaxed about it, and much more interested in finding out how I got caught up in this. It became more like an intellectual exercise to just try and follow the trail of it.'

Martin too was listed as a member of one of the 'clusters' and found himself once again under attack. But like Deborah, he found that once the nature of that attack and of the people backing Russia and joining in with it locally became clear, the pressure was off. 'In 2017, the campaign against me had been quite successful. In 2019, it was the opposite,' Martin says. In fact, just like Laura Walters in Chapter 5, Martin found that being caught up in a Russian campaign – and accused of being an agent of MI6 because his name appeared on a document leaked by Russia – actually helped him professionally. 'It was peculiar because I was vindicated by what happened to Integrity Initiative – it proved that I had been right all along. So a lot of people who had previously been silent or neutral or even critical of my work in this area now openly supported me because of the recognition that maybe I was, in fact, onto something.'

But while for some people being targeted in the campaign against Integrity Initiative was of little concern or even a positive experience, the effect on the staff members there and on the organization itself was far more severe. Deborah Haynes was able to shrug off the online abuse: 'It was totally libellous but I decided ignoring them was the best policy, because the sort of people who believe that stuff are a small noisy corner of the internet,' she says. But staff members suffered the results in real life, having their names and home addresses and personal information published online, and losing their reputations and their livelihoods as the project was first suspended and then effectively forced to close – representing a complete success for the attackers. And features of the operation continue to be useful to Russian propagandists today. My name was on one of the 'cluster' lists too – which Russian propaganda outlets and useful idiots have used since then to call me a 'participant in the Integrity Initiative MI6 anti-Russian project' whenever the opportunity presents.[54]

54. 'Британская разведка МІ-6 реализует "лицензию на разрушение России"' (British Intelligence MI6 puts 'licence to destroy Russia' into action), *Newsland*, 30 May 2021, https://newsland.com/user/4296825048/content/britanskaia-razvedka-mi-6-realizuet-     litsenziiu-na-razrushenie-rossii/7405048.

A major factor in this success was the UK's Labour Party getting involved, and taking the opportunity to go on the offensive against Integrity Initiative for quoting and retweeting blog posts and newspaper articles critical of Labour leader Jeremy Corbyn and his communications director Seumas Milne, pointing out how their policies and rhetoric were aiding Russia and damaging British interests. In this way the Integrity Initiative attack demonstrated a key feature of Russian hack and leak operations: to succeed in their objectives, they depend on willing enablers in the target country. The allegations against Integrity Initiative proved to be a magnet not only for propagandists overtly on Russia's payroll, but also for a wide range of conspiracy theorists and pro-Russia activists. The 'propaganda professors' we met in Chapter 6 seized on the leaked documents and studied them closely for material to use against their critics, despite there being little if anything of relevance to Syria.[55] Activists and Sputnik staffers harassing the staff of the group and its supposed 'cluster members' in person were joined by then Labour MP Chris Williamson, who went further and suggested to RT that in a giant conspiracy, most media were not covering the story not because they were practising responsible journalism by not amplifying the attacks, but because 'they themselves are implicated'.[56] (It's reasonable to assume that the operation's planners were delighted that in attacking the UK, they could be aided by a British politician eager to go on RT and help.)

The Integrity Initiative attack was a demonstration of how Russia could achieve success abroad through a combined programme of information and intimidation, mobilizing local backers. A programme built to bolster the UK and Europe's resilience to malign influence was effectively eliminated, in part through highly targeted use of that same influence. But on a personal level, that story is repeated many times over across Europe. In the same way that it is impossible to tell how many people have been murdered by Novichok because we only hear from the survivors, it is hard to assess how many individuals have shied away from working to counter Russia's hostile campaigns because they have been deterred by the campaigns of harassment and intimidation.

Once journalists, researchers, authors and others working on Russia produce work that is considered sufficiently important or influential to pose a risk of discrediting Moscow, they trigger a response in the form of harassment and intimidation or worse, sometimes just online, but often in person. The result is that writing about Russia entails either compromise or accepting a significant amount of risk. Some people, like the ones we have already met in this book, take this risk, accept the consequences and continue to work. Others, completely understandably,

55. Paul McKeigue et al., 'Briefing note on the Integrity Initiative', Working Group on Syria, Propaganda and Media, 21 December 2018, https://syriapropagandamedia.org/working-papers/briefing-note-on-the-integrity-initiative.

56. 'Media not covering Integrity Initiative scandal because they might be "involved" – Labour MP to RT', RT, 9 January 2019, https://www.rt.com/uk/448393-chris-williamson-integrity-initiative-rt/.

decide that too much is at stake and retreat. While those who put their heads back below the parapet can hardly be blamed, this chilling effect not only represents a victory for Russia and its backers' policy of harassment, but encourages them to continue because it works.

Kasimir is one of those who now does his best to stay out of public view. He experienced a combination attack in his own country like the one on Integrity Initiative described above. But the effects on him personally were far more severe than on others. 'I lost my job because of a Russian hack and leak attack,' he says. 'Russia hacked the organization I was working for, and released documents they stole in a selective and misleading and mislabelled way. And they managed to manipulate groups and individuals in this country into attacking the organization, and it had to close, so I lost my job. That's already a pretty big impact when you're a parent. But what went along with that were all the so-called journalists for Kremlin propaganda channels, harassing people and making false allegations and insinuations. You know, if you're not a hardened internet type of person, that's really distressing and unpleasant. Some people get attacked by these so-called journalists and their friends, the other friends of the Kremlin, and they fight back and they're good at it, but I'm not that kind of person. I just found it really unpleasant and distressing and just wanted to sort of hide away.'[57]

Kasimir was also concerned about potential reprisals against his extended family. 'I did worry, yes, because we have other family in a country that's been attacked by Russia in real life. And my name was out there, so I wondered if they might face consequences. And also they published my home address. And I wondered if the people in this country who they've managed to co-opt for this, the extremists and cranks who latch on to these things, might decide to take action against my home.'

This sounded familiar. 'Doxxing', or publishing a target's personal information, is a favoured technique for intimidating them or complicating their life. In 2018, during one of the periodic surges of malice towards me from a UK-based network of enablers, an 'activist' published on social media not only my address but what they thought were pictures of my house. In characteristic fashion, though, they skimped on their research and failed to realize that I had moved six months previously.

Just as with Integrity Initiative, the hack and leak attack that Kasimir was caught up in appeared coordinated between the Russian intelligence services and their local facilitators. 'We know it was coordinated because the local harassment started immediately the documents were released,' he says. This swiftly spread beyond

---

57. Another of my interviewees similarly did not want to be identified for the same reason – she said that while she knew some people were capable of coping robustly with online and real-life harassment and abuse, she preferred to avoid confrontation. 'I have no desire to attract their attention any more than I have,' she explained, and added, 'I just don't enjoy the conflict as much as you do, Keir' – which after a little thought I decided to take as a compliment.

Russia's direct enablers, like employees of the local branches of Sputnik and RT, as others piled in. This magnified the effect, Kasimir says. 'Some of the people involved who would attach themselves to the Kremlin's propaganda and harassment are obviously a bit mad. But they can also be very callous and cruel and calculating.'

Kasimir's case is a confirmation of how the effects of being personally targeted go far beyond abuse and have a serious and long-lasting impact. Since the attack he has found it hard to find work. 'Having the organization that was attacked on my resumé makes people say "oh I don't want to have anything to do with that", even if they are fully aware that it was the victim of a Russian state attack. They just don't want to be associated with that sort of noise,' he says.

## Estonia 2007 – not just cyber

The combination of online and real-world effects to deliver the result Russia wants goes back further than is often realized. Estonia is customarily described as the victim of the first generalized cyber attack on a country, in 2007. But the focus on the exciting new aspect of 'cyber war' overshadowed the way Russia was at the same time targeting Estonia with some far more old-fashioned hostile measures in a combined and coordinated operation.

The pretext for Russia mobilizing online armies of bots and volunteers to swamp key online services in the country was Estonia's plans to relocate a war memorial and associated war graves from an incongruous location in a park in south-central Tallinn to an actual military cemetery just over a mile away. The memorial, the *Bronze Soldier*, is a Soviet-era statue of a Red Army soldier in heroic pose, referred to by Russia as a monument to the liberators of Tallinn. This was a permanent affront to Estonians who associate the Soviet past not with 'liberation' by the Red Army, but with occupation, mass repressions, poverty and enslavement and death in Siberia. Russia is highly selective in its application of outrage, as relocation of war memorials is a routine practice in Russia itself.[58] Similar moves of Soviet monuments to military cemeteries in China have caused no protest from Moscow.[59] But the removal of a statue of Ivan Konev, a Soviet general who led the 1956 invasion of Hungary, from Prague in 2020 led to an outburst of Russian diplomatic fury, and a series of murky covert activities which led to media reports of plots to murder Czech mayors.[60] In the Estonian case too, Russia decided to extract maximum benefit from finding something to pick a fight over.

58. 'Памятник советских воинов в Химках. Справка' (Monument to Soviet soldiers in Khimki. Reference note), RIA Novosti, 20 April 2007, https://ria.ru/20070420/64026220.html.

59. 'Застывшие в бронзе' (Frozen in bronze), *Rossiyskaya gazeta*, 6 May 2015, https://rg.ru/2015/05/06/kitay.html.

60. Karel Janicek, 'Czech PM: Russian diplomat spread fake report of poison plot', AP, 5 June 2020, https://apnews.com/article/europe-andrej-babis-prague-czech-republic-russia-0778e80d7982a864338a422f74254c5f.

Three weeks of crude cyber attacks targeted government offices, banks, all three mobile phone service providers and the six largest news organizations. Since government and media websites were under attack, Estonia faced significant difficulty in communicating with the rest of the world about what was going on, but the effect on the general public was more inconvenience than disaster. There were no interruptions in transport or energy supply, and shops and essential services continued to work normally. Meanwhile, however, Russia also made good on overt threats that if the memorial was relocated, it would retaliate using 'diplomatic, economic and political levers'.[61]

At the time of the attacks, Heli Tiirmaa-Klaar was in charge of drawing up a National Cyber Strategy for Estonia. She recalls how the 'cyber siege' was just part of a broader attack, with 'cyber activities carefully coordinated and aligned with larger goals of a hybrid operation. This was something new for the Western strategic community at that time as they never had seen Russian information warfare doctrine implemented so visibly in a NATO member country before. It was also one of the first modern hybrid operations with many elements taking place at the same time.'

The other elements included instigating riots in Tallinn, something the capital had never seen before or since. The rioters were primarily made up of young Russian-speaking males, a group who at the time might well rely first of all on Russian news media for information on what was happening in Estonia. But in addition, ahead of the unrest, 'semi-clandestine' meetings had been observed between Russian diplomats and leading activists, and online disinformation distributed on forums and nascent social media included doctored images suggesting the statue had been cut into pieces. Rioters chanting 'Russia, Russia' took the opportunity to loot shops and kiosks. A photograph of Tallinn resident Yevgeniy Kazakov grinning as he made off with his distinctly modest haul of a bottle of Sprite, some chocolate bars and, apparently, a packet of sanitary towels became one of the defining images of the unrest.[62] The only fatality was a Russian citizen, Dmitriy Ganin, stabbed after attacking a bar not far from the statue site.[63]

The hostile measures extended beyond Tallinn. Despite Russia's duty as host nation to protect embassies on its territory, the Estonian Embassy in Moscow was blockaded for almost two weeks by a well-organized group showing evident signs of official support. The embassy was shot at and attacked with Molotov cocktails, and bodyguards for the ambassador, Marina Kaljurand (later Estonian Foreign

61. Ivo Juurvee and Mariita Mattiisen, 'The Bronze Soldier Crisis of 2007: Revisiting an Early Case of Hybrid Conflict', International Centre for Defence and Security, August 2020.

62. Mihkel Tamm, 'Mis sai pronksiöö esinäost kokk Ženjast?' (Whatever happened to chef Zhenya from the Bronze Night?), *Eesti Päevaleht*, 27 April 2020, https://epl.delfi.ee/artikkel/77857724/arhiivist-mis-sai-pronksioo-esinaost-kokk-zenjast?

63. Dario Cavegn, 'Bronze Night's only death still unsolved', ERR News, 26 April 2017, https://news.err.ee/592217/bronze-night-s-only-death-still-unsolved.

Minister), had to use pepper spray to beat back attackers at a Moscow press conference.[64] Russia also took the opportunity to interfere with goods transit through Estonia in order to promote Russian ports including the one at Ust-Luga on the coast of the Gulf of Finland, reportedly a pet project of President Putin. Arbitrary administrative rules introduced by Russia 'for security reasons' meant the transit of Russian goods via Estonia fell by around 60% amid days-long queues at the border. Instead of crossing the bridge over the Narva River, the main border crossing point between Estonia and Russia, lorries bound for Russia had to take a detour of several hundred kilometres.

A later assessment concluded that although the campaign around the Bronze Soldier was closely coordinated, it had 'no firm plan with a clearly defined desired end-state other than to cause disruption', and the opportunity to boost trade for the Ust-Luga port was taken when it presented itself in passing.[65] But the focus on the measures taken against Estonia as primarily a cyber confrontation obscures the way Russia was practising exerting pressure across a broad front, including diplomacy and causing economic damage. One element that was key to later interventions of the same kind by Russia, but absent in Estonia in 2007, was military intimidation and the overt threat of armed force. This may be a result of the particular circumstances of 2007. Estonia had only recently joined NATO, and Russia may have been hesitant about testing the organization's level of commitment to one of its newest allies. And in Russia itself, the Armed Forces were still chronically underfunded and the huge overhaul of their capability and usability we saw in Chapter 4 had yet to begin.

## *The Night Wolves*

One of the clearest examples of how Russia's tools of power make use of the overlap and interdependence between business, the state and crime is the Night Wolves Motorcycle Club – an apparent paradox of an organization which resembles an outlaw motorcycle gang but which in fact is a multinational commercial enterprise working on behalf of the Russian state to expand its influence and control around the world.[66]

Matthew Lauder is a senior Canadian defence researcher who has been tracking the Night Wolves' evolution and their growing global presence.[67] He says that when

64. Ian Traynor, 'EU protests over Russian attacks on ambassadors', *Guardian*, 2 May 2007, https://amp.theguardian.com/world/2007/may/02/eu.russia.

65. Juurvee and Mattiisen, 'The Bronze Soldier Crisis of 2007'.

66. Katarzyna Jarzynska, 'Russian Nationalists on the Kremlin's Police in Ukraine', *OSW Commentary* 156, 29 December 2014, https://www.osw.waw.pl/en/publikacje/osw-commentary/2014-12-29/russian-nationalists-kremlins-policy-ukraine.

67. Matthew A. Lauder, '"Wolves of the Russian Spring": An Examination of the Night Wolves as a Proxy for the Russian Government', *Canadian Military Journal* 18, no. 3 (Summer 2018): 5–16, http://www.journal.forces.gc.ca/vol18/no3/PDF/CMJ183Ep5.pdf.

the Night Wolves were first founded in Moscow in 1983, they were loosely styled on the Hell's Angels, but were 'less an outlaw motorcycle club as understood in Western terms, and more of a collection of anti-establishment rock music and motorcycle enthusiasts, most of whom were seeking an escape from a society defined by ideological conformity'. That didn't stop them taking advantage of opportunities to dabble in crime, including the ubiquitous protection rackets that sprang up alongside free enterprise during the collapse of communism. But during the 1990s, the group began to transform from a counter-culture movement into a patriotic and pro-state organization. Matthew thinks this may have been under the influence of the Russian security services, which first infiltrated the group to monitor and manage its leanings towards political dissent, but eventually took over running its leadership.[68] At this point a criminal organization had already begun serving the state; but by the end of the decade, like so many others, it had also transformed into a legitimate business, running a range of enterprises including a music venue, tattoo shop, clothing line, custom motorcycle shop and numerous 'biker culture' events like tattoo conventions and motorcycle rallies.

The process of integration continued over the next decade, Matthew says, with personal relationships forming with both the Kremlin and the Russian Orthodox Church. The Night Wolves' services were recognized with land concessions, financial grants and government contracts – but less visibly, Matthew says, this recognition and encouragement implies 'significant operational latitude and protection, particularly from police investigation and criminal prosecution'.

The close nature of the relationship, particularly with Russia's military special forces and intelligence services, was highlighted during the Russian invasion of Ukraine in 2014.[69] The Night Wolves prepared the ground for the seizure of Crimea by 'collecting intelligence, distributing pro-Russian propaganda, organizing protests and recruiting members for self-defence units, and operating vehicle checkpoints and roadblocks', Matthew says. 'As the invasion progressed, the Night Wolves became more involved in combat operations, including the execution of joint raids with Spetsnaz on the Ukrainian naval headquarters in Sevastopol and natural gas facilities. In eastern Ukraine, the Night Wolves played a more active role in fighting Ukrainian defence forces.' Here too the Russian state found links to organized crime useful: after providing Russian travel documents and identification to a number of high-ranking Ukrainian defectors, Matthew noted, the group 'utilized its underworld connections and access to various clandestine networks to smuggle them to Russia during the height of the conflict'. At least eleven members of the group received the Russian campaign medal 'For the Return of Crimea' for

---

68. Matthew's employers have asked me to point out that his comments repeated here are his own views and 'do not necessarily reflect the views or policies of the Government of Canada'.

69. Damon Tabor, 'Putin's Angels: The Ride of Russia's Night Wolves', *Rolling Stone*, 26 November 2015, https://au.rollingstone.com/culture/culture-news/putins-angels-the-ride-of-russias-night-wolves-898/.

their services there, and an unknown number have since then been killed in action in eastern Ukraine.

By 2021, the group had more than fifty branches, or 'chapters', across multiple continents. Unlike the normal picture of a genuine motorcycle gang, each chapter operates as a franchise, owned by partners and operating as a commercial business. But Matthew says that although this network has a presence around the world, including operations in Australia and Asia, the primary security threat posed by the Night Wolves is to Europe, particularly the Balkans, Baltics and Scandinavia, as well as the Caucasus. This is due not only to the availability of criminal networks but also to the size of the Russian populations in these regions, 'which is both the target of its activities on behalf of the Russia government but also provides operational cover'. Outside Russia, the Night Wolves 'have conducted a range of specialized and highly sensitive activities, including conducting influence campaigns, collecting intelligence and executing combat operations, often in collaboration with Spetsnaz or intelligence services'. As such, Matthew goes on, they are a prime example of 'a broader trend by the Russian government towards outsourcing to seemingly arms-length entities the functions traditionally conducted by state security and defence agencies'.

Those functions are by their nature a security threat to the countries where the group operates. Kira Harris, a lecturer at the Australian Graduate School of Policing and Security Studies, has looked closely at the Night Wolves and their Australian branch in particular. Her concern is the implications for host countries of 'supporters who are combat ready and exposed to Russian information campaigns'. 'Russia's use of combat-ready supporters, including some Night Wolves' members and associated right-wing nationalist groups, demonstrates the Russian government's ability to create fifth columns in foreign countries. Some of these actors who developed combat experience in Ukraine likely possess the capability, resources and networks to conduct politically motivated violence,' she explains.[70] In effect, the group is 'a proxy of the Russian state that unites combat-ready diasporas', Kira says. The 'combat-ready' part is significant. Some of the group's commercial offshoots tap into specialist skills, like 'Wolf Security Structures Holding', which provides 'martial arts and tactical military courses to foreign military, law enforcement, and Russian-speaking compatriots from European and Asian States'. As a result, two individuals associated with 'Wolf' have fallen under US sanctions – company president Gennadii Nikulov and combat trainer leader Denis Ryauzov. Nikulov is a senior figure in a number of Cossack and special forces associations and, more significantly, was awarded a Russian Ministry of Defence medal for taking part in the operation to seize Crimea. 'Wolf' itself was sanctioned in 2017 after being identified as providing tactical military training to forces in eastern Ukraine.[71]

70. Kira Harris, 'Russia's Night Wolves in Australia', forthcoming article in the *Journal of Policing, Intelligence and Counter Terrorism*.

71. Robbie Gramer, 'Trump's Renewed Russia Sanctions Look a lot Like Obama's', *Foreign Policy*, 20 June 2017, http://foreignpolicy.com/2017/06/20/trumps-renewed-russia-sanctions-look-a-lot-like-obamas-treasury-department-finance/.

But the Night Wolves also serve a propaganda and PR function, as an overt and visible reminder of the way Russia can present challenges to democracies. Their events outside Russia are highly visible and often seek or gain significant media attention. Matthew warns that this can serve as a distraction by being the most visible part of a much larger effort by the Russian government to generate disruptive effects in the countries it targets, politically, socially, economically or even militarily. In this respect they highlight another consistent principle Russia uses to get the results it wants: drawing all eyes away from where the real action is taking place. When the media is full of a high-profile event run by the Night Wolves, it is always a good idea to look closely at what else is going on in the shadows.

## What to do about it

Resistance to this kind of combined approach to doing damage to target countries requires a comprehensive, and coordinated, strategy for resilience – and one that recognizes how much broader and deeper the threat is than if it were only delivered through arms of the Russian state. The buzz-phrase in most common use is dealing with 'whole of government' threats, meaning it is not just a country's defence ministry that has to be involved in fending them off, but other bodies like law enforcement agencies, and organizations overseeing business and the economy. But the integrated nature of how Russia reaches out to attack its enemies means an even wider focus is needed. Since so much of the threat is not even to governments, what is needed is not a whole of government response, but a whole of society response – since it is civil society and the people within it that are also under attack.

In 2021, the UK appeared only to be starting to think about how to make this work, with a public consultation launched on designing a 'National Resilience Strategy', in part to 'decide how we will shape and agree on the role of many businesses which are vital in delivering essential services to the public'.[72] The front-line states, meanwhile, did not need a pandemic or the assault on Ukraine to help them realize their vulnerability. 'Total defence', protecting the country against all conceivable threats and not only military attack, goes under various names and is at varying stages of development or reconstitution in the many European countries that feel they are at risk from Russia.[73] Possibly the best-developed approach to comprehensive security is seen in Finland – in part because while other countries

---

72. 'Paymaster General Speech on National Resilience Strategy delivered on 13 July 2021', UK government website, 15 July 2021, https://www.gov.uk/government/speeches/paymaster-general-speech-on-national-resilience-strategy-delivered-on-13-july-2021.

73. 'Sweden's security: The long way towards total defence', Justyna Gotkowska, OSW, 27 January 2021, https://www.osw.waw.pl/en/publikacje/point-view/2021-01-27/swedens-security.

relaxed after the Cold War and dismantled or neglected their civil defences, the Finnish system and its underlying rationale was retained intact.

That rationale focuses on national resilience and protecting the integrity of 'functions vital to society' when they are under threat. This means paying attention not just to defence capability and internal security, but also aspects that are more abstract but still critical when considering how Russia carries out its attacks – like 'psychological resilience ... of individuals, communities, society and the nation'.[74] It also means ensuring that when a crisis does arrive, people know what to do. Countries like Latvia and Sweden publish regularly updated guides for what citizens should do in a national emergency or when the country is under attack. Mindful of probable Russian disinformation operations, they tell people unequivocally and in bold red type that there will be no surrender and that any instructions to cease resistance should be disregarded as fakes.[75] The importance of knowing what to do in advance is even more important for people in positions of leadership – so Finland runs regular 'National Defence Courses', bringing together not just government officials and civil servants but people in key roles from all different sectors of society.[76]

But former Finnish military intelligence chief Pekka Toveri thinks proactive measures are vital to blunt Russian capabilities even before national resilience is tested. 'Prevent the clandestine operations of the Russian intelligence and security services in the West by hunting down their operatives aggressively and either disrupting their intel, assassination and recruiting operations or sending them home,' he says. 'Close cooperation between Western border, police and intelligence services is needed to share information on the movements of these operators.' The message of better situational awareness to track threats before they become active is echoed widely. David Kilcullen explains that this is because Russia's planning is in large part driven by the likely or actual responses of the target once an operation is launched. 'They integrate all different elements of physical, cyber, economic, info, political warfare and kinetic manoeuvre along a timeline that is driven by our decision-making processes,' he says. And a key part of that is remaining undetected for as long as possible, and then sowing confusion and uncertainty once discovered. 'Once you cross that detection threshold, the reaction clock starts. It's like the bad guys hitting a bank vault – we've got to be out of here before the cops arrive,' David explains. 'You get as much done as rapidly as possible, then you start the rhetoric about de-escalating. You run your information operations and political warfare to try to extend the enemy's decision time, to delay or prevent a decision on countermeasures.'[77]

Operations launched by Russia can be as small and straightforward as the case of Integrity Initiative – attacking a single limited target primarily through information means, augmented by mobilizing Sputnik staffers and a range of useful idiots in the target country. Or they can be as large and complex as the seizure of Crimea, combining military, intelligence, information and disinformation activities and the Night Wolves in place on the ground in a swift and ruthless move to change national borders. What the whole range has in common is the way it can leave the West confused and uncertain. But proper recognition of the way Russia can use business interests, organized crime, local facilitators and more to achieve what it wants – and being prepared for when this happens – can be an important part of making sure that Western countries are ready for the next challenge from Moscow.

77. 'Russian Spetsnaz in the Grey Zone', Russia Strategic Initiative, 19 August 2021, https://community.apan.org/wg/rsi/project-connect/w/events/29786/rsi-connect-russian-spetsnaz-in-the-grey-zone/.

# Chapter 8

## WHAT COMES NEXT

The invasion of Ukraine marks a turning point in the West and the world's understanding of the threat from Russia. But it will not in itself mark a change in the fundamental nature of the threat. Even in the unlikely circumstances that Russia should suffer a catastrophic defeat in Ukraine, and even if that were then to precipitate a change of leadership in Moscow, the experience of 1991 and what came after shows that it takes far more than a change of ownership in the Kremlin to alter Russia's fundamental attitudes of what it is entitled to, and how it goes about getting it.

Both the catalogue of Russian abuses, and the failures to date of Western governments to deal with them appropriately and prevent them recurring, seem over the years to form patterns that are both repetitive and dismal. In fact, my last book included a more upbeat chapter at the end about how things might possibly, eventually, get better. But that was only included because after reading the rest of it, the publishers insisted that there had to be something at least a little bit optimistic to relieve the persistent gloom. The trouble is, the people who are most accurate at predicting Russia's futures over the long term are the pessimists. And sure enough, many of the predictions in *Moscow Rules* of what would happen in Russia next proved accurate very shortly afterwards – with the main exception being the optimistic part.

This is because Russia is, despite what anybody may claim, predictable. And so, too, are the people who argue Russia's case in the West. And that means that whatever the outcome of the war in Ukraine – which at the time of writing hangs in the balance – the repetitive patterns of the past may well still provide a guide to how Russia, and the West, will respond as the initial shock of the war passes.

For the foreseeable future and beyond, all of the threats emanating from Russia that have been described in this book will continue to affect both those countries and people that stand up in opposition to Russia, and those that would rather stay out of the fight.

Moscow's immediate neighbours may not suffer invasion, especially while Russia remains fully occupied in Ukraine. But irresponsible brinkmanship with aircraft, abuse of electronic warfare capabilities, economic warfare like trade embargoes and energy cut-offs, and soft challenges like migrant dumping and more will continue to form part of the inescapable background noise of living next door to Russia. Countries further away will continue to face attempts at state capture, subversion, destabilization, attacks on democratic processes and state institutions, military intimidation, cyber attacks and – unless and until the UK in particular grips the problem – dirty money and its pernicious effect on societies and governance.

It's important to remember that as well as meeting specific Russian operational objectives, these sub-threshold attacks are also sometimes driven by Russia's craving for recognition of its status and self-perceived importance. The simple fact is that the West matters very much more to Russia than vice versa. This can be demonstrated by a simple test: if you remove crises caused by Russia, what need is there for the West to engage with Moscow? Unfortunately, as we've seen in multiple examples through this book, this also creates an incentive for Moscow to create more crises, in order that the West will come and talk to it. The satisfactory effect for Moscow of the invasion of Ukraine making it the centre of the world's attention may not last indefinitely.

Russia's power will in the long term decline, and that decline may quite possibly be hastened by stalemate or even defeat in Ukraine. But Moscow will retain the capabilities to do harm to other countries for as long as possible. Failure in Ukraine could start the process of Russia relaxing into its new reality as one country among many rather than as a superpower, and adapting as other former empires have done in the past. But that process will be a long and hard one with reverses and setbacks, and in the meantime Russia will continue to fret and posture and lash out. In fact, the Kremlin may well accelerate still further as it sees the light on its global reach and power shift to amber.

Russia's network of propagandists will continue to try to persuade us that actions by the US and its allies in NATO are dangerous, and an inadvertent clash could spiral into all-out war. And people in the West will continue to fall for this, overlooking the fact that this can't be a genuine fear for Russia, because all the actions and provocative behaviour that could trigger an event like that are actually driven by Moscow. The Kremlin and its friends and apologists abroad will continue to point to Western actions that they say 'provoke' Russia. But what all the things they point to have in common is that they are either a response to a hostile act by Russia, or an attempt to prevent a future action that harms Europe or its friends and allies. The pretence that there is a gratuitous, spontaneous campaign to harm a peace-loving Russia that previously was simply minding its own business lives on even after Ukraine, despite being a fantasy that doesn't stand up to a moment's examination. Russia will inevitably also continue to lobby against sanctions and seek to re-enlist interest groups in the West on its side, especially once the initial flood of headlines about atrocities in Ukraine passes. Western businesses will be encouraged to think that they are missing out on business opportunities because of the intransigence of their governments.[1] And many of the enablers described in Chapter 6 will find themselves unable to resist the lure of Russian money once again.

1. Ian Bond and Zach Meyers, 'Russia–Ukraine: The West Needs a Sanctions Strategy', Centre for European Reform, 10 March 2022, https://www.cer.eu/publications/archive/policy-brief/2022/russia-ukraine-west-needs-sanctions-strategy.

But at the same time, we will also soon once again hear arguments that for the West as a whole, Russia isn't really as big a problem as it's painted. The reasons put forward are repeated over and over despite being of little relevance to Russia's current behaviour. 'Russia is a declining power' – which may be true in the long run, but is no help for dealing with Russia using what capabilities it still has in the short and medium term. 'It has a GDP the size of Italy' – but confrontations with Russia aren't about comparing how big each other's economy is; they use far sharper tools. 'China is a bigger problem' – but nobody has the luxury of being able to deal with only one problem at a time. 'The West is just as bad' – true or not, it's not a reason not to defend it when it is under attack.

Arguments will carry on too about the nature of Russia itself – whether it is driven by innate aggression or merely responding to outside events, whether the problem is Putin personally or the Russian state mindset he emerged from, whether Russia is a mafia state or something more complex. But while the answers may tell us *why* Russia behaves as it does, they make no difference to *how* it behaves. Regardless of the roots of Russia's current attitude to the West, how it goes about acting on that attitude remains the same. And the realization will continue to dawn only slowly in the West that there is no reason to assume that what comes after Putin will be an improvement – because Putin and his accomplices are a product of Russia rather than the other way round.

## Danger signs

But there's also a substantial danger that what comes after the war on Ukraine could be even worse.

Ukraine's existential challenge is that the possibility of it becoming a fully independent, fully functional democracy enjoying political, economic, cultural, and social integration with the West was, in President Putin's mind, catastrophic for Russia. But Russia's inability to cope with democracy should never be used as an excuse to deny it to others. In launching the invasion in February 2022, Putin wanted to unite Ukraine with Russia. Instead, he united Ukraine and the West against Russia. His actions created a firm Western coalition against him at a time when most of the West would have preferred instead to ignore Russia's ongoing covert campaigns and just continue to do business.[2] In fact, in an effort to bend reality to his fantasy by conquering Ukraine, Putin brought into existence the united and hostile West he most feared.

But past experience suggests that that unity is fragile. A protracted stalemate in the war brings the risk of compassion fatigue and Ukraine-fatigue in the West. There are two possible harmful outcomes to this. Europe could return to failing to address the core issue of Russia as a rogue state, and to the complacent, stubborn

---

2. 'Ukraine–Russia war: The era of complacency is over', says Liz Truss', BBC, 10 March 2022, https://www.bbc.co.uk/news/uk-politics-60685613.

refusal of the collective West to accept that Russia was at war with it.[3] Routine statements of international condemnation of the latest Russian outrage could once again follow one after the other, as wearily familiar in the West as they are meaningless to Moscow. So too could the repeated surprise each time Moscow behaves according to its own rules rather than those of the West.

This would lead directly to the revival of another factor augmenting the danger of current Russian behaviour: overconfidence by Putin and his entourage. Putin has had such a long series of wins that he may well have started to believe his own propaganda – that Russia could push forward unopposed, and that the weak, decadent West is in rapid and inevitable decline. It is that mental framework that led Russia to underestimate the potential for Ukrainian resistance during the invasion and in the event of possible occupation. But it is precisely the way Russia continues to get it wrong that puts at risk the fragile freedoms that others of Russia's former imperial possessions regained just thirty years ago.

Already in 2015 political analysts were writing of Russia that 'the current trajectory appears to be worse than the worst-case scenario'.[4] But even besides open warfare, there are plenty more ways left that things could get worse still. For all the concern over Russia's increasing repression of its subjects and the rolling back of basic rights, there's still a long way to go before Russia finally replicates the all-pervasive Soviet system of control and punishment. And externally, there are still plenty more weapons in Moscow's arsenal for harming the West beyond Ukraine. For instance, one element that is less prominent in today's Russian practice so far is direct support for anti-Western domestic terrorist groups. During the Cold War the USSR and other members of the communist bloc were the source of 'weapons, training and sanctuary for a worldwide terror network aimed at the destabilization of Western democratic society'.[5] This included, for instance, supplying guns to the Irish Republican Army (IRA).[6] The closest today's Russia is thought to have come so far – at least according to public reporting – is the GRU funding the Taliban to target US servicemen in Afghanistan.[7] But given overall

3. Keir Giles and Toomas Hendrik Ilves, 'Europe must admit Russia is waging war', Chatham House, 23 April 2022, https://www.chathamhouse.org/2021/04/europe-must-admit-russia-waging-war.

4. Maria Lipman and Nikolay Petrov (eds), *The State of Russia: What Comes Next?* (London: Palgrave Pivot 2015), Introduction.

5. Claire Sterling, 'Terrorism: Tracing the International Network', *New York Times*, 1 March 1981, https://www.nytimes.com/1981/03/01/magazine/terrorism-tracing-the-international-network.html.

6. Kieran Fagan, 'Official (and Provisional) secrets', *Irish Times*, 23 October 1999, https://www.irishtimes.com/news/official-and-provisional-secrets-1.242356.

7. John Haltiwanger, 'The shadowy Russian intel unit that allegedly paid Afghan militants to kill US troops is the same one running assassinations in Europe', *Business Insider*, 29 June 2020, https://www.businessinsider.com/unit-29155-russian-intel-branch-allegedly-behind-bounties-us-troops-2020-6.

trends, it should not come as any surprise if Russia in due course corrects this oversight and once again not only sends its own military intelligence officers abroad to carry out terrorist attacks, but starts backing self-starting terror groups of convenience in Europe and beyond.

But the greatest danger of all lies in failing to defeat Russia in Ukraine itself. Unlike other European countries, Russia is not content with the notion that the boundaries to its influence and power should coincide with its national territory – and so has decided unilaterally to revise them at the expense of its neighbour. Containing Russia within its own borders in the future is a challenging, and potentially highly costly, but nonetheless essential contribution to the future security not only of Europe but of any other theatre where a truculent revisionist power may feel emboldened to challenge the West.

As we saw in Chapter 1, President Putin's clearly stated aim is to reconstitute the Russian Empire. If Putin is to be believed – and so far he has acted on his convictions – Russia will not stop its drive to reconquer its former possessions at Ukraine. Putin's lengthy speech in February 2022 justifying the attempted dismemberment of Ukraine said much about Putin himself but also contained chilling warnings for the rest of Europe. And European states must heed those warnings if they do not wish to be the next victims of Russia's imperial ambition. Putin reached back much further than the Cold War to find his grievances. He stated clearly that the processes that led to Russia losing territory a full century ago must be reversed. His warped description of the way countries achieved their independence from Russian rule at the end of the First World War was aimed at Ukraine, but there is little in it that could not also be applied to Poland, Finland and the Baltic states.[8] Russia's 'draft treaties' from December 2021 also demanded rolling back Western protection not only from the territories of the former Soviet Union but all the countries of the former Warsaw Pact too.

All Russia's previous successes in resisting and reversing the rolling back of its power have only reinforced its conviction of entitlement. This is because not only has Russia's claim to greater rights than other states not yet been directly challenged in public, but also Russia has not yet suffered a direct and unambiguous setback demonstrating that it cannot assert those rights through military power. Russia therefore has no reason, until unarguably defeated, to question the beliefs that underpin its current demands.

If some – or any – of these demands are met in Ukraine, it will confirm for Moscow once again that actual or threatened military force is the best means of achieving international political goals. So there will be every reason for Russia to adopt the same approach the next time it wants to present demands to the US or Europe. Russia may need a pause to regroup, rebuild its Armed Forces and reorient its economy under the impact of new sanctions. But after the pause, the process

---

8. 'Address by the President of the Russian Federation', Russian presidential website, 21 February 2022, http://en.kremlin.ru/events/president/news/67828.

will continue unless and until the US, with support from its European allies, decides it must stop – and is willing to meet the costs of stopping it. There can be no future security for Europe without a clear demonstration to Russia that the age of empires there is over, and it does not have the rights it claims over the futures of independent and sovereign states. At that point it will no longer be the time to discuss how to deter Russia, since it has long been clear that deterrence has failed. It is essential to be ready, in advance, to move from attempting to deter Russia to succeeding in defeating it.

## *What can be done?*

Meanwhile, the West's awakening to the nature of the Russian threat has, as yet, had little impact in addressing the wide range of means Russia has to do damage beyond its borders, as outlined in this book.

Getting a true picture of how to deal with Russia means stepping back from individual cases of hostile behaviour – even ones of the enormity of the assault on Ukraine – and looking instead at the big picture and long-term trends. There's a choice between constantly reacting to Russian damage and probing, and looking for a long-term solution to it at an international level. But the first step towards this is actually recognizing the broader and deeper nature of the challenge than its immediate focus in Ukraine. The problem for Russia is not just Ukraine, and not even necessarily anything the West is doing. Instead, the West presents a challenge to Russia simply by existing as free and democratic societies, largely governed through rule of law. Russia cannot change at home, so seeks to change the world around it – sowing misery in the attempt.

The permanent search for anything the West can do to foster a more benign Russia, one that doesn't terrorize its subjects or threaten its neighbours, will continue – and continue to be frustrated. Moscow's inability to enter a normal, cooperative relationship over not just decades but centuries is so startlingly consistent that it seems perfectly reasonable that it will be extended into the future too. That means Russia will continue to be a problem for the West – and as in so many examples throughout this book, nobody is too insignificant to be affected. But it also means that the West has some clear choices available for how to tackle that problem and reduce its impact on ordinary people living there. Tom Tugendhat, the former soldier who is now chair of the UK Parliament's Foreign Affairs Committee, says the West faces a choice. 'We have the financial, commercial, intellectual, military, developmental and cultural ability to defend our interests,' he writes. 'We know that when free people choose, they choose freedom ... So far we're choosing to lose.'[9]

---

9. Twitter thread by @TomTugendhat, 12 August 2021, https://twitter.com/TomTugendhat/status/1425919651469565955.

While the nature of Russia's war on Ukraine is obvious enough, Western publics still lack a clear picture of all of the other ways in which Russia targets and harms other countries and their citizens. Western publics have to be better informed of the extent of hostile Russian activity, in order that they can understand the need for defensive measures and support them at election time. Talking about security problems in Russia's neighbourhood mustn't continue to gloss over the fact that they emanate almost exclusively from Russia – but also Russia's malignant reach and influence further abroad has to be coldly and soberly discussed, without playing Moscow's game of making its intelligence services look omnipotent. And for Russia itself, clear statements of Western determination to respond are essential – that even after unprecedented levels of sanctions, its target countries still have both the capability to inflict damage in return and the will to use it if Russia does not rein in its hostility.[10]

Honesty is also needed in accepting reality. The first step towards that is recognizing that each new shock from Russia, including open warfare against Ukraine, isn't a 'current crisis' but a symptom of an enduring reality. Russia will continue to see itself as being in conflict with a far wider range of countries than Ukraine and will continue to prioritize ways and means of doing its adversaries harm.

Paradoxically, the acceptance of reality has to include acceptance that the Kremlin exists in a different version of it. Robert Pszczel says that 'If you actually respect [Russia], then you have to take them as they are' – rather than patronizing the Kremlin by pretending they do not mean what they say or do and it is all a huge misunderstanding. And that's crucial for understanding what Russia might do next, and how to prevent it. Any predictions of how Russia might react to any given situation have to be grounded in the Kremlin's view of the world, rather than what 'makes sense' in the West. This includes the basic assumption of hostility and a state of conflict, where aggression holds little to lose and much to gain. It also turns on a very different set of measures for what constitutes success or failure – repeatedly we have seen how Russia shrugs off what for the West would be major setbacks, because they're not relevant to the end goal Moscow had in mind.

Once Western countries have individually or together fully accepted that the nature of their relationship with Russia will not change, they face the question of what to do about it. But whatever they do, it is vitally important that they do it together. No individual European country can withstand Russia alone – the continent's power lies in unity. Joint responses have exponentially higher value, both in effect delivered and in demonstrating that individual partners cannot be picked off one by one. NATO and the Joint Expeditionary Force (JEF) are in place to ensure countries can respond together to military threats from Russia. But

10. Dr James Lewis, Senior Vice President and Director, Strategic Technologies Program, CSIS, at Oral evidence: The Integrated Review – Threats, Capabilities and Concepts, HC 834, House of Commons Defence Committee, 10 November 2020, https://committees.parliament.uk/oralevidence/1174/pdf/.

coalitions of the willing, small or large, should form to tackle both military and non-military challenges, through increased resilience and a demonstrated willingness to take countermeasures.

The argument persists that NATO is to blame for conflict with Moscow, for accepting new member states close to Russia. It's an argument that will grind on, regardless of how distant it may be from the truth; after all, Russia never needed an excuse of NATO being anywhere nearby to invade its neighbours beforehand, and as we saw in Chapter 4, membership in NATO has actually proven to be the strongest stabilizing factor of all in the Baltic Sea region. But the argument over cause has been allowed to obscure the more important issue of effect. The alternative to NATO enlargement either implicitly or explicitly endorsed by its critics is to suggest that Russia is entitled to a sphere of influence, and that countries within it making their own free and democratic choices would pose a threat to Moscow which would entitle it to invade those countries to remove it. To accept this is to return Europe to a previous century and to wind back the clock in precisely the way President Putin is demanding. If, on the other hand, we accept that sovereign nations like Finland, Poland, Ukraine and more have the right to govern themselves and determine their own future, then there is no choice but to confront Russia over its demands that it has privileges over them and that their sovereignty should be restricted. It's vital to remember that for the front-line states, how larger powers of the West decide to deal with Russia is a matter of national survival. Linas from Lithuania is concerned that the behaviour of countries like France and Germany, repeatedly willing to pander to Russia regardless of Moscow's behaviour, will soon revert to type regardless of the invasion of Ukraine.

The West should also have more confidence in itself and its power of attraction. Sami Siva concluded from his reporting from Russia's borderlands that 'the EU and US should have clear and coordinated plans to implement cultural and economic projects in the near abroad community in order to remind people how their lives are better in the West compared to Russia'. And that confidence should extend to belief in what Western liberal democracies stand for. If Western nations abandon their morals and values in order to resist Russia, there is little point in resisting further because Russia has won.

This does of course mean that the range of available responses to Russia will be limited and constrained by comparison to the Kremlin's anything-goes approach. The West has limited tools and levers that can directly cause damage to Russia and still be compatible with Western values. But this makes defensive measures even more important. For as long as Russia has no incentive to change its attitude and behaviour towards the West, the West should work hard on mitigating as far as possible the damage that Russia will inevitably cause. Because of Russia's own attitude to military force, this still includes a need for Western countries to maintain capable and substantial armed forces, however unfashionable and expensive they may be. In particular, an armed force that is not capable of engaging in high-attrition warfare – like the UK's – has only limited deterrent value against Russia.

Russia exploits the opportunities it is provided with, whether weaponizing corruption, infiltrating insecure cyber systems or amplifying and radicalizing the voices of disaffected groups in society. It follows that a large part of the answer is reducing those opportunities to a minimum, in order to prevent Russia pocketing easy wins. For resisting Russia's probing and prodding for weaknesses, the remedies remain the same, including finding and patching the target country's vulnerabilities in law enforcement, counter-intelligence, border and financial controls, and situational awareness overall. This isn't a one-time remedy, but instead needs to be a constant process; one of my interviewees working for a government agency called this a 'race of imagination' where as the West detects and tackles one problem, the Kremlin and its servants are busily thinking up more. But in particular it means doing the opposite of the glaring failures of government identified in the UK Parliament's 'Russia Report' – a lack of relevant legislation meaning agents of influence were operating freely because they were entirely legal, and a lack even of interest in what Russia was doing and how.

Meanwhile the West should strengthen its resolve in responding to hostile Russian actions, at the least by building on the successful policy of decisively and systematically exposing, attributing and discrediting them. Consistent determined action is essential in order to raise the cost of hostile action and diminish Moscow's inclination and incentive to act nefariously. The risk that the Kremlin might escalate its hostile activities against the West still further should be weighed against abundant evidence that firm responses consistently lead to Russia cutting its losses and withdrawing, rather than persisting with a strategy whose costs outweigh its benefits. By contrast, Russia has shown consistently that failure to react to its crimes and aggression, and exercise meaningful deterrence, leads only to greater excesses in attacks on Western countries, societies and citizens.

Confidence in the robust commitments of alliances like NATO are vital for dissuading Russia from acts of harm, from those carried out against individual citizens up to major encroachments on the sovereignty and rights of whole nations. Where Russia does hold back – for instance, avoiding open military clashes with members of alliances – it is because it knows it cannot withstand the combined strength of NATO or the EU and the damage that open conflict would cause. This means, in particular, going beyond responses that consist of words alone, which Russia has shown itself consistently content to ignore – as with former British prime minister Theresa May telling Russia that 'we know what you are doing' in late 2017, but not stating any consequences for doing it.[11] The lack of firm and meaningful consequences for Russia's actions even when they are known in advance in effect means giving Russia permission to carry on – as in the period before the invasion of Ukraine, when intelligence disclosures by the US and UK of Russian plans not only showed that Western powers were

11. 'Theresa May accuses Russia of interfering in elections and fake news', *Guardian*, 14 November 2017, https://www.theguardian.com/politics/2017/nov/13/theresa-may-accuses-russia-of-interfering-in-elections-and-fake-news.

fully aware of Russian intentions, but also confirmed for the Kremlin that they were not planning on doing anything about them.

One tool that's underused by the West in responding to Russia is unpredictability. So many Russian plans, and the calculation for whether Moscow can get away with implementing them, depend on Russia's opponents behaving in a predictable way – and as such, they are ideally suited to taking on the EU and NATO. David Kilcullen thinks that a Russian weakness is 'relying on predictable opponent decision-making behaviour, and structuring your entire campaign around an understanding of how your opponent works'. Sulev Suvari agrees, and says that Russian planners 'also take for granted that we follow our plans, and it becomes very frustrating to them when we don't follow our strategy, or our documents, or our plans as they have read them. When we're not so predictable in our movements, it does confuse them.' The multinational diplomatic response over the Salisbury attack startled Russia, and led to major setbacks, because it was a clear departure from previous behaviour. The principle can be extended into far more robust counters to Russian actions than diplomatic manoeuvring and expulsions. At the very least, less predictable responses to the things Russia does will introduce far more uncertainty into Russian planning for hostile action, and so make it less likely that those plans will be approved and carried out.

But overall, more thought needs to be given to what motivates Russia to carry out these attacks against countries and people – because that will provide the key to removing that motivation and making Russia less likely to attack. There's no point in looking for a change in Russia's behaviour when that behaviour results not from short-term challenges but from the long-term and deeply embedded convictions within the Kremlin about the nature of the world and Russia's place in it that we saw in Chapter 1. In particular, Westerners like to think that the age of empires in Europe is over. If they sincerely believe that, then they need to convince Russia of it too. And that means that Russia needs to be confronted with the limitations of its own power – and those limitations need to be demonstrated, if necessary, by responding to Russia in the language that it itself prefers to use.

What stops Russia, and has done reliably over centuries, is credible and visible potential to do damage in return being present and ready in advance. Dialogue and diplomacy, the first resorts of Western statecraft, have been shown to have no impact on a country that is operating on a different plane of reality and in a different century. Russia's confidence to act against Ukraine stems from the failure of deterrence by the West overall. It is vital that the West relearns what it takes to put up a stop sign for Moscow.

## Coda

As this book goes to press, the future of Ukraine hangs in the balance. But so too does the future of Russia. Success or failure in Ukraine will not only determine how soon Russia will make its next push to regain territories lost decades ago. The dissent at all levels of society unleashed by the invasion, and by the subsequent

Western sanctions and resulting economic upheaval, represents the closest Russia has come yet to meaningful opposition to Putin's rule. If Russia were to fail badly, and suffer an unambiguous setback, that could be exactly the shock the country needs to start the long, hard process of transitioning from a frustrated former imperial power to a normal country that can coexist with Europe. But it could also potentially be the trigger for political change.

Putin's Russia has built an apparently strong and tight system of domestic control. Change from the bottom up would require a spectacular failure of Russia's internal security apparatus – but the opening days of the military campaign in Ukraine showed that spectacular failures are possible. More likely would be opposition to Putin emerging from within the power structures themselves. If the war on Ukraine grinds on and the damage it causes to Russia grows deeper, and there is no change in the self-destructive policy enacted from the top, there will a limit to how much of Russia's self-inflicted injuries can be blamed on the scheming of the West – and senior appointees may eventually be faced with the choice of loyalty to Putin or to Russia itself.

Past experience suggests the fallout of uncontrolled regime change in Moscow would be felt far beyond Russia itself – and once again, it's a dangerous delusion to think that Russia's current behaviour is so driven by one man that once Putin is out of the picture, things will automatically improve. The youngest generations in Russia have known nothing but Putin. But their successors will have known nothing but a highly aggressive, militarist, xenophobic nationalist culture, where fundamental personal freedoms are an irrelevance and any misfortune, however irrationally, is blamed on the campaigns and encroachments of the hostile West. In this view, the safety and security of Russia – often measured by criteria that make little or no sense in the twenty-first century – outweigh a flourishing economy or a rising standard of living for ordinary people. And all the while, the grudge against the West for the outcome of the Cold War is nurtured and fanned. Once again the disturbing parallels are not only with the Soviet Union, but with Nazi Germany before the Second World War.

That highlights the fragility of freedom in Russia's front-line states, especially those that rely on foreign support to bolster their national militaries. The danger of a return to appeasement of Russia is still present and could even be augmented by the suffering of Ukraine. Alex Grigorievs, a member of the Latvian parliament that took his country into independence at the end of the Cold War, is alarmed for the future today. 'I don't want to be living under the Soviet Russian hegemony again,' he says. 'I've lived a good part of my life under that. But I think that the countries on the perimeter of Russia are in danger. If they are vulnerable, they will be attacked one way or the other. And they can be made vulnerable by the wrong policies of western Europe and the United States.' But it's not just the front-line states, and it's not just the threat of renewed direct domination by Moscow, that should concern us. Far more people in far more places suffer directly as a result of Russia's attitude and actions, and it's a dereliction of any country's duty not to admit and address that threat. Regardless of the outcome of the overt war on Ukraine, Russia's covert war on everybody is likely to continue. Russia is everybody's problem, and it's not going away any time soon.

# APPENDIX: INTERVIEWEES

*All posts are correct as of the early summer of 2021. First names in quotation marks are pseudonyms, where the interviewees need them for their own protection.*

Anneli Ahonen – Finnish journalist and former head of an EU agency working against disinformation

Valeriy Akimenko – Ukrainian expert in media in the former Soviet Union, living and working in the UK since the 1990s

Timothy Ash – British economist specializing in Turkey, Ukraine and Russia

Adam Blake – British cybersecurity expert

Justin Bronk – British expert on air power with the RUSI think tank in London

Tor Bukkvoll – Norwegian researcher and academic at the Defence Research Establishment (FFI) in Oslo

Nick 'Bane' Caraballo – US Air Force fighter pilot, currently with the Fighter Weapons School at Nellis Air Force Base in Nevada

'Darth Putin KGB' – International Twitter account parodying Vladimir Putin

Samantha de Bendern – British expert in financial crime and corruption and former banker, based in Europe

'Gavril' – Disinformation researcher

Alex Grigorievs – Latvian journalist and former politician

Laura Halminen – Finnish journalist and expert on cybersecurity, malign influence and online threats

Deborah Haynes – British journalist specializing in defence and security issues

'Janis' – Government official from an EU country bordering Russia

Jakub Kalenský – Czech counter-disinformation activist and former EU official

'Kasimir' – European former staff member of a group working against disinformation and malign influence

Martin Kragh – Swedish researcher and academic specializing in Russia

'Lars' – Serving officer with the counter-intelligence service of a Northern European nation

Matthew Lauder – Canadian senior researcher in defence and security threats

Jean le Roux – South African researcher in online disinformation and influence

'Linas' – Lithuanian Army officer currently attached to NATO

Jüri Luik – Former Minister of Defence of Estonia, now Estonian permanent representative at NATO

Andrey Makarychev – University professor living in Estonia

'Maria' – Official with the European External Action Service in Brussels

John Mooney – Irish author and journalist focusing on defence, security and crime

'Nicola' – Serving officer with a British law enforcement agency

'Peter' – British Army lance-corporal, currently posted to Estonia

Robert Pszczel – Polish NATO official and the organization's representative in Moscow from 2010 to 2015

Sven Sakkov – Estonian government official and former head of defence research agencies, currently ambassador to Finland

Raphael Satter – American journalist based in Europe

Reiner Schwalb – Former German Army officer, who served as Defence Attaché in Moscow from 2011 to 2018

Sami Siva – Canadian photojournalist working in the Baltic states

Sulev Suvari – Former American bomb disposal officer and Russia expert for the US Army, now managing international security for a major US IT company

Heli Tiirmaa-Klaar – Estonian expert on cyber law and Ambassador at Large for Cyber Diplomacy

Pekka Toveri – Retired major-general, former head of Finnish Military Intelligence

Nathalie Van Raemdonck – Belgian expert in cybersecurity and cyber law

Laura Walters – New Zealand journalist

Vilde Skorpen Wikan – Norwegian journalist working on international security and defence

Kyle Wilson – Australian lecturer in Russian history, culture and language, and former diplomat

# SELECTED READING

Akimenko, Valeriy and Keir Giles, 'Use and Utility of Russia's Private Military Companies', *Journal of Future Conflict* 01 (Fall 2019), https://www.queensu.ca/psychology/research/journal-future-conflict/journal-future-conflict-issue-01-fall-2019.

Allan, Duncan, 'Managed Confrontation: UK Policy Towards Russia After the Salisbury Attack', Chatham House, 30 October 2018.

Blake, Heidi, 'From Russia With Blood', *Buzzfeed*, 15 June 2017, https://www.buzzfeed.com/heidiblake/from-russia-with-blood-14-suspected-hits-on-british-soil.

Bond, Ian, 'Stronger sanctions on Russia: Essential, but not a strategy', Centre for European Reform, 25 February 2022, https://www.cer.eu/insights/stronger-sanctions-russia-essential.

Colliver, Chloe et al., '"Smearing Sweden": International Influence Campaigns in the 2018 Swedish Election', ISD, October 2018, https://www.lse.ac.uk/iga/assets/documents/arena/2018/Sweden-Report-October-2018.pdf.

Crankshaw, Edward, *Putting up with the Russians*, London: Macmillan, 1984.

Gaddis, John, *Strategies of Containment*, Oxford: Oxford University Press, 1982.

Galeotti, Mark, 'Free Sergei Lavrov!', *Foreign Policy*, 17 February 2016, https://foreignpolicy.com/2016/02/17/free-sergei-lavrov-putin-russia-syria/.

Galeotti, Mark, 'Crimintern: How the Kremlin Uses Russia's Criminal Networks in Europe', European Council on Foreign Relations, April 2017, https://ecfr.eu/publication/crimintern_how_the_kremlin_uses_russias_criminal_networks_in_europe/.

Galeotti, Mark, 'The Minsk Accords: Should Britain declare them dead?', Council on Geostrategy, 24 May 2021, https://www.geostrategy.org.uk/britains-world/the-minsk-accords-should-britain-declare-them-dead/.

'George Kennan's "Long Telegram"', 22 February 1946, http://digitalarchive.wilsoncenter.org/document/116178.

Giles, Keir, 'Moscow Rules: What Drives Russia to Confront the West', Chatham House, 2019.

Giles, Keir, 'What deters Russia: Enduring principles for responding to Moscow', Chatham House, September 2021, https://www.chathamhouse.org/2021/09/what-deters-russia

Glenny, Misha, *DarkMarket: How Hackers Became the New Mafia*, London: Vintage, 2012.

Jonsson, Oscar, *The Russian Understanding of War: Blurring the Lines between War and Peace*, Washington, DC: Georgetown University Press, 2019.

Juurvee, Ivo, '"The resurrection of 'active measures'": Intelligence services as a part of Russia's influencing toolbox', *Hybrid CoE* (April 2018): 3, https://www.hybridcoe.fi/wp-content/uploads/2018/05/Strategic-Analysis-2018-4-Juurvee.pdf.

Juurvee, Ivo and Mariita Mattiisen, 'The Bronze Soldier Crisis of 2007: Revisiting an Early Case of Hybrid Conflict', International Centre for Defence and Security, August 2020.

Juurvee, Ivo et al., 'Falsification of History as a Tool of Influence', NATO Strategic Communications Centre of Excellence, December 2020.

Lanoszka, Alexander, 'How NATO should greet Russia's "draft treaty"', Council on Geostrategy, 20 December 2021, https://www.geostrategy.org.uk/britains-world/how-nato-should-greet-russias-draft-treaty/.

Marten, Kimberly, 'President Trump, keep in mind that Russia and the West think about negotiations very, very differently', *Washington Post*, 25 July 2017, https://www. washingtonpost.com/news/monkey-cage/wp/2017/07/25/president-trump-keep-in-mind-that-russia-and-the-west-think-about-negotiations-very-very-differently/.

McGlynn, Jade, 'Moscow Is Using Memory Diplomacy to Export Its Narrative to the World', *Foreign Policy*, 25 June 2021, https://foreignpolicy.com/2021/06/25/russia-puting-ww2-soviet-ussr-memory-diplomacy-history-narrative/.

'Myths and Misconceptions in the Debate on Russia: How they Affect Policy: and What Can Be Done', Chatham House, May 2021, https://www.chathamhouse.org/2021/05/myths-and-misconceptions-debate-russia.

Radin, Andrew et al., 'Understanding Russian Subversion: Patterns, Threats and Responses', RAND, 2020, https://www.rand.org/pubs/perspectives/PE331.html.

'Russia', Intelligence and Security Committee of Parliament, 21 July 2020, http://isc. independent.gov.uk/committee-reports

'Russia's Global Reach: A Security and Statecraft Assessment', George C. Marshall European Center For Security Studies, http://www.marshallcenter.org/en/publications/marshall-center-books/russias-global-reach-security-and-statecraft-assessment.

'Russia's Toolkit', in 'The Russian Challenge', Chatham House, June 2015, http://www. chathamhouse.org/publication/russian-challenge-authoritarian-nationalism.

Seely, Bob, 'Foreign Interference Unchecked: Models for a UK Foreign Lobbying Act', Henry Jackson Society, 10 February 2021, https://henryjacksonsociety.org/publications/uk-foreign-lobbying-act/.

Soldatov, Andrey and Irina Borogan, *The Red Web: The Struggle between Russia's Digital Dictators and the New Online Revolutionaries*, New York: PublicAffairs, 2015.

'The UK's kleptocracy problem: How servicing post-Soviet elites weakens the rule of law', Chatham House, 8 December 2021, https://www.chathamhouse.org/2021/12/uks-kleptocracy-problem.

Weiss, Michael, 'You Don't Have to Be Recruited to Work for Russian Intelligence', *Newlines*, 4 February 2021, https://newlinesmag.com/reportage/you-dont-have-to-be-recruited-to-work-for-russian-intelligence/.

# INDEX